KNOWLEDGE OF GOD
IN THE GRAECO-ROMAN WORLD

ÉTUDES PRÉLIMINAIRES
AUX RELIGIONS ORIENTALES
DANS L'EMPIRE ROMAIN

PUBLIÉES PAR

M.J. VERMASEREN†

M.E.C. VERMASEREN-VAN HAAREN ET **MARGREET B. DE BOER**

TOME CENT DOUZIÈME

**KNOWLEDGE OF GOD
IN THE GRAECO-ROMAN WORLD**

EDITED BY

R. VAN DEN BROEK,
T. BAARDA, AND J. MANSFELD

KNOWLEDGE OF GOD
IN THE GRAECO-ROMAN WORLD

EDITED BY

R. VAN DEN BROEK,
T. BAARDA, AND J. MANSFELD

E.J. BRILL
LEIDEN · NEW YORK · KØBENHAVN · KÖLN
1988

LIBRARY OF CONGRESS
Library of Congress Cataloging-in-Publication Data

Knowledge of God in the Graeco-Roman world / edited by R. van den
Broek, T. Baarda, and J. Mansfeld.
    p.   cm. -- (Etudes préliminaires aux religions orientales dans
l'Empire romain, ISSN 0531–1950 ; t. 112)
    Includes bibliographies and indexes.
    ISBN 9004086889 (pbk.)
    1. God--Knowableness--Comparative studies--Congresses. 2. God-
-Knowableness--History of doctrines--Early church, ca. 30–600-
-Congresses.   I. Broek, R. van den. II. Baarda, Tjitze.
III. Mansfeld, Jaap. IV. Series.
BL473.K56 1988
291.2'11'0938--dc 19   88-5064
                                                       CIP

ISSN 0531-1950
ISBN 90 04 08688 9

PRINTED IN THE NETHERLANDS BY E.J. BRILL

CONTENTS

PREFACE

This volume contains most of the papers read at an international symposium on "Knowledge of God in Philosophy and Religion from Alexander the Great to Constantine," which was held at the University of Utrecht 26–30 May 1986, on the occasion of the University's 350th anniversary.

The theme of the symposium is related to our research project concerned with the Literary, Religious and Philosophical Background of Early Christianity, in which members of the Faculties of Theology and of Philosophy participate.

Two contributions, by C. Colpe on Euhemerism and by E.P. Meijering on Irenaeus, are to appear elsewhere.

We gratefully acknowledge the financial support provided by our University and by the Netherlands Organization for the Advancement of Pure Research (ZWO).

Utrecht, April 14th 1987   R. van den Broek
                                                        T. Baarda
                                                        J. Mansfeld

ABBREVIATIONS

AC	Antiquité Classique
AJPh	American Journal of Philology
BSOAS	Bulletin of the School of Oriental and African Studies
CIMRM	Corpus Inscriptionum et Monumentorum Religionis Mithriacae (ed. M.J. Vermaseren)
CPJ	Corpus Papyrorum Judaicarum (ed. V.J. Tcherikover)
CQ	The Classical Quarterly
CR	The Classical Review
CRAI	Académie des Inscriptions et Belles-Lettres. Comptes Rendus
CSEL	Corpus Scriptorum Ecclesiasticorum Latinorum
EPRO	Etudes préliminaires aux religions orientales dans l'Empire Romain
GGA	Göttingische Gelehrte Anzeigen
IG	Inscriptiones Graecae
JA	Journal Asiatique
JbAC	Jahrbuch für Antike und Christentum
JBL	Journal of Biblical Literature
JHS	Journal of Hellenic Studies
JSNT	Journal for the Study of the New Testament
HAA	Hamburger Arbeiten zur Altertumswissenschaft
HThR	Harvard Theological Review
Mnem	Mnemosyne
MH	Museum Helveticum
NH	Nag Hammadi, Codices I–XIII
NTT	Nederlands Theologisch Tijdschrift
OGIS	Orientis Graeci Inscriptiones Selectae (ed. W. Dittenberger)
PG	Patrologiae cursus completus, Series Graeca
Phron	Phronesis
PhW	Philologische Wochenschrift
PL	Patrologiae cursus completus, Series Latina
RAC	Reallexikon für Antike und Christentum
RE	Realenzyclopädie der klassischen Altertumswissenschaft (Pauly-Wissowa)
REA	Revue des Études Anciennes
REAug	Revue des Études Augustiniennes
REG	Revue des Études Grecques
RFNS	Rivista di Filosofia Neo-Scolastica
RhM	Rheinisches Museum
RHR	Revue de l'Histoire des Religions
RPh	Revue Philologique
SC	Sources Chrétiennes
SGM	Sources Gnostiques et Manichéennes
SO	Symbolae Osloenses
SPAW	Sitzungsberichte der preusischen Akademie der Wissenschaften zu Berlin
TAPA	Transactions and Proceedings of the American Philological Association
TS	Texts and Studies. Contributions to Biblical and Patristic Literature
TU	Texte und Untersuchungen zur Geschichte der altchristlichen Literatur
VC	Vigiliae Christianae
ZDMG	Zeitschrift der deutschen morgenländischen Gesellschaft
ZNW	Zeitschrift für die neutestamentliche Wissenschaft und die Kunde der älteren Kirche

IDENTIFICATION AND SELF-IDENTIFICATION OF GODS IN CLASSICAL AND HELLENISTIC TIMES

BY

GERARD MUSSIES (UTRECHT)

The notion 'Knowledge of God' which figures in our jubilee-theme more or less presupposes a stage of religion which is past polytheism, but as the period indicated, 'from Alexander to Constantine,' can hardly be considered to have been heno- or monotheistic only, the polytheistic variant of this subject also deserves to receive some attention. This means that in this case we are not so much dealing with 'knowledge of God' but rather with 'knowledge of the gods,' which above all amounts to the questions of how such knowledge worked in practice, how people recognized gods when they appeared to them and how gods in their turn made themselves known to mankind. For that such encounters could offer problems was acknowledged already by Homer.

As a matter of fact he describes the Greek gods as having themselves no difficulty in recognizing one another. Hermes, the messenger of the gods, quite unexpectedly arrives at the grotto where the nymph Calypso lives and is then weaving and singing. Being herself a daughter of the god Atlas she immediately recognizes him 'because' says Homer 'the immortal gods are not ἀγνῶτες, unknown to each other, not even if one of them lives in a mansion far away' (*Od.*5,79–80). With regard to the meetings of gods and humans, however, he seems to hold no uniform opinion. For on the one hand he makes Odysseus say to Athena that it is hard for a mortal to recognize her, even for one who is well acquainted with her, as she is wont to change her real figure into that of all kinds of human persons (*Od.*13,311–313), and exactly the same remark is made in the *Hymn to Demeter* when ordinary people fail to recognize this goddess in her disguise of an old woman (1,111). Athena once even bestows the recognizing of gods as a special gift on her favourite hero Diomede so as to enable him to wound Aphrodite, her personal enemy, in the battles at Troy (*Il.*5,127–132; cf. *Od.*10,573–574).

On the other hand, however, there is in Homer also the story of the sea-god Poseidon who in the disguise of a priest visits the two Ajaxes to urge them to go on fighting against the Trojans. After this conversation he jumps so quickly away from them that he is immediately found out as a god. 'I easily recognized his steps and gait when he went' remarks one of them, 'gods are ἀρίγνωτοι, well distinguishable' (*Il.*13,45–72; cf. *Od.*6,108). The much later novel writer Heliodorus (ca A.D.235) relates how Apollo and Artemis appear at night to

the Egyptian priest Kalasiris with the command to escort the lovers Theagenes
and Charicleia, the principal persons of the book, to Egypt. On being asked
how exactly he knows that what he has seen was no dream (ὄναρ) but a real
apparition (ὕπαρ) he answers by referring to the Iliad lines just quoted. He
interprets, however, the word ῥεῖ' there (*Il.*13,72) not as an apocopated ῥεῖα
'easily' but as the verb ῥεῖ which then means 'glide' and he comments as follows: 'The wise man recognizes the gods from ... the way they move, in which
they do not separate their feet and make steps, but glide throug the air' adding
that for that reason the statues of Egyptian gods always have joint feet, which
form as it were one whole (*Aeth.*3,11,5–3,13,3).

From all these passages it is apparent that once they had given up their disguise gods could be distinguished from mortals, and that the remarks about
difficulties in this connection have to do only with 'gods incogniti'. The gods
themselves sometimes think that even in this case people should be able to see
through their cover. When he is back in Ithaca without realizing it Odysseus
is first addressed by Athena disguised as a young prince who tells him the name
of the island. Next she changes into a beautiful woman who reproaches him
for his fencing answers and says in the end: 'Haven't you now recognized me
yet as Pallas Athena, Zeus' daughter, who is always by your side in all your
troubles?' (*Od.*13,222–301; cf. *Il.*21,550–22,21). This episode also shows that
it was thought possible to recognize the gods as specific individuals.

Generally speaking one may say that in Antiquity any one who did something that was not understood or that was considered miraculous ran himself
the risk of being looked upon as a god. But even in situations where no further
living beings were present people could get the idea, for instance when something turned out remarkably well, that a deity was there to help them, or that
a god was working against them when things went wrong contrary to all expec-
tation. When his ship safely put into a bay in the midst of a dark night, the
moon being shrouded in clouds, Odysseus comments that 'some god' (τις
θεός) was guiding him safely through the surf.[1] The opposite situation was ex-
perienced by the Romans during their siege of Syracuse. Their opponents
directed by the scholar-engineer Archimedes, constructed such a diversity of
war-engines which harmed them in so many different and unorthodox ways,
that they seemed to themselves 'to be fighting against the gods now that count-
less evils were poured out on them, seemingly from nowhere' as Plutarch relates (*Marcell.*16).[2]

---

[1] *Od.*9,142–148; cf. 10,140–141 and also 19,33–40 (miraculous light). Later he identifies this
invisible helper as Athena (13,317–319). The rhetor Aelius Aristides quotes *Od.*9,142 when he
related his experience (A.D.167) of travelling along a miraculously sharp dividing line between
rainfall and dry weather on his way to Pergamum, which seemed to lead him straight to the temple
of Asklepios (*Sacred Tales* 5,26–27).

[2] Cf.Acts 5,17–39 Gamliel I warns the Sanhedrin not to prosecute the apostles who had so

More often, however, there is someone present who performs the miraculous. On several occasions in Homer ordinary men or women who have been helpful in some way or other disappear in the end in the shape of a bird and thus give themselves away as gods.[3] In Lystra in Asia Minor when Paul has performed the prodigious healing of a crippled man, the crowds present immediately want to venerate him and his companion Barnabas as gods. They decline this honour with the utmost vigour, saying that they are humans ὁμοιοπαθεῖς ὑμῖν 'who suffer the same things as you do.'[4] In fact they were considered to be Zeus and Hermes in human shape, apparently so because these two were reported to have paid a visit to an elderly couple in nearby Phrygia and likewise disguised as ordinary men, Hermes having laid down his wings according to Ovid: 'positis Caducifer alis.' They went there to check the hospitability of the population but were sheltered only by Philemon and Baucis, and then there happened all kinds of wonders: the wine which these very hospitable people offered to their divine guests was automatically supplied, and when they wanted to dish up their fatted goose for them, their only one, the bird keeps escaping them and even takes refuge with the guests, so that Philemon and his wife get frightened and the gods blow their own cover so to say and reveal their identity by saying 'di sumus' and grant them to make a wish.[5]

Apart from all such miraculous activities gods could also make themselves known simply by their outward appearance. That the full revelation of a deity could be unbearable for a human is shown by the well-known myth of Semele. She wanted to see her lover Zeus only for once in his divine glory and not in some disguise, but when he appeared with lightnings and all she could not bear the sight and was killed by a thunderbolt.[6]

On the other hand gods are also reported to have shown themselves in their full glory to mankind without inflicting any harm by it. One of the most outspoken and personal reports of such a manifestation is that of Apuleius, who

---

miraculously escaped from prison, so as not to become 'fighters against God'. Conversely, according to Philostratus, one could even give thanks in Athens to 'unknown gods' (ἄγνωστοι δαίμονες) in order to avoid being ungrateful for unexpected and 'anonymous' blessings (*Life of Apoll.*6,3,5); see also P.W. van der Horst's contribution to this volume, below 19–42.

[3] *Od.*1,319–323; 420; 3,371–372. Someone seen in mutually exclusive situations is suspected to be a god in *Od.*4,653–656; Telemachus thinks the same of his rejuvenated father in *Od.*16, 181–212).

[4] Acts 14,8–18, esp. 15; Odysseus also denies divinity in front of his son because he has suffered many evils (*Od.*16,205 παθὼν κακά).

[5] Ovid. *Met.*8,616–724. For such stories see: D. Flückinger-Guggenheim, *Göttliche Gäste. Die Einkehr von Göttern und Heroen in der griechischen Mythologie*, Europäische Hochschulschriften, Reihe 3, Nr.237, Frankfurt am Main – Bern – Las Vegas 1984.

[6] Apollodorus, *Libr.*3,4,3; Ovid *Met.*3, 253–315; Hyginus *Fab.*179. Less disastrously humans could not look gods in the face or bear their regard and had to look away: *Od.*16,179; *Hymn Aphr.*1,181–182. Cf. also in the O.T.: Exod.19,21; 33,12–23; 1 Kingd.19,9–18.

finally after all his journeys is deemed worthy to look upon the god into whose mysteries he has been initiated: 'In the end just after a few days the god of the gods, more powerful than the great (gods) and the highest of the greater (gods), the greatest of the highest and the ruler of the greatest (gods), Osiris, appeared in my sleep, not disguised as another person whosoever, but in his own essence and granting me (to be addressed by) his own venerable voice . . .' (*Met.*11,30). And his consort Isis, too, is said to have shown her own likeness in dreams (Diod.Sic.1,25,3), as it in fact befell Apuleius as well, be it that he was then still an ass (*Met.*11,3–4).[7]

What then exactly were the outward features which distinguished deity from human? It appears that there were several of them, but that the most general characteristic of the gods was deemed their excessive beauty. The mere sight of human beauty, especially in a woman, was often enough to consider her for the time being as a goddess. Aphrodite, the goddess of love, was once condemned by Zeus to fall in love herself and that with a mortal man. She then visits Anchises, a prince of Troy, as a young beautiful girl in a shining robe and as soon as he has set eyes on her he takes her for a goddess, although he does not know which one, as he says himself. Odysseus has similar thoughts when he is washed ashore and sees the beautiful princess Nausikaa,[8] and many more stories and texts can be adduced, both from literature and inscriptions, which make mention of the beauty of gods and goddesses. There is even the story of a mortal man, Philip of Croton, who was according to Herodotus (5,47) the most beautiful Greek of his time. Because of this he was honoured as no one else: when he had been killed although he had taken refuge on an altar of Zeus, the inhabitants of Segesta in Sicily where this took place, deified him by building a chapel upon his grave and bringing offerings to him.[9]

Above all else it is the eyes of the gods that are described as having a special quality, either bright and shining (*Il.*3,397; *Hymn Aphr.*1,181) or frightening (*Il.*1,200). It is again the novelist Heliodorus who also comments on this latter case saying that the passage indicates that gods look straight and without blinking and can so be recognized (*Aeth.*3,13,2–3).

A further characteristic which is often mentioned is that the appearance of gods as a whole, that is including their clothing, was shiny and had a peculiar lustre which surpassed the glow of fire. Aphrodite, although disguised, dis-

---

[7] Cf. also Quintus of Smyrna 4, 110–117 where Thetis attends the funeral games of her son Achilles apparently not disguised and causing no panic.

[8] *Od.*6,151–152; cf. *Il.*3,396–397 (Aphrodite disguised as an old woman recognized by her beauty).

[9] 'Beautiful of face' (*nfr-ḥr*, Nopheros, Pnepheros) was in Egypt the epithet both of anthropomorphic and theriomorphic gods. Especially with regard to the crocodile-god Suchos this epithet has been thought to be euphemistic (so Helck in *Der Kleine Pauly* s.v. Nopheros), but more likely it underlined the benevolent aspect of such a dangerous looking god.

plays it in front of Anchises (*Hymn Aphr.*1,86), it is mentioned about Demeter when she has revealed her divinity to her mortal hostess (*Hymn Dem.*1,189, 278,280) and as a matter of fact it is said of Apollo, the god of light (*Hymn Ap.*1,440ss.); the Egyptian god Imuthes-Asklepios is clothed in white shining garments (P.Oxy. 1381), and who would not also think in this connection of the angels in the N.T. who are clothed in the same way (e.g. Matt.28,3; Luk.24,4), or of the appearance of Jesus during the glorification on the mountain (Matt.17,2)?

A third characteristic is the very special fragrance which accompanies the gods when they appear to man, for instance Demeter and Apollo (*Hymn Dem.*1,277; *Hymn Ap.*1,184); when the latter was born on Delos, an ambrosian odour is said to have filled the whole island (Theognis 1,5–10). And Aeneas recognizes his mother Venus, who first appeared to him as some other woman, both from her divine fragrance and lustre, says Virgil (*Aen.*1, 402–409). Apuleius finally, although he had been converted into a stupid ass, was not so insensible that he could not smell the godess Isis' odoriferous feet as well as the incense of Arabia Felix when she appeared to him (*Met.*11,4).

Most conspicuous and often mentioned in combination with their beauty was the more than human size and length of all gods. After Aphrodite has shared the bed of Anchises she rises and lays off her human appearance, which means that she is now so tall that she all of a sudden touches the roof with her head while beauty 'shines' on her cheeks; exactly the same is told of Demeter once she has disclosed her divine nature.[10] On their voyage to the East the Argonauts run into the harbour of the island of Thynias in the Black Sea. At dawn they see the god Apollo silently pass by. They recognize him from his golden hair and the silver bow which he holds. Apparently he was so huge that the island trembled under his feet and the waves surged high on the beach (Apoll. Rhod.*Arg.*2,669–684). The sea-god Triton is likewise so gigantic that he can hold the ship Argo in one hand and stear her (*Arg.*4,1609–1610).[11] Obviously size was the first divine characteristic which the gods had to get rid of when they wanted to look like humans. Aphrodite took care before going to Anchises to look like a girl μέγεθος καὶ εἶδος 'both in length and appearance' (*Hymn Aphr.*1,82; cf. *Hymn Dem.*1,275).

---

[10] *Hymn Aphr.*1,173–174; *Hymn Dem.*1,188–189. In vase paintings, too, gods may seem almost to touch the roof, see in H. Walter, *Griechische Götter. Ihr Gestaltswandel aus den Bewusztseinstufen des Menschen dargestellt an den Bildwerken*, München 1971, illustrations on pp. 223,322,323. The statues of Athena Parthenos and Zeus made by Phidias were both 12 m. giants (Pausanias 1,24,7; Strabo 8,3,30).

[11] In *Il.*13,18–39 a similar description is given of Poseidon's gait. In *Hymn. Ap.*1,70–74 it is feared that baby Apollo, yet to be born, will be such a giant that he will be able to push Delos under water with his feet.

Well known, too, are the stories about two beautiful warriors, 'who are taller than a normal man' and who help the Greeks in the battle against the Persians, and the Romans against the Tarquinians, bringing in the latter case the good news of the victory back to the City. These couples are later on identified respectively with Phylakos and Antinoos, two local heroes from the neighbourhood of Delphi, and with Castor and Pollux.[12]

Tall persons were sometimes because of their length taken for gods. Plutarch tells in the *Life of Aratus* how in the Aetolian War the town of Pellene was being plundered by Aratus' enemies and their officers each put his own helmet on the head of the captive woman of his choice, so that the different helmets could show after the battle to whom the woman belonged. One of these women who excelled in beauty and stateliness, was sent to the temple of Artemis. When, however, Aratus came to help the Pellenians this woman appeared in the front-portico of the temple, wearing the three-crested helmet of the captain of the cracked regiment of the enemy and looking down on the combattants from on high. And then by both sides she was thought to be the apparition of Artemis herself, so that the Pellenians were encouraged and the enemies no longer thought of defending themselves (*Aratus* 31−32). This happened more or less by accident, but a similar event was once staged on purpose and for political reasons.

When the tyrant Pisistratus had been expelled from Athens for the first time his opponents soon became divided among themselves, so that one of them wanted him to return. In order to make his return acceptable to the citizens one dressed up a beautiful tall girl in full armour, so as to make her look like the goddess Athena. She was called Φύη or 'Growth', an appropriate name at least in Antiquity, for she was almost four cubits long, that is about 1 m. 80 cm. She then entered the city standing in a war-chariot and preceded by heralds who urged the citizens to accept Pisistratus again, proclaiming that it was the goddess herself who brought him back to Athens, and so it was believed by the people (Hdt 1,60).

---

[12] Hdt 8,38; Dion.Hal.6,13; Plutarch *Aem.*25; and cf. e.g. Philostratus *Life of Apoll.*4,16 (Achilles first five cubits tall, then twelve), and Cassius Dio 55,1.3−4 (huge German goddess appearing to Drusus). In dreams gods likewise may appear as giants; unidentified instances: Hdt.5,56; 7,12; Xenophon *Eph.*1,12,4; Achilles Tat.1,3,4; Tacitus *Hist.*4,83 (Sarapis); P.Oxy. 1381 (Imuthes);Philostratus *Life of Apoll.*4,34 (nurse of Zeus); cf. also the huge god appearing to king Gudea, who was later identified as Ningirsu (Cylinder A 4,14). − This trait was also present in Hermetism (CH 1,1−2: Poimandres), Judaism (mystic texts: giant Kabod), Gnosis (the giant Anthropos), Christianity (Apc 10,1−2: gigantic angel; *Gospel of Peter* 10,40: Christ a giant at resurrection; *Vision of Dorotheus* 233; 297−301; 329: angels and Dorotheus 'like Christ' are giants; see Dutch translation by Van der Horst-Kessels in NTT 40(1986) 97−111), and Islam (according to Ibn-Ishaq's *Sirat Rasul Allah* 153 or 'Life of the Prophet': Muhammad saw the angel Gabriel reaching up to the azimuth); finally also in personifications outside of religion such as the giant Lady Philosophy in the opening chapter of Boethius' *Consolation of Philosophy.*

A final distinguishing mark of the gods, not mentioned by Pfister in his article *Epiphanie* in Pauly-Wissowa, was the loud and far-reaching sound of their voice. At the Odyssey's very end, Athena, who according to Homer's last lines was then still disguised as Mentor (24,548), ordered the inhabitants of Ithaca to stop their civil war, and then, he says, 'green fear catches them, the weapons fall out of their hands to the ground, when the goddess had raised her voice' (24,529−535). Even Hector is frightened when hearing Apollo's voice, although this god was on the side of the Trojans (*Il.*20,375−380).

The divine voices are compared either with the sound of the thunder or with that of musical instruments. Jason and his Argonauts are warned by Hera to stop their expedition. Sitting on the Hercynian Rock (to be vaguely equated with some Middle-European mountain chain) she cries out to them 'and they were stricken with fear for mighty crashed the firmament' (*Arg.*4,640−642). And in the overture of Sophocles' *Aias* Athena addresses Odysseus when she is still invisible to him and making no allusions to her identity. His answer is: 'Oh word of Athana, goddess most dear to me, how clear, although you are still out of sight, do I hear your voice and grasp it with my mind like the sound of an Etruscan bronze-voiced gong' (14−18).

Both comparisons or associations are also known from the New Testament. On the occasion of Jesus' entrance into Jerusalem God speaks from heaven according to the 4th Gospel in response to his request: 'Father glorify Thy name' the words: 'I have glorified it and will glorify it again.' The people present say, however, that they have heard a thunder-clap or that an angel had spoken (John 12,27−29). And when the author of the Apocalypse hears God's or Christ's voice for the very first time and from behind, he can only describe it as the loud sound of a trumpet (Apc.1,10−11), and we may add that all the voices from heaven or of angels are in that book said to be μεγάλαι, loud, in some twenty passages in all.

Such are the outward features in general of the ancient gods in the Classical and Hellenistic periods through which, if so wished, they could allow themselves to be known as divine beings, apart from the supernatural actions that lay within their power. These features are the same as those by which humans may seem impressive, only, the gods possessed them as a matter of fact and to a much greater extent.[13] It was, however, also necessary for people to be able to tell their many gods apart by more personal characteristics. How else could they be certain with whom they were dealing when a god or goddess appeared to them in a dream and ordered them, for instance, to make specific

---

[13] For more material on the gods' length and beauty, lustre and fragrance in ancient literature, papyri and inscriptions we refer to Pfister's article *Epiphanie* in Pauly-Wissowa, Supplement IV, Stuttgart 1924, 277−323, especially 314−316; W.J. Verdenius, ΚΑΛΛΟΣ ΚΑΙ ΜΕΓΕΘΟΣ, *Mnemosyne*, Series IV, 2 (1949) 294−298.

sacrifices in his or her temple? In Homer it is clear, as remarked above, that the gods when they were not somehow disguised were usually recognized as specific individuals. This is no surprise because in some cases he describes such personal distinguishing marks as the caduceus of Hermes and Poseidon's trident. And from many more sources it is known that the gods were not supposed to look alike or to wear the same clothes, that they had their own attributes, their distinctive emblem-birds or other animals to accompany them, and even had their specific sacred trees. And so Apollo, for instance, is said to be beardless, to hold bow and arrows, to wear a quiver, to have a falcon on his helmet (although according to Plutarch the raven was his bird), while his sacred tree was the laurel. And when the Argonauts are sailing between Scylla and Charybdis close to Sicily and its volcanoes, where Hephaestus was supposed to have his smithy, they actually see him once while he is watching their ship from a high peak leaning on his sledgehammer[14] etc.

Turning to vase paintings we perceive that this whole so-called 'system' of personal distinguishing marks is handled with much more consistency than in literature where such marks are mentioned only occasionally. All the gods are almost without exception consistently portrayed with attributes in hand, in fact it is often the only way to determine them, especially so on geometrical vases. Zeus always holds a thunderbolt, not our modern zig-zag lightning, but a rather short javelin with several points on both ends, and not only so when he is fighting a giant, but also when sitting at ease on his throne. His brother Poseidon is not at all like our modern portrait of Neptune, half fish half man, which seems to have been inspired rather by the picture of Triton (cf. Ap.Rhod.*Arg.*4.1601−1616). He is a purely human primitive fisherman who has no boat and holds a trident, a kind of harpoon, in one hand and a fish in the other. The other brother Hades-Pluto usually has a cornucopia, Apollo a bow or a lyre, sometimes also a branch from his laurel tree, etc.

Other gods wear uniform clothing: Athena always wears her helmet, Dionysos his ivy-garland. In fact these two are portrayed as wearing these head-gears already at the very moment when they were born, respectively out of the head and the knee of their father Zeus. All such attributes are so permanently present in these pictures[15] that it strikes our modern mind as superfluous when we see that in addition to all this in many cases the names of the gods have been written underneath.

Apart from attributes, clothing, etc., gods could also be recognized and mutually distinguished by their personal features. Odysseus thinks that Nau-

---

[14] *Od.*5,44ss. and 292; Cicero *Nat.Deor.*1,82−83; Aristophanes *Aves* 515−516 (cf. Plutarch *De Iside* 379d); Phaedrus *Fab.*3,17; Ap.Rhod.*Arg.*2,678−679; 4,1709 and 956−958.

[15] See the ilustrations in Walter, *o.c.*, pp. 30,34,38,39,58,59,60,66,120,149,152,206,248, 322,323.

sikaa is Artemis because of her appearance and stature (*Od.*6,149–152); Diomedes recognizes the goddess of love when she is in battle and certainly not accompanied by any of her sacred birds (*Il.*5,330–348); Achilles knows Athena from her glaring eyes (*Il.*1,197ss), which according to Cicero were bluish grey (*Nat.Deor.*1,83); in a number of cases the personal sound of a god's voice seems to play a role as well (*Il.*2,182; 20,380). Only once do we hear that a person is aware that he is talking to a god without knowing which. Curiously enough this is Hector who does not know Apollo the helper of his own people (*Il.*15,236–254).

Finally, when outward characteristics were of no help, a special activity could be considered to belong rather to one god than another, and for that reason the citizens of Lystra thought that Paul was Hermes, 'because he was the spokesman' (Acts 14,12).

We have to admit that many of the examples thusfar adduced stem from art, either from literature or from vase painting. The question is now, of course, whether the situation was different in reality, that is in the actual religious practice of the people at large and also in the theory based on this practice.

The religious theory as far as apparitions are concerned may well be represented here by a man who wrote a systematically ordered work on the explanation of dreams, including dreams about gods, Artemidorus from Daldis in Lydia, who lived about A.D.175. His work is divided into five books, four being theoretical and predictive, mainly of the content: 'if someone dreams this, it means that.' The fifth book is of a more descriptive nature and relates in a very brief form the contents of no fewer than 95 dreams and also what happened afterwards to the persons who had had these dreams. Since among the great many subjects which one can dream about the gods ranked first in Antiquity Artemidorus devoted nine rather lengthy chapters to them, in which he discusses the good or bad significance of the appearances in dreams of some 55 divinities, a number of them even in several varieties. He discusses, for instance, seven different manifestations of Artemis, subdividing them into 'long-robed' and 'short-robed' appearances. With regard to their recognizability distinctions are sometimes made between the god as he really is, the image of the god as people suppose him to be, and the statue of the god, either with proper dress and attributes or without.[16]

To quote an example: 'To see Zeus himself as we suppose that he is or his statue in heaven, and having his own attire, is good for a king or a rich

---

[16] *Onir.*2,33–40; 44. This distinction between gods as they really are and as humans imagine them is probably also the background of the remark made by Aelius Aristides (*Hymn to Poseidon* XLVI, p. 373,5–7 Keil), that Homer portrays the gods as speaking and conversant with mankind. Compare the observation made by Xenophanes that the Ethiopians have black gods with flat noses, the Thracians blond gods with blue eyes (in Clemens Alex.*Strom.*7,22,1; see the reconstructed hexameters in J.Mansfeld, *Die Vorsokratiker*, I, Stuttgart 1983, 222 nr. 27.

man ... It is always better to see the god when he is standing still or sitting and does not move. For if he were moving he would be auspicious if (he moved) to the East, but if to the West he would be inauspicious, just as (he is) when he does not have his own attire ...'. Hera signifies the same to women, but worse things to men (2,35; cf. 2,40). With regard to the sun he first discusses its appearance in dreams as a celestial body and then goes on to say: 'The Sun, not as he is, but such as he is considered to be when seen in the semblance (ἰδέα) of a man, having the attire of a chariot-driver, is favourable to athletes, to those who plan to go abroad, and to charioteers ... It is always better to see a statue of this god set up in a temple, standing on a pedestal, than the god himself as he is supposed to be. For such a dream foretells that the good things (which it predicts) will be more definite and the bad things even worse. As he is and as he is seen when shining in the sky, as such he will also be favourable' (*Onir.*2,35 and 36).

The recognizability of gods seems to be no point at all, not even when it depends on personal features only. For he says that it is unfavourable to see Artemis wholly naked (2,35) and remarks the same about Aphrodite, with the exception that it means business when prostitutes see her like that (2,37), so Artemidorus assumes that people could even tell the two goddesses apart when both were naked.

In all these cases it is of course difficult, if not impossible, to estimate the amount of the author's own theorizing creativity, or to say how many of all these gods had actually been seen in dreams. He also has a chapter on the identification of those gods that did not allow themselves to be recognized, τοὺς ἀγνοουμένους θεούς τε καὶ θεάς: 'The gods appear in the semblance and form of humans because we have always considered them to be outwardly like ourselves. One should therefore determine (κανονίζειν)' the gods who avoid to be known 'by their age, by their outward appearance or their profession ... A young boy indicates Hermes, a young man Heracles, a grown-up Zeus, an old man Kronos, two boys the Dioskouroi, a girl either Hope, Artemis or Athena, if she laughs Hope, if she is solemn Artemis, if she looks grim Athena.' He then goes on to say that a man with the attribute of a specific god stands for that god, and that someone carrying out a specific profession stands for the protective deity of that profession. This would imply that a man with a lyre means Apollo, and that a smith means Hephaestus (2,44). The same holds good of sacred animals and trees, so to dream of an owl is equal to dreaming of Athena, to dream of a pine-tree means dreaming of Cybele (4,56–57).

Among the actual dreams which he describes in his last book the following about gods are worthy of note: 'Someone dreamt that he was chained to the pedestal (of the statue) of Poseidon on the Isthmus: he became a priest of Poseidon' (5,1); 'A sick woman dreamt that she asked Aphrodite if she would live. The goddess nodded (ἀνένευσε) and the woman stayed alive' (5.72);

'Someone dreamt that he had been thrown by Sarapis in the kalathos (or basket) which is on the head (of that god). He died, for Sarapis is considered to be the same as Pluto, the god of the netherworld' (5,93).

The dreams about sickness and healing which he relates were certainly taken out of a religious context and this context was of course the practice of incubation. In such cases the identity of the appearing god was no problem. He or she was simply the deity in whose temple one went to sleep in order to get a dream and possibly regain health. In the inscriptions of Epidaurus which report of such healings through instructions of Asclepius, he is simply referred to as 'the god' (ὁ θεός). Only once it is said there that the god explicitly mentioned his own name. A sick woman had gone to the temple at Epidaurus, but had not received a dream. On her way back home, however, she encountered a beautiful man who ordered the men who carried her to put down the litter, and then he operated upon her by the side of the road. She was cured and the man told her that he was Asclepius (Dittenberger, *Sylloge* 1169,95ss.).

More of such religious practice is to be found in the autobiographical *Sacred Tales* of the sickly orator Aelius Aristides. He often had dreams in which Asclepius gave him instructions to help him to better his apparently very frail bodily condition. He likewise very simply refers to 'the god' or has such cryptic phrases as 'next night he said to me . . . .' Asclepius was, however, not the only god to appear to him. He also saw Isis, Sarapis, Hermes, Telesphorus, and a mixed apparition, a god who was Sarapis and Apollo at the same time.[17] A number of times, too, he says that the gods who appeared to him were like their statue in a specific temple. In the summer of the year A.D.165, for instance, he saw Athena in all her beauty and magnitude, like the statue of Phidias at Athens, and he adds very significantly, that from her shield there came a sweet scent, like that of wax.[18]

Such and similar texts prove without a doubt that the whole system of gods' characteristics was not only present in painting and literature but really formed part of the religious experience of ancient man.

One could say that by all these outward signs and features the gods allowed themselves to be identified in a somewhat passive way. When gods were not recognized they sometimes kept silent about their identity, like the tall and handsome man who announced imminent death to Hipparchus tyrant of Athens, and the other one who forbade Xerxes to make war against the Greeks (Hdt 5,56; 7,12). The god may also give a clue in the form of a riddle: when Alexander the Great had found the temple and the statue of Sarapis, whom he did not yet know, and this god appeared to him in a dream he did not mention

---

[17] *Sacred Tales* 1,18; 71.2,7; 9; 13; 18. 3,21–23; 45; 47. 4,30–31; 40; 50; 56; 57.
[18] *Sacred Tales* 2,40–41; cf. 3,21–23;47. 4,50; and Xenophon *Eph.*4,1,4; IG IV 956 (224 A.D.); Aelian *frg.*106; Libanius *Or.*11,114 (Hdt 2,41).

his name as such, but only the numerical values of the letters making up his name.[19] In other cases they had themselves identified only afterwards by a priest or an oracle: the beautiful young man of more than human size who appeared to king Ptolemy I and ordered him to fetch his statue from Pontus, was only later identifided by a priest as Sarapis.[20]

A much more active way of self-identification was, as a matter of fact, for gods to reveal their own name without any restriction. In Homer this does not happen very often (e.g. *Od.*11,252), and if so it is only to put an end to a mystifying situation, and in the Hymns to Aphrodite and Demeter it is not otherwise. In the Western world the best known instances of ancient self-identification, self-presentation or -manifestation—the dividing lines are not always clear—are of course those that are described in the Bible, such as to Abraham 'I am Yhwh who led you out of Ur' (Gen.15,7) and 'I am El the Almighty' (Gen.17,1), or to Moses: 'I am the god of your father (Sam.: 'fathers'), the god of Abraham, Isaac and Jacob' (Ex.3,6; Matt.22,32). As the first instance shows the identification etc. in the strict sense can be followed by a descriptive addition, and there is also a type which consists of such descriptions only: 'I am the alpha and the o(mega) ... who is, and was and who will come' (Apc.1,8). Such formulae have parallels in many cultures, and as Abraham is said to have come from Ur, one may be inclined to look in Sumeria for formulae comparable to 'I am Yhwh ....' At first sight there seems indeed to be some parallel material there, which has been quoted by E. Schweizer.[21] Gudea king of Lagash, who was also king of Ur (c.2144–2124 B.C.), had a dream in which he saw a man of gigantic size whom he recognized as a god by his head-gear and who was also accompanied by a sacred bird, but whom Gudea did not know. As this god ordered him to have his temple repaired the king prayed to a special goddess for an explanation of this dream, and she answered that the god was Ningirsu. When he appeared to Gudea for the second time he repeated his command and said: 'I am Ningirsu, who checks the raging water, the great

---

[19] Ps-Callisthenes, *Life of Alexander*, 1,33,10. The name 'I am who I am' has often been considered to be such a mysterious way to underline the divinity of the speaker, but this was hardly the intention of Exod.3,14, cf. J. Kinyongo, *Origine et signification du nom divin Yahvé à la lumière de récents travaux et de traditions sémitico-bibliques (Ex.3,13–15 et 6,2–8)*, Bonner Biblische Beiträge 35, Bonn 1970, 102–118, and M. Weippert, art. Jahweh, in *Reallexikon der Assyriologie* 5, Berlin – New York 1976–1980, 246–253. In later times, however, this name and also 'I am' were certainly used in this way in magic etc., see the instances in Y. Naveh – Sh. Shaked, *Amulets and Magic Bowls. Aramaic Incantations of Late Antiquity*, Jerusalem – Leiden 1985, 44s, 50s, 54s, 90s, 94s, 222s, 237.

[20] Tacitus *Hist.*4,83–84; cf. Ps-Call. 1,8: Philip II dreams of a horned god who is later identified by a priest as Ammon; Pausanias 1,32,5 has a story about identification by an oracle of an unknown god. In Ps-Call.1,4–5 Olympias dreams about a god who had been described to her by a priest beforehand (cf. Anonymi *Vita Alexandri* 2,4).

[21] E. Schweizer, *Ego Eimi. Die religionsgeschichtliche Herkunft und theologische Bedeutung der johanneischen Bildreden*, Göttingen [2]1965, 12; 31 n. 191.

warrior of Enlil's place, the lord who has no equal.'[22] Later analysis, however, of this famous text, as well as recent developments in Sumerian linguistics have made it clear that the translation 'I am N.' has no foundation in the Sumerian original.[23]

Moreover, as all these self-presentations of God to Abraham happen already within the geographical context of Palestine, it is more likely that they are the product of an independent, local development. They are also the background of the N.T. instances, which were, however, certainly reinforced by the rather abundant instances from the Hellenistic world from which we shall quote some instances.

In the first tractate of the Corpus Hermeticum which as a whole has an Egyptian background, the person who sees a formidable apparition, again of gigantic size, asks: 'But who are you?' and receives the answer: 'I am Poimandres, the mind with absolute authority' (C.H.1,2). And from Egypt stems also the famous aretalogy of the goddess Isis, which begins with line 3a: 'Isis I am, the mistress of all land,' and this line is then followed by 55 more lines of a descriptive character, all in the first person or containing the pronoun 'me'. Among these further lines are such self-descriptions as: 'I made justice strong' (16); 'I brought wife and husband together' (17); 'I made it a law that parents should be loved by their child' (19); 'I dissolved the reigns of tyrants' (25); 'I put an end to killing' (26); 'I made justice stronger than gold or silver' (28); 'I am the one who is called the Lawgiver' (52).[24] Such an elaborate self-description is also found in the tractate 'The Thunder' which forms part of the mostly gnostic Nag Hammadi library, but which itself may also be Jewish or Christian. It is a revelation delivered by a female who says of herself that she has been sent by 'the Power' and is almost wholly made up of sentences beginning with 'I am' and containing some paradox like 'I am the one whom they call Life, and whom you have called Death,' 'I am the mother of my father and the sister of my husband and he is my offspring,' 'I am the one whom they call Law and whom you have called Lawlessness.'[25]

Now Schweizer has pointed out with some emphasis when tracing the back-

---

[22] M. Thureau-Dangin, *Die sumerischen und akkadischen Königsinschriften* Leipzig 1907, p. 99 (cylinder A 9,20).

[23] A. Falkenstein – W. v.Soden, *Grammatik der Sprache Gudeas von Lagas*, II, Rome 1950, 21: there is no copula-sentence here, and the same holds good of "I am the shepherd" (cyl.A 1,26) according to p. 34 sub 4.

[24] IG 12, Suppl. 98–99.

[25] J.M. Robinson, (ed.) *The Nag Hammadi Library in English*, New York etc. 1977, 271,272, 274. The paradoxical definitions probably serve, as some elaborate enigma, to bring out the divine character of the speaker, cf. note 19. The name of the female speaking is mentioned in the title "The Thunder: Perfect Mind": the word used there is feminine: [T]EBPONTH, the connection with the second part NOYC·ÑTEΛEIOC is unclear from the point of Coptic grammar (NHC VI-2,13 and 16).

ground and origin of this formula, that there are hardly any parallels in the Classical Greek and Roman texts. This is certainly true, but only so if one strictly clings to the exact wording ἐγώ εἰμι or *ego sum*, and does not admit as roughly equivalent material passages like 'nomen Mercurio'st mihi' (Plautus *Amphitr*.19), and ἥκω followed by the god's name, and still other phrases, which may have been used to avoid the uniform 'I am' and in the case of ἥκω also to underline a specific mission. A good instance is the prologue of the *Bacchae* of Euripides: 'I have come, Zeus' son, to this country of the Thebans, I Dionysos, to whom once the daughter of Kadmos gave birth, Semele'[26]: if such material is also allowed as equivalent with 'I am' etc. somewhat more parallels can be adduced than the few now listed by Schweizer from tragedy or comedy.[27]

With regard to all these passages, however, one may posit the same question that arose in connection with the written gods' names accompanying many vase paintings. It is well known that gods when appearing on the stage had been perfectly dressed up and were quite recognizable. Nevertheless the tragedians always take care to have the gods' names explicitly mentioned, either by the gods themselves or by an antagonist either before or after their actual appearance. Aristophanes does not keep up this practice, but the much later Roman comedian Plautus maintained it and so did probably Menander, at least so in the *Dyscolus*, the only play left of his in which a god has a part.

The mention of the god's name in a play was probably not some kind of hidden stage instruction, because it may be supposed that shifts of roles were indicated in the text in margine, as appears from the Bodmer-papyrus of the *Dyscolus*, although this papyrus is of a much later time than the autograph. Neither does it seem plausible to assume with Schweizer that this practice was there because the audience had no programmes in hand and the roles had somehow to be introduced to them.

In order to find a more satisfying answer to this question it should be kept in mind that ancient tragedy owed its origin ultimately to the cult of Dionysus.

---

[26] Lines 1–3. It is true, of course, that both in Greek and in Latin the more normal unemphatic construction has no pronoun e.g. *Od*.13,9 and *Hymn Dem*.1,268, but cf. *Od*.6,196; 11,252; and Plautus, *Capt*.863, where the pronoun is present (metri causa?), while the emphasis seems to rest rather on the predicate, the name. However this may be, it seems to us that the Hellenistic standard manifestation formula: ἐγώ εἰμι plus name, was influenced by the fact that in the Biblical Hebrew and Egyptian models there was no copula verb but only a personal pronoun, which may have looked rather emphatic and was so translated (sometimes even in verbal sentences e.g. Judges 5,3 (B) ἐγώ εἰμι ᾄσομαι = I shall sing)

[27] Such as Euripides *Hec*. 1–4; *Hippol*. 1–2; *Ion* 1–5; *Troad*. 1–3; Aeschylus *Aetniae* frg.195, 15; Menander *Dysc*.11–12; IG 12,3,421; P. Giss.I 3; Plautus *Amph*.19; *Cist*.154; *Trin*.8–9; cf. O. Weinreich, De dis ignotis quaestiones selectae, *Archiv für Religionswissenschaft* 18(1915) esp. 34–45. It is, of course, clear that Schweizer's purpose was different from ours and that he had to leave out the purely identificational formulae.

And second we shall have to see what can be said about the origin of such texts as the Isis-aretalogy. When discussing this latter Greek text, as well as the Isis- and Osiris-inscriptions mentioned by Diodorus of Sicily (1,27,3–5), the Swedish scholar Jan Bergman has shown that these texts have their counterparts in Egyptian literature and inscriptions, and were certainly copied from such models. He adduces for instance a comparable text from the temple at Edfu which runs: 'I am Thoth, the oldest son of Re, whom Atum has created, ... I have come from heaven ... Today I arrived in Pe' etc. This text is preceded by the words 'ḏd mdw' which mean 'to recite' or 'for recitation,' and embody an instruction for the priest who in the performance of the cult had to play the role of the appearing god, wearing no doubt in this case the mask of an ibis,[28] or speaking perhaps from behind the god's statue when it was displayed or moved to the fore. The priest thus played an active role in the revelation or epiphany of the god who was in either case, as a masked impersonation or as the cultic statue, perfectly known to the worshippers who had gathered in the temple. Why should the god then begin his address here as well by stating his name? No doubt so because a god's name was such an integral and indissoluble element in his manifestation to mankind, being an important vehicle of the power emanating from him. Without it his manifestation would be incomplete and less effective.

It is not to be wondered at that likewise in Egyptian surroundings Moses, after the divinity has revealed himself to him in the desert only as 'the god of your father, the god of Abraham ...,' does not feel at ease when on the authority of such a vaguely described divinity he had to perform such an important task in Egypt, where a god who had only a paraphrased name may have seemed to be not a very powerful deity. It may well be that indications like 'the god of Abraham' were characteristic of the gods worshipped by desert nomads. The Nabataeans, who were desert merchants, have left us at least a number of such inscriptions dedicated 'to the god of' someone and they are also found in adjacent regions. In one case the one 'whose god' is venerated even bears a Greek name: in the 4th century a certain Abedrapsas had an inscription set up to honour 'the god of Arkesilaos, the god of his father.'[29] Curiously enough some later Christian inscriptions in nearby Jordania show the same

---

[28] J. Bergman, *Ich bin Isis. Studien zum memphitischen Hintergrund der griechischen Isisaretalogien*, Uppsala 1960, esp. 219–228 and 287s. cf. also in the *Book of the Dead*: 'I am Thot the perfect scribe, whose hands are pure. I am the lord of purity ...' (183,41) and 'I am the great Phoenix which is in Heliopolis, the inspector of that which exists' (17a); for the impersonation of the mourning Isis e.g. H. Bonnet, *Reallexikon der ägyptischen Religionsgeschichte*, Berlin 1952, 378, s.v. Klageweib.

[29] CIG 3,4464. These inscriptions have been collected by A. Alt, *Der Gott der Väter. Ein Beitrag zur Vorgeschichte der israelitischen Religion*, Beiträge zur Wissenschaft vom Alten und Neuen Testament, 3.F.H.2, Stuttgart 1929, 74–84.

pattern, but the 'owner' of the god is now a saint: 'oh God of St.Lot and of St.Procopius ....'[30] Such a god was, however, an anonymous god in Egypt, and therefore Moses asked for God's name.

If we now turn again to Greek tragedy we think that a similar explanation will apply. There is a consensus about the fact that tragedy had arisen from the cult of Dionysus, and that its most original portion is the chorus. According to Aristotle the tragedy owed its existence to the improvisation of the one who started the dithyrambic song that was sung by the chorus in honour of the god.[31] It is difficult to imagine, however, how a difference in roles could develop in this way, unless the improvisation was a prelude to the dithyramb and of such a kind that the impression was created that the chorus sang in response to the choir-leader or commented on his song. It is also thinkable that this improvised part had gradually developed from a song that was originally sung by a priest.

As is well known, the statue of the god Dionysus was before his festival removed from his temple in Athens, taken outside the city walls and brought back on the eve of the festivities of which the performance of tragedies formed part. This happened no doubt in order to create the illusion of an epiphany or arrival of the god, especially so as Dionysus was so often abroad in his mythology, on his journeys through the Orient, which were no doubt a reminiscence of the East-Anatolian origin of vineculture.[32] In this cultic connection it seems rather logical to assume that a priest, either impersonating Dionysus or speaking in his name, made a solemn announcement of the god's arrival in which it was essential that his awe-inspiring name be mentioned, and that the dithyramb was a response. This annunciation, if it ever was a fixed formula, may have become more freely phrased in the course of time and was then taken over by a member of the chorus. This liturgical situation, to which the first 170 lines of the *Bacchae* still come very close, may explain also why other gods, after they had been introduced into tragedy in the course of its further theatrical development, are at least once expressly called by name and that this happens often already in the first lines of the play. Even the superfluous name inscriptions on vases mentioned above might be a relic of the same nature,

---

[30] *Revue Biblique* 43(1934) 395; cf. C.H. Kraeling, *Gerasa: City of the Decapolis* ..., New Haven – Connecticut 1938, nr. 311: 'oh Lord, God of the Holy Cosmas and Damianus;' *Quarterly of the Department of Antiquities in Palestine* 3(1933) 105: 'Lord, God of the Holy Mary' (Kh. ʿAhya); Cyril of Scythopolis, *Vita Sabae* p. 254A (ed. E. Schwartz, 1933, 109): 'Lord, God of my father Sabas.' The instances of the god Men, such as 'Men of Pharnakes,' 'Men of Artemidorus,' 'Men of Tiamos (?),' Μὴν ἐξ Ἀπολλωνίου are different cases because the name of the god is here mentioned and followed by that of the builder of the altar or the temple, see: E. Lane, *Corpus Monumentorum Religionis Dei Menis (CMRDM)*, EPRO 19, Leiden 1976, III, 67ss.

[31] *Poetica* 4,14.

[32] That Dionysus makes war even against the Indians (Nonnus, *Dionysiaca*, book XIV) is certainly a later expansion due to the conquests of Alexander.

because vase paintings seem so often to have been inspired by stage scenes.

That the Greek conception of gods' names was not much different from that in Egypt is among other things shown by the positive evaluation of the phenomenon of a number of gods like Zeus, Aphrodite, Apollo, Artemis, having so many cultic names under which they were worshipped. Pausanias listed already 59 different titles and manifestations of the goddess Athena,[33] and Isis, that Hellenistic deity par excellence, had so many names that she was called both in literature and inscriptions μυριώνυμος, 'having ten thousand names,' and Bergman says that she was the only god to bear this epithet.[34] This may be true, but that other virtually synonymous epithet πολυώνυμος, 'with many names' occurs in connection with Pluto and Artemis already in the *Hymn to Demeter* I 18 and Aristophanes *Thesm.* 320.[35] The Alexandrian poet Callimachus was of course well aware of all this and makes πολυωνυμία even a bone of contention between the Olympians. In his *Hymn to Artemis* he depicts this goddess, who was then still a very young girl, as sitting on the knee of her father Zeus and asking of him all kinds of gifts, one of her very first wishes being that he grant her to keep: 'eternal virginity, Daddy (ἄππα), and many names so that (my twin brother) Apollo will not be able to contend with me' (1–7; 33–35). In the much later Orphic Hymns πολυώνυμε figures as one of many epithets of no fewer than 14 different divinities.[36]

Finally, it is a further and perhaps only modern development to ask the apparition of a well-known and recognizable god or goddess under what additional name he or she appears this time. When Mary started to appear to six children simultaneously in Medyugorye—Yugoslavia some years ago, and these appearances took place very regularly, every afternoon around

---

[33] See the edition by W.H.S. Jones—R.E. Wycherley, V, Cambridge-Mass. 1965, 206; sometimes the gods are sworn by under two different additional names in one and the same inscription: Zeus Diktaios and Zeus Agoraios in Syll.526, Zeus Tallaios and Zeus Agoraios, Apollo Delphinios and Apollo Poitios (= Pythios) in Syll.527; even Bona Dea, whose real name was probably secret, but may have been Fauna (Macrobius *Sat.*1,12,27), had some 35 different epithets, see H.J.J. Brouwer, *Bona Dea. De bronnen en een beschrijving van de cultus* (Bona Dea. The sources and a description of the cult), thesis Utrecht 1982, 111–116. In addition to this epithet-system all kinds of equations could also multiply the name of one specific god, either within the same pantheon, e.g. Zeus Helios, or outside, e.g. Zeus Sarapis. The former process probably underlies Exodus 6,1–2 'I am Yhwh, I appeared to Abraham, to Isaac and to Jacob as El-Shadday;' the latter is meant by Cicero when he says: 'quot hominum linguae tot nomina deorum' (*Nat. Deor.*1, 30/84).

[34] *o.c.*, 300; e.g. Plutarch *De Iside* 372e; OGIS 695,2, etc.; in Latin inscriptions *myrionyma* e.g. CIL 5,5080; a list of the names of Isis is found in P. Oxy.1380; G.H.R. Horsley, *New Documents Illustrating Early Christianity*, I, Macquarie University 1981, 16 wonders whether Philemon 2,9 'the name above all names' might be a reaction against the very phenomenon of polyonymia.

[35] Isis is called '*multinominis*' in Apuleius *Met.*11,22.

[36] 2,1; 10,13; 11,10; 16,9; 27,4; 36,1; 40,1; 41,1; 42,2; 45,2; 50,2; 52,1; 56,1; 59,2. (ed. G. Quandt, Berlin 1962).

six o'clock, the children were advised to ask the Holy Mother for her name. This they did and Mary answered that she was 'The Queen of Peace,' which meant, as she herself explained, that her appearances had the special purpose of bringing all people together, the Roman-Catholics, the Eastern Orthodox and the Muslims, the three religions that meet one another in Yugoslavia.[37] Whatever we may think or believe of these appearances, they are at any rate acceptable when they carry a message of this kind, which, of course, is also a message to the whole world.

---

[37] R. Laurentin—L. Rupčić, *La Vierge apparaît—Elle à Medjugorje? Un message urgent donné au monde dans un pays marxiste*, Paris 1984, 75.

THE UNKNOWN GOD (ACTS 17:23)

BY

Pieter Willem van der Horst (Utrecht)

At some time in the last quarter of the first century CE an early Christian author, of whom we know next to nothing, composed a highly original twofold work, which for the sake of convenience we call 'Luke-Acts'. Luke was the first to write not only a volume on the life of Jesus but also one on the careers of some of his earliest followers. Whereas in book I, the Gospel, Luke gives his language the bouquet of Jewish Palestine by a purposeful use of Semitisms, or rather Septuagintisms, in book II, the Acts of the Apostles, this stylistic device is used less and less in proportion to the degree in which the preaching of the Christian message moves away from Palestine into the non-Jewish world. Luke shows his linguistic skill especially in the missionary and defence speeches of the apostle Paul, who is the protagonist from chapter 13 onwards. In chapters 13–20 Luke has Paul deliver three great missionary speeches (besides a number of summaries of minor ones): one before a Jewish audience in Pisidian Antioch (13:16–41), one before a pagan audience in Athens (17:22–31), and one before a Christian audience in Miletus (20:18–35). In chapters 21–28 Paul gives three great defence speeches: the first before the inhabitants of Jerusalem (22:1–21), the second before Felix, the Roman procurator (24:10–21), the third one before king Agrippa (26:2–23). This structure seems to indicate that Luke regarded Paul's speech in Athens as the summit of his missionary career.[1] This speech, the most Hellenistic part of the most Hellenistic book of the New Testament,[2] was delivered in one of the most prestigious cities of the Hellenistic and Roman world. For in spite of Athens' political and economic decline during the Hellenistic period, the city was still an important cultural centre, much visited by scholars and artists from all over the world who were attracted by its symbolic status.[3] It is on a detail of Paul's speech in Athens that we will focus now.

It should be stated clearly at the outset that, although the historicity of Paul's visit to Athens is not open to any doubt, I do not regard the Areopagus

---

[1] J. Dupont, Le discours à l'Aréopage (Ac 17,22–31), lieu de rencontre entre christianisme et hellénisme, in: idem, *Nouvelles études sur les Actes des Apôtres*, Paris 1984, 380–423, esp. 382–384.

[2] Ed. Meyer, *Ursprung und Anfänge des Christentums* III, Stuttgart—Berlin 1923, 89, calls Acts 17:22–31 "das Glanzstück der Apostelgeschichte."

[3] W. Elliger, *Paulus in Griechenland*, Stuttgart 1978, 117–126.

speech, as reported by Luke, to be the *ipsissima verba Pauli*. "A prevailing convention among ancient historians was the custom of inserting speeches of the leading characters into the narrative."[4] These often occupied large sections of their historical work. The chief requisite of such speeches was appropriateness to the speaker and to the occasion. Five centuries before Luke, the Greek historian Thucydides had already said: "As to the speeches that were made by several men (. . .), it has been difficult to recall with strict accuracy the words actually spoken. (. . .) Therefore they are given in the language in which, as it seemed to me, the several speakers would express, on the subjects under consideration, the sentiments most befitting the occasion" (I 22). Since it is obvious that both the ancient historians and their readers considered the speeches more as a vehicle for editorial and dramatic comment than for historical tradition, we should not try to find the words of the apostle in Paul's address. From beginning to end it is a Lucan composition.[5] It is a composition in which Luke demonstrates his skill as a Hellenistic writer.[6] Already in the introduction to the speech he shows his knowledge of the contemporary philosophical scene by introducing Stoics and Epicureans as Paul's antagonists and by alluding to Socratic traditions in v. 18 (for ξένων δαιμονίων δοκεῖ καταγγελεὺς εἶναι cf. Xenophon, *Memorabilia Socratis* I 1 καινὰ δαιμόνια εἰσφέρων). In the speech itself, Paul begins his *captatio benevolentiae* with the well-known topic of Athens' piety (v.22). Then he uses the traditional literary device of taking a starting-point in an (altar) inscription (v.23). In v.25 he airs the current idea that God is self-sufficient and not in need of anything. V.27 states that God can be found since he is not far from each of us, a thought paralleled in several contemporary Greek and Latin authors. V.28 gives a quotation from Aratus' *Phaenomena* and perhaps even one from a poem of Epimenides. And this is only a random selection. The whole section teems with Hellenistic motifs (besides Jewish and, at the end, Christian elements, of course) to which a plethora of parallels can be adduced and has been adduced.[7] For the moment we will have to leave this aside; we hope to return to

---

[4] H.J. Cadbury, *The Making of Luke-Acts*, New York 1927 (repr. London 1958), 184.

[5] Cadbury, *Making* (n. 4),184 ff. See esp. the valuable discussion of this matter by M. Dibelius, The Speeches in Acts and Ancient Historiography, in his *Studies in the Acts of the Apostles*, London 1956, 138–185. For literature since Dibelius see A. Weiser, *Die Apostelgeschichte, Kapitel 1–12*, Gütersloh—Würzburg 1981, 97–100.

[6] E. Plümacher, *Lukas als hellenistischer Schriftsteller*, Göttingen 1972, 32 ff.

[7] Abundant comparative materials can be found in, e.g., E. Norden, *Agnostos Theos. Untersuchungen zur Formengeschichte religiöser Rede*, Leipzig 1913 (repr. Darmstadt 1956), 1–140. C. Clemen, *Religionsgeschichtliche Erklärung des Neuen Testaments*, Giessen 1924², 290–304. W. Schmid, Die Rede des Apostels Paulus vor den Philosophen und Areopagiten in Athen, *Philologus* 95 (1942) 79–120. W. Jaeger, Review of Norden, *GGA* 175 (1913) 569–610. M. Dibelius, Paul on the Areopagus, *Studies* (n. 5), 26–77.

it on another occasion.[8] It is now the much discussed altar-inscription to which we wish to turn. In v.23 the speaker says: "As I strolled around, looking at your sacred monuments, I found even an altar with the inscription: To an Unknown God" (διερχόμενος γὰρ καὶ ἀναθεωρῶν τὰ σεβάσματα ὑμῶν εὗρον καὶ βωμὸν ἐν ᾧ ἐπεγέγραπτο · Ἀγνώστῳ θεῷ). I want to try to find an answer to the following questions: I. Was there such an altar in Athens or elsewhere? II. If so, what was the meaning of this or a similar inscription?

I

The evidence for the existence of altars for unknown gods was presented in a masterly fashion by Eduard Norden in his magnificent work *Agnostos Theos* of 1913[9] in which he tried to prove that the idea of an 'unknown god' is utterly un-Greek. In the almost three quarters of a century that have lapsed since then, only one or two pieces of evidence have been added to Norden's dossier (see below). In our presentation we will first give the evidence from non-Christian sources and then consider whether additional information may be gathered from patristic writings. All our sources are later than the Acts of the Apostles.

In the third quarter of the second century CE Pausanias wrote his *Description of Greece*. He begins his first book, on Attica, with a description of the harbours of Athens.[10] After having dealt with Piraeus (I 1,1–3), he continues:

Ἔστι δὲ καὶ ἄλλος Ἀθηναίοις ὁ μὲν ἐπὶ Μουνυχίᾳ λιμὴν καὶ Μουνυχίας ναὸς Ἀρτέμιδος, ὁ δὲ ἐπὶ Φαληρῷ, καθὰ καὶ πρότερον εἴρηταί μοι, καὶ πρὸς αὐτῷ Δήμητρος ἱερόν. ἐνταῦθα καὶ Σκιράδος Ἀθηνᾶς ναός ἐστι καὶ Διὸς ἀπωτέρω, βωμοὶ δὲ θεῶν τε ὀνομαζομένων Ἀγνώστων καὶ ἡρώων καὶ παίδων τῶν Θησέως καὶ Φαληροῦ· τοῦτον γὰρ τὸν Φαληρὸν Ἀθηναῖοι πλεῦσαι μετὰ Ἰάσονός φασιν εἰς Κόλχους. ἔστι δὲ καὶ Ἀνδρόγεω βωμὸς τοῦ Μίνω, καλεῖται δὲ Ἥρωος· Ἀνδρόγεω δὲ ὄντα ἴσασιν οἷς ἐστιν ἐπιμελὲς τὰ ἐγχώρια σαφέστερον ἄλλων ἐπίστασθαι (I 1,4).[11]

---

[8] See my series "Hellenistic Parallels to the Acts of the Apostles" of which the first instalments have been published in *ZNW* 74 (1983) and *JSNT* 25 (1985). Other instalments are in preparation.

[9] Norden, *Agnostos Theos* (n. 7), 1–140, esp. 31 ff., 56 ff. For other presentations of this material see Th. Zahn, Die auszerbiblischen Zeugnisse für die Altarinschrift Ἀγνώστῳ θεῷ in Athen, in: idem, *Die Apostelgeschichte des Lukas* II, Leipzig 1921, 870–882; A. Wikenhauser, Der Altar des "unbekannten Gottes" in Athen, in: *Die Apostelgeschichte und ihr Geschichtswert*, Münster 1921, 369–394; K. Lake, The Unknown God, in: *The Beginnings of Christianity* V, London 1933, 240–246. A short summary of the evidence in Dibelius, *Studies* (n. 5), 38–41, and in R. Turcan, Agnostos theos, *Encycl. of Religion*, 1 (1987) 135–138.

[10] For a short survey of the archeology of Athens in the first two centuries CE see O. Broneer, Athens, 'City of Idol Worship,' *Biblical Archaeologist* 21 (1958), 2–28, and especially W. Elliger, *Paulus in Griechenland* (n. 3), 117–199.

[11] "The Athenians have also another harbour, at Munychia, with a temple of Artemis of Munychia, and yet another at Phalerum, as I have already stated, and near it is a sanctuary of Demeter. Here there is also a temple of Athena Skiras, and one of Zeus some distance away, and

The reason why I quote this passage at length will become apparent presently. Pausanias speaks about altars of gods called 'unknown gods' near one of the harbours of Athens. Immediately the question arises: what was the inscription on these altars? It has been argued that of the plural βωμοὶ θεῶν ἀγνώστων the singular is not βωμὸς θεῶν ἀγνώστων but βωμὸς θεοῦ ἀγνώστου.[12] When Greek and Latin authors speak of βωμοὶ θεῶν or *arae deorum*, they usually mean a number of altars dedicated to a number of individual gods (e.g. Homer, *Iliad* XI 808, Juvenal, *Satura* III 145), not altars dedicated to a plurality of gods. So logically and grammatically it might seem to be defensible that Pausanias is talking about several altars each of which was dedicated to an unknown god in the singular, but it should be borne in mind that the use of the plural βωμοί may have been occasioned by the fact that he mentions here three groups of altars, *sc.* of unknown gods, of Heroes, and of the sons of Theseus. Be that as it may, what could have been the text of the inscription? In his final remark Pausanias says that the altar of Androgeos was called the altar 'of a heros,' because one did not know for certain for whom it had been erected. Elsewhere (VI 20, 15 – 19; VI 24, 4; X 33, 6) Pausanias mentions other altars of unknown heroes.[13] And we do possess altar-inscriptions which read ἥρωος or ἥρωι, 'of/for a heros.'[14] So it might well be that the inscriptions on the altars for unknown gods just read θεῷ or θεοῦ, 'for/of a god,'[15] without the name of the deity added for the reason that it was unknown. But one cannot exclude the possibility that the inscription was indeed θεῷ ἀγνώστῳ. More probable, however, would seem to be a dedication θεοῖς ἀγνώστοις, for in V 14,8 Pausanias says in his description of the sanctuaries in Olympia:

τὰ δὲ ἐς τὸν μέγαν βωμὸν ὀλίγῳ μέν τι ἡμῖν πρότερόν ἐστιν εἰρημένα, καλεῖται δὲ Ὀλυμπίου Διός. Πρὸς αὐτῷ δέ ἐστιν ἀγνώστων θεῶν βωμός.[16]

---

altars of gods named Unknown, and of heroes, and of the children of Theseus and Phalerus; for this Phalerus is said by the Athenians to have sailed with Jason to Colchis. There is also an altar of Androgeos, son of Minos, though it is called that of Heros; those, however, who pay special attention to the study of their country's antiquities know that it belongs to Androgeos" (translation by W.H.S. Jones in the Loeb Classical Library: *Pausanias, Description of Greece* I, London 1918, 7).

[12] Th. Birt, Ἄγνωστοι θεοί und die Areopagrede des Apostels Paulus, *RhM*, N.F. 69 (1914) 342–392, esp. 349 f.

[13] See E. Rohde, *Psyche*, Leipzig 1898² (repr. Darmstadt 1961), I, 173 f. In this connection we may also refer to the curious report about a cult of heroes called "the unknown ones" in Pollux, *Onomasticon* VIII 118–119: μετὰ γὰρ Τροίας ἅλωσιν Ἀργείων τινὰς τὸ Παλλάδιον ἔχοντας Φαληρῷ προσβαλεῖν, ἀγνοίᾳ δὲ ὑπὸ τῶν ἐγχωρίων ἀναιρεθέντας ἀπορριφῆναι. καὶ τῶν μὲν οὐδὲν προσήπτετο ζῷον, Ἀκάμας δὲ ἐμήνυσεν ὅτι εἶεν Ἀργεῖοι τὸ Παλλάδιον ἔχοντες. καὶ οἱ μὲν ταφέντες ἀγνῶτες προσηγορεύθησαν τοῦ θεοῦ χρήσαντος.

[14] *IG* II 2, 1546.1547. See Birt in *RhM* (n. 12) 350 f.; C.G. Yavis, *Greek Altars*, St. Louis 1949, 170; *Suppl. Epigr. Gr.* 31 (1981) 639, etc.

[15] Both genitive and dative are possible; see Lake in *Beginnings* (n. 9), 242.

[16] "An account of the great altar I gave a little way back; it is called the altar of the Olympian

There are two important differences with the previous passage (I 1, 4): Here
there is an explicit statement that there was *one* altar dedicated to a *plurality*
of unknown gods. Second, here Pausanias does not say that they were *called*
'unknown gods' (as in I 1, 4) but he simply states that there was an altar ἀγνώστων θεῶν. This makes it very probable that ἀγνώστοις θεοῖς or ἀγνώστων
θεῶν was the actual inscription on the altar. So this passage seems to turn the
scales in favour of the possibility of an inscription in the plural, the more so
since Pausanias never writes about βωμοὶ ἀγνώστου θεοῦ.[17]

A passage in Diogenes Laertius, however, seems to point in another direction. In his *Lives and Opinions of Eminent Philosophers* (written in the early
third century CE) he tells us that when the Athenians were attacked by pestilence, they sent a ship to Crete to ask the help of Epimenides, the famous religious teacher and miracle-worker from Cnossos.[18] In order to bring about
atonement for the city, Epimenides took black and white sheep and brought
them to the Areopagus.

> κἀκεῖθεν εἴασεν ἰέναι οἷ βούλοιντο, προστάξας τοῖς ἀκολούθοις ἔνθα ἂν
> κατακλίνοι αὐτῶν ἕκαστον, θύειν τῷ προσήκοντι θεῷ· καὶ οὕτω λῆξαι τὸ
> κακόν. ὅθεν ἔτι καὶ νῦν ἔστιν εὑρεῖν κατὰ τοὺς δήμους τῶν Ἀθηναίων βωμοὺς
> ἀνωνύμους, ὑπόμνημα τῆς τότε γενομένης ἐξιλάσεως (I 110).[19]

It is hard to say what is meant by ὁ προσήκων θεός. I have translated it
vaguely by "the divinity concerned" (n.19), but others translate it by "the
local divinity,"[20] taking it to be the god worshipped in the *demos* within which
or near the spot on which the sheep lay down. But the fact that Diogenes says
that in his day[20a] 'anonymous altars' were still visible in Attica suggests that
the Athenians did not know whom they had to placate in order to get rid of
the plague. The προσήκων θεός probably was the unknown deity who had sent
them the pestilence. Hence the altars bore no name. Of course they were not
inscribed τῷ προσήκοντι θεῷ. Most probably they bore the simple inscription
θεῷ, 'to a god,' of which we do indeed have some epigraphic examples.[21]

Zeus. By it is an altar of unknown gods" (transl. W.H.S. Jones in LCL ed. of Paus. vol. II, London 1926, 463).

[17] See O. Weinreich, *De dis ignotis quaestiones selectae*, diss. Halle 1914 (= *Archiv für
Religionswissenschaft* 18, 1915, 1–52), 27 f.

[18] The legendary traditions about this person make it impossible to fix the dates of his life-
time, but he most probably lived somewhere in the sixth century (maybe into the fifth century)
BCE.

[19] "And there he let them go whither they pleased, instructing those who followed them to
sacrifice to the deity concerned on the spot where each sheep lay down. And thus, it is said, the
plague was stayed. Hence even to this day altars may be found in different districts of Athens with
no name inscribed upon them, which are memorials of this atonement" (revised version of R.D.
Hicks' transl. in LCL ed. of Diog. Laert. vol. II, London 1925, 115.117).

[20] So Hicks, *op. cit.*, 115.

[20a] Though the words ἔτι καὶ νῦν may have come from one of Diogenes' sources.

[21] E.g. *IG* II 2, 1601. Other instances are mentioned by Birt, *RhM.* (n. 8), 351, and can be

Before we ask the question whether there is epigraphic evidence for either θεῷ ἀγνώστῳ or θεοῖς ἀγνώστοις, let us look at the final piece of literary evidence, a much debated passage in Philostratus' *Life of Apollonius of Tyana* (written in the early third century CE). In *VA* VI 3 Philostratus reports a conversation on the Nile between Apollonius and a certain Timasion from Naucratis (in Egypt). Timasion had left his home in order to escape the affection of his stepmother, which was like that of Phaedra for Hippolytus. Unlike Hippolytus, however, he had not insulted Aphrodite but had constantly sacrificed to her. Apollonius says that in this respect Timasion was wiser than Hippolytus.

> καὶ αὐτὸ δὲ τὸ διαβεβλῆσθαι πρὸς ὀντιναδὴ τῶν θεῶν, ὥσπερ πρὸς τὴν Ἀφροδίτην ὁ Ἱππόλυτος, οὐκ ἀξιῶ σωφροσύνης· σωφρονέστερον γὰρ τὸ περὶ πάντων θεῶν εὖ λέγειν, καὶ ταῦτα Ἀθήνησιν, οὗ καὶ ἀγνώστων δαιμόνων βωμοὶ ἵδρυνται.[22]

The parallellism of θεῶν and δαιμόνων in these lines proves that, as so often, the words are identical in meaning. The most hotly debated problem of this passage need not detain us here, since it is hardly of relevance for our discussion. To summarize it briefly: Norden argued that the words καὶ ταῦτα Ἀθήνησιν κτλ. made no sense in a conversation on the Nile and hence he assumed that originally they came from another context, *sc.* Apollonius' speech before the Athenians which had been incorporated into his now lost treatise Περὶ θυσιῶν. This speech or treatise Norden supposed to have been the source of the story in Acts 17.[23] This ingenious but artificial construction did not meet with much approval and was decisively disproved by Eduard Meyer and others.[24] Be that as it may, here again it is said that in Athens there were

---

found by consulting the indexes of *SEG*. For this use of θεός see W.H.S. Jones, A Note on the Vague Use of ΘΕΟΣ, *CR* 27 (1913) 152–255.

[22] "The mere aversion to any one of the gods, such as Hippolytus entertained in regard to Aphrodite, I do not class as a form of prudence; for it is a much greater proof of prudence to speak well of all the gods, especially in Athens, where altars are set up in honour even of unknown gods" (slightly revised version of F.C. Conybeare's transl. in LCL ed. of Philostratus' *VA*, vol. II, London 1912, 13).

[23] Norden, *Agnostos Theos* (n. 7), 37–55.

[24] See Ed. Meyer, Apollonios von Tyana und die Biographie des Philostratos, *Hermes* 52 (1917) 371–424, esp. 400f.; Th. Plüss, Apollonios von Tyana auf dem Nil und der unbekannte Gott zu Athen, in: *Festgabe Hugo Blümner*, Zürich 1914, 36–48; P. Corssen, Der Altar des unbekannten Gottes, *ZNW* 14 (1913) 309–323; F.C. Burkitt, *Agnostos Theos, Journal of Theological Studies* 15 (1914) 455–464; E. von Dobschütz, Agnostos Theos, *Sokrates* 67 (1913) 625–630; Th. Birt, Ἄγνωστοι θεοί (n. 12), 346 ff; Norden's thesis was defended by O. Weinreich, Agnostos Theos, *Deutsche Literaturzeitung* 34 (1913) 2949–2964; R. Reitzenstein, Die Areopagrede des Paulus, *Neue Jahrbücher für das klassische Altertum* 31 (1913) 393–422; W.W. Jaeger, Agnostos Theos, *Göttingische gelehrte Anzeigen* 175 (1913) 569–610; H. Lietzmann, Zu Nordens Agnostos Theos, *RhM* 71 (1916), 280f. A list of reviews is given by L. Deubner in: *Archiv für Religions-Wissenschaft* 20 (1920/21) 422 n. 1.

altars for unknown gods, both 'altars' and 'gods' being in the plural, so that
we have here the same interpretative problem as in the first-mentioned passage
from Pausanias. Whether we should consider Philostratus to be an independent witness is uncertain, since we can certainly not exclude the possibility that
he got his information from Pausanias.

We now turn to the archeological evidence. Most unfortunately the only
piece of epigraphic material adduced so far in the last 75 years is a mutilated
inscription which breaks off at the decisive point.[25] In 1909 Hugo Hepding ex-
cavated a small altar from the second century CE within the precinct of the
great sanctuary of Demeter in Pergamon. He published it in 1910.[26] The inscription reads:

ΘΕΟΙΣΑΓ⸌

Κ Α Π Ι Τ⸌

Δ Α ΔΟΥ Χ Ο

Hepding restored it to:

ΘΕΟΙΣΑΓΝΩΣΤΟΙΣ

Κ Α Π Ι ΤΩ Ν

Δ Α ΔΟΥ Χ Ο Σ

If this restoration is correct, this altar-inscription would be really 'hard' evidence for the existence of altars for unknown gods in antiquity. But Hepding's
restoration has met with much criticism and has been rejected by many scholars
in the field of both classics and New Testament studies.[27] The fact, however,
that the three greatest experts in the religious world of Hellenistic-Roman
times, *sc.* Otto Weinreich, Arthur Nock, and Martin Nilsson, have firmly
defended Hepding's reading,[28] should give us cause to think. Let us weigh the
pros and cons for the various restorations proposed.

The first thing to note is that the reading of the lines 2–3, Καπίτων δαδοῦ-
χος, is certain. The *dadouchos*, 'torch-bearer', was one of the highest hereditary

---

[25] Weinreich, *De dis ignotis* (n. 17), 29: "Fortuna, qua est inconstantia et malitia, lapidem mutilum esse voluit."

[26] H. Hepding, Die Arbeiten zu Pergamon 1908–1909. II: Die Inschriften, *Mitteilungen des kaiserlich deutschen archäologischen Instituts, Athenische Abteilung* 35 (1910) 454–457. A photo can also be found in A. Deissmann, *Paulus. Eine kultur- und religionsgeschichtliche Skizze*, Tübingen 1925², Tafel IV (see his discussion at pp. 226–229).

[27] To mention only one recent authoritative commentary: E. Haenchen, *Die Apostel-geschichte*, Göttingen 1968⁶, 458–9 n. 6. Norden, *Agnostos Theos* (n. 7), 56 n. 1, also summarily dismisses this inscription.

[28] O. Weinreich, Agnostos Theos (n. 24) 2958ff.; idem, *De dis ignotis* (n. 17), 29 ff.; idem, *Triskaidekadische Studien*, Giessen 1916 (repr. Berlin 1967), 71 f.; A.D. Nock, *Sallustius, Concerning the Gods and the Universe*, Cambridge 1926, XC–XCI n. 211; M.P. Nilsson, *Geschichte der griechischen Religion* II, München 1961², 355; idem, Zu den Inschriften in dem Demeterheiligtum in Pergamon, in: idem, *Opuscula Selecta* III, Lund 1960, 188.

priests at the mysteries of the Eleusinian Demeter, a cult that had been exported from Attica to Pergamon.[29] Did this priest of Demeter erect an altar θεοῖς ἀγρίοις or ἀγροτέροις or θεοῖς ἁγίοις or ἁγιωτάτοις or θεοῖς ἁγνοῖς or ἁγνοτάτοις or ἀγγέλοις or ἀγνώστοις? All these restorations have been proposed, all of them with a Γ, Ρ, Ι or Ν as the third letter after ΑΓ, since the vertical stroke of which the lower part is visible after the Γ must have been of one of these letters. The shorter suggestions (ἀγρίοις, ἁγίοις, ἁγνοῖς, also ἀγγέλοις) can be rejected immediately since the clearly symmetrical construction of the inscription enables us to determine that after the Γ there most probably followed 7, perhaps 8, other letters, no less. The reading ἀγροτέροις is extremely unlikely. Meaning 'wild' or 'fond of hunting', it is not a suitable epithet of gods, except of Artemis, the only deity to whom it is sometimes applied. Ἁγνότατοι as an epithet of gods is so rare as virtually to preclude that this was what the inscription read (we know of only one other instance).[30] The reading ἁγιωτάτοις, defended by Otto Kern,[31] at first sight seems to be an attractive filling of the gap. It is an epithet that is frequently applied to deities, especially to oriental gods, and it nicely fits the available space. But, as Weinreich has pointed out, the improbability of this restoration lies in the fact that ἁγιώτατος/ἁγιώτατοι always precedes θεός/θεοί and is almost always accompanied by the name of the deity/deities. Moreover, if the torch-bearer had meant Demeter and her daughter to be the "most holy goddesses," he certainly would have used the article and have said ταῖς θεοῖς ἁγιωτάταις, or, using the dual, as in CIG I 1449 τοῖν ἁγιωτάτοιν θεοῖν, sc. Demeter and Kore. And, finally, if ἁγιωτάτοις were written, then the left horizontal stroke of the Ω would probably have been visible, just as it is in the second line after the Τ of Καπίτων.[32] That leaves us with ἀγνώστοις as the most feasible restoration of the inscription. In my opinion, there can be little doubt that Hepding's proposal to read the altar-inscription as θεοῖς ἀγνώστοις is correct.

Apart from these epigraphical and stylistic probabilities, there are other factors that may serve as corroborative data for the proprosed reconstruction of the inscription. Pausanias reports the existence of altars for unknown gods in Athens and in Olympia. Pergamon falls outside the scope of his work, which is limited to Greece. Most striking, however, is the similarity between the situation described by Pausanias for Athens and Olympia (as far as their *sebasmata* are concerned) and the situation discovered by archeologists in the nineteenth and twentieth century in Pergamon. To be more precise, Pausanias describes

---

[29] See e.g. P. Stengel, *Die griechischen Kultusaltertümer*, München 1920³, 178.

[30] Weinreich, *De dis ignotis* (n. 17), 30–31, mentions two instances but one is an improbable restoration of *CIG* 6857, the second is in the singular, followed by the name of the deity.

[31] O. Kern, Das Demeterheiligtum von Pergamon und die orphische Hymnen, *Hermes* 46 (1911) 431–436, esp. 434.

[32] Weinrich, *De dis ignotis* (n. 17), 30–32.

Athens and Olympia as cities crammed with sanctuaries and altars of all kinds, not only of the official Olympian gods but also of a great number of other deities and also of personified abstractions: in Athens there were in the neighbourhood of the great temples altars for e.g. Ἔλεος, Αἰδώς, Φήμη, Ὁρμή (Pausanias I 17,1), in Olympia for Ὁμόνοια, Καιρός, etc. (Pausanias V 14,1ff.).[33] Moreover, in both cities there were altars of 'all gods' (θεῶν πάντων βωμοί). (The cult of πάντες καὶ πᾶσαι θεοί or even ὁ πάνθεος or τὸ πάνθειον was widespread in the Greek world of the Hellenistic-Roman period, more so in fact than the cult of personalized abstractions).[34] And, as if all that was not yet enough, in both cities there were altars ἀγνώστων θεῶν. What do we find in Pergamon? Exactly the same situation: again altars by the dozens, altars for the traditional gods (Zeus, Hermes, Demeter, etc.), for less traditional deities like Helios and Selene, for abstractions like Ἀρέτη, Σωφροσύνη, Πίστις, Τελέτη, Ὁμόνοια, even τὸ Αὐτόματον, of θεοὶ πάντες καὶ πᾶσαι and τὸ πάνθειον, and, finally, of θεοὶ ἄγνωστοι.[35] This last item, the 'unknown gods,' may now safely be added. In these three great religious centres of the early imperial period we find an almost identical situation: around or in the vicinity of one of the main altars or temples there is a gradual accumulation of minor altars, and the further this process goes, the stronger becomes the tendency to strive for completeness. There is what appears to be an anxious endeavour not to pass over or omit any inhabitant whatsoever of the divine world. That this tendency did indeed exist in priestly (and probably also in other) circles is demonstrated by an illuminating inscription from Miletus (of the end of the second or beginning of the third century CE), in which the *prophetes* Damianus asks Apollo permission to complete the πάνθεος περιβωμισμός of the Didymeion by adding a still missing altar of Apollo's sister, which the god permits.[36] A πάνθεος περιβωμισμός, a precinct for altars of all the gods without exception, is exactly what we have in Pergamon.

---

[33] On the cult of personified abstractions see e.g. L.R. Farnell, *The Cults of the Greek States* V, Oxford 1909, 443 ff.; H. Dörrie, Gottesvorstellung, *RAC* XII (1983), 117 f. F.W. Hamdorf, *Griechische Kultpersonifikationen aus vorhellenistischer Zeit*, Mainz 1964.

[34] F. Jacobi, Πάντες θεοί, diss. Halle 1930 (p. 53 f. on our altar in Athens); K. Ziegler, Pantheion, *RE* XVIII 3 (1949) 697–747; O. Kern, *Die Religion der Griechen* III, Berlin 1938, 126–144.

[35] Nilsson, *Gesch. der gr. Rel.* (n. 28), 355 ff. Note that in Philostratus, *Vita Apoll.* VI 3, too, first πάντες θεοί are mentioned and then the ἄγνωστοι δαίμονες.

[36] The inscription was published by Th. Wiegand, Siebenter vorläufiger Bericht über die von den königlichen Museen in Milet und Didyma unternommenen Ausgrabungen, *Abhandlungen der königlich preussischen Akademie der Wissenschaften zu Berlin*, Phil.-hist. Klasse, Berlin 1911, 63–64: lines 1–14 Ὁ προφήτης σου Δαμιανὸς ἐρωτᾷ· ἐπὶ (= ἐπεὶ) ἐν τῷ ἱερῷ σου καὶ πανθέῳ περιβωμισμῷ οὐδέπω ὁρᾷ ἱδρυμένον βωμὸν τῆς ἁγιωτάτης σου ἀδελφῆς, τῆς πατρίου αὐτοῦ θεᾶς σωτείρας Κόρης, φιλόθεον δὲ αὐτὸν ὄντα λυπεῖ τὸ τοιοῦτον, δῖται (= δεῖται) σου, δέσποτα Διδυμεῦ Ἥλιε Ἄπολλον, θεσπίσαι αὐτῷ παρὰ τὸν τῆς καρποφόρου Δήμητρος βωμὸν ἱδρύσασθαι βωμὸν τῆς παιδὸς αὐτῆς. Lines 20ff. ἐπέτρεψας αὐτῷ ἐν τῷ ἱερῷ σου περιβωμισμῷ ἱδρύσασθαι βωμὸν κτλ.

In order to make the *pantheos peribomismos* as complete as possible, one includes not only the gods one knows, but one includes *expressis verbis* also the
gods one does not know. Hence dedications of altars not only to 'unknown
gods,' but also, still safer, to 'all the gods.'[37] All deities shoud receive their
fair share of honour and worship, for otherwise one of them might manifest
himself and take revenge for the neglect, whether by sending pestilence or
causing an earthquake or some other disaster.[38] This fear is described by John
Chrysostom when in one of his homilies on the Acts of the Apostles he says,
referring to the altar in Athens:

δεδοικότες μή ποτε καὶ ἄλλος τις ἦ αὐτοῖς μὲν οὐδέπω γνώριμος, θεραπευόμε-
νος δὲ ἀλλαχοῦ, ὑπὲρ πλείονος δῆθεν ἀσφαλείας καὶ τούτῳ βωμὸν ἔστησαν,
καὶ ἐπειδὴ οὐκ ἦν δῆλος ὁ θεός, ἐπεγέγραπτο· ἀγνώστῳ θεῷ.[39]

As I said above, this is the only piece of archeological evidence that has played
a part in the research of this century. I would now like to suggest that there
is yet another piece of evidence that has been overlooked. It is an inscription
on a marble stele, found near Dorylaeum in the northern part of Phrygia, and
published 50 years ago.[40] Unfortunately the editors do not date the monument
but I presume that, like most other inscriptions from that area, it dates from
the imperial period. Once again the text is badly mutilated. The readable part
runs as follows:

Φ[   ]
ΥΠΕΡΕΑΥ[   ]ΩΝ
[   ]ΙΔΙΩΝΘΕ
[   ]ΟΙΣΕΥ
[   ]

The editors restore as follows:

Φ[. . . . .   ]
ὑπὲρ ἑαυ[τ]ῶν
[καὶ τῶν] ἰδίων θε –
[οῖς . . . . .]οις εὐ –
[χήν]

---

[37] Ziegler, Pantheion (n. 34), on the Miletus inscription: "Dies kann nicht nicht anderes be-
deuten, als dasz der heilige Bezirk des Gottes für die Aufstellung von Altären für alle anderen
Götter zur Verfügung gestellt war."

[38] Nilsson speaks of "das *ängstliche Bemühen*, alle Götter zu erfassen" (Zu den Inschriften (n.
28) 188; my italics).

[39] "Since they (*sc.* the Athenians) feared that there might be some other (god) not yet known
to them but worshipped elsewhere, *to be on the safe side* they erected an altar for him as well; and
as (the nature or name of) the god was not clear, it was inscribed: to an unknown god" (*Homil.
38 in Acta Apost.*, in *PG.* 60, 268). See E. Bickerman, The Altars of Gentiles, in his *Studies in
Jewish and Christian History* II, Leiden 1980, 345.

[40] C.W.M. Cox and A. Cameron (edd.), *Monumenta Asiae Minoris Antiqua* V: *Monuments
from Dorylaeum and Nacolea*, Manchester 1937, 56 (no. 107).

"F... (have fulfilled their) vow to the (...) gods on behalf of themselves and their own family/families."

The first line is irreparably damaged, but it has certainly contained only the name of a collective or two short proper names. The restoration of lines 2–3 is certain because these are standard formulas; the same applies to line 5. The crux is line 4, the only one where the editors have not filled the gap, apart from the ending *ois* to *theois*, an obviously correct reading since the adjective that follows ends in *ois*. Between this *ois* and the supposed *ois* at the beginning of the line there is room for at least five but probably six letters. Moreover, before *ois* after the gap there is visible "part of an upper horizontal bar,"[41] which must belong to a Τ, a Γ, a Σ, or an E. Given these restrictions, many restorations are precluded. For these reasons, e.g., ὁσίοις, ἁγίοις, ἀγρίοις and ἁγνοῖς are impossible (too short, and *iota*, *rho* and *nun* do not fit the horizontal bar). Ἁγιωτάτοις and ἁγνοτάτοις are too long for the space availabe and, as said above, should precede θεοῖς. Other suggestions meet with the same difficulties. To my mind, there is only one word that does not run up against all these problems, viz. the word ἀγνώστοις. Firstly, it fits exactly the availabe space, αγνωστ being six letters. Second, it fits excellently from a paleographical point of view since the Τ has the required upper horizontal bar. And third, it fits perfectly the rest of the inscription since no names of deities are mentioned. This absence of the names of the gods is no longer strange once one reads θεοῖς ἀγνώστοις, unknown gods having no names *per definitionem*. All this makes it well-nigh certain that the lacuna has to be filled according to my proposal. This is a conclusion of some importance since it doubles our archeological evidence for the existence of dedications to unknown gods.[42] It is not difficult to see what the dedicators meant by their inscription. One can imagine that they had prayed to a well-known Olympian or local god for help or relief in a situation which was difficult to bear for them, but gained no answer. Then they tried another known deity or several of them or even all of them at the same time, again without success. Finally, at their wits' end, they concluded that there might be deities unknown to them who caused them these troubles and whom they had to placate in order to get relief. This time their prayers were answered and in gratitude they erected this marble slab, expressing thereon that by this action they fulfilled the vow they had made in their prayers.

---

[41] Cox in *MAMA* V (n. 40), 56.

[42] The lists in M. Santoro, *Epitheta deorum in Asia graeca cultorum ex auctoribus graecis et latinis*, Milano 1974, do not yield viable alternatives to my proposal. G. Ronchi, *Lexicon Theonymon rerumque sacrarum et divinarum ad Aegyptum pertinentium quae in papyris ostracis titulis graecis latinisque in Aegypto repertis laudantur* IV, Milano 1976, 742–3, yields as only alternative μεγίστοις, but apart from the times that μέγιστοι θεοί refers to either the Ptolemaic kings or the Roman emperors, these gods are either identified and named or they have the definite article, none of which is the case in our inscription; see B. Müller, ΜΕΓΑΣ ΘΕΟΣ, diss. Halle 1913, 377 ff.

The material adduced so far has not enabled us to cut the knot with regard to the question of whether the inscriptions on such altars used the singular or the plural in the dedication, although by now it would seem more probable that usually the plural was used. It is exactly on this point that the later Christian sources may turn out to be helpful. At first sight, it might seem to be a strange procedure to expect new light in this matter from Christian writings, since it may be assumed in advance that their authors will not contradict the statement of the Bible that the inscription was in the singular. But let the facts speak for themselves.

In the first three centuries after the composition of Luke's Gospel and Acts, the passage under discussion is referred to by some Christian authors but no problem is noticed. It has been argued that it is highly significant that some of these writers were Athenians by birth (Aristides, Athenagoras, Clement of Alexandria) and that not even they criticize Paul or Luke for lack of accuracy in quoting the altar-inscription, although they could have corrected the statement if it was necessary.[43] By itself this argument is not very impressive, but is should be conceded that it gains more weight once one sees that there are other authors who do correct the statement. There may be an implicit correction already in Tertullian, *Ad nationes* II 9, 3–4:

> Sed et Romanorum deos Varro trifariam disposuit in certos, incertos et electos. Tantam vanitatem! Quid enim erat illis cum incertis, si certos habebant? Nisi si Attico⟨s⟩ stupore⟨s⟩ recipere voluerunt, nam et Athenis ara est inscripta: ignotis deis.[44]

And in *Adversus Marcionem* I 9:

> Persuade deum ignotum esse potuisse. Invenio plane ignotis deis aras prostitutas, sed Attica idololatria est. Item incertis deis, sed superstitio Romana est.[45]

These passages do not explicitly refer to Acts 17:23, but since Tertullian knew the book, he must have been aware that his words were at variance with those of Acts. Nevertheless he did not feel obliged to contradict the biblical author *expressis verbis*. It comes a bit as a surprise that almost two centuries later (in the eighties of the fourth century) the great scholar and Bible translator Jerome does do so explicitly. In his *Commentary on the Epistle to Titus* I 12 he says:

---

[43] So esp. Zahn, *Apostelgeschichte* (n. 9), 871 ff., 881 f.

[44] "But Varro made a threefold division of the gods of the Romans into certain, uncertain and select deities. What a vanity! What did they have to do with uncertain gods, if they had certain gods? Unless they wished to admit Athenian stupidities, for in Athens there is an altar inscribed: to unknown gods." I follow the edition by J.G.P. Borleffs, *Q.S.F. Tertulliani Ad Nationes Libri duo*, Leiden 1929, 54.

[45] "Prove to me that a god can ever have been unknown. I know, of course, of altars prostituted to unknown gods, though that is Athenian idolatry; also to gods undefined, though that is Roman superstition" (transl. by E. Evans, Tertullian, *Adversus Marcionem* I, Oxford 1972, 23).

nec mirum si pro opportunitate temporis gentilium poetarum versibus abutatur, cum etiam de inscriptione arae aliqua commutans ad Athenienses locutus sit: "pertransiens enim," inquit, "et contemplans culturas vestras inveni et aram in qua superscriptum est 'ignoto deo;' quod itaque ignorantes colitis hoc ego annuntio vobis." Inscriptio autem arae non ita erat, ut Paulus asseruit, 'ignoto deo,' sed ita: 'Diis Asiae et Europae et Africae, diis ignotis et peregrinis.' Verum quia Paulus non pluribus diis indigebat sed uno tantum ignoto deo, singulari verbo usus est.[46]

About ten years later (ca. 397/8) Jerome repeats this statement in one of his letters, when he writes: *pro Christo causam agens etiam inscriptionem fortuitam arte torquet in argumentum fidei.*[47]

When a well-informed scholar like Jerome explicitly states that the apostle *torquet* the text of the inscription, one cannot lightly dismiss such a statement. It has been argued that the fact that scholars like Clement of Alexandria and Origen, who knew Athens, did not have such critical comments, proves that an altar with an inscription in the singular could still be seen in Athens in the third century, but that in the fourth the altar had disappeared so that Jerome only knew the altars with inscriptions in the plural.[48] Of course that is a possibility, but it is doubtful whether such a conclusion may be drawn from an *argumentum e silentio*. The silence of earlier authors, even when they knew Athens, may have been caused by other motives, perhaps of an apologetic nature.[49] It needs to be added here that it cannot be ruled out that Jerome drew part of his information from a remark in a commentary on Paul's Epistles to the Corinthians by Didymus of Alexandria, who wrote probably no more than one or two decades before Jerome. In a fragment preserved in a so-called *catena*, Didymus reflects upon the meaning of 2 Cor. 10:5 ('we compel every human thought to surrender in obedience to Christ') and says that this principle is well exemplified by Paul's own behaviour in Athens:

οὕτω γὰρ τὸ Ἀθήνησιν ἀνακείμενον βωμῷ ἐπίγραμμα ἐμφαῖνον πολλῶν θεῶν νόημα ἑλκύσας ὁ ταῦτα γράφων μετήνεγκεν εἰς τὸν μόνον ἀληθινὸν θεόν.[50]

---

[46] "It is not strange if he (Paul) uses verses from pagan poets when there is an opportunity to do so, because in his speech to the Athenians he even changed some elements from the altar-inscription. For he says, "When I walked around and looked at your cultic sites, I found even an altar with the inscription 'to an unknown god.' What you now worship without knowing it, I proclaim to you." But the altar-inscription was not, as Paul asserted, 'to an unknown god,' but as follows: 'To the gods of Asia, Europe, and Africa, to the unknown and foreign gods.' But since Paul did not need a number of gods but only one unknown god, he used the singular" (*PL.*26, 607).

[47] "In his plaidoyer for Christ he even skilfully rephrases an inscription he came across by chance so as to turn it into an argument for faith" (*Epistula 70 ad Magnum*).

[48] Wikenhauser, *Die Apostelgeschichte* (n. 9), 376.

[49] Is it purely accidental that before Constantine there is silence on this point, but that after Constantine corrective statements occur?

[50] "For thus the one who wrote this twisted the inscription put upon an altar in Athens which displayed a thought concerning many gods, and he transferred it onto the only true god" (text

So the opinion that Paul changed the text of the inscription in order to get a suitable starting-point for his speech may derive from Didymus, but that cannot be said of the wording of the inscription. Didymus does not give any, whereas Jerome has: *Diis Asiae et Europae et Africae, diis ignotis et peregrinis.* It has beèn suggested that Jerome had seen such an altar-inscription in Rome,[51] but one cannot see why beside the deities of the whole *oikoumene* the addition 'to unknown and foreign gods' had to be made, for the latter category was fully included in the first.[52] Perhaps, if such an altar ever existed at all, it was an altar with inscriptions at both sides. The original inscription may have been *diis ignotis et peregrinis*, and later, after a rededication, the other side read *Diis Asiae et Europae et Africae* or its Greek equivalent,[53] in order to make the dedication still more comprehensive. Rededication of altars was not an uncommon phenomenon in antiquity. As a matter of fact, the Pergamon altar discussed above has, besides θεοῖς ἀγνώστοις on one side, τοῖς ἀνέμοις ('to the winds') on the other, the latter inscription being made on the occasion of a rededication.[54] At any rate, although the source of Jerome's knowledge about the text of the inscription remains unknown, Jerome's witness, as well as that of Tertullian and Didymus of Alexandria, strengthens the impression we already had on the basis of the non-Christian material, *sc.* that there was perhaps no altar-inscription 'to an unknown god' in the singular, either in Athens or elsewhere.[55]

Euthalius Diaconus, however, a Christian author of whom we know very little but who was probably a near contemporary of Jerome, says in his *Elenchus Capitum Septem Epistolarum Catholicarum* that the text of the inscription was: Θεοῖς ᾿Ασίας καὶ Εὐρώπης καὶ Λιβύης θεῷ τε ἀγνώστῳ καὶ ξένῳ.[56] Here we have a Greek version of Jerome's text with the exception of

---

in K. Staab, *Pauluskommentare aus der griechischen Kirche*, Münster 1933, 37). Both Didymus and Jerome may have got their information from Origen.

[51] Minucius Felix, *Octavius* VI 2, says about the Romans: *aras extruunt etiam ignotis numinibus et Manibus* ("they raise altars even to unknown deities and spirits of the dead"), probably writing about the Rome of his days.

[52] "Gods of Asia, Europe, and Africa" is of course equivalent to θεοὶ πάντες καὶ πᾶσαι.

[53] In a slightly different form this suggestion was done by Th. Zahn, *Apostelgeschichte* (n. 9), 882.

[54] See Hepding, *Arbeiten* (n. 26), 457 for a publication of the inscription and Deissmann, *Paulus* (n. 26), Tafel V for a photo.

[55] Birt, Ἄγνωστοι θεοί (n. 12), 356 ff., asserts that there were no altars at all in antiquity with the word ἄγνωστος in the dedication. He assumes that the inscriptions have been just θεοῖς or maybe θεῷ. His theory is that there were anonymous altars (cf. Diog.Laert.I 110) from archaic times, possibly with the inscription ΘΕΟΙ, to be read as θεῷ since in archaic script *omicron* and *omega* were not distinguished. In later times this ΘΕΟΙ was mistakenly read as θεοί, so that it became a dedication to a plurality of gods. This is not very likely.

[56] "To the Gods of Asia, Europe, and Africa, and to an unknown and foreign god" (*PG.*85, 692). Libya was a common name for Africa among the Greeks; see e.g. Pliny, *Naturalis historia* 5:1 *Africam Graeci Libyam appellavere.* On Euthalius see W. Christ/W. Schmid/O. Stählin,

the plural in the second half. Although the view that this must have been the original text of the inscription[57] has been defended, this seems to me to be improbable. If that were the case, one cannot imagine how in Christian circles the singular could have been changed into a plural, whereas it is not only thinkable but even likely that a tradition about an inscription in the plural would be changed so as to accord with the biblical text.[58] What we can observe is that in all the other Christian evidence from the fourth century onwards, traditions concerning the altar-inscription do indeed mention only the singular, as was to be expected.[59]

In his commentary on the Acts of the Apostles, the Nestorian Church-Father Ishodad of Merv reports that Theodorus of Mopsuestia[60] wrote that:

"the Athenians were once upon a time at war with their enemies, and the Athenians retreated from them in defeat; then a certain *daimon* appeared and said unto them, 'I have never been honoured by you as I ought; and because I am angry with you, therefore you have had a defeat from your enemies.' Then the Athenians were afraid and raised to him the well-known altar. And because they dreaded lest this very thing should happen to them, having secretly neglected one who was unknown to them, they erected this altar and wrote upon it, 'Of the Unknown and Hidden God,' wishing in fact to say this, that though there is a God in whom we do not believe, we raise this altar to his honour that he may be reconciled to us, although He is not honoured as a known deity."[61]

We see here a clear tendency to create aetiological stories which might explain the origin of the inscription. This tendency is manifest also in other, comparable stories. E.g., the same Ishodad reports the fourth century Syrian Church Father Ephraim as saying that according to some sources the Athenians in a time of drought and earthquakes prayed to all the gods they knew, but without success. Then they overturned their altars and wondered which god it might be that sent them these plagues. Eventually they erected an altar for a hidden god, whoever he was, worshipped him, and their prayers were answered.[62] A different story but one that may be not far beside the truth, is told by John Chrysostom. He says that at a certain moment the Athenians realized that not all the gods they worshipped had been known to them from

---

Geschichte der griechischen Litteratur II, München 1924[6], 1351–52, esp. n. 14.

[57] Zahn, *Apostelgeschichte* (n. 9), 874.

[58] U. von Wilamowitz-Moellendorff, *Der Glaube der Hellenen* II, Darmstadt 1955[2] (= 1932), 340 n. 1.

[59] The most extensive collection of these later Christian sources is Wikenhauser, *Apostelgeschichte* (n. 9), 373–380.

[60] He says: 'the interpreter,' which in Ishodad's usage is Theodorus, as is confirmed by my colleague Prof. T. Baarda.

[61] Syriac text and English translation may be found in M.D. Gibson, *Horae Semiticae* X, Cambridge 1913, 28.

[62] Text in Gibson, *Horae Semiticae* X (n. 61), 28.

the beginning but that several of them, especially foreign ones, had been introduced gradually in the course of time, some of them even quite recently. Hence they concluded that there was a distinct possibility that there existed still another god whose existence was unknown to them but who nevertheless should be worshipped. So they erected an altar to the unknown god.[63]

In the fifth century CE we see for the first time that the question of the origin of the altar-inscription is connected with a story in Herodotus, where he tells that the Athenian generals in the time of Miltiades sent a swift-footed messenger, called Pheidippides, to Sparta. On his way he met the god Pan, who told him to ask the Athenians why they paid him no attention, in spite of his friendliness towards them and the fact that he had often been useful to them in the past and would be so again in the future. When the Athenians heard this, they built a shrine to Pan under the Acropolis (*Histories* VI 105). According to the Christian adaptation of the story they built an altar to him with the inscription 'To an unknown god,' which gives the story an odd twist, since the name of the god was not unknown at all. We find this for instance in Isidorus of Pelusium (5th cent.), but also in several later writers.[64] Of course the name of Pan disappears in later versions so as to make the tale more suitable for the purpose it was used for. But these later versions, in medieval authors (Theodorus bar Koni, Theophylactus, Oecumenius, Dionysius bar Salibi, Barhebraeus, etc.), need not detain us here because they do not yield any material that is of importance for the present investigation.[65]

It is time to draw some provisional conclusions. On the basis of the literary evidence, both pagan and Christian, it can be regarded as an established fact that there were cults of unknown gods in antiquity and accordingly altars to these unknown gods. Whether there was a fixed formula for an inscription on such altars and, if so, what that formula was, is less definitely established, but the combination of the literary data and the, admittedly scanty, archeological evidence makes it highly probable that such altar-inscriptions usually ran: ἀγνώστοις θεοῖς. But a probability that something was usually the case definitely does not exclude the possibility that there were deviations from this rule, either due to local or regional customs or to personal beliefs. The next paragraph may help us to gain some more insight into the various possible backgrounds of these cults and hence into the possible variations of the inscriptional formula.

---

[63] Text in his *Sermo ad eos qui conventum ecclesiae deseruerunt (...) et in inscriptionem altaris* (*PG*.51,73).

[64] Details in Wikenhauser (n. 9), 377 ff. Isidorus' text is interesting in that he gives two alternative aetiologies in his *Epistula* IV 69 (*PG*.78,1128).

[65] Quite isolated stands the late notice by Ps-Athanasius in his Ἐξηγητικὸν περὶ τοῦ ἐν Ἀθήναις ναοῦ (*PG*.28,1428): σοφός τις ὀνόματι Ἀπόλλων ... ἔκτισε τὸν ἐν Ἀθήναις ναὸν γράψας ἐν αὐτῷ βωμῷ· ἀγνώστῳ θεῷ. See W. Göber, *Theoi agnostoi*, *RE* V A (1934), 1993; Wikenhauser (n. 9), 380.

II

We have already incidentally touched upon the meaning of altar-inscriptions for unknown gods in the previous paragraph, both when discussing the milieu of the Pergamon altar and when reporting some of the aetiological tales of later Christian writers. We will now briefly examine whether, apart from texts that speak of altars of unknown gods, there is other evidence that might help us to see more clearly the background of such cults and hence the meaning of the inscriptions.

It needs to be borne in mind that the term ἄγνωστος θεός is not unequivocal. It may mean a god who is quite well-known to one people but not or not yet known to another, i.e. a foreign deity whose name and function are in principle knowable by asking the people who do know it. It may mean a deity whose name nobody knows either because it has been forgotten (altar-inscriptions may have become unreadable) or because there is no way of knowing which god—maybe even which of the known gods—is the author of either a calamity or of good fortune. Further it may mean: a god unknown to those who did not receive a special initiation or revelation; or unknown or unknowable—ἄγνωστος can have both meanings—to humanity because of the limitations of human knowledge; or in essence unknowable but partially knowable by inference from his work; or unknowable in his positive character but definable by negations; or unknowable but accessible in a *unio mystica* which is not properly speaking knowledge, being suprarational.[66] In this paper we will leave the four last-mentioned positions out of consideration because they are of a philosophical nature, whether Skeptic or Platonic.[67] We are not concerned at this moment to study the speculations about divine transcendence by the philosophers but the religious feelings and practices of the common people. What induced men and women to worship and bring sacrifices to unknown gods? The first three meanings of ἄγνωστος θεός listed above may be of some help: a foreign god whose name and function is (as yet) unknown; a deity about whose identity one is in doubt; a god who is unknown to outsiders but has been revealed to insiders and whose name should not be mentioned.

As to the first possibility, the god of the Jews fitted such a description. To many Greeks the god of the Jewish religion was definitely an unknown god *par excellence* because he could not be called by name and he had no image, not even in the inmost recess of his single, unapproachable sanctuary in Jerusalem.

---

[66] See Birt, Ἄγνωστοι θεοί (n. 12), 344, and esp. E.R. Dodds, The Unknown God in Neoplatonism, Appendix I in his *Proclus, The Elements of Theology*, Oxford 1963², 310–313.

[67] The three last-mentioned positions correspond, of course, to the *via analogiae*, the *via negationis*, and the *via mystica* (or *via ecstaseōs*) of the later Platonic tradition. See A.-J. Festugière, *La révélation d'Hermès Trismégiste IV: Le dieu inconnu et la gnose*, Paris 1954³, esp. 92–140.

A god without a name and without an image was an unknown god,[68] but yet one who was worshipped not only by masses of Jews all over the Hellenistic-Roman world but also by many so-called 'God-fearers' among the gentiles. One can very well imagine that one of the many diaspora Jews who took little heed of the official restriction of sacrifices to the Jerusalem temple, erected a small altar to his god on his own.[69] He may even have believed that all the gods were only different expressions for one and the same god, *sc.* the god of Israel. That this kind of beliefs did exists among Jews may perhaps be gathered from the fact that in the temple of Pan in Edfu two Jewish inscriptions were found in which ὁ θεός is thanked for his deliverance.[70] Another possibility, advocated by Bickerman, is that such an altar was set up by a gentile worshipper for the (to him) unknown god of the Jews. "Paul could have seen the inscription on a private altar, which would not be mentioned in guide-books, a block raised by a God-fearing Athenian before his house on some side-street."[71] If such were the case, then of course the inscription would be in the singular! It must be conceded that this view cannot be excluded, since we have data which indicate that the god of the Jews could indeed be called an ἄγνωστος θεός.

Johannes Lydus, a late antiquarian author who wrote in the middle of the sixth century CE, says in his *De mensibus* IV 53 Λίβιος δὲ ἐν τῇ καθόλου Ῥωμαϊκῇ ἱστορίᾳ ἄγνωστον τὸν ἐκεῖ [*sc.* in Judaea] τιμώμενόν φησι.[72] Most probably Lydus got this information on Livy from scholia to Lucan's *Pharsalia*, which often were his source.[73] In *Pharsalia* II 592−3 Lucan writes:

> Cappadoces mea signa timent et dedita sacris
> incerti Iudaea dei mollisque Sophene.[74]

And the scholium *ad locum* says:

> Livius de Iudaeis: 'Hierosolimis fanum cuius deorum sit non nominant, neque ullum ibi simulacrum est, neque enim esse dei figuram putant.'[75]

---

[68] See K. Bornhäuser, *Studien zur Apostelgeschichte*, Gütersloh 1934, 143 f. B. Gärtner, *The Areopagus Speech and Natural Revelation*, Uppsala 1955, 247. Note Philostratus' remark in *Vit.Ap.*I 1 on θεοὺς ἑτέρους ὢν τὰ εἴδη καὶ τὰ ὀνόματα οὔπω τοὺς ἀνθρώπους γιγνώσκειν.

[69] For a recent survey of Jewish temples outside Jerusalem and Palestine in the Hellenistic and Roman period see M.E. Stone, *Scriptures, Sects and Visions. A Profile of Judaism from Ezra to the Jewish Revolts*, New York—London 1980, 77−82.

[70] *OGIS*, 73−74. See E. Schürer, *The History of the Jewish People in the Age of Jesus Christ*, rev. ed. by G. Vermes and F. Millar, III, Edinburgh 1986, 58. Text of the inscriptions also in *CPJ* III, nos. 1537−1538.

[71] Bickerman, The Altars of Gentiles (n. 39), 345.

[72] "Livy says in his general Roman History that the god worshipped there is unknown." See M. Stern, *Greek and Latin Authors on Jews and Judaism* I−II, Jerusalem 1974−1980, no. 134.

[73] See Norden, *Agnostos Theos* (n. 7), 59 f.

[74] "My standards overawe Cappadocia, and Judaea given over to the worship of an unknown god, and effeminate Sophene." See Stern, *Greek and Latin Authors* (n. 72), no. 191.

[75] "Livy on the Jews: They do not mention the name of the deity to which the temple in

We see here a two-staged process of interpretation. In his lost 102nd book Livy stated no more than that the Jewish god has neither a name nor an image. Lucan, whose principal authority was Livy, interprets Livy's statement in typically Varronian terminology by speaking of Judaea's *incertus deus*. Varro, as we have seen above in Tertullian's *Ad nationes* II 9, divided the gods into *dei certi* and *dei incerti*, the former being the gods of whose meaning and function he had a clear idea, the second category being those gods of whom he did not have such a clear idea with the result that he, Varro, was uncertain about them.[76] So originally this distinction had little to do with the difference between θεοὶ γνωστοί and ἄγνωστοι. As a matter of fact, Varro himself did not regard the god of the Jews as an *incertus deus*.[77] But soon this terminology was adopted by others for other purposes, e.g. here by Lucan in order to reduce Livy's description to a short formula, no doubt indicating thereby that to him the god of the Jews belonged to the category of the 'unknown gods.' And this is exactly what Lydus says, but—and here we have the second phase of interpretation—this author uses the Neoplatonic terminology familiar to him in order to designate the highest deity, which was the ἄγνωστος worshipped by the Jews. The Varronian stage of interpretation can also be seen in the *Scriptores Historiae Augustae* where it is said that astrologers hold that no one will live longer than 120 years,

> etiam illud addentes Mosen solum, dei, ut Iudaeorum libri locuntur, familiarem, centum viginti quinque annos vixisse; qui cum quereretur quod iuvenis interiret, responsum ei ab incerto ferunt numine neminem plus esse victurum (*Divus Claudius* 2:4).[78]

Although Lydus' text, in which ἄγνωστος is used to designate the god of the Jews, is late, there is no doubt that the earlier Latin texts about the *incertus deus* of the Jews mean the same thing. (The passages quoted above from Tertullian testify to the close connection, if not complete identification, that was felt between *incerti dei* and ἄγνωστοι θεοί). And we have Josephus to prove that as early as the first century even Jews could speak of their own god as an

---

Jerusalem pertains, nor is any image found there, since they do not think the god partakes of any figure." See Stern, (n. 72) no. 133. It is significant that Josephus reports (*Ant.*XII, 259.261) that the Samaritans call their YHWH-temple on Mt. Garizim an ἀνώνυμον ἱερόν.

[76] See G. Wissowa, Die varronischen *di certi* und *incerti, Hermes* 56 (1921) 113–130; B. Cardauns, *M. Terentius Varro, Antiquitates rerum divinarum*, 2 vols., Mainz—Wiesbaden 1976, I 63, II 183 (there literature).

[77] See Norden, *Agnostos Theos* (n. 7), 61; Stern, *Gr. and Lat. Authors* (n. 72) I, 439.

[78] "They even tell us that Moses alone, the friend of God, as he is called in the books of the Jews, lived for one hundred and twenty five years, and that when he complained that he was dying in his prime, he received from the unknown god, so they say, the reply that no one should ever live longer." Stern, *Gr. and Lat. Authors* (n. 72) no. 526. That in this passage *incertum numen* equals ἄγνωστος θεός is also defended by W. Schmid, Bilderloser Kult und christliche Intoleranz, in *Mullus. FS Th. Klauser*, Münster 1964, 305 f.

'unknown one.' In *Contra Apionem* II 167 he states that Moses represented God as one who is δυνάμει μὲν ἡμῖν γνώριμον, ὁποῖος δὲ κατ' οὐσίαν ἐστὶν ἄγνωστον.[79]

The second category mentioned above is that of gods about whose identity one is in doubt. In a papyrus of the first half of the second century CE, a prologue of a drama has been preserved in which the god Apollo announces that the emperor Trajan has ascended to heaven and that Hadrian is his successor. He says:

> ἅρματι λευκοπώλῳ ἄρτι Τραϊανῷ συνανατείλας ἥκω σοι, ὦ δῆμε, οὐκ ἄγνωστος Φοῖβος θεὸς ἄνακτα καινὸν Ἀδριανὸν ἀγγελῶν (Pap. Gissen 3, 1–3).[80]

The fact that this self-identification is phrased with the words οὐκ ἄγνωστος θεός suggests that a god whose identity was uncertain or unknown *was* called an ἄγνωστος θεός.

In ancient religions it was of great importance to know the right name of the deity. Errors in invoking a god's name could, for instance, impede effective prayer. From Homer onwards we find prayer formulas which aim to prevent that the god invoked would be offended by an incorrect invocation. Homer, *Od.*V 445 κλῦθι, ἄναξ, ὅτις ἐσσί, κτλ.[81] Aeschylus, *Agam.*160–1 Ζεύς, ὅστις ποτ' ἐστίν, εἰ τόδ' αὐτῷ φίλον κεκλημένῳ.[82] Cf. also Plato, *Cratylus* 400d6–e4 ναὶ μὰ Δία ἡμεῖς γε, (...) εἴπερ γε νοῦν ἔχοιμεν, ἕνα μὲν τὸν κάλλιστον τρόπον, ὅτι περὶ θεῶν οὐδὲν ἴσμεν, οὔτε περὶ αὐτῶν οὔτε περὶ τῶν ὀνομάτων, ἅττα ποτὲ ἑαυτοὺς καλοῦσιν · δῆλον γὰρ ὅτι ἐκεῖνοί γε τἀληθῆ καλοῦσι. δεύτερος δ' αὖ τρόπος ὀρθότητος, ὥσπερ ἐν ταῖς εὐχαῖς νόμος ἐστὶν ἡμῖν εὔχεσθαι, οἵτινές τε καὶ ὁπόθεν χαίρουσιν ὀνομαζόμενοι,

---

[79] "In his power he is known to us, but in his essence he is unknown." On the philosophical background of this statement see Festugière, *Le dieu inconnu et la gnose* (n. 67), 6–17. Of course it is imaginable that other 'nameless' gods as well could be considered to qualify for the title ἄγνωστος θεός, e.g. the socalled 'anonymous god of Palmyra,' whose name is never mentioned in the inscriptions but who is always called "the one whose name is blessed for ever" (*bryk šmh l 'lm'*); cf. Ps.72:19. See the evidence in M. Gawlikowski, *Recueil d'inscriptions palmyréniennes*, Paris 1974, nos. 106–123,129–130,134–138,140, 142,144, and the discussions in J. Teixidor, *The Pagan God. Popular Religion in the Greco-Roman Near East*, Princeton 1977, 122–130, and idem, *The Pantheon of Palmyra*, Leiden 1979, 115–119. But this cult is attested only from the beginning of the second century CE onwards.

[80] "On a chariot with white horses I have accompanied Trajan in his ascension, I, Apollo, a god not unknown to you, and I have come to announce the new ruler, Hadrian." The best discussion of these lines is still Weinrich, *De dis ignotis* (n. 17), 34–45.

[81] "Hear, Lord, whoever thou art."

[82] "Zeus, whoever he may be, if this name pleases him in invocation." Cf. e.g. Catullus 34:21f. *sis quocumque tibi placet sancta nomine*, with W. Kroll *ad loc.* (*C. Valerius Catullus*, Stuttgart 1959³, 64); Apuleius, *Metamorphoses* XI 2 *Regina caeli, sive tu Ceres (...), seu tu caelestis Venus (...), seu Phoebi soror (...), seu (...) horrenda Proserpina (...), quoquo nomine, quoquo ritu, quaqua facie te fas est invocare*, with J. Gwyn Griffiths *ad loc.* (*Apuleius of Madaurus, The Isis-Book*, Leiden 1975, 119–120). More instances in Norden, *Agnostos Theos* (n. 7), 143 ff.

ταῦτα καὶ ἡμᾶς αὐτοὺς καλεῖν, ὡς ἄλλο μηδὲν εἰδότας.[83] The same ignorance as to the name of the deity concerned is also evident in the story about
the anonymous altars in Athens reported by Diogenes Laertius I 110 (discussed
above, p. 23). In this connection mention should also be made of the ancient
Roman prayer preserved in Macrobius' *Saturnalia* III 9, 10: *Dis pater Veiovis
Manes, sive vos quo alio nomine fas est nominare.*[84]

With regard to the typically Roman material, however, it has to be said that
the Romans developed a specific formula that is often found in prayers or
dedicatory formulas both in inscriptions and in literary texts, *sc.* the formula
sive deus sive dea.[85] This formula had its origin in the ritual of the so-called
evocatio, in which, before the attack on or conquest of a foreign city, the tute-
lary deity of that city was bidden to leave the place.[86] The *evocatio* began with
si(ve) deus si(ve) dea es(t), or one of its variations, in order to ensure that the
deity concerned would not feel offended by a wrong identification. But gradually the formula was used on other occasions as well, for Aulus Gellius reports:

> "The Romans of old (...), whenever they felt an earthquake or received report
> of one, decreed a holy day on that account, but forbore to declare and specify in
> the decree, as is commonly done, the name of the god in whose honour the holy
> day was to be observed, for fear that by naming one god instead of another they
> might involve the people in false observance. If anyone had desecrated that fes-
> tival, and expiation was therefore necessary, they used to offer a victim *si deo si
> deae* (...) since it was uncertain what force and which of the gods or goddesses
> had caused the earthquake" (*Noctes Atticae* II 28, 2–3).[87]

So we see that this and related formulas developed into what the most recent

---

[83] "By Zeus, (...), if we are sensible, we must recognize that there is one most excellent kind
[*sc.* of correct speaking about the gods], since of the gods we know nothing, neither of them nor
of their names, whatever they may be, by which they call themselves, for it is clear that they use
the true names. But there is a second kind of correctness, that we call them, as is customary in
prayers, by whatever names and patronymics are pleasing to them, since we know no other"
(transl. by H.N. Fowler in LCL ed. of Plato, vol. V, London 1926, 63.65).

[84] "Dis pater, Veiovis, Manes, or by whatever other name it is allowed to address you." Cf.
Statius, *Thebais* III 497–8 ... *tunc plura ignotaque iungit | numina et immensi fruitur caligine
mundi* ("then to his prayer he adds more deities, unknown ones, and holds converse with the dark
mysteries of the illimitable heaven").

[85] The relevant material has been collected by J. Alvar, Matériaux pour l'étude de la formule
sive deus sive dea, Numen 32 (1985) 236–273.

[86] See V. Basanoff, *Evocatio. Étude d'un rituel militaire romain*, Paris 1947; also J. le Gall,
Evocatio, in *Mélanges J. Heurgon* I, Rome 1976, 518 ff.

[87] *(Romani ...), ubi terram movisse senserant nuntiatumve erat, ferias eius rei causa edicto
imperabant, sed dei nomen, ita uti solet, cui servari ferias oporteret, statuere et edicere quiesce-
bant, ne alium pro alio nominando falsa religione populum alligarent. Eas ferias si quis polluisset
piaculoque ob hanc rem opus esset, hostiam 'si deo, si deae' immolabant (...) quoniam et qua
vi et per quem deorum dearumve tremeret incertum esset.* Cf. also Vergil, *Aen.*VIII 351–2 *'hoc
nemus, hunc,' inquit, 'frondoso vertice collem—quis deus, incertum est—habitat deus'* ("This
grove, he says, this hill with its leafy crown is a god's home—though it is uncertain which god
it is").

authority on this matter has called "formules préventives (. . .) par lesquelles on voulait empêcher le rejet divin d'une action religieuse et obtenir que celle-ci puisse atteindre le but proposé;" the same scholar concludes: "On peut affirmer qu'il y a une tres grande affinité entre cette formule et l'*ágnostos theós*, le 'dieu inconnu' grec qui eut son propre culte, comme divinité indépendante qu'il fallait vénérer. La formulation même: *sive deus sive dea/ágnostos theós* rend évident l'abime existant entre la capacité d'abstraction conceptuelle des Grecs et celle des Romains."[88] However great the 'capacité d'abstraction conceptuelle' of the Greeks may have been, behind the more abstract formula lurk the same feelings as are described by Aulus Gellius: fear or anxiety that by naming one god instead of another their acts of worship would not yield the results desired.[89] To be on the safe side, a Greek could use the formula 'unknown god.'

The third possibility, that an *agnostos theos* is a god unknown only to uninitiated outsiders, applies to gnosticism where the *gnostikoi* are the only ones who 'know' the highest deity. But gnosticism falls outside the scope of our investigation. And although it has been suggested that the term *agnostos theos* had its 'Sitz im Leben' in Hellenistic mystery cults, I have not been able to find evidence in support of this hypothesis.[90] Another suggestion, however, is somewhat less unlikely, sc. that *agnostoi theoi* may have been chthonic deities whose names one preferred not to mention. The names of the χθόνιοι θεοί, the gods of the nether-world, had magical power *in malam partem*. To pronounce these names meant the provocation of dangerous powers.[91] Sometimes we find the term ἄγνωστος/*ignotus* in connection with these dreaded deities and with the associated practices of black magic. Already in Euripides the Erinyes are called ἀνώνυμοι θεαί (*Iph.Taur.* 944), which is a related concept.[92] In a papyrus of the second century CE, containing a hymn to Apollo probably dating from Hellenistic times, we have a mutilated line containing the clearly legible words ἐπ' ἀγνώστοις ἐπιλοιβαί.[93] There is little doubt that in the lacuna before ἐπ' the word θεοῖσιν should be read, for ἐπιλοιβαί are drink-

---

[88] Alvar, Matériaux (n. 85), 236, 269.

[89] Also J.G. Frazer stresses that the background is the same; see his *Pausanias's Description of Greece translated with a commentary* II, London 1898 (1913²), 34. He also mentions interesting parallels from Zulus and Incas.

[90] Wikenhauser, *Apostelgeschichte* (n. 9), 389, says that, for instance, the real names of the Kabeiroi, the gods of the Samothracian mysteries, are unknown (though their official cultic names are known), because only the initiated learnt them; and these unnamed gods could be worshipped as 'unknown gods.' But this is no more than a guess.

[91] E. Rohde, *Psyche* I (n. 13), 206 ff.; H. Dörrie, Gottesvorstellung, *RAC* XII (1983), 92–93; cf. B. Gladigow, Gottesnamen, *RAC* XI (1981) 1218; A. Harder, *Euripides' Kresphontes and Archelaos*, Leiden 1985, 86f.

[92] On anonymous gods see J.A. MacCulloch, Nameless gods, *Encyclopaedia of Religion and Ethics* 9 (1917) 180; E. Bikerman, Anonymous Gods, *Journal of the Warburg Institute* 1 (1937/38), 187–196; now in: idem, *Studies in Jewish and Christian History* III, Leiden 1986, 270–281

[93] Pap. Chicago inv. no. 1061, VI 26. *Editio princeps* by E.J. Goodspeed, Alexandrian Hexa-

offerings to the gods. It is significant, however, that it was chthonic deities that were most often the recipients of libations.[94] This fact and the several occurrences of the word χθών in the immediately preceding lines (although mostly in obscure contexts) make it highly probable that we have here a reference to drink-offerings to the gods of the nether world, here called ἄγνωστοι θεοί. More evidence is found in Ovid who says about the powerful magician Circe: *verba precantia dicit/ignotosque deos ignoto carmine adorat*.[95] And in this same mysterious sphere of black magic lies what Statius says in his *Achilleis* I 135–40:

> hos abolere metus magica iubet ordine sacri
> Carpathius vates puerumque sub axe peracto
> secretis lustrare fretis, ubi litora summa
> Oceani et genitor tepet inlabentibus astris
> Pontus, ubi ignotis horrenda piacula divis
> donaque: sed longum cuncta enumerare vetorque.[96]

More instances could be quoted but these few examples may suffice to demonstrate that the term ἄγνωστοι (or ἀνώνυμοι) θεοί and its Latin equivalents were applied to the much dreaded deities of the nether-world.[97]

We have briefly sketched three possible backgrounds to our formula, of a different nature. It may be a designation of a foreign god whose name is unknown (e.g. the god of the Jewish people). It may be an expression of doubt concerning the correct name or identity of the god who brought about a certain phenomenon (defeat, earthquake, pestilence, etc.). It may be a formula meant

---

meter Fragments, *JHS* 23 (1903), 237–247, text on p. 244; further in J.U. Powell, Fragments of Greek Poetry from Papyri in the Library of the University of Chicago, *The Journal of Philology* 34 (1915), 106–128, text on p. 111, comments on p. 126: "Line 26 contains a new reference to θεοί ἄγνωστοι which may be added to Norden's instances." Also in Powell's *Collectanea Alexandrina*, Oxford 1925, 85. This papyrus is the second piece of evidence unknown to Norden, although published already 10 years before the appearance of *Agnostos Theos*.

[94] See Stengel, *Kultusaltertümer* (n. 29), 103 ff.; D. Wachsmuth, Trankopfer, *Der Kleine Pauly* 5 (1975), 922f.

[95] "She utters praying words and worships her unknown gods with an unknown charm" (*Metamorphoses* XIV 365–6). The *ignotum carmen* is the mysterious magic formula in *Ephesia grammata*.

[96] "The Carpatian seer bids me banish these terrors by the ordinance of a magic rite, and purify the lad in secret waters beyond the bound of heaven's vault, where is the farthest shore of Ocean and father Pontus is warmed by the ingliding stars. There are awful sacrifices and gifts to gods unknown—but 'tis long to recount all, and I am forbidden" (J.H. Mozley in the LCL ed. of Statius, vol. II, London 1928, 519).

[97] More passages are mentioned by Norden, *Agnostos Theos* (n. 7), 115 ff.; cf. also O. Kern, *Die Religion der Griechen* I, Berlin 1926, 125–134. It is not certain whether two passages that are sometimes referred to in this connection, really belong here. The first is Herodotus II 52, where he says: ἔθυον δὲ πάντα πρότερον οἱ Πελασγοὶ θεοῖσι ἐπευχόμενοι (...), ἐπωνυμίην δὲ οὐδ' ὄνομα ἐποιεῦντο οὐδενὶ αὐτῶν· οὐ γὰρ ἀκηκόεσάν κω. The second is a passage in Strabo III 4, 16 where he says of the Celtiberian tribe of the Callaici that they offered their sacrifices ἀνωνύμῳ τινὶ θεῷ. The two passages are related, but since we know very little about the religious beliefs of either Pelasgi or Callaici, we can only guess at the background of this custom.

to avoid the naming of gods whom, for safety's sake, one preferred not to mention. The first two positions, especially the first, leave open the possibility that in such a case an altar-inscription was in the singular: ἀγνώστῳ θεῷ.[98] But if such inscriptions did occur, they will probably have been far less numerous that those in the plural. For it has to be stressed that in most cases the dominant background of such altars and such a cultus in all likelihood was what Nilsson has called "das ängstliche Bemühen, alle Götter zu erfassen."[99] This concern, as we have seen in the previous paragraph, had the same background as the cult of πάντες καὶ πᾶσαι θεοί, which gained such great popularity in Hellenistic-Roman times.[100] In this period the waning of belief in the traditional individual Olympians, strongly stimulated by the great influx of oriental religions, created a tendency to avoid the risk that one did not know and hence did not worship the best divine helper and so failed to obtain the help one so badly needed. This danger could be warded off by a "möglichst vollständige Berücksichtigung der Gottheiten, also auch der 'unbekannten'."[101]

We may now draw the following conclusions. It is not only possible but even highly probable that in Athens (and elsewhere) there were altars to unknown gods. It is also probable that there were more than one of such altars[102] and they may have had different backgrounds. (The one Paul saw need not have been the one(s) seen by Pausanias[103]). It is not improbable that there were altars with dedications in the singular, though it is likely that they were an exception to the rule, most dedications being in the plural. And, finally, Norden's thesis that the motif of an 'unknown god' is utterly un-Greek and must have been imported from the oriental world, has found no support whatsoever in the present investigation.[104]

---

[98] It should also be borne in mind that in the first centuries CE in philosophical circles the concept of an unknown/unknowable deity was much discussed. And, although this abstract notion never led to a cult in these circles, it cannot be excluded that some individual who knew these discussions, erected an altar to this deity.

[99] Nilsson, *Opuscula* III (n. 28), 188; also his *Gesch. der griech. Rel.* (n. 28), 357.

[100] See the studies referred to in n. 34.

[101] D. Wachsmuth, Theoi agnostoi, *Der Kleine Pauly* 5 (1975), 708.

[102] "vermutlich überall wo es Pantheen gab," thus W. Schmid, Kritisches zum ἄγνωστος θεός, *Wochenschrift für klassische Philologie* 35 (1918), 257.

[103] E. des Places' remark, "c'est sans doute celui de Phalère que Paul avait observé en passant" (*La religion grecque*, Paris 1969, 333), has no basis.

[104] As to the philosophical aspects, Norden's thesis had already convincingly been refuted by Dodds, *Proclus* (n. 66), 310 ff., and Festugière, *Le dieu inconnu* (n. 67), 1–140. For the religio-historical aspects, there has not been such a full-scale refutation, but see the remarks by Th. Plüss, Ἀγνώστῳ θεῷ, *Woch. f. klass. Phil.* 30 (1913), 553–558, and idem, Typisches Beweisverfahren im Falle Ἀγνώστῳ θεῷ, *ibid.* 31 (1914), 852–861, but esp. Weinreich's studies mentioned in nn. 17 and 24. It has to be added here that two passages in Ps-Lucian's *Philopatris* 9 and 29 have been left out of account in our discussion since this whole treatise is a Christian forgery of the 10th or 11th century. Both passages speak about ὁ Ἄγνωστος ἐν Ἀθήναις with an obvious reference to Acts 17:23. See on this treatise e.g. W. Buchwald/A. Hohlweg/O. Prinz, *Tusculum-Lexikon griechischer und lateinischer Autoren des Altertums und des Mittelalters*, München—Zürich 1982³, 635.

ZUR THEOLOGIE DES XENOKRATES

VON

Matthias Baltes (Münster)

"I. Xenokrates, der Sohn des Agathenor aus Chalkedon, nennt die Monas und die Dyas Götter.

Die eine (die Monas) sei männlich(es Prinzip) und nehme daher die Stellung eines Vaters ein und herrsche als König am Himmel (ἐν οὐρανῷ); diese nenne er auch Zeus und Ungerades und Nus, der für ihn der erste Gott ist.

Die andere (die Dyas) sei weiblich(es Prinzip) und führe daher nach Art einer Göttermutter (μητρὸς θεῶν δίκην) den erlosten Bereich unter dem Himmel an; diese sei für ihn die Seele des Alls.

II. Eine Gottheit aber sei auch der Himmel, und die feurigen Sterne seien olympische Götter; auch andere (Gottheiten gebe es), die sublunaren, unsichtbaren Dämonen.

III. Er lehrt aber auch, daß es ⟨gewisse göttliche Kräfte⟩ gibt und daß diese die stofflichen Elemente durchdringen. Von diesen nennt er die eine, ⟨die die Luft durchdringt, Hades, weil sie⟩ gestaltlos (unsichtbar) ⟨ist⟩,[1] die andere, die das Feuchte durchdringt, Poseidon, die dritte, die die Erde durchdringt, pflanzenerzeugende Demeter.

Diese Lehren hat er an die Stoiker weitergegeben;[2] den ersten Teil hat er aus Platon übernommen und in die eigene Terminologie übertragen.''

Dies ist der Wortlaut des bei Stobaios/Aetios I 7, 30 überlieferten Xenokratesfragments (= fr. 15 Heinze). Das Fragment ist grundlegend für die Götterlehre des Platonschülers, doch gehen darüber, wie sein Inhalt zu verstehen ist, die Ansichten der Interpreten auseinander.[3] Der doxographische Bericht unterscheidet deutlich drei Gruppen von göttlichen Wesen:

---

[1] Die Ergänzungen nach Heinze.

[2] χορηγήσας ist natürlich nicht vorzeitig; vgl. Kühner-Gerth I 199, 8.

[3] A.B. Krische, *Die theologischen Lehren der Griechischen Denker*, Göttingen 1840, 313 ff.; R. Heinze, *Xenokrates*, Leipzig 1892 (= Hildesheim 1965), 72 ff.; E. Zeller, *Die Philosophie der Griechen in ihrer geschichtl. Entwicklung*, [6]Darmstadt 1963, Bd II 1, 1021 ff.; P. Boyancé, Xénocrate et les Orphiques, *REA* 50 (1948) 218 ff., bes. 227 ff.; H.J. Krämer, *Der Ursprung der Geistmetaphysik*, Amsterdam 1964, 35 ff.; *Senocrate-Ermodoro, Frammenti*. Edizione, traduzione e commento a cura di M. Isnardi Parente, Napoli 1982, 400 ff.; H.J. Krämer, Ältere Akademie, in: *Grundriß der Geschichte der Philosophie. Die Philosophie der Antike*, Bd 3, hgg. von H. Flashar, Basel/Stuttgart 1983, 58 ff., um nur die Wichtigsten zu nennen. J. Dillon, Xenocrates' Metaphysics. Fr. 15 (Heinze) Re-examined, *Ancient Philosophy 5 (1985* (ersch. 1987)), 47 ff., untersucht die ersten Zeilen des Fragmentes und stellt die Verläßlichkeit des überlieferten Textes in Frage.

I. Monas und Dyas
II. Himmel, Sterne und sublunare Dämonen
III. Göttliche Elementarkräfte.

Ganz offensichtlich haben wir es hier mit einer jener von Xenokrates bevorzugten Dreiteilungen zu tun, wie wir sie vor allem aus frr. 5 und 56 kennen. Betrachten wir nun die drei Klassen von Gottheiten im einzelnen.

I

An der Spitze der Götterhierarchie steht ein Götterpaar, Monas und Dyas, die einander zwar nicht gleichgeordnet, aber ganz aufeinander bezogen sind, was grammatikalisch in der beinahe vollständigen Parallelität der Aussagen über beide Gottheiten zum Ausdruck kommt:

a) τὴν μὲν ὡς ἄρρενα	a) τὴν δὲ ὡς θήλειαν
b) πατρὸς ἔχουσαν τάξιν	b) μητρὸς θεῶν δίκην
c) ἐν οὐρανῷ	c) τῆς ὑπὸ τὸν οὐρανὸν λήξεως
d) βασιλεύουσαν	d) ἡγουμένην
e) ἥντινα προσαγορεύει	e) ...
καὶ Ζῆνα καὶ περιττὸν	
καὶ νοῦν	
f) ὅστις ἐστὶν αὐτῷ	f) ἥτις ἐστὶν αὐτῷ
πρῶτος θεός	ψυχὴ τοῦ παντός

Schon diese Gegenüberstellung macht einiges deutlich. Sie zeigt,
1. daß die von P. Boyancé[4] vorgeschlagene Großschreibung von δίκην sich nicht empfiehlt, weil δίκην dem ἔχουσαν τάξιν entspricht;
2. daß unter e) im Falle der Dyas eine Reihe von Prädikationen ausgefallen ist; dort muß u.a. das Prädikat ἀρτίαν gestanden haben, auch der Name der Gottheit wird dort gefallen sein.
    Was haben wir uns nun konkret unter den beiden höchsten Gottheiten vorzustellen? Am Ende heißt es, Xenokrates habe mit den in der ersten Hälfte vertretenen Lehren Platons Ansichten umformuliert. In der Tat erinnert in diesem Fragment vieles an Platon. Folglich haben wir uns außer in den spärlichen Berichten über Xenokrates' Götterlehre vor allem im Werk Platons umzusehen, um uns dem zu nähern, was Xenokrates gemeint hat. Bekanntlich galt Xenokrates von allen Schülern Platons als *der* Exeget und Verteidiger der Philosophie des Schulgründers,[5] der die Ansichten, die Platon mündlich und

---

[4] *REA* 50 (1948) 227 f.; vgl. auch H.J. Krämer, Grundfragen der aristotelischen Theologie, in: *Theologie und Philosophie* 44 (1969) 483, Anm. 76; skeptisch gegenüber Boyancés Vorschlag sind: J. Dillon, *The Middle Platonists*, London 1977, 25, Anm. 1 und Isnardi Parente, 404; ablehnend H. Schwabl, *RE* s.v. Zeus II, Suppl. XV, 1978, 1345.

[5] Vgl. Ps. Galen, *Hist.philos.* 3 = *Dox.Gr.* 599, 16 f.: τῶν Πλατωνικῶν δογμάτων ἐξηγητήν;

schriftlich geäußert hatte, in systematischer Form weiterzugeben bemüht war.[6]

Die Gegenüberstellung von erstem Gott und Weltseele hat die Interpreten immer an den platonischen *Timaios* erinnert, wo sich "der Gott' (ὁ θεός = ὁ δημιουργός) und die Weltseele in ähnlicher Weise gegenüberstehen wie in unserem Fragment. Der Demiurg wird in diesem Dialog zwar nicht ausdrücklich als "Noûs" bezeichnet, doch hat die antike Tradition ihn—im Anschluß an die berühmte Stelle *Tim.* 39e7 ff. (ᾗπερ οὖν νοῦς ἐνούσας ἰδέας ... καθορᾷ ...)—immer als solchen verstanden (vgl. auch *Tim.* 47b7/c3). Auch "Zeus" wird der Demiurg im *Tim.* nicht genannt, doch lag diese Identifizierung umso näher, als der Gott im *Tim.* in ähnlicher Weise als Göttervater gekennzeichnet ist wie der homerische Zeus. Zudem läßt der zweite Dialog der ursprünglich geplanten Trilogie, der *Kritias* (121b7 ff.), "Zeus, den Gott der Götter", in vergleichbarer Weise eine Rede an die übrigen Götter halten wie der *Tim.* den Demiurgen 41a7 ff., wobei die im *Krit.* zusammengerufenen Götter ähnliche Funktionen ausüben wie die Götter des *Tim.* (vgl. z.B. *Krit.* 109b1 ff. mit *Tim.* 41d2 f., 42e1−3). Die Identifizierung von erstem Gott und Zeus wird noch verständlicher, wenn Zeus im *Kratylos* also ὁ ἄρχων τε καὶ βασιλεὺς τῶν πάντων bezeichnet wird (396a7 f.). Daß er die Stellung eines Vaters einnimmt (πατρὸς ἔχουσαν τάξιν), steht mit dem *Tim.* in vollem Einklang; denn dort bringt der Demiurg den Kosmos und die Untergötter hervor (γεννᾷ, z.B. 37c7, 40d4) und wird als Vater der geschaffenen Götter und des Kosmos bezeichnet (z.B. 28c3, 37c7, 42e6 f.). Die Prädikate "Monas", "männlich" und "ungerade" lassen sich in den platonischen Dialogen nicht nachweisen, sind aber möglicherweise auf mündliche Äußerungen Platons zurückzuführen.[7]

---

fr. 33 H: ὑπεραπολογούμενος τοῦ Πλάτωνος; fr. 54: er kam der Lehre Platons zu Hilfe.

[6] Neben dem Werk Platons haben wir auch die Lehren zu berücksichtigen, die Aetios selbst als platonisch angesehen hat; denn sein Urteil wird ja weitgehend davon beeinflußt gewesen sein, was zu seiner Zeit als platonisch galt. Ferner ziehen wir zuweilen Aetios' Berichte über angebliche Lehren des Pythagoras heran, soweit sie nämlich für uns relevant sind und aus der Alten Akademie stammen. Zu diesen Zeugnissen vgl. W. Burkert, *Weisheit u. Wissenschaft*, Nürnberg 1962, 50 ff.; H. Happ, *Hyle*, Berlin/New York 1971, 249.

[7] Vgl. Krämer, *Ursprung* 379. Für 'Monas' vgl. Platon (*De bono*) bei Alex. Aphr. *In Met.* S.56,7 ff. = fr. 22 B Gaiser; Platon (*De bono*) bei Simpl. *In Phys.* 454, 33 ff. = fr. 23 B Gaiser; Sext. Empir. *Math.* X 261 ff. = fr. 32 Gaiser; vgl. Burkert 51 f. Vgl. ferner das bei Aetios auf das Xenokratesfragment folgende Platonzeugnis (I 7,31): Platon nennt Gott τὸ μοναδικόν.

Man fragt sich, ob τὸ ἕν und ἡ μονάς identisch sind (so Krische 315; Heinze 46,51; H. Dörrie, *RE* s.v. Xenokrates, Bd IX A 2, 1967, 1523; Krämer, *Ursprung* 37, 377; ablehnend Happ, *Hyle* 247, 250 f.) wie bei Aetios I 7, 18: Πυθαγόρας τῶν ἀρχῶν τὴν μονάδα θεὸν καὶ τἀγαθόν, ἥτις ἐστὶν ἡ τοῦ ἑνὸς φύσις, αὐτὸς ὁ νοῦς, wovon dann I 7,20 Speusipp abgehoben wird: Σπεύσιππος τὸν νοῦν οὔτε τῷ ἑνὶ οὔτε τῷ ἀγαθῷ τὸν αὐτόν, ἰδιοφυῆ δέ. Die Identifizierung von τὸ ἕν, τὸ μοναδικόν und ὁ νοῦς wird I 7,31 auch für Platon in Anspruch genommen (vgl. Krämer *a.O.* 57 ff.).—In diesem Fall ist der Gott-Noûs für Xenokrates Ursache auch der Ideen; denn ἕν und ἀόριστος δυάς bringen die Zahlen = Ideen hervor (fr. 33, fr. 68; vgl. Happ, *Hyle* 245 f.). Dann aber liegt es nahe, die Ideen = Zahlen als Gedanken Gottes anzusehen (vgl. dazu Krämer *a.O.* 41 ff.; Isnardi Parente 400 ff., ablehnend), wie Aetios I 10,3 und andere das für Platon postulieren.

Der Ausdruck ψυχὴ τοῦ παντός klingt wie eine wörtliche Übernahme aus *Tim.* 41d4 f., was umso auffallender ist, als Platon nur an dieser Stelle von einer Allseele spricht; sonst nennt er sie einfach ψυχή. Die Allseele kann als weiblich bezeichnet werden, weil sie im *Tim.* aufnehmendes und bergendes Prinzip ist; denn sie nimmt den Kosmoskörper gleichsam in ihrem Schoß auf (*Tim.* 36d9 f.), so wie die Gestirne in ihren Umläufen Platz finden (*Tim.* 38c7 ff., 40a4 f.). Weil sie den Gestirngottheiten in ihren Umläufen Raum bietet, kann sie auch mit Recht mit einer Göttermutter verglichen werden.[8] Mit noch größerem Recht kann die Weltseele als "Dyas" bezeichnet werden, da sie nach dem *Tim.* deutlich eine dyadische Struktur hat, sofern sie aus zwei "Kreisen" besteht, dem sog. Umlauf des Selben und dem des Anderen (36b5–d1).

Zu erinnern ist hier ferner an die xenokratische Erklärung von Platons Seelenmischung (*Tim.* 35a1–5; fr. 68): Hier entsteht in einem ersten Schritt aus der Mischung von ἀμέριστος οὐσία = τὰ ἕν und μεριστὴ οὐσία = ἀόριστος δυάς "die Zahl" (ὁ ἀριθμός), d.h. *die Dyas als erste aller Zahlen.* In einem zweiten Schritt wird dieser Zahl das Gegensatzpaar ταὐτόν und τὸ ἕτερον (*Tim.* 35a4 f.) beigemischt, die Prinzipien von Ruhe und Bewegung, so daß aus der ἀκίνητος δυάς die zu Ruhe und Bewegung fähige Seelenzahl wird: ἀριθμὸς ἑαυτὸν κινῶν (fr. 60 ff.).

Wie wir sehen, lassen sich nahezu alle Aussagen über die beiden höchsten Gottheiten unseres Fragments als Interpretationen von Ansätzen verstehen, die sich in den Dialogen Platons finden. Schwieriger ist das Problem der genauen Zuordnung der beiden Gottheiten. Wir wollen mit der Frage nach der Lokalisierung und den Herrschaftsbereichen beginnen, weil gerade diese in der

---

Daher kann Aetios I 7,4 (nach *Tim.* 29e, 50d) formulieren, nach Platon habe Gott die Welt πρὸς ἑαυτοῦ ὑπόδειγμα geschaffen (vgl. dazu Tauros bei Philoponos, *De aet. mundi* VI 8 S. 147,6 f.; Diog. Laert. III 69, 72, 76 u.ö.), und I 3, 8 werden—nach der Lehre des Pythagoras—τὸ ποιητικὸν καὶ τὸ εἰδικόν identifiziert (ähnlich Numenios bei Calcidius 296 S.298, 13 ff.; vgl. Waszink z.St.; vgl. Aetios I 7,31: τὸ ἕν = τὸ μοναδικόν = τὸ ὄντως ὄν, und Krämer *a.O.* 59 f.). Aus dem Zusammenfall von Noûs und Zahl wäre dann auch die Nachricht des Aetios IV 2,3 f (= Xenokr. fr. 60) zu verstehen: Πυθαγόρας ἀριθμὸν αὐτὸν κινοῦντα (ἀπεφήνατο τὴν ψυχήν) τὸν δὲ ἀριθμὸν ἀντὶ τοῦ νοῦ παραλαμβάνει. Ὁμοίως δὲ καὶ Ξενοκράτης. Denn die Zahl wäre im Noûs selbst Noûs. Dazu würde auch fr. 16 passen: *estque numerus, ut Xenocrates censuit, animus ac deus:* als Seele ist sie *bewegte* Zahl, als Gott-Monas-Noûs unbewegte Zahl. Auch fr. 36 ließe sich einfügen: Xenokrates lege dem Demiurgen eine arithmetische Verfassung (ἀριθμητικὴν ἕξιν) bei (vgl. Krämer *a.O.* 408). Xenokrates hätte dann den ersten Gott Monas genannt, weil er als Monas Prinzip der Zahlen wäre und diese ursprunghaft in sich umschlösse (vgl. Krämer *a.O.* 63, Anm. 140). Gott = Zahl: die Pythagoreer Lysis und Opsimos bei Athenagoras, *Leg.* 6; Pythagoras bei Clemens *Protr.* 6, 69, 2 und Tertull. *Apol.* 47,5; August. *De genesi ad litt.* 4,4; Hierokles, *In C.A.* 87, 16 ff. K. Die Gegensatzpaare περιττόν—ἄρτιον, ἄρρεν—θῆλυ galten als pythagoreisch (vgl. Arist. *Met.* 986a23 ff.) und weisen auf Diskussionen in der Alten Akademie. Vgl. Burkert 45 f.; vgl. zudem Arist. *Met.* 1004b31 f.; *Phys.* 192a22 f.

[8] In der *Epinomis* bringt die Weltseele—ψυχὴ νοῦν κεκτημέη (982b5)—die den Elementen entsprechenden Lebewesen hervor (981c7–984d2), wozu auch die Gestirne zählen (981d5ff.).

Literatur umstritten ist. W. Theiler[9] hat zur Interpretation unseres Textes das 18. Xenokratesfragment herangezogen, in dem von einem Ζεὺς ὕπατος ἐν τοῖς κατὰ τὰ αὐτὰ καὶ ὡσαύτως ἔχουσιν ein Ζεὺς νέατος ὑπὸ σελήνην gesondert wird. Er identifiziert den ersteren mit dem ersten Gott, den letzteren mit der Weltseele des 15. Fragments, so daß nach dieser Interpretation die Weltseele auf den sublunaren Raum beschränkt wäre, während der erste Gott im supralunaren Bereich regieren würde. Die Identifizierung von Monas (fr. 15) und "höchstem Zeus" (fr. 18) ist sicher richtig; denn "der erste Gott" und "der höchste Zeus" müssen identisch sein. Doch wird man gegen eine Gleichsetzung von Dyas und "unterstem Zeus" starke Bedenken haben. Denn es ist doch zu fragen, wieso die Seele ψυχὴ τοῦ παντός sein kann, wenn ihr Aufenthaltsort und Wirkungsbereich auf den relativ kleinen Raum unter dem Mond beschränkt ist, während gleichzeitig die ihr analoge Menschenseele (*mens*)[10] *per totum corpus sparsa discurrit* (fr. 71). Wie könnte sie noch mit einer Göttermutter verglichen werden, da die Gestirne doch auch zu den Göttern zählen? Wie wäre diese Ansicht mit dem *Tim.* in Einklang zu bringen, nach welchem die Seele sich durch das *ganze* All erstreckt (34b3 f., 36e2 f.)? Wäre es ferner vorstellbar, daß Xenokrates den "untersten Zeus" als weibliches Prinzip bezeichnet hat? Nein, Theilers Interpretation führt in allzu große Schwierigkeiten und kann daher nicht richtig sein. Das hat auch H.J. Krämer[11] gesehen, der eine andere Lösung vorschlägt: "Die Lokalisationen im Fr. 15 umschreiben den Wirkungsbereich, nicht den Standort von Demiurg und Weltseele." Aber auch mit dieser Modifizierung ist nicht viel gewonnen; denn eine Beschränkung des Wirkungsbereiches der *All*-Seele auf den sublunaren Raum widerspricht nicht nur Platons Lehren, die Xenokrates doch umformuliert haben soll, sondern auch allen antiken Nachrichten.[12]

Wenn es im 15. Fragment heißt, der erste Gott herrsche als König[13] ἐν οὐρανῷ, die Weltseele aber über den erlosten Bereich ὑπὸ τὸν οὐρανόν, so ist mit οὐρανός m.E. die Fixsternsphäre gemeint.[14] Mit anderen Worten: der

---

[9] JHS 77 (1957) 130 = *Untersuchungen zur antiken Literatur*, Berlin 1970, 316.

[10] *Mens* steht in diesem Fragment wohl für ψυχή; Zeller II 1, 1026, Anm.7; vgl. z.B. Apul. *De Platone* I 9 S.92,7 ff. Th.

[11] *Grundfragen* 485, Anm. 81; ähnlich, wenn auch abgeschwächter, ders., *Platonismus und hellenistische Philosophie*, Berlin—New York 1971, 125, Anm. 84; vgl. *Ursprung* 39, Anm. 65; vgl. Happ, *Hyle* 247, Anm. 850.

[12] Auch der Ausdruck ἐν οὐρανῷ βασιλεύουσαν widerspricht m.E. der Auffassung Krämers. Bei seiner Interpretation würde man im Text doch eher τοῦ οὐρανοῦ erwarten.

[13] Zur Königs-Metapher im Platonismus vgl. H. Dörrie, *Der König. Ein platonisches Schlüsselwort, von Plotin mit neuem Sinn erfüllt*, in: *Platonica Minora*, München 1976, 390 ff.

[14] So schon Krische 316 und Heinze 12 ff.; Dillon, *Middle Platonists* 25 f. Vgl. Anon. Photii (*Bibl.* cod.249) S.439b26 f.: ἐν τῇ ἀπλανεῖ τὸ πρῶτον αἴτιόν ἐστιν; b18 f: τὴν ἀπλανῆ σφαῖραν, ἐν ᾗ ἐστιν ὅ τε πρῶτος θεός ...; Ps.Justin, *Cohort.* 6; Ps.Arist. *Mu.* 397b25ff., 398b8 f., 400a6 ff.; Arist. *Cael.* 278b14 f.: εἰώθαμεν γὰρ τὸ ἔσχατον καὶ τὸ ἄνω μάλιστα καλεῖν οὐρανόν, ἐν ᾧ καὶ τὸ θεῖον πᾶν ἱδρῦσθαί φαμεν. Auch bei Herakleides Pontikos fr. 95 Wehrli erhält Zeus

Noûs als der erste Gott hat Sitz und Herrschaft in der Fixsternsphäre,[15] die Seele dagegen in dem von der Fixsternsphäre umfaßten innerkosmischen Raum.[16]

Diese Interpretation läßt sich weiter erhärten: Das 15. Fragment ist eine Systematisierung platonischer Lehren, wie der Doxograph am Ende betont. Nun hat aber Platon nach Xenokrates, den fünf sog. platonischen Körpern entsprechend, eine Fünfelementenlehre vertreten (fr. 53); dabei muß er—immer aus der Sicht des Xenokrates—den Dodekaeder dem Äther zugewiesen haben, weil die übrigen Körper schon an die bekannten vier Elemente vergeben waren.[17] Es heißt ja an der berühmten *Timaios*stelle 55c4−6, der Demiurg habe den Dodekaeder "für das All" verwandt. Da der Dodekaeder der Kugelform sehr nahe kommt, hat man die Stelle meist so gedeutet, daß der Dodekaeder dem äußeren Allrund zugewiesen wird, dem οὐρανός im Sinne der Fixsternsphäre.[18] Eine solche Interpretation konnte sich darauf berufen, daß nach *Tim.* 33b4 ff. der Kosmos zwar σφαιροειδής ist, aber erst dadurch zur eigentlichen Kugel wird, daß der Gott ihn "drechselt" (κυκλοτερὲς αὐτὸ ἐτορνεύσατο, 33b5) und außen abschleift (λεῖον ... πᾶν ἔξωθεν αὐτὸ ἀπηκριβοῦτο, b7 f.).

Die Vorstellung, daß der Äther zur Fixsternsphäre gehört, liegt nun aber offensichtlich auch dem 15. Xenokratesfragment zugrunde, dessen Kosmographie wie folgt aussieht:

1. οὐρανός   = Fixsternsphäre   ~ ⟨Äther⟩   (*Tim.* 55c4−6)[19]
2. ᾿Ολύμπιοι θεοί   = Planeten, Sonne,   ~ Feuer   (*Tim.* 40a2−4,
                        Mond   31b4−8)
3. Hades   ~ Luft   ⎫
4. Poseidon   ~ Wasser ⎬   (*Tim.* 32b u.ö.)
5. Demeter   ~ Erde   ⎭

---

die Fixsternsphäre. Da Herakleides sich auf die berühmte Aufteilung des Kosmos *Ilias* 15,187 ff. stützt (dazu auch unten S. 59 f.), interpretiert er den οὐρανός (ebd. 15, 192) als Fixsternsphäre.

[15] οὐρανός = Fixsternsphäre: fr. 17 H.; vgl. Arist. *Cael.* 278b11 ff.

[16] Dieser Raum wird als λῆξις, "ausgeloster Anteil" bezeichnet. Krämer, *Ursprung* 36, Anm. 51, weist auf fr. 5 hin, wo Λάχεσις die οὐσία αὐτοῦ τοῦ οὐρανοῦ zugeordnet ist, d.h. die Gestirnsphäre (Krämer).

[17] Vgl. Isnardi Parente, 434 f. Zur Fünfelementenlehre in der Platonischen Akademie vgl. L. Tarán, *Academica: Plato, Philip of Opus and the Pseudo-Platonic Epinomis*, Philadelphia 1975, 36 ff.; M. Baltes, *Philologus* 122, 1978, 190 ff.

[18] Vgl. *Timaios Lokros, Über die Natur des Kosmos und der Seele,* kommentiert von M. Baltes, Leiden 1972, 124.

[19] Vgl. Tarán, *Academica* 39 f. Nach fr. 57 liegen die Sterne in einer Ebene; die auffällige Parallele zu diesem Fragment in *Mu.* 392a16 ff. zeigt, daß die Fixsterne gemeint sind (vgl. Isnardi Parente, 397 f.), die also in der Ebene der Dodekaederfläche liegen. Auch die *Timaios*exegese bei Hippol. *Ref.* IV 8,3 kann man vergleichen. Eine andere Interpretation findet sich bei K. Gaiser, *Das Philosophenmosaik in Neapel*, Heidelberg 1980, 79. Nach ihm will das Fragment besagen, "daß Sonne, Mond und Planeten allesamt in der schräg zur Himmelsachse liegenden Ekliptikebene angeordnet sind."

Wenn Xenokrates davon spricht, daß Zeus "am Himmel als König regiert," so scheint er sich außer von Platon auch von Hesiod und Homer leiten zu lassen. Beide galten ja als die Begründer der Theologie der Griechen (Herodot II 53). Nun sagt Hesiod einerseits, daß Zeus οὐρανῷ ἐμβασιλεύει (*Theog.* 71; vgl. *Ilias* 15,192), andererseits, er sei αἰθέρι ναίων (*Op.* 18, ebenso *Il.* 2,412). Es scheint, als habe Xenokrates die Anschauungen der Dichter-Theologen aus der Sicht Platons interpretieren wollen, indem er Zeus zwar den Himmel = Äther zuwies, diesen aber mit der Fixsternsphäre identifizierte. Für die Weltseelen-Dyas blieb dann nur noch der Raum unterhalb der Fixsternsphäre übrig. Diese Aufteilung stimmt vordergründig zunächst nicht zum *Tim.*, wo die Weltseele sogar die Fixsternsphäre "von außen umhüllt" (34b4, 36d9 f., e3), muß aber schon frühzeitig aus dem *Tim.* herausgelesen worden sein, da sich dieselbe Lehre bei Ps. Timaios Lokros § 44 f., Philon u.a. findet (s.u.), die sich wahrscheinlich alle auf die Interpretation des Xenokrates stützen. Anhaltspunkte für diese Modifizierung der Lehre gab es bei Platon genug: *Tim.* 39c2 und 40a5 wird der "Umlauf des Selben" in der Weltseele (vgl. 36c4 f.) als φρονιμωτάτης κυκλήσεως περίοδος bzw. als ἡ τοῦ κρατίστου φρόνησις bezeichnet, und 37c1 ff. ist "der Kreis des Selben" das Vermögen von Noûs und Epistēmē. Wenn es zudem *Tim.* 30b3 f. (vgl. 46d5 f., *Phileb.* 30c) heißt, daß die Seele Voraussetzung für die Gegenwart des Noûs ist, dann kann man leicht verstehen, daß antike Interpreten den Umlauf des Selben *in der Seele* gern als den νοῦς ἐν ψυχῇ (*Tim.* 30b4) ansahen.[20] Andere Interpreten deuteten *Tim.* 36c2 f. im Sinne eines dritten Umlaufs, der die beiden innerseelischen Umläufe umfassen sollte, und identifizierten diesen mit dem Noûs *über der Seele*.[21] Platon spricht dort davon, daß der Demiurg die *beiden* Umläufe in der Seele mit der Bewegung, die sich immer im selben Sinne und am selben Ort vollzieht, umschloß. In dieser Bewegung sahen einige Interpreten einen Hinweis auf den Noûs über der Seele. Welche der beiden Interpretationen auf Xenokrates zurückgeht, ist auf den ersten Blick nicht ganz klar. Doch scheint bei einem genauen Vergleich der xenokratischen Lehre mit den Lehren Platons die erste Möglichkeit den Vorzug zu verdienen. Denn der erste Gott des Xenokrates erscheint zwar einerseits als ein (unabhängiger) König in seinem Bereich "am Himmel," andererseits aber ist er deutlich auf die Weltseele bezogen, wie die Ausdrücke Monas-Dyas, männlich-weiblich, Vater-Mutter, ungerade-gerade zeigen, so daß man sich fragt, ob beide trotz ihrer Trennung nicht doch zusammengehören und eine Einheit bilden, dergestalt, daß Xenokrates unter dem

---

[20] Vgl. Plut. *Virt. mor.* 3 (441E f.); Hermeias, *In Phaedr.* 89,26 f., 124,8 ff.; Albinos' νοῦς οὐράνιος: *Didask.* X 164,36 ff.; XXVIII 181,36 ff H.

[21] Jamblich bei Prokl. *Tim.* II 250,20 ff., 251,11 ff., 252,7 ff.; Hermeias, *In Phaedr.* 124,23 ff.; (Porphyrios bei) Calcidius 92 S.145,7 ff. Waszink; Albinos' νοῦς ὑπερουράνιος: *Didask.* XXVIII S.181,36 ff.

Noûs denjenigen "Teil" oder Aspekt der Weltseele Platons verstanden wissen wollte, der sich in der Fixsternsphäre befindet und den Kosmos von außen umhüllend transzendiert (*Tim.* 34b4, 36e3). Eine solche Interpretation ließe sich leicht durch andere Platonstellen stützen, etwa durch *Phileb.* 30d, wo es heißt, in der Natur des Zeus gebe es eine königliche Seele und einen königlichen Noûs. Hier werden Weltseele und Noûs in der Gestalt des Zeus zur Einheit verbunden, sind gleichsam zwei Aspekte der Natur des Zeus. Auch der *Phileb.* geht dabei von dem Lehrsatz aus, daß Noûs niemals ohne Seele existiert (30c).[22] Wenn der Noûs im *Phileb.* als "König des Himmels und der Erde" (28c), als Herrscher über das All (30d), als kosmologisches Ordnungsprinzip (28de, 30c) und als demiurgische Ursache (27b) erscheint, dann konnte man das so verstehen, als stehe hier der Noûs—pars pro toto—für Zeus, in dessen Natur Noûs und Seele vereinigt sind.

Im 10. Buch der platonischen *Nom.* haben wir das umgekehrte Verhältnis: hier tritt die Seele stärker in den Vordergrund, ohne daß jedoch der Noûs ganz verschwunden wäre. In den *Nom.* ist die Seele das kosmologische Ordnungsprinzip (892a, 898c, 899b8), allerdings eine Seele, die Noûs besitzt (897b1 f., c5 f., e4 ff., 892b8; vgl. 966e4; *Epin.* 982b5). Sie ist—wie *Tim.* 34c—die Herrscherin über den Weltkörper (896c) und das Prinzip der Bewegung am Himmel und auf der Erde (896e8 f.). Die Weltseele wird—wie auch die Gestirnseelen—als Gottheit bezeichnet (899a ff.), und in der anschließenden Behandlung der Frage nach der Fürsorge der Götter für die Welt ist von einem τοῦ παντὸς ἐπιμελούμενος die Rede (903b4 f., 904a3 f.),[23] der auch als König bezeichnet wird (904a6). Nach dem Voraufgehenden kann man darin aber niemand anderes als die Weltseele sehen.

Versucht man, die Angaben Platons auf einen Nenner zu bringen, so führt das zu folgendem Ergebnis: Noûs und Weltseele sind göttliche Prinzipien, die eines vom anderen nicht getrennt gedacht werden können; vielmehr kann das eine Prinzip das andere mitvertreten, und beide können auch als Einheit aufgefaßt werden. Auf dem Hintergrund dieser Platonstellen liegt es nahe, auch die beiden höchsten Gottheiten des 15. Xenokratesfragments als Aspekte eines einheitlichen göttlichen Wesens zu sehen, als männlich-weibliches Prinzip und als gerade-und-ungerade, wie man im späteren Platonismus die höchste Gottheit gerne bezeichnete. In dieser Einheit hat jedoch keine Vermischung der Prinzipien stattgefunden, sie ist vielmehr eine differenzierte Einheit, in der der Noûs als das männliche Prinzip gegenüber der Seele als dem weiblichen Prinzip

---

[22] Weitere Beziehungen des *Phileb.* zum *Tim.*: der Nus des *Phileb.* ist wie der Demiurg des *Tim.* das syndetische Prinzip (*Phil.* 27d9 – *Tim.* 31c ff.); er wird—wie der Demiurg des *Tim.*—mit Hilfe des Satzes erschlossen, daß alles Entstehende eine Ursache habe (*Phil.* 26e3 – *Tim.* 28a4 ff.). Auf die Chora des *Tim.* scheint *Phil.* 24d anzuspielen; vgl. bes. *Tim.* 52bc.

[23] Vgl. *Phaidr.* 246b6, wo die Seele παντὸς ἐπιμελεῖται τοῦ ἀψύχου.

dominiert.[24] Und wie der Noûs zur Menschenseele θύραθεν hinzukommt und im menschlichen Körper *in vertice praesidet secundum Xenocratem* (fr. 72), so kommt auch im Kosmos der Noûs zur Seele hinzu (vgl. *Nom.* 897b1 f., *Epin.* 982b5) und präsidiert in der höchsten kosmischen Region, dem Fixsternhimmel.[25] Ja, wie die Spitze der platonischen Weltseele transzendiert die Noûs-Monas als Ζεὺς ὁ ἐν τοῖς κατὰ τὰ αὐτὰ καὶ ὡσαύτως ἔχουσιν (fr. 18) selbst die Fixsternsphäre; denn die κατὰ τὰ αὐτὰ καὶ ὡσαύτως ἔχοντα sind ja wohl identisch mit den Ideen,[26] die Xenokrates—nach Plat. *Phaidr.* 247c1 ff.[27]—im ὑπερουράνιος τόπος lokalisiert (fr. 5).[28] ἐν οὐρανῷ (fr. 15) bedeutet also "am Himmel", d.h. "*in* der Fixsternsphäre" und "*auf* der Fixsternsphäre."[29]

Vom fr. 5 her läßt sich das Wesen der Weltseele und ihr Verhältnis zur Noûs-Monas noch etwas näher bestimmen. Es heißt dort, daß es ἐπιστήμη nur von den νοητὰ ἔξω τοῦ οὐρανοῦ gibt, δόξα vom οὐρανός (d.h. den Gestirnen) und αἴσθησις von den sublunaren Dingen. Diese Dreiteilung ist eine Interpretation von *Tim.* 37b6 ff., wo der Umlauf des Selben νοῦς (= νόησις) und ἐπιστήμη erzeugt, wenn er sich mit τὸ λογιστικόν beschäftigt, der Umlauf des Anderen aber δόξαι καὶ πίστεις, wenn er sich mit τὸ αἰσθητόν befaßt. Xenokrates hat nun τὸ λογιστικόν als τὸ νοητὸν ἔξω τοῦ οὐρανοῦ gedeutet und τὸ αἰσθητόν als τὸ δσξαστὸν καὶ αἰσθητόν (vgl. *Tim.* 27d5–28a4). Da nun aber νοῦς und ἐπιστήμη eindeutig der Noûs-Monas zukommen, weil nur sie den οὐρανός transzendiert, müssen δόξα καὶ αἴσθησίς der Seele zugewiesen werden. D.h. die Seele ist nach Xenokrates—wie später bei Ps.Timaios Lokros[30]—bloßes δοξαστικὸν καὶ αἰσθητικόν, also letztlich "an irrational entity requiring informing and intelligizing at the hand of the Monad," wie J. Dillon[31] mit

---

[24] Vergleichbar ist Plotin III 5,8.

[25] Ähnlich ist das Verhältnis im *Tim.*: vgl. 44d3 f., 90 A2 ff.

[26] Der Ausdruck meint die Ideen, nicht den οὐρανός; vgl. *Staat* 500c2 f.; *Politikos* 269d5 ff.; *Tim.* 38a3; anders Heinze, 76 f.; Isnardi Parente, 407. Zur Vorstellung, daß Gott unter den Ideen ist: *Phaidr.* 249C6; Seneca, *Epist.* 65,24; Plut. *Quaest. Plat.* III 2 (1002B); *Quaest. conviv.* VIII 2 (718 F); *De sera num. vind.* 5 (550D); Numenios fr. 24 Leemans = 15 des Places.

[27] Auch in Platons *Staat* 517b5 ist der νοητὸς τόπος (= νοητὸς κόσμος) ganz räumlich als der Ort oberhalb der Höhle = Kosmos gefaßt; vgl. ebd. 526e2–4.

[28] Zur Lokalisierung der Ideen im ὑπερουράνιος τόπος: Arist. *De philos.* fr. 8 Ross; *Cael.* 279a18 ff. (und dazu I. Düring, *Aristoteles*, Heidelberg 1966, 360 f.; B. Effe, *Studien zur Kosmologie und Theologie der Aristotelischen Schrift 'Über die Philosophie'*, München 1970, 102 ff.; F. Solmsen, *MH* 33 (1976) 29 ff., der auch auf die gegenteilige Äußerung des Aristoteles in *Phys.* 203a8 f. eingeht).

[29] Vgl. *Asclepius* 27: *deus supra verticem summi caeli consistens*; Arist. bei Aetios I 7,32: Ἀριστοτέλης τὸν μὲν ἀνωτάτω θεὸν εἶδος ⟨χωριστὸν⟩ (ὁμοίως Πλάτωνι) ἐπιβεβηκότα τῇ σφαίρᾳ τοῦ παντός (vgl. dazu P. Moraux, *RE* s.v. Quinta essentia, Bd XXIV 1, 1963, 1227 f.); Philon, *Heres* 301; *QG* IV 51; *Somn.* II 294; Boethius, *Consol.* IV 12 (Gedicht), 17 ff. Analog dazu ist die plutarchische Vorstellung vom Noûs des Menschen als ἔξω, ἀκρόπλουν, ἐπιψαῦον ἐκ κεφαλῆς τοῦ ἀνθρώπου ... ἄρτημα κορυφαῖον (*De gen. Socr.* 22 591D f.).

[30] Vgl. Baltes, *Timaios Lokros*, 145, 148.

[31] Dillon, *Middle Plat.* 26.

Recht urteilt. Man darf daran erinnern, daß nach akademischer Lehre die Weltseele erst dann zum Ordnungsfaktor in der Welt wird, wenn sie den Noûs hinzunimmt νοῦν προσλαβοῦσα, *Nom.* 897b1 f; *Epin.* 982b5; vgl. *Tim.* 46d5 f. mit e3 ff.).

Wie bekannt, hat die xenokratische Interpretation Platons weitreichenden Einfluß ausgeübt.[32] Es empfiehlt sich also, auch die Nachwirkungen der Lehre von fr. 15 zu untersuchen, zumindest soweit sie die bisher vorgetragene Interpretation tangieren und in der Forschung bisher nicht oder nicht genügend berücksichtigt worden sind.

Bei Philon, *Decal.* 103 finden wir folgenden Text:[33]

> "Das All (ὁ οὐρανός) ist fest gefügt aus der unteilbaren Natur und der teilbaren (ἔκ τε τῆς ἀμερίστου φύσεως καὶ τῆς μεριστῆς, vgl. *Tim.* 35a1–4). Die unteilbare Natur hat den ersten, höchsten und niemals irrenden Umlauf erlost (εἴληχεν), über den *die Monas* Aufsicht führt, die teilbare den zweiten (Umlauf) der Kraft und der Ordnung nach; diesen verwaltet *die Hebdomas*, die—sechsfach geteilt (vgl. *Tim.* 36d2)—die sieben sog. Planeten hervorgebracht hat."

Das dem Philontext—aufgrund einer Interpretation von *Tim.* 35a1–36d7— zugrundeliegende kosmographische Schema sieht wie folgt aus:

1. Fixsternsphäre ~ ἀμέριστος φύσις, regiert von der Monas
2. Planetenbereich ~ μεριστὴ φύσις, regiert von der Hebdomas
   (weil 6fach geteilt)

Monas und Hebdomas als Aufseher im Fixstern- und Planetenbereich—das erinnert auffällig an Xenokrates' Noûs-Monas und Weltseelen-Dyas. Sollten bei Philon mit den beiden Prinzipien Noûs und Weltseele gemeint sein? Nun weiß Proklos an mehreren Stellen (*Tim.* II 302,1 ff., 270,9 ff., 271,15 ff), die Philon nahe verwandt sind, von einer Noûs-Monas und einer Weltseelen-Hebdomas, und man wird mit gutem Grund vermuten, daß beide der gleichen Tradition folgen.[34] Denn sowohl Philon als auch Proklos berufen sich im Zusammenhang mit ihrer Argumentation auf 'Pythagoreer'.[35] Bei beiden hat die Monas im Fixsternbereich, die Hebdomas in den Planetensphären ihren Ort.[36] Beide beziehen sich deutlich auf dieselben *Timaios*passagen. Es scheint

---

[32] Krämer, *Ursprung* 21 ff.

[33] Dazu Boyancé, *REG* 76 (1963) 84 f.; D.T. Runia, *Philo of Alexandria and the Timaeus of Plato*, Philosophia Antiqua 44, Leiden 1986, 210 f.

[34] Dafür spricht auch *Leg. all.* I 19, wo der λόγος, der bei Philon oft die Funktionen der platonischen Weltseele übernimmt, ὁ κατὰ ἑβδομάδα κινούμενος genannt wird. Allerdings ist der λόγος nicht auf die Planetensphären beschränkt.

[35] οἱ περὶ τὰ μαθήματα διατρίψαντες (Philon) sind Pythagoreer, wie die Prädikate der Hebdomas παρθένος und ἀμήτωρ zeigen (vgl. Arist. *De Pythag.* fr. 13 Ross; Colson z.St.; Boyancé, *REG* 76 (1963) 94). Proklos gibt als Begründung für das Prädikat ἀμήτωρ: die Hebdomas stammt nur vom Vater-Noûs: *a.O.* 203,5 f. Auch betont er *a.O.* 236,18 f. die Nähe der Hebdomas zur Monas—wie Philon *Decal.* 102; *Op. mundi* 100; *Post. Caini* 64; *Immut.* 11; *Decal.* 159.

[36] Proklos identifiziert die Fixsternsphäre mit der Monas und den Planetenbereich mit der

also, daß bei Philon und Proklos—trotz einiger Abweichungen im Detail—die gleiche Lehre vorliegt, letztlich xenokratische Lehre, wie ich behaupten möchte. Denn an Xenokrates erinnert—abgesehen von der Systematisierung des *Timaios*—der Ausdruck, die Monas und die Hebdomas hätten ihren jeweiligen Bereich "erlost"; bei Xenokrates war von der λῆξις der Weltseelen-Dyas die Rede. Der Platonschüler vergleicht die Weltseele mit der "Mutter der Götter" (d.h. u.a. der Planetengötter), bei Philon erschafft die Hebdomas die sieben Planeten. Die Monas ist bei Philon der ἀμέριστος φύσις (~ ἀμέριστος οὐσία, *Tim.* 35a1) zugeordnet; Xenokrates hatte diese ἀμέριστος οὐσία im fr. 68 mit τὸ ἕν identifiziert.[37] Bei Proklos ist die Monas—wie bei Xenokrates—identisch mit dem δημιουργικὸς νοῦς (*Tim.* II 203,4).

Nur eine entscheidende Schwierigkeit bleibt zu lösen: Warum sprechen Philon und Proklos von der Weltseelen-Hebdomas, während Xenokrates von der Weltseelen-Dyas gesprochen hatte? Die Lösung dieser Frage ergibt sich aus dem beiden Interpretationen zugrundeliegenden *Timaios*stück 35a1–36d7; denn dort finden wir

1. eine *Zwei*teilung der Seelensubstanz (36b6–d1)
2. zwei Teilungen in *sieben* Teile:
   a) Einteilung der Grundsubstanz der Seele in sieben μοῖραι im Verhältnis 1:2:3:4:9:8:27 (35b4–c2)
   b) Aufteilung der θατέρου φορά der Seele in sieben κύκλοι (36d1–7).

Man hat nun—wie wir aus Proklos, *Tim.* II 246,22 ff. erfahren—versucht, die Zweiteilung mit der ersten Siebenteilung in Einklang zu bringen. Schon früh[38] hatte man ja die sieben Grundeinheiten in Form eines Lambda angeordnet:

Diese durch den Text von *Tim.* 35b4–c2 nahegelegte[39] Trennung von geraden und ungeraden Zahlen ermöglichte auch die Erklärung, die Aufteilung der gesamten Seelensubstanz in zwei 'Bänder' (*Tim.* 36b6ff.) erfolge in der Weise, daß dem einen 'Band' die geraden, dem anderen die ungeraden Zahlen zugewiesen werden, also:

Hebdomas (*a.O.* 271,16 ff). Daß Philon die beiden Prinzipien *in* den genannten Bereichen lokalisiert, zeigt seine Angabe, die Hebdomas sei wie die Planetensphären in sieben Teile geteilt.

[37] Vgl. oben S. 45, Anm. 7.

[38] Vgl. Krantor und Klearchos von Soloi bei Plut. *De an. procr.* 20 (1022C–E). Krantor war Schüler des Xenokrates.

[39] Vgl. Plut. *De an. procr.* 30 (1027D f.).

1 – 2 – 4 – 8 – – – θατέρου φορά⎫ vgl. Prokl. *Tim.* II
1 – 3 – 9 – 27 – – – ταὐτοῦ φορά ⎬ 239,29 f.

Damit war die Zweiteilung von *Tim.* 36b6 ff. als ein bloßer Aspekt der Siebenteilung von 35b4 ff. erwiesen, die ihrerseits wieder—nach Auffassung der antiken Interpreten—die Grundlage für die Siebenteilung von *Tim.* 36d1 ff. war.[40]

Mit anderen Worten: Man konnte die Seele nach Tim. 35b4ff. (und 36d1ff.) als eine Hebdomas oder nach Tim. 36b6ff. als eine Dyas betrachten. Letztlich war immer dasselbe gemeint. So wird denn in den späteren Darstellungen bald die dyadische, bald die hebdomadische Struktur der Seele hervorgehoben;[41] und wenn die hebdomadische Struktur später häufiger betont wird als die dyadische, so liegt das daran, daß die hebdomadische Struktur kosmologisch relevanter war, weil sie in den 7 Planeten deutlich in Erscheinung trat; auch ist zu bedenken, daß man der Siebenzahl größere Bedeutung beimaß als jeder anderen Zahl innerhalb der Dekade, mit Ausnahme der Monas. Man betrachtete sie als μονάδος οἰκειοτάτη καὶ ἀρχῆς (Phil. *Decal.* 102; vgl. Macr. *Somn.Sc.* I 6, 11), vor allem aber setzte man sie mit der mutterlosen, aus dem Haupt des Zeus entsprungenen Athene gleich:[42] auch die Weltseele des *Tim.*—nach Xenokrates das weibliche Prinzip schlechthin—war ja vom Demiurgen ohne weibliche Mithilfe "gezeugt" worden (vgl. z.B. 37c7).

Eine weitere Nachwirkung der xenokratischen Lehre finden wir bei Ps.Timaios Lokros § 45 f. wieder, wo—wie anderenorts nachgewiesen[43]—die Fixsternsphäre der Bereich des Noûs und die Planeten der Bereich der Seele sind. Daß Ps.Timaios Lokros von Xenokrates beeinflußt ist, zeigt vor allem der § 18. Die gleiche Lehre findet sich andeutungsweise auch bei Plotin II 2 [14] 3,1 ff.

Vergleichen läßt sich ferner Varro bei Augustinus, *De civ. dei* VII 23 (= *Antiq.rer. div.* fr. XVI 4 Agahd = fr. 227 Cardauns),[44] wo drei *animae gradus in omni universaque natura* unterschieden werden:

a) *summum animae, quod vocatur animus, in quo intellegentia praeminet … hanc partem animae mundi dicit deum;* er ist identisch mit dem Äther (~ νοῦς ἐν ψυχῇ);

---

[40] Vgl. z.B. Plut. *De an. procr.* 31 f. (1028A ff.); Platoniker bei Hippol. *Ref.* IV 8,5 ff.; Prokl. *Tim.* II 212,12 ff. Man berief sich dabei zu recht auf das κατὰ τὴν τοῦ διπλασίου καὶ τριπλασίου διάστασιν von *Tim.* 36d3.

[41] Die dyadische Struktur: Prokl. *Tim.* II 241,18 ff., 242,14 ff. u.ö.; zur dyadischen Struktur der Weltseele bei Plotin vgl. Krämer, *Ursprung* 296, Anm. 407. Die hebdomadische Struktur: Poseidonios bei Theo Smyrn. *Expos.* 103,16 ff.; Macrobius, *Somn.Scip.* I 6,45.

[42] Vgl. dazu Boyancé, *REG* 76 (1963) 92 ff.; die Gleichsetzung mit Athene findet sich zuerst bei Arist. *De Pyth.* fr. 13 Ross.

[43] Vgl. Baltes, *Timaios Lokros*, 145 f., 148.

[44] Vgl. die Interpretation von Boyancé, *REA* 57 (1955) 79 ff., der die Lehren des Fragments über Antiochos von Askalon auf Xenokrates zurückführt.

b) *secundus gradus animae, in quo sensus est;* dieser befindet sich im Planetenbereich, denn *solem ... lunam, stellas ... esse sensus eius* [sc. *dei*][45] (= αἰσθητικὴ ψυχή);

c) *unum, quod omnes partes corporis, quae vivunt, transit et non habet sensum, sed tantum ad vivendum valetudinem* (= φυτικὴ ψυχή).

Von Xenokrates unterscheidet sich diese Dreiteilung dadurch, daß sie eine Dreiteilung *der Weltseele* ist. Aber wir haben ja schon gesehen, daß nach platonischer Lehre der Noûs nur in der Seele sein kann und daß auch nach Xenokrates Noûs-Monas und Weltseelen-Dyas wie ἄρρεν und θῆλυ zusammengehören. Die φυτικὴ ψυχή wird in den Xenokratesfragmenten nicht erwähnt. Da aber Platon im *Timaios* (77b1 ff.) sie kennt,[46] dürfte auch Xenokrates sie akzeptiert haben. Die Identifizierung von *animus* und Äther scheint stoisch zu sein, geht aber vielleicht insofern auf Xenokrates zurück, als dieser wahrscheinlich den Äther in der Fixsternsphäre, dem Bereich des Noûs, angesetzt hat (s.o. S.48).[47] Als Ergebnis unserer Untersuchungen dürfen wir also festhalten: Die Nachwirkungen der xenokratischen Lehre zeigen, daß unsere Interpretation, die Noûs-Monas regiere am Fixsternhimmel, die Weltseelen-Dyas im Planetenbereich, richtig war.

Die xenokratisch-akademische Ansicht, daß die Seele im Grunde eine irrationale Wesenheit ist, die erst durch das Hinzukommen des Noûs zum Ordnungsfaktor der Welt wird, finden wir im späteren Platonismus in mehreren Varianten wieder, so etwa im Ordnen der ungeordneten Seele durch den Gott-Noûs bei Plutarch und Attikos (Plut. *An.procr.* 9, 1016C u.ö.; Attikos bei Proklos. *Tim.* I 381,26 ff. u.ö.) oder im Wecken der Seele aus dem Schlaf durch den Gott und im Hinwenden auf ihn (Albin, *Did.* 10, S.165, 1 ff.; 14, S.169,30 ff.; vgl. Plut. *An.procr.* 24, 1024D).

---

[45] Boyancé, *REA* 57 (1955) 82 verweist für diese seltsame Lehre auf Pythagoreer bei Epiphanius, *Dox.Gr.* 589,3 ff.; Plut. *De facie* 15 (928B); Plin. *N.H.* II 10. Vgl. auch *Orphicor.fr.* 168,16 Kern.

[46] Im Gegensatz zu Varro gesteht Platon dieser Seelenart eine bestimmte Art von αἴσθησις zu, die αἴσθησις ἡδεῖα καὶ ἀλγεινή. Weder Aristoteles noch die Stoiker haben sich ihm angeschlossen (vgl. Aetios V 26,1 ff.). Hat schon Xenokrates die αἴσθησις der Pflanzenseelen geleugnet oder liegt bei Varro lediglich stoischer Einfluß vor?

[47] Letztlich xenokratisch scheint auch die Aussage bei Varro zu sein, die *vis animi, quae pervenit in astra, ea quoque facere deos*; denn bei Xenokrates übt die Noûs-Monas gegenüber den Gestirngottheiten die Funktion eines Vaters aus (vgl. o. S. 45). Nachwirkungen xenokratischer Lehren sehe ich auch in der Fortsetzung des zitierten Satzes: *et per ea* (sc. *astra*) *quod in terram permanat, deam Tellurem* (= *Cererem*, August. *Civ. dei* VII 16 = *Ant. rer. div.* XVI 49 A Ag. = fr. 270 Card.); *quod autem inde permanat in mare atque oceanum, deum esse Neptunum* (vgl. unten S. 60 ff.). Denn als Göttervater und Göttermutter sind Noûs-Monas und Weltseelen-Dyas Ursachen auch von Poseidon und Demeter, die ihrerseits durch ihre "göttlichen Kräfte" in den beiden Elementen wirken. Anders ausgedrückt: die Noûs-Monas wirkt zusammen mit der Weltseelen-Dyas durch die olympischen Götter (*per ea*) bis zur Erde hinab.

II

Weiter soll Xenokrates nach dem 15. Fragment den οὐρανός als Gott bezeichnet haben, ferner die feurigen Sterne als "olympische Götter", und
schließlich habe er auch die sublunaren, unsichtbaren Dämonen als eine
Gruppe von Gottheiten angesehen.

Was hier unter οὐρανός zu verstehen ist, ist nicht ganz klar. Nach dem
Voraufgehenden wird man an die Fixsternsphäre denken, deren Sterne nach fr.
17 zusammen als eine einzige Gottheit angesehen wurden: *unum* [sc. *deum*],
*qui ex omnibus sideribus, quae infixa caelo sunt, ex dispersis quasi membris
simplex sit putandus deus.* Diese Auffassung hätte im Werk Platons keine Entsprechung, obschon man sie schon früh in *Tim.* und *Nom.* hineingelesen hat,
wie Cicero *N.D.* I 30 bezeugt: *(Plato) et in Timaeo dicit et in Legibus et mun-
dum deum esse et c a e l u m et astra et terram* . . . Dagegen ist festzuhalten, daß
die Fixsterne bei Platon immer als *Einzel*gottheiten erscheinen, nie als eine
einzige Gesamtgottheit (*Tim.* 40a4–b6; vgl. *Nom.* 899b). Als eine einzige
δύναμις neben den 7 δυνάμεις der Planeten erscheinen die Fixsterne dagegen
in der *Epinomis* 986a8 ff.[48]

Die zweite Möglichkeit bestände darin, unter οὐρανός den Gesamtkosmos
zu verstehen (οὐρανός = Kosmos: *Tim.* 28b2 ff., u.ö.), wie dies das Zeugnis
des Clemens (fr. 17) nahelegt, der den Kosmos als achten Gott neben den sieben
Wandelsternen nennt.[49] Auch nach Platon ist der Kosmos ein großer Gott
(etwa *Nom.* 821a2), der durch die Parusie der Weltseele zum "glückseligen
Gott" wird, wie es *Tim.* 34a8–b9 heißt. So gewiß nun Xenokrates—wie alle
Philosophen der Alten Akademie—den Kosmos als einen Gott angesehen hat,
so gewiß hat fr. 15 diesen Kosmos nicht im Sinn, wenn es vom οὐρανός als
einem Gott spricht. Denn wir haben wieder einmal eine der bei Xenokrates
beliebten vertikalen Dreiteilungen vor uns, in welcher der οὐρανός an der
Spitze steht, gefolgt von den Planeten (τοὺς ἀστέρας) und den sublunaren
Dämonen. Οὐρανός meint also—wie in fr. 17—die aus allen Fixsternen be-
stehende Gesamtgottheit.

Gottheiten sind nach dem *Tim.* (z.B. 40b5, 41a3) auch die Sterne. Sie sind—
wie in unserem Fragment—feurige Substanzen (*Tim.* 40a2–4, 31b, 63b), doch
werden sie im *Tim.* nicht "olympische Gottheiten" genannt.[50] Wie bei Xeno-

---

[48] Siehe auch oben S. 52, Anm. 36.

[49] Vergleichbar wäre Aetios I 7,33 von den Stoikern: θεοὺς δὲ καὶ τὸν κόσμον καὶ τοὺς
ἀστέρας καὶ τὴν γῆν, τὸν δ' ἀνωτάτω πάντων νοῦν ἐν αἰθέρι (*SVF* II 1027).

[50] Vielleicht darf man *Nom.* 717ab erinnern, wo neben den "olympischen Gottheiten" die
Stadtgötter und die chthonischen Gottheiten aufgezählt werden; diesen Gottheiten folgen dann οἱ
δαίμονες und οἱ ἥρωες. Hier scheint eine deutliche Stufung vorzuliegen, denn es heißt, man solle
μετ' Ὀλυμπίους τε καὶ τοὺς τὴν πόλιν ἔχοντας θεοὺς den χθόνιοι θεοί Ehre erweisen, μετὰ θεοὺς δὲ τούσδε καὶ τοῖς δαίμοσιν . . . ἥρωσιν δὲ μετὰ τούτους (717b). Vorher (716c) war von ὁ
θεός als dem μέτρον πάντων die Rede. Diese Ausführungen konnten leicht im Sinne einer

krates neben den Gestirngottheiten ἕτεροι stehen—die unsichtbaren sublunaren Dämonen—so stehen bei Platon neben den Sternengöttern ἄλλοι δαίμονες (*Tim.* 40d6 ff.),[51] auch sie unsichtbar, doch heißt es, sie seien imstande zu erscheinen, wenn sie wollten (41a4).

Auf dem Hintergrund der bisherigen Ausführungen wird nun auch fr. 17 klarer. Nach diesem hat Xenokrates 8 Götter anerkannt: fünf Planetengötter, Sonne, Mond und die Fixsterne, die gleichsam eine einzige Gottheit aus vielen Gliedern seien.[52] Diese acht Götter[53] sind natürlich nicht die einzigen Götter, die Xenokrates anerkannt hat, es sind nur die Götter *einer Gruppe*, nämlich der ὁρατοὶ καὶ ἐγκόσμιοι θεοί—im Gegensatz zu den ἀόρατοι δαίμονες—die ihrerseits von der Noûs-Monas und der Weltseelen-Dyas (-Hebdomas) regiert werden. Der Epikureer, auf den fr. 17 zurückgeht, hat die xenokratische Lehre verkürzt und dadurch mißverständlich gemacht.

Auch das 19. Xenokratesfragment[54] muß hier betrachtet werden, nach welchem er zwei Götterarten (*bifariam formam divinitatis*) eingeführt hat, indem er von den olympischen die titanischen Götter unterschied. Die olympischen Gottheiten, zu denen das Fragment nichts weiter sagt, sind natürlich die Götter des Planetenbereichs. Von den titanischen heißt es, sie seien *de Caelo et Terra* entstanden. Arkesilaos hat nach demselben Fragment die Lehre des Xenokrates abgewandelt und eine Dreiteilung der Götter vertreten: olympische Götter, Gestirne, titanische Gottheiten. Die Abwandlung der Lehre durch Arkesilaos scheint lediglich im Abtrennen der olympischen Götter von den Sternen bestanden zu haben; denn seine Titanen entstammen ebenfalls *de Caelo et Terra*.[55] Mit anderen Worten: die im fr. 19 aufgeführten Sukzessionen der Götter (*de Caelo et Terra*: ⟨ . . . . . ⟩[56] *ex Saturno et Ope Neptunum*

Götterhierarchie ausgelegt werden, an deren Spitze ὁ θεός steht, gefolgt von den "olympischen Gottheiten", den Stadtgöttern, den chthonischen Gottheiten, den Dämonen und den Heroen (vgl. Aetios I 8,2). Hier ist nicht davon die Rede, daß die "olympischen Götter" die Sterne seien, aber von *Nom.* 899a ff. her ist dieser Schluß naheliegend, wie denn auch *Epin.* 977b2 Himmel und Olymp identifiziert. Nach Plut. *De Is. et Os.* 26 (361A) bezeugt die *Nomoi*stelle, daß Platon die "olympischen Götter" von den 'Dämonen' geschieden hat. Vorher und nachher wird Xenokrates zitiert (vgl. Heinze, 155). Zur Zuordnung von Planeten und "olympischen Göttern" vgl. W. Gundel/H. Gundel, *RE* s.v. Planeten, Bd XX 2, 1950, 2115 ff.

[51] Vgl. *Phaidr.* 246e, wo dem Gefährt des Zeus 1. die Götter folgen und 2. die δαίμονες.

[52] Ähnlich *Epin.* 987b1−c7, wo auch die Fixsternsphäre—dort κόσμος genannt—den sieben Planeten als eine einzige gegenübersteht.

[53] Zur Achtzahl der (sichtbaren) Götter vgl. Theo Smyrn. *Expos.* S. 104,20 ff.

[54] Das bei Tertullian, *Ad nat.* II 2 überlieferte Fragment geht wahrscheinlich auf Varro zurück: Varro, *Ant. rer. div. fr.* I 12b Ag. = fr. 23 Card.; Boyancé, *REA* 57, 1955, 74.

[55] So schon bei Hesiod, *Theog.* 133 ff.

[56] Nach *Tim.* 40e5 ff. ergänzte P. Boyancé, *REA* 50, 1948, 225, Anm. 1, die von ihm bemerkte Lücke, wie folgt: ⟨*Oceanum et Tethyn, ex Oceano et Tethyde Saturnum et Opem,*⟩ *ex* . . . Ob es sich um eine wirkliche Lücke im Text oder eine bewußte Abänderung des Xenokrates handelt, muß allerdings offen bleiben, da Kronos und Rhea gewöhnlich als direkte Kinder von Uranos und Ge galten (Hes. *Theog.* 133 ff.). Der überlieferte Text scheint anzudeuten, daß Xenokrates Kronos und Rhea mit Uranos und Ge identifizierte (Rhea = Ge: *SVF* II 1076,1084)

Iovem Orcum et ceteram successionem) gehören wohl dem Xenokrates. Gestützt wird diese Annahme durch die Parallele *Tim.* 40e5 ff., wo *aus Erde und Himmel* Okeanos und Tethys entstehen, aus Okeanos und Tethys Phorkys, *Kronos und Rhea* (= Ops) und deren Geschwister, aus Kronos und Rhea aber *Zeus*, Hera und deren *Brüder und Schwestern*. Erneut scheint Xenokrates eine *Timaios*stelle zum Ausgangspunkt seiner systematischen Theologie gemacht zu haben. Doch hat er die im *Tim.* nur angedeutete Generationenfolge weiter ausgeführt. Dies zeigt nicht nur die Erwähnung von Hades und Poseidon neben Zeus sowie der Hinweis auf die *cetera successio*, sondern auch das 20. Xenokratesfragment, nach dem die Τιτανική in Dionysos kulminierte.[57] Wer sind nun aber die titanischen Gottheiten des Xenokrates? Nimmt man die Angaben von fr. 15 über die zweite Gruppe von Gottheiten mit der *Timaios*parallele zusammen, so können nur die sublunaren Dämonen gemeint sein.[58] Diese Erklärung wird sich alsbald erhärten lassen.

Versuchen wir nun, die Angaben von fr. 15 und fr. 17 mit fr. 19 in Einklang zu bringen, so geraten wir in große Schwierigkeiten, da der Zeus von fr. 15, der dort der *erste* Gott genannt wird, nicht mit dem Zeus von fr. 19 identisch sein kann, der nur eine nachgeordnete Gottheit zu sein scheint; denn er steht nicht nur in der Generationenfolge der titanischen Gottheiten weit unten, sondern ist offenbar auch den olympischen Göttern nachgeordnet. Sind aber der Zeus des 15. und der des 19. Fragments nicht identisch, so haben wir mit mehreren Arten dieser Gottheit zu rechnen. Diese Annahme wird durch fr. 18 bestätigt, das, wie schon gesagt, einen Ζεὺς ὕπατος ἐν τοῖς κατὰ τὰ αὐτὰ καὶ ὡσαύτως ἔχουσιν von einem Ζεὺς νέατος ὑπὸ σελήνην scheidet. Mit anderen Worten: es gibt bei Xenokrates einen höchsten Zeus ἐν οὐρανῷ und einen unteren Zeus ὑπὸ σελήνην, d.h. im Bereich der Dämonen. Auch die frr. 23/24 können für diese Ansicht als Bestätigung herangezogen werden, nach welchen die Schilderung der Dichter über unwürdiges Verhalten der Götter—also auch des Zeus—τὰ Γιγαντικὰ καὶ Τιτανικά werden u.a. als Beispiele aufgeführt— nicht auf die Götter, sondern auf "große Dämonen" zu beziehen seien.[59] Xenokrates hat also tatsächlich mehrere Arten einer Gottheit unterschieden. Der in fr. 19 genannte titanische Zeus, der Zeus der Mythologie, ist also ein großer Dämon, kein Gott im strengen Sinne. Er gehört zu den sublunaren Dämonen der II. Göttergruppe und ist wahrscheinlich mit dem sublunaren Zeus von fr. 18 identisch. Nun fragt man sich allerdings, ob es neben dem Zeus

---

[57] Vgl. auch fr. 24, wo vom Kampf Apollons gegen den Pythondrachen, von der Flucht des Dionysos und dem Herumirren der Demeter die Rede ist.

[58] So Heinze, 149 ff.; Boyancé, *REA* 50, 1948, 224,226; Burkert, 228, Anm. 40; Isnardi Parente, 411. Vgl. Plut. *Def. orac.* 21 (421E): Jeder Dämon wird mit dem Namen eines Gottes benannt, dem er folgt (*Phaidr.* 246e) und an dessen δύναμις und τιμή er teilhat.

[59] Vgl. Heinze, 94 f. Dagegen M. Detienne, *REA* 60 (1958) 272 f.—ohne genügende Berücksichtigung von fr. 19 und fr. 20. Vgl. auch, Anm. 58.

am Himmel und dem sublunaren Zeus als dritten nicht auch einen olympischen Zeus gegeben haben muß. Denn 1. wissen wir von Xenokrates' Vorliebe für Dreiteilungen, wobei dem Mittelglied jeweils syndetische Funktionen zukommen, und 2. gibt es ja unter den Sternen einen mit Namen Zeus.[60] Sieht man sich nun den Kontext von fr. 18 bei Plutarch (*Quaest.Plat.* IX 1 1007F) näher an, so zeigt sich, daß Xenokrates höchstwahrscheinlich auch von einem Ζεὺς μέσος gesprochen hat,[61] da bei Plutarch von der Trias Nete—Mese—Hypate die Rede ist. Plutarch übergeht den "mittleren Zeus" mit Stillschweigen, weil es ihm einzig und allein um die Bedeutung von ὕπατος und νέατος zu tun ist. Xenokrates hat also aller Wahrscheinlichkeit nach drei Arten der Gottheit Zeus unterschieden:

1. den Zeus ἐν οὐρανῷ (καὶ ἐν τοῖς κατὰ τὰ αὐτὰ καὶ ὡσαύτως ἔχουσιν),
2. den olympischen Zeus im Bereich der Sterne,
3. den titanischen Zeus im sublunaren Bereich.

Neben dem titanischen Zeus gibt es weitere titanische Gottheiten, z.B. Kronos, Hades und Poseidon (fr. 19), Apollon, Python (?), Demeter und Dionysos (fr. 24, 20), neben dem olympischen Zeus weitere olympische Gottheiten, die allem Anschein nach den Namen der Sterne entsprechen (*qui in stellis vagis nominantur*, fr. 17, vgl. aber unten S.60 ff.).

Die Nachwirkungen der Aufteilung in drei Arten des Zeus sind aufschlußreich. So spricht Proklos, *In Crat.* 148/150 von der δημιουργικὴ τριάς, die er unterteilt in;

a) ὁ ἀρχικὸς Ζεύς, der μοναδικῶς Ζεύς und πατήρ genannt wird und über τὸ ἀπλανές herrscht;

b) ὁ δεύτερος δὲ δυαδικῶς καλεῖται Ζεὺς ἐνάλιος καὶ Ποσειδῶν = αἴτιος (bzw. ἐξάρχων) κινήσεως = Herrscher über den Planetenbereich;

c) ὁ δὲ τρίτος τριαδικῶς Ζεύς τε καταχθόνιος καὶ Πλούτων καὶ "Αιδης = Herrscher über die Region unter dem Mond.

Ganz ähnlich ist die Behandlung der δημιουργικὴ τριάς in *Theol. Plat.* VI 6–10, wo sich die entscheidenden Worte über die Zuweisung der kosmischen Bereiche S. 368, 4 ff. finden.

Wie die Proklosstellen klar zeigen, steht im Hintergrund dieser Aufteilung die berühmte *Ilias*stelle 15,187 ff., die schon Platon *Gorg.* 523a3–5 herange-

---

[60] Zum erstenmal belegt *Epin.* 987c6.

[61] So schon Krische, 324; dann Krämer, *Ursprung*, 37, Anm. 58 und 82, Anm. 209; ders. *Platonismus und hellen. Philosophie*, 124; H. Happ, *Kosmologie und Metaphysik bei Aristoteles*, in: *Parusia, Festgabe für J. Hirschberger*, Frankfurt/M 1965, 178, Anm. 101). Skeptisch sind Heinze 76 f., H. Cherniss in seiner Loeb-Ausgabe von Plutarch, *Quaestiones Platonicae*, London 1976, 92, Anm. *a* und Isnardi Parente, 405. Man vergleiche jedoch Plut. *Quaest. conviv.* IX 14,4 (745B)—eine Stelle, die letztlich auf Xenokrates fußt (vgl. fr. 5)—, wo der Fixsternsphäre, dem Planetenbereich und der Region unter dem Mond eine Ὑπάτη Μοῦσα, eine Μέση Μοῦσα und eine Νεάτη Μοῦσα zugewiesen werden.

zogen hatte und die wohl auch Xenokrates im Auge hatte. Jedenfalls wird später die Aufteilung in drei Δίες (fast) immer mit einem Hinweis auf die *Ilias*stelle erklärt (z.B. Hermeias, *In Phaedr.* 136,19 ff.).

Damit man aber nicht argumentiere, hier handle es sich um eine typisch neuplatonische Erfindung, sei verwiesen

1) auf Herakleides Pontikos, fr. 95 Wehrli, der den Kosmos (nach *Il.*15,187 ff.) wie folgt aufteilt:

   a) Zeus regiert über die Fixsternsphäre,
   b) Poseidon über den Bereich darunter bis zur Sonne einschließlich,
   c) Pluton über den Bezirk vom Mond[62] abwärts,
      wobei jeder der drei Kroniden, wie Pausanias 2,24,4 zeigt, als Zeus bezeichnet werden konnte;

2) auf Athenagoras, *Legatio* 23, wo unterschieden werden

   a) ὁ μέγας ἡγεμὼν ἐν οὐρανῷ Ζεύς = ὁ ἀίδιος νοῦς καὶ λόγῳ καταλαμβανόμενος = ἡ πρώτη δύναμις = ὁ ποιητὴς τῶν ὅλων = ἀγένητος θεός = ὁ οὐράνιος;
   b) ὁ χαμᾶθεν Ζεύς = ὁ Κρόνου (nach *Tim.* 41a1) = δαίμων = γενητός.

Nur scheinbar ist bei Athenagoras lediglich von zwei Arten des Zeus die Rede; denn aus dem Kontext geht klar hervor, daß seine Vorlage drei Arten von Gottheiten kannte: neben dem ἀγένητος θεός die Planeten und die Fixsterne einerseits und die Dämonen andererseits. Daß dabei die Sterne einem einzigen Prinzip zugeordnet werden, zeigt das Zitat aus dem berühmten 2. ps. platonischen *Brief* 312e1–4, das von *drei* Prinzipien spricht. Athenagoras übergeht den mittleren Zeus, weil es ihm um den Gegensatz Gott—Dämonen zu tun ist und er beweisen will, daß nicht Gott, sondern die Dämonen die wunderbaren Erscheinungen an den Götterbildern hervorrufen.

Daß Athenagoras' Vorlage wirklich drei Gottheiten erwähnt hat, legen die Interpretationen von *Ep.* II 312e bei Justin, *Apol.* I 60 und Kelsos bei Origenes, *C. Cels.* VI 18 nahe (vgl. auch Numenios fr. 1 S. 115, 1 f. Leemans = fr. 24,51 f. des Places und dazu das Vorwort S. 10).

III

Die dritte Gruppe hat—wie Stobaios/Aetios andeutet—bei Platon keine genaue Entsprechung; doch ist sie kosmologisch die folgerichtige Fortsetzung der zweiten Gruppe. Denn Xenokrates ließ sich offensichtlich von dem Gedanken leiten, daß jedem Element eine göttliche Wesenheit entsprechen müsse. Dabei gelangte er zu der oben S.48 dargestellten Systematik.

Die Wesenheiten dieser dritten Gruppe sind keine Dämonen, auch keine Götter—diese waren ja in den beiden voraufgehenden Gruppen genannt—

---

[62] Den Mond sah er dabei wohl als die Grenzscheide zwischen dem Bereich der ewig gleichen Bewegung und der veränderlichen γένεσις an.

sondern θεῖαι δυνάμεις nach der Ergänzung von Zeller und Heinze (θεῶν δυνάμεις, Krische), die durch das bei Aetios sich anschließende Referat über Platons Lehre (I 7,31) gestützt wird—ein Referat, das, wie H.J. Krämer[63] gezeigt hat, auf Xenokrates zurückgeht: πρὸς δὲ τούτοις ἐναιθέριοί τινες δυνάμεις[64] (λόγοι δ' εἰσὶν ἀσώματοι[65]) καὶ ἐναέριοι καὶ ἔνυδροι.

Diese δυνάμεις sind offenbar Ausstrahlungen der Götter bis in die untersten Bereiche des Kosmos; sie durchdringen die ὑλικὰ στοιχεῖα und lassen auch diese teilhaben an der Göttlichkeit des ganzen Alls.

Die Zuweisung der Luft an Hades und des Wassers an Poseidon erinnert zusammen mit der Zuweisung des Himmels an Zeus (Gruppe I) erneut an die berühmte Aufteilung des Kosmos in *Il.*15,187 ff., nach der Poseidon das Meer (πολίην ἅλα), Hades den ζόφος ἠέριος und Zeus den weiten Himmel erlost hat. Es scheint also, daß Xenokrates die berühmte *Ilias*stelle in mehrfacher Weise in seine Überlegungen miteinbezogen hat.

Der Zuordnung von Demeter und Erde liegt dagegen offenbar die Etymologie Δημήτηρ = Γῆ μήτηρ zugrunde, die möglicherweise aus orphischer Umgebung stammt (fr. 302 Kern).[66] Die Etymologie Ἅιδης < ἀ[ε]ιδής, mit der Xenokrates bei der Zuordnung von Luft und Hades arbeitet, war schon Platon bekannt (*Gorg.* 493b4 f.; *Krat.* 403a5 ff.; *Phaid.* 81c11).

Wenn nun aber die θεῖαι δυνάμεις von den Göttern stammen, Hades, Poseidon und Demeter also keine Dämonen, sondern Götter sind, dann ist nach ihrer Zugehörigkeit zu fragen. Nach allem, was wir bisher über die Theologie des Xenokrates eruiert haben, können sie nur *olympische* Götter sein. Denn nach der eben angeführten *Ilias*stelle (15,187 ff.) ist der Olymp—d.h. bei Xenokrates der Planetenbereich—der gemeinsame Sitz *aller* Götter. Zudem gehören zumindest Poseidon und Demeter traditionell zu den olympischen Göttern. Da nun aber Hades, Poseidon und Demeter[67] keine der traditionellen Planetengottheiten sind, haben wir im olympischen Bereich mit mehr als sieben Gottheiten zu rechnen. Es stellt sich somit die Frage nach der Zahl der olympischen Götter. Nun heißt es im *Phaidros*, daß ὁ μέγας ἡγεμὼν ἐν οὐρανῷ Ζεύς bei seiner Auffahrt zum ὑπερουράνιος τόπος von 11 Göttern begleitet wird (246e/247a). D.h. Platon geht im *Phaidr.* von den traditionellen 12 olympischen Göttern aus und lokalisiert sie ἐν οὐρανῷ.[68] Das gleiche scheint auch

---

[63] *Ursprung*, 59 f.

[64] Hier scheint der Äther als ein fünftes Element angesehen worden zu sein (Vgl. Xenokrates fr. 53; Aetios II 7,4), der entsprechend der Lehre der *Epin.* unterhalb der Feuerregion gesetzt ist. Anders als bei Xenokrates fr. 15 wird hier auch für den Äther eine eigene göttliche δύναμις angenommen—wie z.B. bei Sallust, u. S. 67.

[65] Ein stoisierender Zusatz.

[66] Vgl. die weiteren Belege im Kommentar von A.S. Pease zu Cicero, *N.D.* II 67.

[67] Vgl. Hesiod, *Theog.* 453 ff. mit 633 f.; *homer. Demeterhymnus* 84 f., 92, 331 f., 441 ff., 483 ff.

[68] Vgl. R. Hackforth, *Plato's Phaedrus*, Translated with an Introduction and Commentary,

Xenokrates getan zu haben, wie im folgenden, so hoffe ich, erhärtet werden kann, nur lokalisiert er die olympischen Götter im Planetenbereich.

Da die antiken Zwölfgötterlisten nicht immer die gleichen Gottheiten nennen, ist danach zu fragen, *welche* Gottheiten Platon und Xenokrates zur Gruppe der 12 olympischen Götter gezählt haben.

Die Listen enthalten in ihrer kanonischen Form folgende Namen: Zeus, Hera, Poseidon, Demeter, Apollon, Artemis, Ares, Aphrodite, Hermes, Athene, Hephaistos, Hestia. Davon nennt Platon im *Phaidr.* nur die Namen Zeus, Hestia, Ares, Hera, Apollon (246e f., 252c ff.),[69] in den *Nom.* (745b ff., 828b ff., wo ebenfalls von den Zwölfgöttern die Rede ist) Hestia, Zeus, Athene, Pluton. Die Zuweisung von Pluton (Hades) zur Gruppe der Zwölfgötter ist ungewöhnlich. Sie kommt sonst nur noch im Scholion zu Apollonios Rhodios II 532 vor, weshalb Weinreich[70] annahm, sie gehe auf Platons *Nom.* zurück. Die Zuweisung steht im übrigen im Einklang mit der bekannten *Ilias*stelle 15,187 ff., wo nach der gleichberechtigten Nennung von Zeus—Poseidon—Hades der Olymp als allen Göttern (also auch Hades) gemeinsam angesehen wird.

Die Gruppe der olympischen Götter des Xenokrates umfaßte die 7 Planetengötter sowie 5 weitere Gottheiten. Die Namen der Planetengötter der Akademie waren: Kronos, Zeus, Ares, Aphrodite, Hermes, Helios und Selene (*Epin.* 987bc; *Tim.* 38d; Arist. *Met.* Λ 8). Hinzu kommen aus fr. 15 Hades, Poseidon und Demeter, aus fr. 22 Apollon. Dabei mögen—wie später häufig belegt—Apollon mit Helios und Artemis mit Selene gleichgesetzt worden sein.[71] Wir kämen dann zu folgender Liste des Xenokrates:

> Kronos
>
> Zeus
>
> Ares
>
> Aphrodite
>
> Hermes
>
> Helios = Apollon

Cambridge 1952, 72 f.; Höfer s.v. Olympioi Theoi, in: Roscher, *Ausführliches Lexikon der griech. und röm. Mythologie* III 1, 838: "Die Ὀλύμπιοι θεοί sind gleichbedeutend mit den οὐράνιοι θεοί (Hesych: Ὀλύμπιος · οὐράνιος), den Himmelsbewohnern; denn der Olympos [...] ist der himmlische Sitz und insofern mit dem Himmel gleichbedeutend." Die Identifizierung von Olymp und Uranos findet sich seit dem 5. Jh. mehrfach belegt: ebd. 852 f.; vgl. H. Herter, *RE* s.v. Olympioi Theoi, Bd XVIII 1, 1939, 230.—Zu den Zwölfgöttern vgl. O. Weinreich, *Ausgewählte Schriften* Bd II, Amsterdam 1973, 555 ff. (= Roscher, *Ausführl. Lexikon* VI 764 ff.), 435 ff.

[69] Prokl. *In Remp.* I 108,9 ff. zählt auch die 265b genannte Aphrodite dazu.

[70] *a.O.* S. 653 ff. (840 f.).

[71] Vgl. Schwenn, *RE* s.v. Selene, Bd II A 1, 1921, 1142; W. Otto, *RE* s.v. Helios, Bd VIII 1, 1912, 75 f. Beide Identifizierungen finden sich seit dem 5. Jh. v. Chr. belegt. Zur Identifizierung von Helios und Apollon vgl. Speusipp fr. 61 Lang = fr. 85 Tarán.

> Selene = Artemis
>
> Hades
>
> Poseidon
>
> Demeter

Von den Namen dieser Liste zählt Kronos gewöhnlich nicht zum Kreis der Zwölfgötter;[72] er gehört ja eigentlich auch nicht zu den olympischen Göttern, sondern zu den Titanen (= Dämonen, fr. 19). Also muß die erste Planetensphäre bei Xenokrates einem anderen Gott zugewiesen worden sein. Die Bezeichnung der Planeten mit Götternamen war zu seiner Zeit ja noch ziemlich neu,[73] und auch später waren die Benennungen nicht immer einheitlich. Welche Gottheit Xenokrates der ersten Sphäre zugewiesen hat, ist nicht sicher auszumachen (s.u. S. 65 ff.).

Es ist anzunehmen, daß Xenokrates auch die anderen bei Platon vorkommenden olympischen Götter in seine Liste aufgenommen hat, also Hera, Athene und Hestia, so daß nunmehr folgende 12 olympischen Gottheiten für Xenokrates wohl feststehen:

> Zeus–Hera
>
> Poseidon–Demeter
>
> Hades–Hestia
>
> Ares–Aphrodite
>
> Apollon–Artemis
>
> Hermes–Athene

Dies ist die kanonische attische Zwölfgötterliste mit einziger Ausnahme von Hades, der Hephaistos verdrängt hat.[74]

Daß Xenokrates wie Platon im *Phaidr.* wirklich an *zwölf* olympische Gottheiten gedacht hat, soll nun noch von einer anderen Seite her bestätigt werden: Im fr. 58 heißt es, daß nach Xenokrates die Zahl Neun dem Mond angemessen und verwandt sei. Das ist auffällig, da dem Mond gewöhnlich die Zahl Sieben oder Acht, der Erde dagegen die Zahl Acht oder Neun zugewiesen wird. Doch stimmt die Angabe des Fragments mit dem überein, was wir bisher herausgefunden haben. Denn wenn der Mond (= Artemis) in der Folge der olympischen Götter der neunte ist,[75] dann entsprechen der Luft (Hades), dem

---

[72] Einzige Ausnahme ist die Zwölfgötterliste von Olympia (*FGrHist* 31 F 34a), die auch sonst Abweichungen gegenüber der kanonischen Form enthält: Weinreich, *a.O.* 578 (782).

[73] Vgl. F. Cumont, *AC* 4, 1935, 9 ff.; W. Gundel/H. Gundel, *RE* s.v. Planeten, Bd XX 2, 1950, 2113 f.

[74] Es fällt auf, daß die ersten drei Götterpaare identisch sind mit den von Hesiod, *Theog.* 453 ff. aufgezählten Kronoskindern, während die drei letzten Paare Zeuskinder sind. Hat deswegen Hades den Hephaistos verdrängt, weil er Sohn nur der Hera allein ist (Hes. *Theog.* 927 ff.) und nicht in das Schema paßt?

[75] Zu der Zuordnung von Artemis zur Zahl Neun vgl. Hermeias, *In Phaedr.* S. 139,8.

Wasser (Poseidon) und der Erde (Demeter) die Zahlen Zehn—Zwölf. Mit
anderen Worten: die Hierarchie des Götterkosmos ist ganz analog zur Hierarchie des sichtbaren Kosmos. Damit bestätigt sich die Angabe des Theophrast
im fr. 26, daß Xenokrates in gewisser Weise alles um den (sichtbaren) Kosmos
herum gruppiert habe, auch τὰ θεῖα.[76] Zugleich darf man an das Wort Platons in den *Nom.* erinnern (899b; *Epin.* 991d), daß alles voll von Göttern sei.

Es ist zu fragen, in welchem Verhältnis die olympischen Götter zu ihren
Sphären stehen. Platon (*Nom.* 898e ff.) hatte es offen gelassen, ob die Götter
in den Gestirnkörpern wohnen und sie so bewegen oder ob sie, von ihnen
getrennt, die Gestirne von außen bewegen. Wir haben schon gesehen, daß
Hades, Poseidon und Demeter in der sublunaren Welt nur durch ihre θεῖαι
δυνάμεις anwesend sind und wirken; sie selbst wohnen im olympischen
Bereich, und nur durch ihre δυνάμεις treten sie in Kontakt mit der (unreinen)
sublunaren Materie, dem Ort der Vergänglichkeit und des Bösen.[77] Über das
Verhältnis der übrigen Gottheiten zu den Himmelskörpern bei Xenokrates ist
eine sichere Aussage nicht möglich, doch legt der Wortlaut von fr. 15 und fr.
17 es nahe, daß Xenokrates Gestirne und olympische Götter identifiziert hat—
ganz ähnlich wie der *Timaios*, wo die Gestirne sichtbare Götter (40d4, 41a3 f.)
und die Seelen der Gestirne (= die Gottheiten: *Nom.* 899b7) mit den Gestirnkörpern verbunden sind (*Tim.* 38e5 f., 40b5).

Kommen wir nun auf das schwierige fr. 20 zu sprechen, in dem es heißt, die
φρουρά, in welcher wir Menschen uns nach dem *Phaidon* (62b3 f.) befinden,
sei die Τιτανική, die ihre Spitze in Dionysos habe. Die Τιτανικὴ φρουρά ist
nach dem oben S.58 f. Gesagten der sublunare Bereich der Dämonen, zu welchem auch Dionysos gehört. Was aber bedeutet die Aussage, Dionysos sei die
Spitze der Τιτανικὴ φρουρά? Nun sagt der Neuplatoniker Hermeias in seinem
Kommentar zum *Phaidros*, nachdem er S. 136,25 ff. ausführlich über die
Zwölfgötter als dem τέλειον μέτρον καὶ πᾶν πλῆθος θεῶν (137,4; vgl. 138,13)
gehandelt hat,[78] Dionysos habe die dreizehnte τάξις erhalten ὡς μετὰ θεοὺς
ὤν (138,23 ff.). Es scheint somit, als stehe Dionysos nach Hermeias und
Xenokrates an der Spitze der Titanen, die den sublunaren Raum regieren.[79]

Nachdem Ps. Olympiodor = Damaskios, *In Phaed.* S. 84,21 ff. Norvin (I
§ 2 West.) das 20. Xenokratesfragment gebracht hat, heißt es bezeichnender-
weise S. 85,4 ff. (I § 3 West.), es gebe zwei Arten von δημιουργία, die eine

---

[76] Dazu Krämer, *Ursprung*, 33 ff.
[77] Dort leben ja die bösen Dämonen (fr. 24, fr. 25).
[78] Die Namen dieser Zwölfgötter (ebd. 139,3 ff.) sind die traditionellen der attischen Liste.
Zur Zwölf als der geeigneten Zahl für die Begleitung eines ἡγεμών Prokl. *In Remp.* I 153,3 ff.
(dazu Festugière in seiner Übersetzung z.St.); *In Euclid.* 174,8 ff.
[79] Vgl. Boyancé, *REA* 50 (1948) 220 ff.; vgl. auch Ps. Olympiodor = Damaskios, *In Phaedr.*
172,2 Norvin (I § 378 West.): der sublunare Kosmos ist Διονυσιακός; Olympiodor, *In Alcib.* I
2,56: Dionysos ist ἔφορος ... τῆς γενέσεως; ebenso Hermeias, *In Phaedr.* S. 54,33 f.

unteilbar, die andere teilbar; an der Spitze der ersteren stehe Zeus, an der der letzteren Dionysos;[80] dem Zeus sei die Anzahl der olympischen Götter untergeordnet, dem Dionysos die Titanen. Das ist letztlich xenokratische Lehre, und es scheint somit, als sei Dionysos nach Xenokrates als Sohn des Zeus dessen Stellvertreter im Bereich der Dämonen. In welchem Verhältnis er zum sublunaren Zeus steht, ist leider nicht auszumachen.[81] Es wäre zu fragen, ob Xenokrates nicht auch die titanischen Dämonen—ähnlich wie die olympischen Götter—in 12 τάξεις aufgeteilt hat. Denn schon Hesiod kennt eine Gruppe von 12 Titanen (*Theog.* 133 ff.), wenn auch seine Namen mit denen des Xenokrates nicht übereinstimmen. Und in Platons *Phaidr.* (246e6 f.) ist nicht nur das Heer der Götter, sondern auch das der Dämonen in 12 μέρη geteilt. Eine solche Einteilung auch der Dämonen wäre der systematisierenden Denkweise des Xenokrates angemessen und würde vortrefflich in das von uns rekonstruierte Gedankengebäude passen. Aber leider verlassen uns hier die Zeugnisse sämtlich.

IV

Die Ergebnisse unserer bisherigen Untersuchungen lassen sich in folgender Übersicht zusammenstellen:

1. Ideen-Zahlen (ὑπερουράνιος τόπος)   Nus-Monas, Zeus, Göttervater

2. Fixsternsphäre (*Äther*)
3. Saturn : ?
4. Jupiter : Zeus   Hera   ⎫
5. Mars   : Ares   Athene   ⎪ *Feuer*
6. Venus   : Aphrodite Hestia   ⎬ Zwölf
7. Merkur : Hermes   ⎧ Hades   ⎫ Olympische   Weltseelen-Dyas
8. Sonne   : Apollon   ⎨ Poseidon   Götter   Göttermutter
9. Mond   : Artemis   ⎩ Demeter ⎭
10. *Luft* ⎫ θεῖαι   ⎧ (Hades)   Dämonen = Titanen
11. *Wasser* ⎬ δυνάμεις ⎨ (Poseidon) Kronos, Rhea,
12. *Erde* ⎭   ⎩ (Demeter)   Zeus, Poseidon,
                                     Hades, Demeter,
                                     Apollon, Python
                                     (?) ... Dionysos

Wie wir sehen, sind in unserer Rekonstruktion drei Gottheiten ohne Zuweisung

---

[80] Vgl. Hermeias, *In Phaedr.* S. 155,7, 54,34; Prokl. *Tim.* III 310,30 ff.
[81] Möglicherweise hat Dillon, *Middle Platonists* 27, recht, wenn er meint, Xenokrates habe Dionysos mit Hades identifiziert; vgl. W. Fauth, *RE* s.v. Zagreus, Bd IX A 2, 1967, 2231 ff. Dagegen spricht allerdings die unterschiedliche Abstammung der beiden.

von Bereichen geblieben, Hera, Athene und Hestia. Es wäre möglich, mit Calcidius 178 S. 207,1 (ff.)—einer Stelle, die sicherlich in letzter Konsequenz xenokratische Lehre wiedergibt, allerdings vermischt mit Lehren der *Epinomis*—Hestia der Weltseele zuzuordnen.[82] Wir haben ja gesehen, daß in fr. 15 der Name der Weltseelen-Dyas ausgefallen ist. Hestia wäre dann als Weltseelen-Dyas Herrscherin über den olympischen Feuerbereich,[83] und Xenokrates hätte die Worte Platons im *Phaidr.* (247a1 f.), nach welchen Hestia allein im Hause der Götter bleibt, so gedeutet, daß nur die Weltseele und Göttermutter im 'Olymp' verweilt,[84] wenn die übrigen 11 Götter zur Apsis des Himmels auffahren; denn nur der ψυχῆς κυβερνήτης νοῦς (*Phaidr.* 247c7 f.), d.h. die der Weltseele zugeordnete Noûs-Monas, kann das transzendente Seiende schauen.

Athene könnte dann als die Gottheit, die aus dem Kopf des Zeus entsprungen ist, dem Bereich der Ideen-Zahlen zugeordnet sein—wie später bei Varro (*Ant. rer. div.* fr. XV 4 Ag. = fr. 206 Card. = August. *Civ. dei* VII 28).[85] Dann aber bliebe für Hera nur noch die Sphäre des Saturn übrig.

Auch eine andere Aufteilung wäre denkbar: daß nämlich die Weltseele als Hebdomas (s.o. S. 53 f.) Athene benannt worden ist; denn Athene ist wie die Weltseele vom Vater Zeus geschaffen ohne jede andere Mithilfe.[86] Dann müßte man Hestia, deren Name nach *Krat.* 401c auf οὐσία weist, der Sphäre der Ideen-Zahlen zuweisen. Porphyrios jedenfalls hat Hestia als πηγαία οὐσία ἱδρυμένη ἐν τῷ πατρί zur ὀντότης gemacht (Lydus, *Mens.* S. 138,20 ff.). Für Hera bliebe auch bei dieser Aufteilung die erste Planetensphäre übrig.

---

[82] Allerdings sagt Calcidius *a.O.*: *Vestam scilicet animam corporis universi m e n t e m q u e eius a n i m a e.* Wahrscheinlich handelt es sich hierbei um eine Art Hendiadyoin, denn nach dem voraufgehenden Kapitel (S. 206,3) *ist* die Weltseele *(secunda) mens.*

[83] Zur Zuordnung der Hestia zum häuslichen Herd und überhaupt zum Feuer vgl. Süß, *RE* s.v. Hestia, Bd VIII 1, 1912, 1257 ff; M. Terentius Varro, *Antiquitates rerum divinarum*, Teil II: Kommentar von B. Cardauns, Wiesbaden 1976, 236 f. Varro kannte die Ansicht, daß *ignis mundi levior* der Vesta zugesprochen wurde (*Ant. rer. div.* fr. XVI 64a Ag. = fr. 281 Card. = August. *Civ. dei* VII 16).

[84] Die Identifizierung von Olymp = Planetenbereich mit dem Haus der Götter könnte sich auf *Krit.* 121c stützen, wo die τιμιωτάτη οἴκησις τῶν θεῶν *in der Mitte* des Alls liegt und auf alles herabsieht, was am Werden teilhat (d.h. den sublunaren Bereich).

[85] Vgl. dazu W. Theiler, *Die Vorbereitung des Neuplatonismus*, Berlin 1930, 18 f.; Boyancé, *REA* 57 (1955) 77 f.; Cardauns 221. Die Lehre geht vermutlich über Antiochos von Askalon, den Lehrer Varros, auf Xenokrates zurück; denn es ist ja bekannt, wie sehr Antiochos die Alten schätzte. Schon Plat. *Krat.* 407b hatte Athene als νοῦς τε καὶ διάνοια, θεονόα und τὰ θεῖα (!) νοοῦσα gedeutet; vgl. W. Kraus, *RAC*, Bd I s.v. Athena, 1950, 879 f. Nach einem weiteren Varrofragment (*Ant. rer. div.* fr. XV 3a Ag. = fr. 205 Card.; vgl. fr. XVI 60f Ag. = fr. 277f Card.) ist Athene = *summum aetheris cacumen*, während Zeus mit dem *medius aether* identifiziert wird (vgl. dazu Boyancé, *REA* 57 (1955) 71, Anm. 5); bei Servius, *Aen.* IV 201, finden wir die Nachricht: *Minerva, quae s u p r a a e t h e r e m est, unde de patris capite procreata dicitur*; vgl. fr. XV 3b Ag. = fr. 205 Card.; Arnobius 3,31: *aetherium verticem et summitatis ipsius esse summam.*

[86] Schwierig bliebe bei dieser Erklärung des Prädikat 'Göttermutter', da Athene die παρθένος par excellence ist.

Die genaue Zuordnung der drei genannten Gottheiten muß also offen bleiben.

Später finden sich andere Spielarten der Zuordnung der Zwölfgötter zu den 12 Sphären des Kosmos. Die bekannteste ist die des Neuplatonikers Sallustios, *De dis* 6, die wie folgt aussieht:

1. οὐρανός	: alle Götter	
2. Saturn	: Demeter	
3. Jupiter	: Zeus	
4. Mars	: Ares	*Äther*: Athene
5. Merkur	: Hermes	
6. Venus	: Aphrodite	
7. Sonne	: Apollon	
8. Mond	: Artemis	
9. *Feuer*	: Hephaistos	
10. *Luft*	: Hera	
11. *Wasser*	: Poseidon	
12. *Erde*	: Hestia	

Die Zwölfgötterliste des Sallust ist identisch mit der kanonischen attischen Form; von der xenokratischen und platonischen unterscheidet sie sich lediglich dadurch, daß Hephaistos nicht durch Hades verdrängt worden ist.

Sallust behandelt die Zwölfgötter als ἐγκόσμιοι θεοί. Daher muß er den ὑπερουράνιος τόπος unberücksichtigt lassen. Stattdessen führt er den Äther, das Element der Himmelskörper, als gesonderte Sphäre ein und muß infolgedessen das Feuer unter dem Mond ansetzen. Der Erde hat er—wie es gewöhnlich geschah[87]—Hestia zugeordnet, Hera und Hephaistos—wie es die Stoa zu tun liebte[88]—der Luft und dem Feuer, während Demeter—was ganz ungewöhnlich ist—die Sphäre des Saturn erhalten hat. Stoisch scheint auch die Zuordnung der Athene zum Äther zu sein.[89]

Die übrigen mir bekannten Zuordnungen sind weniger vollständig. Nach Prokl. *Remp.* II 46,14 ff. besteht der ganze Kosmos aus 12 Sphären, von welchen jede mit einer der 12 Gottheiten des *Phaidros* verbunden ist. Bei Calcidius 178 S. 207,1 ff. findet sich folgende Aufteilung der *caelestes et angelicae*[90] *potestates* des *Phaidros*:

---

[87] Vgl. H. Cherniss, *Aristotle's Criticism of Plato and the Academy* I, Baltimore 1944, 564; Baltes, *Timaios Lokros*, 107.

[88] Vgl. z.B. *SVF* I 169, II 1079.

[89] Vgl. Cornutus, *De natura deorum* 20; Varro bei August. *Civ. dei* VII 16, IV 10 = *Ant. rer. div.* fr. XVI 60f Ag. = fr. 277 Card.; Sallustius, *Concerning the Gods and the Universe*, ed. ... by A.D. Nock, Cambridge 1926, LX, Anm. 99. Übrigens weiche ich mit Weinreich, *Ausgew. Schr.* Bd II, 648 (= Roscher VI 836) bewußt von der Planetenordnung ab, wie Nock *a.O.* sie empfiehlt, da nichts im Text des Sallust für Nocks Anordnung spricht.

[90] Auch *Anon.Proleg. 12,10 West.* kennt die Erklärung, daß die δαίμονες des *Phaidros* (246e6) ἄγγελοι seien.

1. *aplanes*: ὁ μέγας ἡγεμὼν ἐν οὐρανῷ Ζεύς,
2. – 8. *septem planetes*,
9. *aetheris sedes (quam incolunt daemones)*,
10. *aerea substantia*,
11. *humecta substantia*,
12. *terra*.

Die Hestia ordnet Calcidius, wie schon gesagt, der Weltseele zu. Vielleicht war *die Erde* in seiner Vorlage—*Nom.* 955e entsprechend—ἱερὰ πᾶσι πάντων θεῶν.

Beim Anonymus Photii schließlich (Phot. *Bibl.* cod. 249 S. 439b17 ff.) finden wir folgende zwölf Ordnungen des Kosmos aufgezählt:[91]

1. Fixsternsphäre: ἡ ἀπλανής, ἐν ᾗ ἐστιν ὅ τε πρῶτος θεὸς καὶ ... αἱ ἰδέαι[92],
2. – 8. die Planeten, benannt mit den traditionellen Planetennamen (Kronos, Zeus, Ares, Aphrodite, Hermes, Helios, Selene),
9. – 12. die vier Elemente Feuer, Luft, Wasser, Erde.

An Xenokrates erinnert hier besonders die Aussage, in/auf der Fixsternsphäre befänden sich der erste Gott und die Ideen, wobei der Gott offenbar als Monas verstanden wurde (438b34, 439b19 ff.). Eine weitere Zuordnung von Göttern und Sphären bringt der gekürzte Bericht des Photios leider nicht.[93]

---

[91] Vgl. dazu W. Theiler, *Philo...*, in: *Parusia* (s.o. Anm. 61) 209 ff., bes. 211.

[92] Vgl. zur Lokalisierung der Ideen in/auf der Fixsternsphäre Ps. Justin, *Cohort.* 6 und oben S. 51.

[93] Eine unvollständige Aufzählung findet sich bein Philon, *Decal.* 54 f. und bei Varro bei August. *Enarratio in Psalmos* CXIII 4 = fr. XVI 6 Ag. = fr. 225 Card.

NAMING AND KNOWING

THEMES IN PHILONIC THEOLOGY WITH SPECIAL REFERENCE TO THE *DE MUTATIONE NOMINUM*

BY

DAVID T. RUNIA (SOEST)

Philo, the loquacious yet often inscrutable Jew from Alexandria, has had the honour of being called "the first theologian."[1] Whether one agrees or disagrees with this, it is surely fitting that, during a symposium on knowledge of God from Alexander to Constantine, at least one paper should be devoted to Philo's theological ideas. Which other author writing in Greek could we summon, in whose works the word θεός—as we shall see, only one of the supreme Being's names—is the most commonly occurring noun?[2] Yet, much though Philo wrote on God, far more has been written by modern scholars about what Philo wrote on God, or, we might add, about what Philo might or should have written on God. Is there anything to add to the accumulated weight of studies on Philo's theology? Should we join the prevailing consensus that his thoughts are stimulating but disorganized and ultimately dissatisfying? It is with some brief remarks on Philonic scholarship, at any rate, that I wish to begin.

I

There are, *grosso modo*, three ways of approaching Philo's theology. The first I would call the *systematic* approach, for it can not unfairly be described as the attempt to put together, on Philo's behalf, the systematic presentation of his doctrine of God which he never managed (or dared) to publish. The climax of this attempt is represented by the two large volumes of Wolfson. But behind

---

[1] W. Bousset/H. Gressmann, *Die Religion des Judentums im späthellenistischen Zeitalter*, Tübingen 1926³, 445, cited with approval by I. Heinemann, *Philons griechische und jüdische Bildung*, Breslau 1932, 5. For J. Daniélou, *Message évangélique et culture hellénistique aux IIe et IIIe siècles*, Tournai 1961, 300, Philo is "le premier théologien de la transcendance."

[2] The top-twelve of nouns in Philo is, according to Mayer's (not fully complete) lexicon: θεός, ψυχή, λόγος, φύσις, ἄνθρωπος, ἀρετή, γῆ, μέρος, νοῦς, τρόπος, κόσμος. Compare Plato's list, according to Brandwood: λόγος, ἄνθρωπος, πόλις, ἀνήρ, θεός, Σωκράτης, ψυχή, νόμος, σῶμα, φύσις, τέχνη, ἀρχή (note that if θεός was confined to usage in the singular, it would fail to gain a place).

him lies a long tradition, in which the names of Goodenough, Bréhier, Drummond, Gförer and Von Mosheim span a period of nearly two centuries.[3] Wolfson notoriously overtrumped his predecessors by banning every form of inconsistency from Philo's thought and claiming the foundation of a religious philosophy that was to last until Spinoza. It has generally been recognized that the clarity thus achieved was of a rather artificial kind. Since then attempts at systematic elucidation have been more modest, e.g. in the sparkling survey of Philo's theological ideas published recently by David Winston.[4]

The systematic approach has made significant contributions to our understanding of Philo's theological ideas. It does, however, run into certain problems. It has proved, *pace* Wolfson, very difficult to remove inconsistencies, contradictions and obscurities from Philo's thinking. It has not been easy, moreover, to come to terms with the nature of Philo's writings, which have been described as unfortunate or artificial, or even as designed to mask his true thought. Most importantly there has been insufficient awareness of the dangers involved in looking at Philo retrospectively, i.e. from the perspective of later developments in philosophy which he may have set in motion, but could not all foresee.

In the last thirty years or so research on Philo's theology has been undertaken from another angle, which we might call the *historical* (or doxographical) approach. Strenuous efforts, pioneered by Theiler and Boyancé, have been made to locate the sources of Philo's ideas in the philosophical developments taking place in the three centuries between Posidonius and Plotinus. Many distinctive Philonic notions can be paralleled and illuminated by doctrines in Middle Platonism and Neopythagoreanism. In this context Philo is a source of evidence and a fascinating figure in his own right, but not a protagonist on the intellectual stage. Exemplary studies using the historical approach are Boyancé's account of Aristotelianizing theological motifs in Philo and John Dillon's balanced and sympathetic survey in his well-known book on the Middle Platonists.[5]

The historical approach too has had to pay a price for its undoubted successes. Time and time again researchers have had to confront the harsh reality that it is easier to use Philonic evidence to illuminate his surroundings than to

---

[3] J.L. Von Mosheim, 'De Philone' in his translation of R. Cudworth, *The true intellectual system of the universe*, Lugd. Bat. 1773², 1.828–839; A.F. Gförer, *Philo und die jüdisch-alexandrinische Theosophie*, Stuttgart 1831, 1835², 2 vols.; J. Drummond, *Philo Judaeus*, London 1888, 2 vols.; É. Bréhier, *Les idées philosophiques et religieuses de Philon d'Alexandrie*, Paris 1908, 1950³; E.R. Goodenough, *By Light, Light*, New Haven 1935; H.A. Wolfson, *Philo: Foundations of religious philosophy in Judaism, Christianity, and Islam*, Cambr. Mass. 1947, 2 vols.

[4] D. Winston, *Logos and mystical theology in Philo of Alexandria*, Cincinatti 1985.

[5] P. Boyancé, Le dieu très haut chez Philon, in: *Mélanges d'histoire des religions offerts à H.-C. Puech*, Paris 1974, 139–149; J. Dillon, *The Middle Platonists*, London 1977, 139–183.

use his surroundings to illuminate him. In my study on Philo's knowledge and use of Plato's *Timaeus*, which also had to deal with diverse theological themes, I concluded that, though it is very tempting to label Philo as a 'Middle Platonist', we do so at the peril of misrepresenting his loyalties and violating his own self-awareness.[6] It is possible, however, to give a much more radical critique of the historical approach.

I am referring to a paper comparing the Alexandrians Philo and Clement recently presented by the Australian theologian Eric Osborn.[7] Having written highly respected studies on early Christian thinkers, Osborn felt the need to confront the ostensible source of many of their ideas. But how much did these men actually learn from Philo? Osborn's argument moves in two steps. First he denounces historians who try to explain the development of ideas by hunting sources, by tracing the careers of terms and concepts, by presenting doctrines in neatly packaged parcels. This doxographic approach is comparable to the taxonomic efforts of a stamp-collector. Terms, concepts, and even doctrines are fluid, their meaning dependent on the context in which they are put forward. Proper to historical enquiry in the domain of philosophy is the method of problematic elucidation.[8] It is necessary to ask what *problems* a thinker posed and to analyse the *arguments* he put forward in order to resolve those problems. We now come to the second step in Osborn's argument. When Philo and Clement are compared, it emerges that there is much common ground, but that what Clement takes over from Philo are not the interesting and important things. Clement makes grateful use of the language of biblical Hellenism developed by Philo and the many exegetical themes found in his works. The crucial difference, however, is that Philo does not offer argument, whereas Clement does. For Philo scripture gives immediate access to the plain of truth; reasoning is inappropriate. Philo is not a philosopher but a theosophist, closer to the Gnostics than to Clement.[9] This is a harsh judgment on Philo, which we should not, I think, swallow hook, line and sinker. I shall return to it later.

It is my intention in this paper to pursue a third approach to Philo's theological thought, which for want of a better term, I label the *contextual* approach. There is a growing consensus among Philonic scholars that Philo saw

---

[6] *Philo of Alexandria and the Timaeus of Plato*, Leiden 1986[2], 505 ff.

[7] Philo and Clement, *Prudentia* 19 (1987) 34–49.

[8] Osborn here draws on the work of the Australian philosopher John Passmore; cf. his justification in *The beginnings of Christian philosophy*, Cambridge 1981, 273–288.

[9] Osborn, 40, gives an elegant variation of the *consequentia mirabilis* immortalized in Aristotle's *Protrepticus*: "No one can dispense with argument for, to show that argument is unnecessary, it is necessary to argue." The description of Philo as a theosophist is taken over from the study of Gfrörer cited in n. 3.

himself first and foremost as an exegete of Mosaic scripture, and that a sound way to start understanding him is to begin at the level of his exegetical expositions, i.e. in the context in which his ideas are first developed. Various scholars have contributed in various ways to this movement, among whom I might mention the late Samuel Sandmel, Marguerite Harl, Burton Mack, Peder Borgen and Jacques Cazeaux. But above all it is associated with the scholarly achievement of the late Valentin Nikiprowetzky.[10] A fruitful result of this new approach has been a growing interest in the structure and procedures of Philo's exegetical writings. But does this new awareness of the importance of Philo's exegetical activity mean that he is *no more than* an exegete? In fact the implications for his stature as a philosopher or theologian are as yet by no means clear. Hopefully the present paper can make a contribution to this evaluatory task. My starting point, in accordance with the method I am advocating, will be a concrete example of Philonic exegesis, an extended passage from the treatise *De mutatione nominum* in which Philo reflects on the themes of knowing and naming God.

II

The *De mutatione nominum* is the final treatise still extant of the body of continuous verse-by-verse and exclusively allegorical exegesis that Philo compiled on the book of Genesis.[11] The great *Allegorical Commentary*, as we now call it, is the richest and most rewarding section of the Philonic corpus—also for the study of his theological ideas—, but readers have often been deterred by the extraordinary complexities of its structure. It is only in recent years that we are starting to understand the rationale behind the way these treatises are composed.[12] Like in the exegetical notebooks which constitute his *Quaestiones in Genesim et Exodum*, Philo asks questions of and makes observations on the main biblical text. Unlike in the *Quaestiones*, however, he makes extensive use of secondary biblical texts in order to give the exegesis greater depth and enchains the sequences of exposition in a continuous whole, interrupted only by periodic returns to the main text.[13] The assumption upon which this

---

[10] Cf. above all *Le commentaire de l'Écriture chez Philon d'Alexandrie*, Leiden 1977; also R. Radice, Filone di Alessandria nella interpretazione di V. Nikiprowezky e della sua scuola, *RFNS* 76 (1984) 15–41; P. Borgen, Philo of Alexandria, in: M. Stone (ed.), *Jewish writings of the Second Temple period*, Assen 1984, 259 ff.

[11] The *De somniis*, at least in the books we have, does not continue the verse-by-verse exegesis, but assembles material from the whole of Gen.

[12] See my articles The structure of Philo's allegorical treatises *VC* 38 (1984) 209–56, and Further observations on the structure of Philo's allegorical treatises *VC* 41 (1987) 105–138, which contain surveys on the progress of research.

[13] The *De mutatione nominum* is one of the privileged cases where we can trace the parallelism with the *Quaestiones*, for the same biblical passage is given exegesis in *QG* 3.39–44, 53–60

method is based is the total coherence of Mosaic scripture. Often the only way to retain the thread of the procedure is to keep a good eye out for the biblical texts that Philo summons and for the associations of words and ideas that cause him to summon them. A cornucopia of themes flow in and out of the exegesis, depending on the exigencies of the text and the whims of the interpreter. No attempt is made to integrate these into a rigorously unified whole. But analysis of individual treatises reveals that Philo does locate in the biblical text under discussion a main directive idea, which is able to give the single treatise a loose kind of unity.

The treatise I have singled out for special attention possesses some idiosyncratic features. Because of the poor manuscript tradition the text is in very bad shape, and the exact meaning of many passages is far from clear.[14] We are badly in need of a sound, philologically precise commentary. The section of biblical text which Philo gives exegesis is rather long, and in a number of sections this leads to a sketchy treatment, with less invocation of secondary biblical texts than usual. Nevertheless the reader will soon observe, also in the passage we will be looking at more closely, that Philo makes extensive use of other Pentateuchal material to cast light on the verses that are the special object of his exegesis.

The main biblical text commented on in the treatise is Gen. 17:1−22, the record of an appearance of God to Abraham when he is ninety-nine years old. Philo deletes verses 6−14 from his commentary for two reasons. He has apparently already discussed important aspects of their contents in the lost treatises *On the covenants* (cf. § 53). Moreover the omission allows him to pass directly from the change of name given to Abraham in v.5 to that of Sarah in v.15. The section of the treatise on which I propose to concentrate is what we may call the first chapter, § 1−38.[15]

Without any introductory words Philo begins by quoting the initial biblical lemma:[16]

ἐγένετο Ἀβραὰμ ἐτῶν ἐνενήκοντα ἐννέα, καὶ ὤφθη κύριος τῷ Ἀβραὰμ καὶ εἶπεν αὐτῷ· ἐγώ εἰμι ὁ θεός σου.

Abraham was ninety-nine years old, and the Lord appeared to Abraham and He said to him, I am your God. (Gen. 17:1)

(I follow the abbreviations for Philo's works set out in Runia, *op. cit.* [n. 6] xi−xii).

[14] At a conservative estimate 400 emendations have been incorporated into or proposed for the text as printed in Colson's translation. There are only two manuscripts of any value. Some passages are indirectly preserved in the *Sacra Parallela* of John of Damascus.

[15] On the role of the 'chapter' in the structure of the allegorical treatises see Runia, Further observations, 112, 121.

[16] Text as in Philo; LXX twice reads Αβραμ.

Examination of the exegesis in our chapter shows that this lemma gives rise to five problems or *aporiae*, all of them implicit rather than explicitily formulated, which the exegete proceeds to answer one by one.

Aporia 1.   What is the significance of the number ninety-nine? What does it tell us about the man to whom the Lord appears? (§ 1–2)

Aporia 2.   How, or by what means, is the Lord seen? (§ 3–6)

Aporia 3.   Who is it that is actually seen? (§ 7–17)

Aporia 4.   What is meant by 'I am *your* God'? (§ 18–26)

Aporia 5.   What is meant by 'I am your *God*'? (§ 27–33)

At the end of the chapter, after a series of quick thematic shifts, Philo invokes Enoch as an example of a sage who 'pleased God and was not found' (Gen. 5:24) (§ 34–38). The choice of the secondary text clearly anticipates the next main biblical lemma 'be pleasing before Me' discussed in § 39 ff. Philo often uses this technique of anticipation for the fluent enchainment of his exegesis.[17] Later in the treatise there are two further *aporiae*, drawn from Gen. 17:17–18, the response to which illustrates some themes touched on in the first chapter. I add them to the above list.

Aporia 6.   Why does Abraham briefly doubt the birth of Isaac, although he is recorded in Gen. 15:6 as having trusted God? (§ 175–187)

Aporia 7.   If Abraham asks that Ishmael shall live, does that mean he despairs of Isaac's birth? (§ 218–232)

We have thus seven *aporiae*, a suitably Philonic number, but only a limited selection of all the questions and themes raised in this single treatise.

Before we move on, it is worth making a brief remark on the nature of these *aporiae* that Philo raises. As already noted above, the method of asking questions of the biblical text—probably drawn from contemporary synagogal practice[18]—plays an important structural role in Philo's allegorical commentaries. In Hellenistic literature too there was an important genre of ζητήματα καὶ λύσεις, practised on both literary and philosophical texts.[19] *Aporiae* occur, as the word itself indicates, because the road to understanding is blocked. There are obstacles which impede the exegete's path as he tries to gain an adequate grasp of the text. Why should Abraham be ninety-nine when he is told

---

[17] This anticipatory or 'teleological' method of exegesis has been well observed by J. Cazeaux. But I cannot go along with the far-reaching conclusions he draws from it in terms of a structuralist reading of Philo. In his huge monograph on Philo's structures he gives a detailed analysis of *Mut.* 1–38 which well illustrates his methods; cf. *La trame et la chaîne*, Leiden 1983, 476–499.

[18] Cf. *Contempl.* 75 and Nikiprowetzky, *op. cit.* (n. 10), 176 ff.

[19] Cf. H. Dörrie, Erotapokriseis, *RAC* 6, 1966, 342 ff.

of Isaac's impending birth, and not some other (less improbable) age? At the same time, however, the obstacles encountered have a positive effect, for they indicate that the real meaning lies deeper, to be unveiled by the resources of the allegorical method. It is perhaps not entirely inappropriate to compare the list of *aporiae* drawn up by Aristotle in *Metaphysics* B.[20] The difference between Aristotle and Philo—and of course it is a very significant difference—is that the former meets his obstacles in what he regards as a direct theorizing on the nature of reality, whereas the latter confronts them in an authoritative text that interposes itself between the interpreter and that reality.

III

What, then, are the themes of importance for an understanding of Philo's theological thought that these exegetical obstacles in our passage generate? The first two *aporiae* do not cause our author much delay.

The symbolism of the number ninety-nine points to the man of progress (ὁ προκόπτων), for at a hundred years the perfect man Isaac (ὁ τέλειος) is born. Abraham falls short of perfection, but only by a little. The notion of progress and the division of men into the categories 'worthless' (φαῦλοι), 'progressing' and 'perfect'—both doctrines familiar from Stoic ethical theory—are fundamental to the thematics of the treatise.[21]

If the Lord of the Universe is seen by Abraham, then He is obviously not seen by the eyes of the body, but by means of the noetic activity of the eye of the soul, which makes use, not of sense-perceptible light, nor of its own light, but of that light which God himself shines forth. These are again familiar themes, derived ultimately from Plato's *Republic*. Philo has worked them out at greater length elsewhere, and does not dwell on them here.[22] Such cursory treatment should not, however, blind us to the quasi-automatic way in which our author translates the appearance of God in terms of learning and the intellective quest. This is reinforced by the way in which the third *aporia* is tackled.

When scripture declares that 'the Lord was seen,' it must not be thought that τὸ ὄν, the supreme Being, was mentally grasped by any man (§ 7). The experience which Moses, paradigm of the questing mind, had on the mountain as recorded in Ex. 33 is a sufficient guarantee. God does not reveal his Being, but only what comes after him. Once again Philo does not elaborate the theme in the way we find a number of times elsewhere.[23] The crucial distinction

---

[20] Cf. J. Owens, *The doctrine of Being in the Aristotelian Metaphysics*, Toronto 1978³, 211–9.

[21] The standard work on this immensely important theme in Philo is still W. Völker, *Fortschritt und Vollendung bei Philo von Alexandrien*, Leipzig 1938.

[22] Cf. *Post.* 166–9, *Deus* 62, *Spec.* 1.49, *Praem.* 36–46, *QG* 4.1–2 etc.

[23] *Post.* 13–16, 166–9, *Fug.* 164–5, *Spec.* 1.32–50.

between God's existence and essence is not pointed out. Instead Philo invokes the traditional, and not very inspiring, argument which moves by analogy from the unknowability of the human mind to the unknowability of God.[24] The brevity is motivated, I suspect, by his haste to arrive at the theme which occupies the central place in the treatise as a whole.

There is, strictly speaking, no exegetical constraint on Philo to introduce the theme of the naming of God. But the juxtaposition of the two chief Septuagintal names κύριος and θεός in the single biblical lemma is a good pretext. And Philo has prepared the way by already speaking of God as 'Being' (τὸ ὄν § 7, 10). Consequent upon Being's unknowability is the fact that He has no 'proper name' (ὄνομα κύριον). To the reader this statement in § 11 cannot as yet be wholly clear. He or she can be certain that Philo introducing some kind of word-play on the use of the divine name κύριος in the main biblical lemma. But he does not know whether the expression 'proper name' is to be understood as (1) a *legitimate* name as opposed to an 'improper' or metaphorical appellation, or as (2) a *personal* proper name (the ambiguity, we note, is preserved in English as well).[25] Philo does not leave the reader in suspense. First he indicates the secondary biblical text which he is adducing for purposes of elucidation, Ex. 3:14. Then, by immediately introducing the notion of 'improper use of language' (κατάχρησις, already implicit in the words δίδωσι καταχρῆσθαι § 12), he makes it quite clear that he intends the first of the two possible meanings. This notion of *katachrēsis*, taken over from rhetorical theory and given a theological application, is, I submit, the single most interesting feature of our passage. I will discuss it in more detail later on in my paper. For the time being, however, we have enough interpretative problems on our hands.

Interpretation of Philo's discussion on the naming of God in § 11–15 has been complicated by two suppositions made by diverse expositors. The first is that Philo is intentionally mixing up the two usages of 'proper name' in the passage and oscillates from the one meaning to the other.[26] The second is that God's 'proper name' refers to the *tetragrammaton* (as intended in the original Hebrew of the second secondary text Ex. 6:3).[27] If modern scholars have been perplexed by the passage, then it is likely that ancient and medieval scribes were too. Hence, no doubt, the chaotic state of the text.[28]

---

[24] Cf. *Abr.* 74–76, A.J. Festugière, *La révélation d'Hermes Trismégiste*, II, *Le dieu cosmique*, Paris 1949, 83, 544, 609; on the unknowability of the soul/mind see also *Somn.* 1.30 ff.

[25] It is important to note that the ancients did not clearly distinguish between name and word (ὄνομα serving for both); so in this article I will disregard the distinction as well.

[26] Cf. F.H. Colson, *Philo* LCL (London 1929–62) 5.149; W. Theiler, *Philo von Alexandria: die Werke in deutsche Übersetzung* (Cohn/Heinemann/Adler/Theiler), Berlin 1962², 6.110.

[27] Cf. Wolfson, *op. cit.* (n. 3), 2.120–2, whose view is uncritically accepted by Festugière *op. cit.* IV, *Le dieu inconnu et la Gnose* (Paris 1954) 17 n., and followed by J.C. McLelland, *God the Anonymous: a study in Alexandrian philosophical theology*, Cambridge Mass. 1976, 34.

[28] For §§ 11–15 the much emended text as presented by Colson is generally speaking satis-

My view is that both suppositions are incorrect. Philo's thesis is straightforward: because God, as he announces to Moses in Ex. 3:14, is ὁ ὤν, he cannot be legitimately and properly named. Implicit at this point is the Platonist argument, derived from the theological reflection on the first and second hypotheses of the *Parmenides*, that any name or attribute adds to Being. A name entails predication, which necessarily involves a measure of plurality and—the aspect that Philo will later stress (§ 27)—a degree of relationality. If we say 'Being is good' or 'Being is God,' the attribute and the name can only indicate His relation to something else, for Being in Its (essential) nature is unknowable (§ 9). All that one can do is to resort to negative attributes such as 'indescribable' (ἄρρητος), 'unknowable' (ἀπερινόητος), 'incomprehensible' (ἀκατάληπτος) (all three found in § 15), 'unnameable' (ἀκατονόμαστος) (not used here, but cf. *Somn.* 1.67, *De Deo* 4). One might argue that even here there is an implicit comparison with beings which *are* knowable (and a relation to creatures who might desire to know Him). Moreover 'Being' itself might be thought to be a positive attribute. Philo has not worked out the philosophical problematics of the question with the precision that we will later find in Clement and Plotinus.[29] But, to be fair to him, he is primarily interested at this point in the positive divine names θεός and κύριος (and, let us not forget, he is committed to the biblical text in Ex. 3:14).

God cannot legitimately be named, Philo concludes from Ex. 3:14. But, as the very next verse indicates, mankind does need the use of an appellation for Being.[30] God therefore grants the improper use of a name, κύριος ὁ θεός (the Lord God), *as if it were a proper (i.e. legitimate) name* (§ 12 δίδωσι καταχρῆσθαι ὡς ἂν ὀνόματί τῳ κυρίῳ). Philo contends that the formulation in Ex. 3:15 supports his interpretation. God gives an αἰώνιον ὄνομα, a name for the ages of man, but not appropriate for His own ageless existence. It is a name for 'generations' (γενεαῖς), i.e. for those who come into the realm of mortal genesis there is need for the 'improper use' (κατάχρησις) of a divine name, so that if they worship Him they can do so with a best possible name

---

factory. Two phrases, both involving the term ὄνομα κύριον, require comment: § 12 mss. ὡς ἐν ὀνόματι τῷ κυρίῳ, John Dam. ὡς ἂν ὁ ὢν ὀνόματι τοιούτῳ, Wendland's conjecture ὁ ἀκατονομαστος ὢν ὀνόματι τοιούτῳ (!), Colson ὡς ἂν ὀνόματι κυρίῳ τῷ (accepted by Theiler); my own suggestion is ὡς ἂν ὀνόματί τῳ κυρίῳ. § 13 mss. περὶ τοῦ μηδενὶ δεδηλῶσθαι ὀνόματι αὐτοῦ κυρίῳ, John Dam. τὸ ὄνομα αὐτοῦ κύριον (followed by Wendland), Hoeschelius, Mangey, Colson ὄνομά τι αὐτοῦ κύριον (whom I follow) (interestingly exactly the same mistake at Justin *Apol.*2.6.1).

[29] On Clement see below at n. 91; for Plotinus see esp. 6.3.12–17, and R. Mortley, Negative theology and abstraction in Plotinus, *AJPh* 96 (1975) 363–77 (esp. 367 ff.). For Philo the problem of relationality is more important than that of multiplicity.

[30] It might seem in §§ 11–12 that Philo distinguishes between ὄνομα (name) and πρόσρησις (appellation), but it soon becomes clear that he does not follow this through, and prefers to speak of an "improper name."

(§ 13). Colson badly mistranslates here: mortality does not need a 'substitute for the divine name,' for any name applied to God is substitutionary.[31] An impressive confirmation of the interpretation so far is located, Philo now argues, in the parallel text Ex. 6:3, which, because it begins with the word ὤφθην ('I was seen'), brings the problematics of Ex. 3:14–15 even closer to the main biblical lemma from Gen. 17:1. But the exegete has to engage in some fast footwork to get the text to say what he wants. The LXX text τὸ ὄνομά μου κύριος ('my name Lord') is cited by Philo as τὸ ὄνομά μου κύριον. Clearly he has no idea that the *tetragrammaton* is being referred to.[32] Philo argues that we have here a case of *hyperbaton* (unusual word order). The words need to be rearranged, so that we read ὄνομά μου τὸ κύριον ('My proper name').[33] God says, 'My proper (i.e. legitimate) name I did not reveal to them (because, Philo means to say, I do not have one), but instead I gave My improper name.' Moses, as we shall see, speaks here the technical language of Greek grammar and rhetoric.

Philo complicates, but does not confuse, the matter further by adding an *a fortiori* argument (§ 14–15). If God's *logos*, in this case the angel with whom Jacob wrestled, does not disclose his name (Gen. 32:20), then is it any wonder that God himself also does not do so? There is, however, a basic distinction to be made. The angel, situated at a lower level of being, does have a proper name, but refuses to reveal it, whereas God does not have one and cannot reveal it properly. Philo to his credit makes the distinction pellucidly clear in two ways. He describes the *logos* as having a name that is '*personal* as well as proper' (ἴδιον καὶ κύριον). Secondly he distinguishes between God who is 'indescribable' (ἄρρητος) and the *logos* who is 'not described' (οὐ ῥητός), i.e. he is well aware of the difference between a negative and a privative attribute.[34]

Philo concludes (§ 15) that if the supreme Being is indescribable, He is also unknowable and incomprehensible. If we recall § 9–11, it appears that the reasoning is circular, for there Philo deduced unnameability from unknowability. Perhaps, as Wolfson argued,[35] Philo believes the two doctrines are reciprocally reinforcing. Perhaps the conclusion is made only in order to return the commentary back to the main biblical text. However this may be, I believe that, provided we take κύριον ὄνομα to mean 'proper, legitimate name'

---

[31] Colson, *op. cit.* (n. 26), 149.

[32] On Philo and the *tetragrammaton* cf. L. Cohn, Zur Lehre vom Logos bei Philo, *Judaica: Festschrift zu H. Cohns 70. Geburtstage*, Berlin 1912, 309. Philo refers to the *tetragrammaton* at *Mos.* 2.114–5, 132, *Legat.* 353, but he does not attempt to relate this to the question of God's "proper name".

[33] From § 13 (and, if my emendation is accepted, § 12) it emerges that Philo prefers the expression ὄνομά τι κύριον. But the biblical text constrains him.

[34] On this difference cf. Mortley, *art. cit.* (n. 29), 374–5.

[35] Wolfson, *op. cit.* (n. 3), 2.120 (but his reading of the citation of Ex. 6:3 in *Mut.* 13 is wide of the mark!).

throughout, Philo's passage on the naming of God is coherently and not unimpressively argued. A précis of the same argument, with reference to the same biblical text Ex. 6:3, is given at *Somn.* 1.230.[36]

The *aporia* raised in § 7 is now close to solution. God does not appear to Abraham as Being,[37] but in the guise of His ruling power, as indicated by the name κύριος. The learning soul is a late starter. Not long ago as a Chaldean he was still under the delusion that the cosmos possesses autonomous efficient causes. Now he recognizes God as king and ruler. And then immediately he becomes the recipient of a greater act of divine beneficence, when the Lord (κύριος) says to him 'I am your God (θεός).'

In the fourth *aporia* Philo directs his attention to the personal pronoun joined to the divine name (I am *your* God).[38] The supreme Being is not only God of creation as a whole, but also of human souls (§ 18). The relation of God to men was already hinted at when He gave His improper name 'Lord God of Abraham, Isaac and Jacob' (§ 12). It is now worked out with more precision, with reference to the three classes of men outlined at the beginning of the treatise. For the worthless man such as Pharaoh He is κύριος in a relationship of fear; for the man of progress such as Abraham He is θεός in a relationship of beneficence; for the perfect man such as Moses He is both κύριος and θεός, and such a man is honoured with the title 'man of God.' The train of thought is here once again rather labyrinthine. The interpretations that Colson suggests are ingenious but unconvincing. I cannot discuss them now.[39]

But Philo is not finished with the words 'I am your God.' The fifth *aporia* turns to the role of the divine name θεός. Philo is immediately struck by the juxtaposition of εἰμί ('I am') and θεός. The statement can only be spoken 'improperly' (καταχρηστικῶς), not 'properly' (κυρίως). In other words the previous discussion on the supreme Being's unnameability is relevant here too. Philo now focusses in on the ontological aspect (§ 27). Being (τὸ ὄν) exists *qua* Being (ᾗ ὄν), not as belonging to what is relative (πρός τι). This, one might be tempted to say, is a sentence such as only Philo could write. Platonic being,

---

[36] But in *Abr.* 51, 121, where he is concerned with exegesis of Ex. 3:15 and Gen. 18:1–3 without reference to Ex. 6:3, the explanations of God's name are not strictly speaking consistent with *Mut.* 11–15.

[37] Philo writes οὐχ ὡς ἐπιλάμποντος καὶ ἐπιφαινομένου τοῦ παντὸς αἰτίου, by which he must mean τὸ ὄν but at the same time refers back to the discussion in §§ 5–6. I regret having given the impression in *VC* 38 (1984) 225, that the phrase might refer to the creative power.

[38] Cf. Cazeaux, *op. cit.* (n. 17), 486.

[39] Colson, *op. cit.* (n. 26), 154–7. The passage should be read in terms of an intended contrast between Moses, who is θεός to Pharaoh, and God, who is θεός to Abraham. Beginners should look to Moses, as is implied in his blessing in Deut. 33:1 (§ 25). Hence κλῆρον αὐτοῦ must (rather surprisingly) refer to Moses and not God, and Colson is obviously wrong in wanting to emend νόμους (cf. the illuminating parallel passage at *Mos.* 1.158). See now my detailed interpretation in God and man in Philo of Alexandria, *JThS* 39 (1988).

Aristotelian substance, Academic categories—all are brought to bear on a personal God who says 'I am'![40] Suffice it to say that the main point is the distinction between what is absolute and what is relative,[41] and it is made clearly enough. God is absolute, unchanging and self-sufficient. Created reality is relative, wholly dependent on divine benevolence. In between, *as if* relative' (ὡσανεὶ πρός τι),[42] stand God's powers, by means of which that benevolence is effectuated. The name θεός, as the etymology indicates, discloses God's creative activity. Thus 'I am your God' is equivalent to 'I am your maker and creator' (ἐγώ εἰμι ποιητὴς καὶ δημιουργός § 29).[43]

So we end up with a brief exposition of the doctrine of the divine powers, probably the best known of all Philo's theological ideas. Yet I would wish to argue that the motivation and the consequences of the doctrine are presented here in a particularly lucid way. Philo is claiming that *every time* we speak of God by means of his names, we are not speaking of Him as He really is, but invariably in terms of His relationality, via the powers, towards that which is other than Him. By making a mental displacement we can understand, I think, how Philo could become enthused about the consistency of the Pentateuch. How accurate that God presents himself as κύριος to the recalcitrant Pharaoh![44] How splendid that right throughout the account of creation the divine name θεός is used![45] How appropriate that only once in the whole Pentateuch the veil of God's relationality is cast aside, when the God-beloved Moses receives the oracle in Ex. 3:14![46] Philo, of course, finds it quite impossible and quite unnecessary to achieve consistency and correctness in the use and non-use of God's names.[47] I myself do no better when I speak of God's names (it goes against the grain to talk continually of Being and Its names). Moses is not superstitious in the use of names, Philo says elsewhere.[48] Nor, he implies,

---

[40] I am not sure Philo intends any kind of allusion to the Aristotelian doctrine of τὸ ὂν ᾗ ὄν. As far as I know it is the only instance in his writings.

[41] On the Academic categories and their use in Eudorus and Middle Platonism cf. R.E. Witt, *Albinus and the history of Middle Platonism*, Cambridge 1937, 66–67; Dillon, *op. cit.* (n. 5), 8, 37, 133, 279.

[42] Cf. Drummond cited by Colson *op. cit.* 587, or compare Albinus' description of ἰδέα in *Did.* 9.1 as relative to God, the thinking subject, matter and the cosmos, but in absolute terms (καθ' αὑτήν) οὐσία.

[43] It is tempting to accept Wendland's proposed conjecture δημιουργὸς ⟨σός⟩.

[44] Philo has to ignore passages such as Ex. 7:16, 9:1, where God speaks as κύριος ὁ θεός to Pharaoh.

[45] Cf. *Plant.* 86, *QG* 2.16. Observations such as these may have something to do with the origin of the doctrine of the powers (and may antedate Philo).

[46] Ex. 3:14, 20:21 (γνόφος), 33:13–23 are the central texts of Philo's theology of transcendence. On his use of the first see the analysis of E. Starobinski-Safran, Exode 3, 14 dans l'œuvre de Philon d'Alexandrie, in; P. Vignaux (ed.), *Dieu et l'être: exégèses d'Exode 3,14 et de Coran 20,11–24*, Paris 1978, 47–55.

[47] E.g. in § 46 he speaks of θεός when τὸ ὄν would seem more correct, whereas in § 82 the reverse applies.

[48] *Somn.* 1.230; on this difficult text see V. Nikiprowetzky, Sur une lecture démonologique de

need we be. What he does expect is that 'we carry along with us' the awareness of God's essential namelessness every time we find ourselves making use of the various names which he possesses.

Time and space forbid more than a passing glance at the last two *aporiae*. I have included them to give some idea of how themes initiated in the first chapter are developed later in the treatise. Both *aporiae* reveal doubts on the part of the progressing soul to whom God appears. But God has said 'I am your God,' affirming His unceasing beneficence. The learner must dispense with all self-assertion (§ 175), recognize his own 'nothingness' (οὐδένεια, § 155) and God's never-ceasing grace (§ 218–9).[49] There is an unbridgeable gap between God and man, for God is uncompoundedly divine, whereas man is a mixture of the divine and mortality (§ 184). Man can only receive the munificence of the divine grace if it is measured out in accordance with what the soul of each person can accept (§ 232).[50] Let the soul therefore be a thankful suppliant of God,[51] hoping for the full measure of proffered knowledge (§ 222–3). But let her in any case be content (ἀγαπητόν § 219) with the fruits of toil and practice, for the highest benefits are reserved for divine natures wholly severed from the body.[52] Philo thinks here not only of angels and departed souls such as Enoch (§ 34), but especially of Moses who entered the 'darkness' of invisible and immaterial being (§ 7), and no doubt also of Isaac who is born 'in the other year' (Gen. 17:21), i.e. in the incorporeal and intelligible realm (§ 267). At the end of the treatise the learner has not quite yet progressed so far. Isaac is not yet born. But God leaves him (Gen. 17:22) perfected as a listener[53] and filled with wisdom, able to stand on his own two feet (§ 270).

As I observed a little earlier, Philo does not attempt to make his allegorical commentaries into thematically unified and coherent literary products, the chief reason for this being his subservience to the main biblical text. But a treatise is not just a potpourri of whatever happens to enter into his head. Our treatise has a main directive idea or theme, which allows a measure of integration. I would formulate it as follows. There is a vast difference between God and

Philon d'Alexandrie, *De Gigantibus* 6–18, in: G. Nahon et C. Touati (eds.), *Hommage à Georges Vajda*, Louvain 1981, 61 f.

[49] The theme of divine grace/benevolence is very prominent in *Mut.*: cf. §§ 30, 52 f., 142, 155, 219, 253, 260, 268.

[50] On the theme of measured distribution of divine beneficence cf. Runia, *op. cit.* (n. 6), 137–8. It looks like the wording of § 232 is meant to remind us of the celebrated text Sapientia Salomonis 11:20.

[51] On the 'Levitic spirituality' cf. M. Harl, *Quis rerum divinarum heres sit* vol. 15 *Les œuvres de Philon d'Alexandrie*, Paris 1966, 130 ff.

[52] The theme of 'contentment' also at §§ 50, 118, 183; cf. the very similar formulation at *Aet.* 2, which adapts Plato's ἀγαπᾶν χρή at *Tim.* 29c8 (cf. Runia, *op. cit.*, 123 ff.).

[53] Not the seer! Philo is unpleasantly constrained by the text of Gen. 17:22, not least because his copy of the LXX apparently read κύριος and not the ὁ θεός in our mss. Understandably Philo does not dwell on the choice of divine name here.

man: God is steadfast, unchanging,[54] whereas man is subject to the vicissitudes of change. The changes of name in scripture are not a matter for ridicule (§ 62), but illustrate a profound truth. Properly speaking God as Being has no name, but through his diverse unchanging improper names he mercifully relates to souls at different levels. Men and women such as Abraham (§ 60) and Sarah (§ 77) receive changes of name because they show progress, or, in the case of Joseph (§ 91), decline. The exceptions are Moses, who is polyonymous (having three names, § 125–9),[55] and Isaac, who alone of the Patriarchs has a single name (§ 88). These are our two great examples, the one as an unwritten law (cf. *Abr.* 5), the other as the great lawgiver (cf. § 26). To say that the title of the *De mutatione nominum* is inappropriate because it covers the contents of only part of the treatise (i.e. the catalogue of name-changes in § 60–129) is clearly very wide of the mark.[56]

IV

In his survey of Philo's debts to Middle Platonism John Dillon states that Philo is the earliest authority for the application of the epithets ἀκατονόμαστος, ἄρρητος, and ἀκατάληπτος to God.[57] Even Festugière, despite his notorious reluctance to credit Philo with any independence of thought whatsoever, could not contest this.[58] But does this entail that we should grant Wolfson's claim that Philo's scripturally based philosophy provided the vital impulse for the development of negative theology in later Greek philosophy?[59] If the line of transmission was confined to Philo, Justin, Numenius, Celsus, Clement, Plotinus, we might be tempted to give Wolfson the benefit of the doubt. I agree with Dillon, however, that the presence of such themes in a broad group of school Platonists (and Neopythagoreans) militates against the thesis, and that exegesis of the first hypothesis of the *Parmenides* was a probable stimulus to reflection in Philo's time or even earlier.[60] Another weakness of Wolfson's

---

[54] On God's stability and immutability cf. §§ 24, 28, 46, 54 f., 87, 176. The last two words of the treatise are (not accidentally I suspect) βεβαιότατον εἶδος.

[55] Another difficult passage, splendidly analysed by V. Nikiprowetzky in a posthumously published article, *Moyses palpans vel liniens*: on some explanations of the name of Moses in Philo of Alexandria, in: F.E. Greenspahn/E. Hilgert/B.L. Mack (eds.), *Nourished with peace: Studies in Hellenistic Judaism in memory of Samuel Sandmel*, Chico California 1984, 117–142.

[56] Cf. the complaints of L. Cohn, Die Einteilung und Chronologie der Schriften Philos, *Philologus* Supplbd. 7 (1899) 396, and Theiler, *op. cit.* (n. 26), 6.104, and the sound remarks of R. Arnaldez, *De mutatione nominum* vol. 18 *Les œuvres de Philon d'Alexandrie*, Paris 1964, 11.

[57] *Op. cit.* (n. 5), 155.

[58] *La révélation d'Hermès Trismégiste*, 4.17, 307. It is true that the paraphrase of *Tim.* 28c in the Epicurean doxography at Cicero *ND* 1.30 approaches negative theology, but the characteristic negative terms are not employed. Aristotle is reported as having called the fifth element ἀκατονόμαστον (*De phil.* fr. 27), but this seems to me clearly a privative use of the term.

[59] *Op. cit.* (n. 3), 2.110–138.

[60] Dillon *ibid.*; cf. also R. Mortley, *Connaissance religieuse et herméneutique chèz Clément*

position is the fact that the *specifically* Jewish prohibitions on pronouncing the *tetragrammaton* and on taking God's name in vain (third commandment) do not appear to have had much impact on Philo.[61]

The subject of negative theology has been much discussed.[62] I would like now, in the space that remains, to focus on a related topic that has gone largely unnoticed. Indeed, as far as I know, Philo's theological application of the notion of *katachresis* has never received any scholarly attention at all.[63] Before commenting on Philo's application we shall have to look at the background and development of the term and what it represents.

κατάχρησις is a technical term belonging to the theory of tropes (τρόποι, i.e. non-literal word usage) in Greek rhetoric and grammar. In general terms one can say that *katachresis* has to do with the extended use or misuse of words or phrases, but it is difficult to give a more precise general definition, for analysis of its development and usage reveals that it is employed in two related but differing ways.[64] These I shall call the soft and hard line respectively. The 'soft line' finds its origins in Aristotle. According to Cicero Aristotle includes *katachresis* under the heading of *metaphora*, the former term being used by grammarians for misuses of language, 'when we say a "minute" (i.e. diminished) mind instead of a "small" mind, and when we misuse related words on occasion because it gives pleasure or it is fitting.'[65] This report is consistent with non-technical usage of the verb καταχράομαι in Aristotle's extant writings.[66] The term κύριον ὄνομα in Aristotle does not yet have its technical meaning of 'proper, legitimate word or name' and indicates no more than 'normal, ordinary usage.'[67] Nevertheless some notion of 'extended' or 'unusual' word-usage must be implied in *katachresis*; otherwise it could not be distinguished from metaphoric usage in general.[68] Cicero and other Latin gram-

---

d'Alexandrie, Leiden 1973, 6–11, and the contribution of J. Mansfeld, this volume, pp. 92 ff.

[61] See above n. 32; cf. also Philo's interpretation of the third commandment at *Decal.* 82–95.

[62] See esp. Festugière's study (cited in n. 58) and the researches of J. Whittaker now collected together in *Studies in Platonism and Patristic thought* London 1984, (notably Neopythagoreanism and the Transcendent Absolute, *SO* 48 (1973) 77–86 and Ἄρρητος καὶ ἀκατονόμαστος, in *Platonismus und Christentum: Festschrift für H. Dörrie, JbAC* Ergbd. 10 (1983) 303–6).

[63] Apart from a brief discussion in Runia, *op. cit.* (n. 6), 438.

[64] For what follows I am partially indebted to J. Cousin, *Quintilien Institution oratoire* vol. 5, Paris 1978, 296–7; cf. also D.M. Schenkeveld, *Studies in Demetrius On style*, Amsterdam 1964, 97–9.

[65] *Orator* 94: *Aristoteles autem tralationi et haec ipsa* [ὑπαλλαγή *et* μετωνυμία] *subiungit et abusionem, quam* κατάχρησιν *vocant, ut cum minutum dicimus animum pro parvo et abutimur verbis propinquis, si opus est, vel quod delectat vel quod decet.* Cf. also *De orat.* 3.169, *Rhet. ad Her.* 4.45.

[66] Note esp *De Caelo* 1.3 270b24; also earlier Plato *Symp.* 205b6.

[67] Cf. *Rhet.* 3.2 1404b6, 3.10 1410b13, *A.P.* 21 1457b1.

[68] As Prof. Schenkeveld points out to me, a lot may depend on how one interprets the words *si opus est* in Cicero. Taken in a very specific way, these might point in the direction of our 'hard line'. But nothing in Cicero's example suggests this.

marians approve of this soft line on *katachresis*. It finds a modern formulation in Smyth's *Greek grammar*, where it is described as 'the extension of the meaning of a word beyond its proper sphere, especially a violent metaphor.'[69]

In Book VIII of the *Institutio oratoria* Quintilian explicitly rejects the Aristotelian-Ciceronian approach, arguing that the term κατάχρησις should only be used to describe the deliberate misuse of a word in order to represent a meaning *for which no correct word is available*, such as when we call the murderer of a mother or a brother a 'parricide' (which word originally only referred to the killing of a father [*pater*], if we accept Quintilian's etymology).[70] In Ps.Plutarch's *Vita Homeri* κατάχρησις is defined as 'the transference of a word-usage from an object which is properly (κυρίως) signified to another object which has no proper name (κύριον ὄνομα).'[71] We note that the technical use of κύριον ὄνομα as 'proper' or 'correct' name is an intrinsic part of the definition. The rhetorical theorist Tryphon, who lived in Alexandria one or two generations before Philo, in his little book Περὶ τρόπων gives a similar definition, and at the end of his discussion specifically addresses the problem of the difference between *metaphora* and *katachresis*. The former, he asserts, involves the transference of a word from one named object to another named object, whereas the latter moves from what is named to what is unnamed (ἀκατονόμαστον).[72] Here, succinctly stated, is the difference between what I have called the soft and the hard line. What the soft line calls *katachresis*, the hard line in many instances regards as no more than *metaphora*. In his standard work on ancient rhetoric Martin follows the latter tradition, when he says that 'die κατάχρησις, *abusio*, besteht darin, daß für ein fehlendes *proprium* ein naheliegendes in seiner Bedeutung dem gesuchten *proprium* ähnliches Wort eintritt.'[73]

It has been argued by Barwick that the origin of the doctrine of tropes is to be sought in the contribution of the Stoa to the study of grammar and rhetoric,

---

[69] H.W. Smyth, *Greek grammar*, Cambridge Mass. 1956, 677.

[70] 8.6.34−5: '... *catachresis, quam recte dicimus abusionem, quae non habentibus nomen suum accommodat quod in proximo est ... discernendumque est ⟨ab⟩ hoc totum tralationis istud genus, quod abusio est ubi nomen defuit, tralatio ubi aliud fuit.*' (ed. Cousin).

[71] 2.18 346.11−13 Bernadakis: κατάχρησις μὲν δή, ἥπερ ἀπὸ τοῦ κυρίως δηλουμένου μεταφέρει τὴν χρῆσιν ἐφ' ἕτερον οὐκ ἔχον ὄνομα κύριον ...

[72] L. Spengel, *Rhetores Graeci*, Leipzig 1856, 3.192.20−193.7: κατάχρησίς ἐστι λέξις μετενηνεγμένη ἀπὸ τοῦ πρώτου κατονομασθέντος κυρίως τε καὶ ἐτύμως ἐφ' ἕτερον ἀκατονόμαστον κατὰ τὸ οἰκεῖον, οἷον γόνυ καλάμου, καὶ ὀφθαλμὸς ἀμπέλου ... διαφέρει δὲ μεταφορὰ καὶ κατάχρησις, ὅτι ἡ μὲν μεταφορὰ ἀπὸ κατονομαζομένου ἐπὶ κατονομαζόμενον λέγεται, ἡ δὲ κατάχρησις ἀπὸ κατονομαζομένου ἐπὶ ἀκατονόμαστον, ὅθεν καὶ κατάχρησις λέγεται. M.L. West, *Tryphon De Tropis*, *CQ* 15, 1965, 230 ff., argues that both this work and the companion piece falsely ascribed in Spengel to Gregory of Corinth, if they are not by Tryphon himself, plausibly contain material going back to him. The *t.a.q.* for the Περὶ τρόπων literature is given by a 2nd century A.D. Würzburg papyrus, but an earlier date, e.g. 1st century B.C., is likely.

[73] J. Martin, *Antike Rhetorik*, München 1974, 266.

and that the Stoa was responsible for introducing the new technical usage of κύριον (ὄνομα) as meaning 'proper'.[74] Whether this was the case or not,[75] it is worth pointing out that certain Stoic doctrines naturally led to reflection (and no doubt polemics) on the subject of word-usage. Chrysippus is known to have written a treatise on 'Zeno's correct usage of words.'[76] If the Stoics claimed that only the sage is a king or a rich man, they are clearly not using the words βασιλεύς and πλούσιος in the usual manner.[77] A neglected text in Philo may be illuminating. In *De Cherubim* 121 he argues that only God is in the true sense (κυρίως) a citizen; men, and this even includes the wise, are actually aliens and foreigners, and if they are called citizens, it is only by misuse of the word (καταχρήσει ὀνόματος). The theological extrapolation is of course Philonic. We may, however, entertain the possibility that the Stoics defended their paradoxes in a similar manner, by arguing that their use of words was legitimate, as opposed to ordinary usage, which might seem correct, but is in fact catachrestic.[78]

Let us return now to Philo's exploitation of the term *katachresis*. He refers to it fourteen times, a comparatively high frequency when compared with other writers.[79] On occasion Philo uses the term quite loosely (e.g. at *Decal.* 94, swearing as misuse of God's polyonymous name); sometimes this loose usage approximates to our 'soft line' (e.g. *Congr.* 161, κάκωσις meaning not 'chastening' but 'toil'); twice, as we have already seen, Philo gives the term a Stoic application (*Leg.* 3.86, *Cher.* 121). Of paramount interest to us, however, are the seven passages in which Philo specifically applies the notion of *katachresis* to man's naming and speaking about God.[80] There can be no doubt that in these passages he has the 'hard-line' interpretation in mind. When we address God by one of His names, or when we speak of Him generally, we use words not legitimately but catachrestically, for we apply names or words to a Being who is properly speaking nameless and indescribable. Naming and

---

[74] K. Barwick, *Probleme der stoischen Sprachlehre und Rhetorik, Abhandlungen der Sächsischen Akademie der Wissenschaften zu Leipzig*, philol.-hist.Kl.49.3, Berlin 1957, 88–97. Not the Old Stoa, Barwick suggests (110), but initiated by Diogenes of Babylon.

[75] The speculative nature of Barwick's investigations is criticized by D. Fehling, *GGA* 212 (1958) 161–173, who argues that the origin of such rhetorical theories should not be sought within the confines of one particular philosophical school.

[76] Περὶ τοῦ κυρίως κεχρῆσθαι Ζήνωνα τοῖς ὀνόμασιν, Diog.Laert. 7.122 (= *SVF* 3.617).

[77] Cf. the complaint of Alexander of Aphrodisias at *SVF* 3.595.

[78] Cf. also *Leg.* 3.86 (health, wealth, fame can be καταχρηστικῶς called ἀγαθά).

[79] *Leg.* 2.10, 3.86, *Cher.* 121, *Sacr.* 101, *Post.* 168, *Her.* 124, *Congr.* 161, *Mut.* 11–14, 27–28, 266, *Somn.* 1.229, *Abr.* 120, *Decal.* 94, implicitly at *De Deo* 4. Cf. also the use of κυριολογέω at *Det.* 58, *Post.* 7, *Deus* 71 (τὸ κυριολογούμενον ἐπ' ἀνθρώπων πάθος ὁ θυμός ... εἴρηται τροπικώτερον ἐπὶ τοῦ ὄντος; Winston and Dillon in their commentary miss the allusion to the theory of tropes), *Somn.* 2.245, *Mos.* 1.75, *Legat.* 6). In Plutarch's *Moralia* once (25B), in Plotinus once (1.4.6.20), in Clement four times.

[80] *Sacr.* 101, *Post.* 168, *Mut.* 11–14, 27–28, *Somn.* 1.229, *Abr.* 120, *De Deo* 4.

speaking about God strains the limitations of language, for the task of language is to give phonetic expression to the factuality and essence of things.[81] Since God's essence is unknown to man, language must necessarily fall short. This can be made clear with reference to a technical term drawn from (philosophically influenced) rhetorical theory.

It would surprise me greatly if we have not encountered here a serendipitous find of Philo himself. May we not surmise that his remarkably associative mind[82] was struck by the word ἀκατονόμαστος in his grammar book (we recall Tryphon's statement above[83]) and that he observed that it was precisely the same term that Platonists were using in their attempts at negative theology. But it is very important not to overlook that even here scripture is pointing the way. As we observed earlier, Philo reads, or rather one should say misreads, Moses as saying that God does not reveal a κύριον ὄνομα. The great nomothete had not, it would seem, forgotten the rhetoric and philosophy that Greek teachers had taught him when he was still a prince of Egypt (*Mos.* 1.23)!

Original and apposite as Philo's idea may have been, it cannot be said to have caught on. This emerges when we examine the early Christian philosophers and exegetes who were acquainted with the Philonic heritage of thought.[84] The doctrine that God is ineffable and nameless, but has made himself known under many names or appellations is already a prominent theme in Justin and other early Apologists.[85] But is there any evidence that Philo's specific application of the notion of *katachresis* was taken over? I have found only two passages which are in any way relevant. In *Stromateis* V Clement in a discussion of God's ineffable transcendence writes that 'if we sometimes name Him, calling Him improperly (οὐ κυρίως) the One or the Good or Nous or Being or Father or God or Demiurge or Lord, we apply these not as His name, but out of embarrassment we take recourse (προσχρώμεθα) to fine names, so that the mind can gain support from these and not be led astray.'[86]

---

[81] Cf. *Leg.* 2.15, *Cher.* 56, *Somn.* 1.230, *QG* 4.194 etc.

[82] Some examples at Runia, *op. cit.* (n. 6), 371.

[83] ἀκατονόμαστος also at Spengel 3.208.30, 217.11,19 (the second work ascribed to Trypho, see n. 72 above), 232.7.

[84] I confine myself to Christian thinkers up to the time of Origen. Prof. G.C. Stead informs me that the subject may be of relevance to the later Arian controversy.

[85] Cf. esp. Justin *Apol.* 2.6.1, also 1.61, Athenagoras *Leg.* 10.1, Theophilus *ad Aut.* 1.3.1, and also the text of Aristides discussed by R. van den Broek, this volume, 202 ff.

[86] *Str.* 5.82.1: κἂν ὀνομάζωμεν αὐτό ποτε, οὐ κυρίως καλοῦντες ἤτοι ἓν ἢ τἀγαθὸν ἢ νοῦν ἢ αὐτὸ τὸ ὂν ἢ πατέρα ἢ θεὸν ἢ δημιουργὸν ἢ κύριον, οὐχ ὡς ὄνομα αὐτοῦ προφερόμενοι λέγομεν, ὑπὸ δὲ ἀπορίας ὀνόμασι καλοῖς προσχρώμεθα, ἵν' ἔχῃ ἡ διάνοια, μὴ περὶ ἄλλα πλανωμένη, ἐπερείδεσθαι τούτοις (text Le Boulluec). A. Le Boulluec (*Clément d'Alexandrie, Les Stromateis V*, SC 278–9, Paris 1981, 2.266) adduces a statement in a speech of the rhetor/philosopher Maximus of Tyre, the formulation of which is almost exactly the same as Clement's (*Or.* 2.10 28.8–29.2 Hobein): ὁ μὲν γὰρ θεός ... κρείττων δὲ χρόνου καὶ αἰῶνος καὶ πάσης ῥεούσης φύσεως, ἀνώνυμος νομοθέτῃ, καὶ ἄρρητος φωνῇ, καὶ ἀόρατος ὀφθαλμοῖς· οὐκ

This reminds us very much of Philo, and a direct debt may be suspected (much Philonic material is absorbed into this book[87]). The second relevant passage is located in the *Cohortatio ad gentiles*, whose anonymous author was probably a contemporary of Origen.[88] Speaking of Plato's doctrine of being, he declares that the Greek philosopher had heard the words spoken to Moses in Ex. 3:14, and had realized that God did not tell him his proper name (κύριον ὄνομα), for no name can properly be ascribed to God (κυριολογεῖσθαι).[89] The last clause is a paraphrase of Philo's words in *Mos.* 1.75, which is clearly the direct source.

Both Clement and the *anonymus*, therefore, come very close to Philo's idea, but the 'technical' notion of *katachresis* is neglected. Origin too does not exploit it in his discussions with Celsus on God's namelessness or in the *De principiis*.[90] Both he and Clement show more sophistication than Philo in their speculations on God's transcendence. It is especially striking that Clement, in contrast to Philo and anticipating Plotinus, disqualifies the epithet 'Being' for God. But, as we saw earlier, Philo cannot accept this on account of his loyalty to Mosaic scripture.[91] Middle Platonists also do not apply the notion of *katachresis* theologically, not even Plutarch, who had a fine opportunity to do so in his mediations on the Delphic E.[92] If we wish to find a creative use of the term *katachresis* which is somewhat comparable to Philo's, we must turn, surprisingly perhaps, to Sextus Empiricus. Sceptics do not use the terms and expressions of their philosophy dogmatically as if they properly reveal facts, but indifferently or catachrestically, in a way that is relative (πρός τι) and so also relative to the Sceptics.[93] The connection between Philo and the Sceptics

---

ἔχοντες δὲ αὐτοῦ λαβεῖν τὴν οὐσίαν, ἐπερειδόμεθα φωναῖς, καὶ ὀνόμασιν, καὶ ζῴοις καὶ τύποις χρυσοῦ ... · ἐπιθυμοῦντες μὲν αὐτοῦ τῆς νοήσεως, ὑπὸ δὲ ἀσθενείας τὰ παρ' ἡμῶν καλὰ τῇ ἐκείνου φύσει ἐπονομάζοντες ... Philo and Clement would of course both aggressively reject the rhetor's reference to "graven images". Human weakness (ἀσθένεια) is also stressed by Philo at *Mos.* 1.75.

[87] Cf. the *index locorum* in Stählin's edition and Le Boulluec's commentary. Note especially the extensive use of *Post.* 12–20 in *Str.* 5.71–74, where in 71.5 Clement adds καὶ ὀνόματος καὶ νοήσεως to Philo's ὑπεράνω καὶ τόπου καὶ χρόνου (*Post.* 14).

[88] Cf. R.M. Grant, *HThR* 51 (1958) 128–134.

[89] *Coh. ad gent.* 20–21, 72.20–73.3 Otto: ἀκηκοὼς [ὁ Πλάτων] γὰρ ἐν Αἰγύπτῳ τὸν θεὸν τῷ Μωϋσεῖ εἰρηκέναι 'Εγώ εἰμι ὁ ὤν, ... ἔγνω ὅτι οὐ κύριον ὄνομα ἑαυτοῦ ὁ θεὸς πρὸς αὐτὸν ἔφη. οὐδὲν γὰρ ὄνομα ἐπὶ θεοῦ κυριολογεῖσθαι δυνατόν. τὰ γὰρ ὀνόματα εἰς δήλωσιν καὶ διάγνωσιν τῶν ὑποκειμένων κεῖται πραγμάτων ...

[90] Note esp. *C. Cels.* 7.42, *De princ.* 1.2.1.

[91] See above at n. 29.

[92] Cf. *Mor.* 388F–389A, 393B–C. With regard to the question being/above being both Plutarch and Numenius are closer to Philo than Clement and Plotinus; cf. J. Whittaker, *CQ* 19 (1969) 189 ff.; *Phoenix* 32 (1978) 144–154. At Seneca *Ep.* 58.11 (in a 'Platonist' context) the words *nomen parum proprium 'quod est'* might suggest an allusion to κατάχρησις, but in fact they refer to the Latin rendering of τὸ ὄν.

[93] *Hyp.* 1.207: φαμὲν δὲ καὶ ὡς οὐ κυρίως δηλοῦντες τὰ πράγματα ... τίθεμεν αὐτάς [φωνάς], ἀλλ' ἀδιαφόρως καὶ εἰ βούλονται καταχρηστικῶς· οὔτε γὰρ πρέπει τῷ σκεπτικῷ

may seem less startling if we bear in mind the contribution of sceptical theories
to what Raoul Mortley has called the gradual move 'from word to silence' in
ancient thought.[94]

Why, we may finally ask, was Philo's idea not more explicitly taken over?
In the case of the author of the *Cohortatio* one might surmise that he did not
recognize the technicalities involved. But I would be very hesitant to say this
of Clement and Origen, who know their rhetorical tropes backwards, front-
wards and sideways, so to speak.[95] A clue may be gained if we observe that,
although quotations of Ex. 3:14 are common in early Patristic literature, references to the other two texts used by Philo, Ex. 3:15 and Ex. 6:3, are exceedingly
rare.[96] When Justin quotes the last-named text to Trypho, he implies that
Christ the Logos was the θεός who appeared to the Patriarchs and that it was
his name that was not disclosed to them.[97] Clement, having just written the
passage on God's unnameability which we discussed, goes on to add that it is
only by divine grace and God's Logos (i.e. Christ) that the Unknown is known
and quotes the words of Paul in Acts which are the subject of Dr. Van der
Horst's paper elsewhere in this volume.[98] Philo's use of the notion of
katachresis, we may conclude, has too negative an emphasis for the Christian
thinkers. The limitations of human thought and language are a fact and a
problem—on this all are in agreement—, but why underline it so heavily when
God has sent His only begotten son, who said to his followers 'if you know me,
you know my Father and have seen Him'?[99] On the other hand, in comparison
with the Platonists, the aim of whose philosophy could also be said to be 'to
see God',[100] the Jew Philo and the Christian Fathers stand side by side. Somewhat simplistically we might formulate the difference as follows: for the Jew
and the Christians God makes sure that he is κατὰ τὸ δυνατόν known to man
(whether via Moses or the incarnation), whereas for the Greeks God is knowable (again κατὰ τὸ δυνατόν) and it is up to man to know him. It might be
argued that this contrast is too absolute. Does not Plotinus emphasize the
passivity of the intellect as it waits for the spark suddenly to jump across from

---

φωνομαχεῖν, ἄλλως τε ἡμῖν συνεργεῖ τὸ μηδὲ ταύτας τὰς φωνὰς εἰλικρινῶς σημαίνειν
λέγεσθαι, ἀλλὰ πρός τι καὶ πρὸς τοὺς σκεπτικούς. Cf. also *Hyp.* 1.135,191. On the use of
the phrase πρός τι cf. above p. 80 on *Mut.* 27, and also Greg.Naz. *Or.* 30.18 (in an exegesis of
Ex. 3:14 quoted by M. Harl on p. 97 of the article cited below in n. 96).

[94] Gnosis I, *RAC* 11 (1981), 526.

[95] Their acquaintance with the trope is clear from passages such as *Str.* 8.26.1, *C. Cels.* 5.4.

[96] Cf. *Biblia patristica, ad locc.* On Patristic use of Ex. 3:14 see M. Harl, Citations et com-
mentaires d'*Exode* 3, 14 chez les Pères Grecs des quatre premiers siècles, in: Vignaux, *op. cit.*
(n. 46), 87–108.

[97] *Dial.* 126.2

[98] *Str.* 5.82.4.

[99] Cf. John 14:6–9, cited by Clement *Str.* 5.16.1, Origen *C. Cels.* 7.43.

[100] Justin *Dial.* 2.6, on which see J.C.M. Van Winden, *An early Christian philosopher*, Leiden
1971, 50–51.

the One and illuminate the soul?[101] Very true. But by then the stage of gaining support from the availability of God's names has long been passed.[102]

In my dissertation I hinted that, though the notion of *katachresis* in its specific application is limited to the problem of naming and speaking about God, nevertheless it might aid us in developing a more general perspective on Philo's theology.[103] For it cannot but draw attention to an unavoidable element of tension in his thinking on God. Philo's loyalty to Judaism, including its central tenet of monotheism, is unconditional. But in his thinking and writing about God he has decided to appropriate ideas from Greek philosophical theology, and he finds that its chief doctrine, a split-level conception of divinity, is not a viable option.[104] God has to be unnameable and named at the same time. Hypostasization, as developed in the doctrine of the powers, is a crutch. Philo would gladly throw it away if he could, but of course he is stuck with it. In Philo's view *katachresis* is a necessary evil, we might be tempted to say, symptomatic of the human condition.[105] But it occurs not without God's connivance. At *Mut.* 12 I am tempted to read, with the direct ms. tradition, δίδωμι καταχρῆσθαι.[106] '*I* bestow the possibility of *katachresis*', says God according to Philo. Perhaps we should better say, for Philo *katachresis* is not a 'necessary evil', but an audible sign of God's grace.

V

Allow me to return, as briefly as I can, to the themes with which I began.

Our reading of a single Philonic text has shown that there are two 'patterns of correlation' in Philo's exegetical works. The diverse themes which Philo develops in his elucidation of the main biblical text and related secondary texts can be analysed (1) in relation to the same themes found elsewhere in his works, and (2) in relation to the Greek philosophical doctrines which give them a

---

[101] Cf. esp. *Enn.* 5.3.17.28−35 (with clear reference to Pl. *Ep.* 7 341c), and the remarks of J. Rist, *Plotinus: the road to reality*, Cambridge 1967, 224 f.

[102] Note too the casualness with which Maximus says (above n. 86) that 'we give to God's nature names that we like.'

[103] *Op. cit.* (n. 6), 438. Particularly important are the passages *Sacr.* 101 and *Deus* 51−71, in which Philo, with reference to his favourite texts Num.23:9 and Deut.8:5, discusses in very general terms our speaking about God. Note that ἀλληγορία too is one of the tropes; cf. Trypho at 3.193.8, 215.31 Spengel.

[104] Cf. Runia, *op. cit.* 442−3; the phrase δεύτερος θεός is found only once in the Philonic corpus, at *QG* 2.62 (on this text 443 n. 196). As J. Mansfeld, in this volume pp. 107 f., shows, Greek philosophical theologies which have a νοῦς as their highest divinity confront the same problem. But by the time of Plotinus these difficulties have been definitively straightened out.

[105] Cf. Origen, *Comm.Joh.* 32.28.351.

[106] Editors since Hoeschelius have read δίδωσι with John Dam. If we retain δίδωμι with the mss., then Philo is quite naturally continuing the first person employed in ἴσον τῷ εἶναι πέφυκα, οὐ λέγεσθαι.

theoretical basis. It is these two 'patterns of correlation' which make the systematic and the historical/doxographic approaches possible and worthwhile, though they are never without their perils. They are hazardous precisely because Philo subordinates himself to the main and associated bible texts at hand, preferring the internal conceptual coherence of a chapter or a treatise to the achievement of a wider consistency. This practice can be highly irritating to modern sensibilities, and we are still far from fully understanding its rationale.[107] I would nevertheless contend that, if Philo is read in smaller sections as we have attempted to do in the present paper, the results can often be quite rewarding.

What, then, should be the response to Osborn's critique? It would be facile to affirm that our analysis of the chapter from the *De mutatione nominum*, the contents of which proved to be coherently thought through, is sufficient to vindicate Philo. The fact of the matter is that Philo *does not* argue as much as we would wish. His method is primarily that of *correlation*, i.e. he relates Mosaic words and concepts (e.g. κύριον ὄνομα) to acceptable philosophical ideas. The notion of *katachresis*, for example, is sound and apposite, but it is left to the reader to determine the precise theological connotations. Clement *does* represent an advance, philosophically speaking, over Philo. It is hardly helpful, though, to describe the difference in terms of theosophy and philosophy. Both men accept divine revelation; both regard it as rationally defensible, Philo perhaps more so than Clement, but the Jew's defences are formulated with less eye for apologetic rigour.

Osborn is right in saying that Clement takes over the language of biblical Hellenism first developed by Philo, but he does not recognize how important and determinative that first step was.[108] Philo, in his exegesis of Mosaic scripture, embarks on the decisive shift from an experience of God that is direct and concrete to an experience of God that is mediated through theoretical reflection on what God's nature is.[109] Hence the discussion on knowing, naming and

---

[107] Much emphasis has recently been placed on the role of tradition in Philo's exegesis, e.g. in the Claremont Philo research project (on which see *Studia Philonica* 3 (1974–75) 71–112), and by T.H. Tobin, *The creation of man: Philo and the history of interpretation*, Washington 1983, but for critical remarks on Tobin's study see Runia, *op. cit.* (n. 6), 556 ff. and D. Winston, *JBL* 104 (1985) 558 ff.

[108] In response to the view (Nikiprowetzky) that Philo is first and foremost a commentator on scripture and that this goes a long way to explaining his lack of consistency, Osborn replies (p. 44): "The difficulty which faces this defence is that Philo is not really subject to the text; his allegorical method is too arbitrary to be governed by its subject matter." Yet for Philo his hermeneutic method is essentially scientific! Here a potential weakness of the method of problematic elucidation becomes apparent, i.e. that it projects modern assumptions onto a past body of thought which as a (Kuhnian) paradigm has its own coherence.

[109] Cf. a penetrating analysis of the confluence of Judaic and Hellenic theological motifs in Hellenistic Judaism by Y. Amir, Die Begegnung des biblischen und des philosophischen Mono-

speaking about God that has occupied us in this paper. For this reason, perhaps, Philo *was* the first theologian, even if, as we have seen, not all his theological ideas caught on.*

---

theismus als Grundthema des jüdischen Hellenismus, *Evangelische Theologie* 38 (1978) 2–19.

* The research for this contribution was supported by a C. & C. Huygens scholarship of the Netherlands Organisation for the Advancement of Pure Research (Z.W.O.).

COMPATIBLE ALTERNATIVES: MIDDLE PLATONIST THEOLOGY AND THE XENOPHANES RECEPTION

BY

JAAP MANSFELD (UTRECHT)

1. Students of Middle Platonism are familiar with the phenomenon that the accounts of the divine provided by various authors of the 2nd cent. CE strike one as incoherent.[1] Qualifications according to the *viae negationis, analogiae*, and *eminentiae*, which to us seem incompatible to a degree, tend to coexist in a peaceful jumble. On the one hand, the essence or nature of God is described by means of a refusal to predicate any attributes whatsoever. Attributes withheld in this way may be arranged in polar pairs. On the other hand, God's existence as a supreme cause tends to be described in a positive way by means, e.g., of varieties of the *argumentum ex gradibus entium*. The theology of ch. 10 of Alkinoos' *Didaskalikos* is a notorious instance of such a medley.[2] That this is not only a problem from an anachronistic modern point of view becomes clear when we adduce important evidence neglected by the students of Middle Platonism, viz. the parallel accounts[3] of the theology of Xenophanes to be found in the ps.-aristotelian treatise *De Melisso Xenophane Gorgia* (hereafter *MXG*), chs. 3−4, and in Simplicius' *Commentary on Aristotle's Physics*, pp. 22.22−23.30 Diels.[4] Here, God is said to be, on the one hand, eternal, one,

---

[1] See the survey and analysis of the traditional evidence in A.-J. Festugière, *La Révélation d'Hermès Trismégiste, 4. Le Dieu Inconnu et la Gnose*, Paris 1954, 92 ff., 135 ff.; cf. also P.L. Donini, *Le scuole l'anima l'impero: la filosofia antica da Antioco a Plotino*, Torino 1982, 106 ff. S.R.C. Lilla, *Clement of Alexandria: A Study in Christian Platonism and Gnosticism*, Oxford 1971, 212 ff., provides a valuable collection of parallels from Plato, Middle Platonists, Early Christians, and Gnostics, concerned with "the doctrine of the transcendence of God," but does not seem to be aware of the problem analysed by Festugière.

[2] See my paper Three Notes on Albinus, I: Problems of Transcendence, *Theta-Pi* 1 (1971) 61−7; G. Invernizzi, *Il Didaskalikos di Albino e il medioplatonismo, I: Saggio introduttivo*, Roma 1976, 43 ff. With some hesitation, I accept the argument that the *Did.* is by the otherwise unknown Alkinoos; see M. Giusta, Ἀλβίνου Ἐπιτομή ὁ Ἀλκινόου Διδασκαλικός?, *AttiAccTorino* 95 (1960−1) 167 ff. (arguments *contra* in C. Moreschini, *Apuleio e il Platonismo*, Firenze 1978, 55 f. n. 7, 62 f.), and J. Whittaker, Parisinus graecus 1962 and the Writings of Albinus, *Phoenix* 26 1974, 320 ff., 450 ff., repr. in: J. Whittaker, *Studies in Platonism and Patristic Thought*, London 1984, Nrs. XXI−XXII. Cf. also W. Deuse, *Untersuchungen zur mittelplatonischen und neuplatonischen Seelenlehre, AbhAkMainz*, geist.-sozwiss. Kl., Sonderabh. 3, Wiesbaden 1983, 81 ff. For further information on this issue and an ingenious suggestion which cannot be discussed here see H. Tarrant, Alcinous, Albinus, Nigrinus, *Antichthon* 19 (1985), 87 ff.

[3] Texts in H. Diels/W. Kranz, *Die Fragmente der Vorsokratiker*, Berlin ⁶1952, 21 A 28, A 31.

[4] For *MXG*, I accept Diels' dating to the 1st-2nd cent. CE (H. Diels, *Aristotelis qui fertur de*

homogeneous, spherical, limited, and unmoved, and, on the other, neither limited nor unlimited and neither at rest nor in motion. Both ps.-Aristotle and Simplicius are aware that one has a problem here. The former dialectically exploits the contradiction between the negated pairs of polar opposites and some of the positive attributes in order to prove Xenophanes' position not acceptable. The latter irons out this contradiction by arguing that 'spherical' means 'homogeneous' and 'unmoved' means 'beyond motion and rest,' i.e. he explains those positive attributes which clash with the negated polar pairs in the sense of precisely these pairs.

The accounts in ps.-Aristotle and Simplicius have as a rule puzzled the students of Presocratic philosophy. What I would like to call the 'doxographical vulgate,' i.e. the plurality of sources Diels (still followed by the majority of experts in the field) wanted, at least to the extent that they agree among themselves or with purported fragments of Theophrastus, to derive from Theophrastus' lost *Physikai doxai*, knows nothing of the negated pairs of polar attributes. Yet Simplicius explicitly attributes these pairs *to Theophrastus*. This attribution, as I argue elsewhere, should be accepted. What Theophrastus, following Aristotle (*Met.* A 5.986b19 ff.), meant was that Xenophanes was not clear about his one principle, neither committing himself to the view that it is limited nor to the view that it is unlimited, and neither stating clearly that it moves nor that it is at rest. It follows that the doxographical vulgate, which holds that Xenophanes' God not only is one and eternal, but also that he is homogeneous, limited, spherical, unmoved, and rational, does not derive from Theophrastus.[5] It also follows that the source from which the description of Xenophanes' doctrine in ps.-Aristotle and Simplicius derives paradoxically combined the entirely positive account to be found in the doxographical vulgate with Theophrastus' negative *non liquet*. The motives which brought about this combination are one of the subjects of the present investigation.

2. We should begin by looking at the texts. Ps.-Aristotle's version can be conveniently quoted from the summary of *MXG* 3.977a14—b19 at b18–20 (for God's holistic rational perception see 977a37–8):

> ... τὸν θεόν, ἀίδιόν τε καὶ ἕνα, ὅμοιόν τε καὶ σφαιροειδῆ ὄντα, οὔτε ἄπειρον οὔτε πεπερασμένον οὔτε ἠρεμοῦντα οὔτε κινητὸν εἶναι.

At 977b1–3 sphericity is deduced from homogeneity; next the pair 'neither unlimited nor limited' is deduced from the four positive predicates *including*

Melisso Xenophane Gorgia libellus, SPAW, Philos.-hist. Kl. Abh. 1900.I, Berlin 1900, 9 ff.). See further my paper 'De Melisso Xenophane Gorgia:' Pyrrhonizing Aristotelianism, forthcoming in *RhM.* 1988, and my paper cited next note, n. 2. Simplicius of course wrote in the 6th cent. CE.
    [5] For the argument, given here only in outline, see my paper Theophrastus and the Xenophanes Doxography, *Mnem.* 40 (1987) 286 ff.

sphericity. As we have noticed above, ps.-Aristotle is aware of the contradiction involved when you posit a series of positive attributes as well as a pair of
negated polar attributes which partly overlaps with one of the positive ones.
He makes good use of this awareness in his counter-argument concerned with
'sphericity' and 'neither limited nor unlimited' at ch. 4.978a15 ff. It is to be
noted that the attribute 'unmoved', which is lacking in ch. 3, appears to be
clearly presupposed in the counter-argument at 4.978b15 ff.

Simplicius' account, *In Phys.* pp. 22.22 ff., presents both pairs of negated
polar attributes as well as a series of positive ones which is virtually identical
with that in *MXG* (and with the strings of attributes to be found in the doxographical vulgate), viz. 'one', 'eternal', 'homogeneous', 'spherical', 'limited',
'unmoved'. The epithet 'limited' (not in *MXG*, which only has 'spherical', but
often found in the vulgate) contradicts the first pair of negated polar attributes
figuring both in *MXG* and Simplicius, just as 'unmoved' contradicts the
second pair to be found in both these sources. As we have noticed above, Simplicius presents an argument intended to prove that no conflict exists between
the positive and the negative qualifications provided by the account of Xenophanes' theology he attempts to explain. Scholars have tended to regard this
attempt as not serious; Zeller's verdict, "was Simplicius . . . zur Lösung dieses
Widerspruchs sagt . . . erklärt nichts,"[6] has never been challenged.

We had better listen to what Simplicius has to say. The formula that God
is 'neither at rest nor in motion', he argues, need not conflict with *Vorsokr.*
21 B 26 [quoted by Simplicius at this point] according to which God is at rest
and does not move: 'he [Xenophanes] does not mean that he [*sc.*, God] is at
rest according to the rest that is opposed to motion, but (that he is so) according
to the abiding that is beyond motion and rest' (*In Phys.* p. 23.13–4). The conflict between the attributes of sphericity or being limited and the formula
'neither unlimited nor limited' may be resolved in a similar manner. Simplicius
argues that the doctrine that God is 'limited and spherical' (as phrased by
Alexander of Aphrodisias, quoted at this point) does not clash with the formula 'neither unlimited nor limited' because Xenophanes meant 'limited and
spherical' in the sense of 'everywhere homogeneous' (πανταχόθεν ὅμοιον, *In
Phys.* p. 23.17–9, *Vorsokr.* I, p. 122.13).[7] Consequently, God's sphericity
would denote his *simplicity*. The sphere, so to speak, is spiritualized away, and
the potentially embarrassing elements of the positive theology are interpreted
in the sense of a sophisticated negative theology.

---

[6] E. Zeller/W. Nestle, *Die Philosophie der Griechen in ihrer geschichtlichen Entwicklung,
I.1,* Darmstadt [7]1963 = Leipzig [6]1919, 630 n. 6. Cf. M.C. Stokes, *One and Many in Presocratic
Philosophy,* Washington D.C. 1971, 72: "Neoplatonic interpretation, drastically forced."

[7] In *MXG* 3.977b1 πάντη δ' ὅμοιον ὄντα σφαιροειδῆ εἶναι (argument *contra* at 4.978a7 ff.)
we have the converse of Simplicius' argument. At *In Phys.* p. 23.19, follow the *ms* not Diels and
read λέγει not λέγειν.

Simplicius twice returns to Xenophanes in the sequel of his account of the principles of the philosophers. The first time is *In Phys.* p. 28.4 ff. (Theophr., *Phys. op.* fr. 8 Diels). Here he says that Leucippus 'did not pursue the same route as Parmenides and Xenophanes as to the things that are, but went the opposite way. For these men said that the All is One and unmoved and ungenerated and limited ...' Scholars have argued that this text is unalloyed Theophrastus[8] and so have used it to shore up the attribution to Theophrastus of the version of the Xenophanean ontology and theology found in the doxographical vulgate. But the argument is inconclusive: at *In Phys.* p. 22.26 ff. we have a nominatim fragment, whereas at p. 28.4 ff. Theophrastus' name is absent. The really important parallel, on the other hand, is at p. 29.5 ff., a to my knowledge utterly neglected text.[9] Simplicius here again discusses Xenophanes Parmenides Melissus. Parmenides and Xenophanes said the principle is 'one and limited' (p. 29.7−8, cf. p. 28.4 ff., quoted *supra*), Melissus said it is unlimited (p. 29.20). But there is something special about Xenophanes, who not only said the principle is one and limited, but stated something else as well, p. 29.12−14:

> 'however, Xenophanes posits it [the principle] as the cause of all things and as transcending all things and as beyond motion and rest and polarities in general,[10] just as Plato in the first *hypothesis* of *Parmenides*.'

The account at p. 29.5−13 not only corroborates that at p. 22.26 ff. as to the blending of negative and positive theology (note that only the latter is at issue in the intermediate passage, p. 28.4 ff.), but usefully complements the earlier argument (p. 23.13 ff.) in favour of a reconciliation of these two ways of approaching the divine.

The word I have translated 'polarities', viz. *antistoichia*, rings a bell. It is synonymous with *systoichia*.

At *Met.* A 5.986a22−b8 (*Vorsokr.* 58 B.5, I p. 452.35 ff.), i.e. immediately before his discussion of the Eleatics (Parmenides Melissus Xenophanes) and their views of the One principle, Aristotle studies and describes the views of certain Pythagoreans who arranged the opposites in a table, or *systoichia*, of polarities. The first pair in this table is 'limit—unlimited' (πέρας—ἄπειρον), the sixth 'at rest—moving' (ἠρεμοῦν—κινούμενον). The Xenophanean One as described and analysed by Simplicius at pp. 22.22 ff. and p. 29.12 ff. may be said to transcend such Pythagorean polar qualities to the extent that the

---

[8] E.g., J. Wiesner, *Ps.Aristoteles MXG: Der historische Wert des Xenophanesreferates. Beiträge zur Geschichte des Eleatismus*, Amsterdam 1972, 222.

[9] Not in H. Diels, *Poetarum philosophorum fragmenta*, Berlin 1901. Not in *Vorsokr.* Not in M. Untersteiner, *Senofane: Testimonianze e frammenti*, Firenze 1955. Not discussed in the secondary literature.

[10] For the Greek text see *infra.*, 97.

qualification 'neither limited nor unlimited and neither at rest nor in motion' entails that it is beyond polarity as such.

Furthermore, Aristotle had studied other Pythagoreans immediately before the Pythagorean dualists (see esp. 986a13–21; cf. *Vorsokr.* 58 B.5, I p. 452.30 ff.). These others had derived all things from number and number from the One, which encapsulates the opposites in that it is both odd and even, both limited and unlimited. A Pythagorean variety of monism, at least according to Aristotle's presentation.[11]

3. In the 2nd half of the 1st cent. BCE, the Platonist[12] Eudorus of Alexandria (quoted verbatim Simpl., *In Phys.* p. 181.10 ff.) described a flexible Pythagorean system. He distinguished two Ones, placing the first *beyond* the table of opposites and the second *in* this table as opposed to the Unlimited Two. Further opposites listed by his Pythagoreans are also enumerated by Eudorus. The pairs of opposites in the table are generated by the first One which is the Supreme God. This reinterpretation, or reception, of Pythagoreanism has been considered a major contribution to the rise of Middle Platonism.[13] It has also been pointed out that this negative theology, just as that of subsequent Middle Platonism and Neoplatonism, is indebted to the spirit of the second part of Plato's *Parmenides*.[14] One should add that there

---

[11] I do not have to take sides here on the issue whether there really were monistic and dualistic currents in Early Pythagoreanism. See, however, Ph. Merlan, Monismus und Dualismus bei einigen Platonikern, in: K. Flasch (ed.), *Parusia. Studien zur Philosophie Platons und zur Problemgeschichte des Platonismus. Festgabe J. Hirschberger,* Frankfurt a.M. 1965, 97 ff., repr. in: Ph. Merlan, *Kleine Schriften,* Hildesheim 1976, 419 ff.

[12] Arius Didymus *ap.* Stob. II p. 42.7 calls him an Ἀκαδημαικὸς φιλόσοφος. See J. Glucker, *Antiochus and the Late Academy,* Hypomnemata 45, Göttingen 1978, 122.

[13] See H. Dörrie, Der Platoniker Eudoros von Alexandreia, *Hermes* 79 (1944) 25 ff., repr. in: H. Dörrie, *Platonica minora,* München 1976, 279 ff.; Festugière, *op. cit.* (*supra,* n. 1), 24 ff.; P. Boyancé, Études philoniennes, *REG* 76 (1963) 85 ff.; W. Theiler, Philo von Alexandria und der Beginn des kaiserzeitlichen Platonismus, in: K. Flasch (*supra,* n. 11), repr. in: W. Theiler, *Untersuchungen zur antiken Literatur,* Berlin 1970, 488 ff.; J. Whittaker, ἐπέκεινα νοῦ καὶ οὐσίας, *VC* 23 (1969), repr. in: *Studies* (*supra,* n. 2), Nr. XIII; P.W. van der Horst/J. Mansfeld, *An Alexandrian Platonist Against Dualism: Alexander of Lycopolis' Critique of the Doctrines of Manichaeus,* Leiden 1974, 10 ff.; J.M. Dillon, *The Middle Platonists: A Study of Platonism 80 B.C. to A.D. 220,* London 1977, 117 ff., 126 ff.; G. Calvetti, Eudoro di Alessandria: Medioplatonismo e Neopitagorismo nel I secolo A.C., *RFNS* 69 (1977) 3 ff.; Donini, *op. cit.* (*supra,* n. 1), 100 ff. See also H. Tarrant, Middle Platonism and the Seventh Epistle, *Phron.* 28 (1983) 86, 88, and H. Tarrant, The Date of Anon. *in Theaet., CQ* 33 (1983) 165 ff., where this commentary is attributed to Eudorus on what seem to me specious grounds. The fragments of Eudorus have now been collected by C. Mazzarelli, Raccolta e interpretazione delle testimonianze e dei frammenti del medioplatonico Eudoro di Alessandria, *RFNS* 77 (1985) 197 ff., 535 ff. (by Sept. 1986, I had not yet seen the promised "interpretazione").

[14] See E.R. Dodds, The Parmenides of Plato and the Neoplatonic 'One,' *CQ* 22 (1928) 136. Dodd's thesis has been disputed by J.M. Rist, The Neoplatonic One and Plato's Parmenides, *TAPA* 93 (1962) 389 ff. Cf. also the discussion in Whittaker, *op. cit.* (*supra,* n. 13), 97 ff., in Lilla, *op. cit.* (*supra,* n. 1), 206, and see further J. Whittaker, Philological Comments on the Neoplatonic

is no prima facie evidence that what we have here is Eudorus' own philosophy or the "system of Eudorus," as it is often called in the learned literature; at the most, his account of Pythagoreanism is part of his own philosophy to the extent that he is practicing history of philosophy as philosophy.

I wish to argue that both as to its doctrine and as to much of its terminology Simplicius' interpretation of Xenophanes at *In Phys.* p. 29.12 ff. is identical with Eudorus' interpretation of Pythagoreanism as quoted verbatim by Simplicius at *In Phys.* p. 181.10 ff. This becomes clear when we use the time-honoured method of the parallel columns:

181.17 ff. (Pythagoreans)

ἀρχὴν ... τῶν πάντων τὸ ἕν, ὡς ἂν καὶ τῆς ὕλης καὶ τῶν ὄντων πάντων ἐξ αὐτοῦ γεγενημένων· τοῦτο δὲ εἶναι καὶ τὸν ὑπεράνω θεόν.[15] [...].

κατ' ἄλλον δὲ τρόπον δύο τὰ ἀνωτάτω στοιχεῖα ... καλεῖν δὲ τὰ δύο ταῦτα στοιχεῖα πολλαῖς προσηγορίαις· τὸ μὲν γὰρ αὐτῶν ὀνομάζεσθαι τεταγμένον ὡρισμένον (κτλ.), τὸ δὲ ἐναντίον τούτῳ ἄτακτον ἀόριστον (κτλ.).[16]

29.12 ff. (Xenophanes)

(τὸ ἕν) ... πάντων αἴτιον καὶ πάντων ὑπερανέχον

καὶ κινήσεως αὐτὸ καὶ ἠρεμίας καὶ ὡς πάσης ἀντιστοιχίας ἐπέκεινα τίθησιν.

Both Eudorus' Pythagoreans and Simplicius' Xenophanes place One *supreme*[17] God beyond the opposites which come forth from him because he is their principle, or cause.

Parallels with both these texts are to be found in two passages in Philo of Alexandria.[18] At *De post. Caini* 14, interpreting Exod 33:13 ('I shall reveal

---

Notion of Infinity, in: R. Baine Harris (ed.), *The Significance of Neoplatonism*, Norfolk, Virg. 1976, repr. in: *Studies* (*supra*, n. 2), Nr. XVIII, 156 ff., who supports Dodd's thesis with further proofs. The Simplicius text (*In Phys.* p. 29.12 ff.) quoted *supra*, p. 95, may be added to the evidence.

[15] Eudorus fr. 4 Mazzarelli.

[16] Eudorus fr. 5 Mazzarelli.

[17] ὑπεράνω ⏤ ὑπερανέχον. For ὑπεράνω in Philo see immediately *infra*. Iamblichus, *Comm. math. sc.* 4, p. 15.6 ff. Festa (= Speusippus fr. 72 Isnardi Parente, in: M. Isnardi Parente, *Speusippo: Frammenti*, La scuola di Platone 1, Napoli 1980), discussing the One (ἕν) and plurality (πλῆθος) as the highest and first principles, argues (p. 16.10 f. Festa, p. 95.18 f. Isnardi Parente) that τὸ ... ἕν οὔτε καλὸν οὔτε ἀγαθὸν ἄξιον καλεῖν, διὰ τὸ καὶ τοῦ καλοῦ καὶ τοῦ ἀγαθοῦ ὑπεράνω εἶναι. But this One is not linked up with a *systoichia*, and is not God. The attribution of this text to Speusippus has been questioned by L. Tarán, *Speusippus of Athens: A Critical Study with a Collection of the Related Texts and a Commentary*, Philosophia antiqua 39, Leiden 1981, 86 ff.—note that Tarán does not include this text among the fragments—, and defended by J.M. Dillon, Speusippus in Iamblichus, *Phron.* 29, 1984, 325 ff. I prefer to leave the matter *sub iudice*; one cannot, at any rate, be certain that the wording *ap.* Iambl. is genuinely Speusippean. The word ὑπεράνω (see L.S.J. *s.v.*) seems to be rather late, and certainly so when used *sensu metaphorico*.

[18] Also quoted by Lilla, *op. cit.* (*supra*, n. 1), 215. Note that the *via negationis*, connected with

myself unto you in the darkness;' cf. also Exod 20:21), Philo explains that God is τὸ αἴτιον, and ὑπεράνω both place and time: τὰ γὰρ γεγονότα πάντα ὑπ-οζεύξας ἑαυτῷ ..., ἐπιβέβηκε δὲ πᾶσιν κτλ. Cf. also *ibid.*, 7: ὁ θεὸς ... τὰς τῶν γεγονότων ἰδιότητας ἀπάντων ἐκβεβηκὼς κτλ. An edited conflation of these two Philonic passages (in the order 14—7) is given, in much of the original wording, by Clement, *Strom.* II 6.1 f. The (Eudorean) pythagoreanizing notion of transcended polarities is not lacking in Philo, for although ἰδιότητας is feeble, the use of the verb ὑποζεύξας entails that the things that are below the transcendent God are arranged in polar pairs (Philo, of course, blends in the image of the good and the bad horse from Plat., *Phaedr.* 264b ff.). Note that the formula τὸν ὑπεράνω θεὸν is further found at Phil., *Congr.* 106 f. Arguably, these Philonic passages betray the influence of Eudorus' reception of Pythagoreanism. At the very least, they belong to the same family as Eudorus' account of the Pythagoreans and Simplicius' of Xenophanes.

4. What precisely were the traditions which have to be assumed as influences upon Eudorus' reinterpretation, or reception, of Pythagoreanism is a moot point. It is of course clear that his first pair of Pythagorean opposites, the One, or Monad, and the Unlimited Two (*In Phys.* p. 181.26—7), originally are the two principles of Plato's 'unwritten doctrines.' For my present purpose I need not discuss the vexed question whether this Platonization of Pythagoreanism derives from Plato's immediate pupils, as Festugière and others have argued.[19] It is sufficient to recall that it is certainly older than Eudorus, because the *Pythagorean Hypomnēmata* (a compilation of partly earlier material to be dated to the 2nd cent. BCE[20]) cited by Alexander Polyhistor *ap.* Diogenem Laertium derive the Unlimited Two from the Monad (Diog. Laert. VII 25 ~

---

the idea that God is ineffable, is first found in Philo (Festugière, *op. cit.* [*supra*, n. 1], 19 ff.; Dillon, *op. cit.* [*supra*, n. 13], 155 f.; D.T. Runia, 'Naming and Knowing,' this vol., 69 ff.). Dillon, *ibid.*, 128, 155, suggests that behind Philo (and Albinus/Alkinoos) we have the reinterpretation of Pythagoreanism by Eudorus. In more general terms, J. Whittaker has called attention to the Neopythagorean background of negative theology, see 'Ammonius on the Delphic E,' *CQ* 19 (1969) 185 ff., repr. in: *Studies (supra*, n. 2), Nr. V; Neopythagoreanism and Negative Theology, *SO* 44 (1969) 109 ff., repr. in: *Studies*, Nr. IX; ἐπέκεινα ... (*supra*, n. 2); Neopythagoreanism and the Transcendent Absolute, *SO* 48 (1973) 77 ff., repr. in: *Studies*, Nr. XI. P. Boyancé, Fulvius Nobilior et le Dieu ineffable, *RÉL* 81 (1955) 172 ff., arguing that the attribution in Lyd., *Ost.* 16, of the expression τοῦ πάντων ἀρρήτου πατρὸς to Fulvius N. (early 2nd cent. BCE) should be accepted, holds that the notion of ineffability is much older. His proof-text (also cited, for a similar purpose, by H. Chadwick, rev. of H.A. Wolfson, *Philo I—II*, Cambridge Mass.—London 1947, *CR* 63 (1949) 24) is Cic., *ND* I 30, *Platonis ... qui in Timeo patrem huius mundi nominari neget posse.* But the sloppy Epicurean doxography used here by Cicero occasionally exaggerates in order the better to strike its targets; *Tim.* 28c is cited in such a stretched form. There is, moreover, no trace of a negative theology in Cic., *loc. cit.* (nor, for that matter, in the passage from Lydus, supposing one were to accept Boyancé's argument).

[19] Festugière, *op. cit.* (*supra*, n. 1), 28 ff.

[20] See A.-J. Festugière, Les «Mémoires Pythagoriques» cités par Alexandre Polyhistor, *REG* 58 (1945) 1 ff., repr. in: A.-J. Festugière, *Études de philosophie grecque*, Paris 1971, 371 ff.

Vorsokr. 58.B1a, I p. 449.1 ff.). Festugière correctly argued[21] that one should assume both monistic and dualistic tendencies in pre-eudorean Neopythagorism; yet much of the evidence at issue cannot be securely dated. Rist interestingly posited that Eudorus' doctrine of the two Ones is not genuinely (Neo)pythagorean, but represents an original interpretation of the evidence in Alexander Polyhistor.[22] There may be some truth in this, but the *Pyth. Hypomn.* present a monistic system in which the first two opposites, which in Eudorus' account are on the *same* level, are to be found on *different* levels. Presumably, both the *Pyth. Hypomn.* and Eudorus provide attempts to reconcile monism and dualism, but in the earlier work dualism effectively disappears, which in Eudorus it does not. Whittaker (not unlike Festugière) believes that Eudorus' account was influenced by a plurality of earlier pseudo-pythagorica. He argues that Syrianus, *In Met.* p. 165.33 ff., tells us that Philolaus, Brotinus, and (*sic*) Archenaetus placed the One beyond the principles and beyond the columns of opposites, and that Proclus, *In Tim.* I p. 176.9 ff., attributes to 'the Pythagoreans' the view that the One is prior to all polarity.[23] But we cannot date the pieces of evidence quoted by these two Late Neoplatonists; as parallels they are important, but they may well be later than Eudorus, or have been cited not in their original form but according to a later *interpretatio*.

E.R. Dodds pioneered the important insight that the first hypothesis of the second part of Plato's *Parmenides* must have been a source of inspiration for Eudorus,[24] but this does not suffice to explain the latter's interpretation of Pythagoreanism in some of its more important and striking details. Another Platonic passage which may have been involved is *Philebus* 16c−17a,[25] cf. the backward reference at *Phileb.* 23c: 'God has made manifest the limited and the unlimited in things.' The transcendentalizing interpretive turn imposed on this passage by Proclus, *In Tim.* I, p. 385.18 ff., is called "évidemment abusive" by Festugière, although the same scholar points out that this reading of the Plato passage is obviously similar to what is characteristic of Eudorus' interpretation of Pythagoreanism.[26]

We should therefore limit ourselves to such (Neo-)Pythagorean notions as are certainly pre-Eudorean. Not only the platonizing Neopythagorean monism described by Alexander Polyhistor will have been known to Eudorus. He will also have been familiar with Neopythagorean varieties of the Early Pytha-

---

[21] See *supra*, n. 19.

[22] *Op. cit.* (*supra*, n. 14), 391 ff.

[23] Whittaker, Neopythagoreanism . . . (*supra*, n. 18), 78; cf. already Festugière, *op. cit.* (*supra*, n. 1), 30.

[24] See *supra*, n. 14.

[25] See Dillon, *op. cit.* (*supra*, n. 13), 127 f.

[26] *Op. cit.* (*supra*, n. 1), 35.

gorean *systoichia*. Varro, several decades before Eudorus, attributes to 'Pythagoras' the doctrine that *omnia rerum initia bina esse, ut finitum et infinitum, bonum et malum, vitam et mortem* (*Ling. lat.* V 11). Cf. Eudorus *ap.* Simpl., *In Phys.* p. 181.12 f., δύο ἀρχὰς κτλ.; p. 181.14, ἀστεῖον— φαῦλον; p. 181.24 ff., ὡρισμένον—ἀόριστον. Accordingly, the suggestion of Festugière and Theiler that in Eudorus' account also the early table of Pythagorean opposites described by Aristotle at *Met.* A 5 is involved provides an important clue.[27] That Eudorus was a close reader of at least part of *Met.* A follows from his famous but puzzling textual suggestion concerned with an important point of exegesis, viz. the issue of Plato's view of the One (*Hen*) as the principle of the Forms at A 6.988a8–14.[28]

In *Met.* A 5, authoritative accounts of both (Early) Pythagorean monism and dualism are to be found.[29] It is an economical assumption that Eudorus attempted to harmonize these two versions of Pythagorean metaphysics by putting the monistic One that contains the opposites 'odd' and 'even', or 'limited' and 'unlimited' (986a18 ff.), on top of the dualistic *systoichia* of 'limit' and 'unlimited' etc. (986a23 ff.). The important difference is that in Eudorus' version the polarities, although produced by the first One, do not seem to be present in it. Yet he seems to come rather close to the view that the opposites are inside a One when stipulating subsequently and to some extent inconsistently that the (second) One and the Unlimited Two 'taken together are, again, One' (p. 181.28, ἀρχαὶ ἄμφω ἓν ὄντα πάλιν[30]). In this way, the distinction between the first One beyond the opposites and the second One, opposed to the Two, which 'they' (*sc.*, the Pythagoreans) 'also call *Monas*' (Eud. *ap.* Simpl., *In Phys.* p. 181.28–31), seems to become blurred.

Presumably, the blur is only apparent. Too little attention has been given to the fact that according to Eudorus as quoted verbatim by Simplicius the monistic and dualistic Pythagorean doctrines are *alternative* ways of contemplating *the same* realities, although the alternatives themselves are of unequal value (*In Phys.* p. 181.10–12). According to the 'highest explanation' (κατὰ τὸν ἀνωτάτω λόγον) there is one causal principle only. According to the 'second-best explanation' (κατὰ ... τὸν δεύτερον λόγον) there is duality. Returning

---

[27] Festugière, *op. cit.* (*supra*, n. 1), 24 n. 1; Theiler, *op. cit.* (*supra*, n. 13), 490 n. 105. W. Burkert, *Lore and Science in Ancient Pythagoreanism*, Cambridge Mass. 1972, 52 n. 119, is more reserved.

[28] See P. Moraux, Eine Korrektur des Mittelplatonikers Eudoros am Text der Metaphysik des Aristoteles, in: *Beiträge zur alten Geschichte und ihrem Nachleben, Festschr. Fr. Altheim, I*, Berlin 1969, 492 ff.; G. Iaksetich, Eudoro e la Metafisica di Aristotele, *Quaderni di filolologia classica Trieste* 4 (1983) 27 ff. Cf. also *infra*, n. 59, *ad finem*.

[29] Cf. *supra*, 96 f.

[30] Cf., on Pythagorean monism, Arist., *Met.* A 5.986b19 f., ... τὸ μὲν ἄπειρον τὸ δὲ πεπερασμένον, τὸ δ' ἓν ἐξ ἀμφοτέρων εἶναι τούτων. Eudorus may have wanted to preserve all the aspects of Aristotle's account.

to the monistic explanation, Eudorus calls it another 'mode' (or 'presentation', p. 181.17, κατ' ἄλλον τρόπον), and he also employs the designation 'mode', or 'presentation', for the dualistic explanation (p. 181.23). I shall revert to this important point.

It should also be acknowledged that the list of opposites as given according to the dualistic account at p. 181.24–7 is incomplete: 'ordered limited (ὡρισμένον) knowable male odd right light—unordered unlimited (ἀόριστον) unknowable female left even darkness.' For one should, of course, place first on this list the One, i.e. Monad, as opposed to the Unlimited Two, and take the fact into account that according to p. 181.13–5 'good—evil' should be included as well. Furthermore, the list of items in the table of opposites at p. 181.24–7 is introduced with the observation that each of the two principles (viz. the One and the Unlimited Two) is called by 'many appellatives.'[31] Finally, we read (p. 181.13–15) that *all* the things that may be conceptualized in a dualistic way may be arranged under each of the opposed principles, viz. what is 'good' (ἀστεῖον) under the One, and what is 'evil' (φαῦλον) under the Unlimited Two. The examples provided by Eudorus, although for the most part traditional, are plainly given *exempli gratia*, and the open-ended table of opposites may therefore be supplemented *ad lib*. Again, it would appear that Eudorus is bent upon working out a synthesis that would be able to accommodate the various views that were available—just as is the case for his reconciliation of monism and dualism. This is much more than eclecticism.[32]

However, we still have to explain how Eudorus came to place the first *Hen* beyond the opposites, and how he came to call it 'God'[33]—in short, for what reason "il s'est élevé jusqu'à un degré plus haut encore de transcendance"[34] than his pythagoreanizing predecessors. Logically speaking (at least in a Greek context), such a most supreme God leaves room for a less supreme God, or even gods, lower on the scale of excellent things. Eudorus' first One beyond the opposites cannot be paralleled from earlier Neopythagorean literature; however, some among the earlier Neopythagorean dualists proclaimed the *Monas* opposed to the Unlimited Two to be God. Aetius I 3.8 ascribes such a system to 'Pythagoras'; here the One and the Unlimited Two are also good and evil, and the Monad is νοῦς ὁ θεός. This lemma is in both ps.-Plutarch and Stobaeus, so the odds are that the doctrine at issue is somewhat earlier than Eudorus. The same view is found Aet. I 7.18, again in both of Diels' contributary sources, and also in the part of ps.-Galen's compilation depending on a

---

[31] Greek text *supra*, 97.

[32] See P.L. Donini's paper on the problematical concept of eclecticism, forthcoming in the *Acts* of the FIEC Colloquium on Eclecticism (Dublin 1984) edited by J.M. Dillon and A.A. Long.

[33] τοῦτο δὲ εἶναι καὶ τὸν ὑπεράνω θεόν, p. 181.19.

[34] Festugière, *op. cit.* (*supra*, n. 1), 29.

source much similar to ps.-Plut., viz. *Philos. hist.* 35[35]. According to Stob. I
1.29*b*; 36.6 ff. Wachsmuth [printed by Diels as Aet. I 7.30, although no
parallels for this rather long and occasionally confused lemma exist in either
ps.-Plut. or ps.-Galen or other related literature], Xenocrates (fr. 15 Heinze =
213 Isnardi Parente) said that the Monad and the Unlimited Two are gods. One
may doubt that this passage gives us Xenocrates' unadulterated view,[36] but it
is a fair enough assumption that his theology is presented in the form of a
perhaps pre-Eudorean pythagoreanizing reception.

Other sources, more difficult to put a date to, although presenting a form
of Neopythagorean monism with the Monad as God, do not place this divine
Monad in opposition (or next) to an Unlimited Two. Athenagoras, *Leg.* 6.1,
p. 12.9–10 Schoedel, quotes a Pythagorean he calls 'Opsimus' who said μονάς
ἐστὶν ὁ θεός, τουτέστιν εἷς; note, though, that again God is not identified with
the *Hen*.[37] Hipp., *Ref.* I 2.2, argues that 'Pythagoras' μονάδα ... ἀπεφήνατο εἶναι τὸν θεόν. In Hippolytus, the doctrines of Empedocles and Heraclitus
have been thoroughly assimilated to the doctrines attributed to 'Pythagoras'.[38] Empedocles is said to have affirmed that τὸ τῆς μονάδος πῦρ νοερὸν
τὸν θεόν (*Ref.* I 3.1), Heraclitus—no mention of the (Pythagorean) Monad
here—that πῦρ νοερὸν τὸν θεόν (I 4.2).[39]

Finally, a distinction between *Hen* and *Monas* which, interestingly enough,
is the opposite of that stipulated by Eudorus is found in ps.-Justin, *Coh.* 19
(*PT*, 186.8 ff. Thesleff; same quotation in Clement, *Protr.* 6, which provides
a *t.a.q.*), and in the possibly early *Anonymus Photii* (*PT*, 237.18 ff. Thesleff).
Both these reports attribute to 'Pythagoras' a monistic system with the Monad
as 'the principle of all things,'[40] but add that the *Hen* belongs to the domain
of arithmetic and the *Monas* to that of the intelligibles. However, they do not
claim that this *Monas* is to be conceived of as God.

Consequently, such partly comparable evidence as is available reveals that
Eudorus' approach, according to which the Pythagorean *Hen* (not: *Monas*) is

---

[35] *Dox. gr.* 618.12 ff.

[36] See the overview of the discussion in M. Isnardi Parente, *Senocrate—Ermodoro: Frammenti*, La scuola di Platone 3, Napoli 1981, 400 ff. Note that M. Baltes, this volume, 43 ff., accepts
the fragment.

[37] Text also in H. Thesleff, *The Pythagorean Texts of the Hellenistic Period* (hereafter *PT*),
ActAcAboensis, Hum. 30.1, Åbo 1965, 141.3.

[38] Diels, *Dox. gr.* 145 f., was horrified.

[39] That this no mere fancy of Hippolytus but represents a definite tradition, or reception, is
proved by a parallel in Clem., *Strom.* V.xiv.103.6–104.1. For the larger setting see W. Burkert,
Plotin, Plutarch und die platonisierende Interpretation von Heraklit und Empedokles, in: J.
Mansfeld/L.M. de Rijk (eds.), *Kephalaion. Studies ... de Vogel,* Wijsgerige teksten en studies
23, Assen 1975, 137 ff.; my paper Resurrection Added: The interpretatio christiana of a Stoic Doctrine, *VC* 37 (1983) 218 ff.; and my paper Heraclitus, Empedocles, and Others in a Middle
Platonist Cento in Philo of Alexandria, *VC* 39 (1985) 131 ff.

[40] Cf. Eudorus *ap.* Simpl., *In Phys.* p. 181.17, quoted *supra*, 97.

the most high God beyond the opposites which spring forth therefrom, is original. Proof for a pre-Eudorean (Neo-)Pythagorean meta-dualistic sole principle of all things *which would be God* I, for my part, have not found; it does not occur either in Aristotle or Alexander Polyhistor or any other account which can be safely dated before Eudorus.

Yet Aristotle provides a clue. We have noticed above that Eudorus had studied the text of *Met.* A.[41] We have also seen that Aristotle's description of Pythagorean dualism was taken into account by Eudorus.[42] In *Met.* A 5, subsequent to his examination of the early physicist monists in the previous chapters and to that of Pythagorean monism and dualism in this chapter itself, Aristotle had studied Eleatic monism (and dualism, in so far Parmenides was taken into account).[43] The idea that the One principle is God he had attributed *to Xenophanes only*,[44] who, as he had argued, unlike Parmenides and Melissus was not clear at all as to this *Hen's*, or God's, being either limited or unlimited, form or matter. It is extremely plausible that Eudorus was aware of the affinity between Aristotle's discussion of 'limited' and 'unlimited' in regard to the Eleatic One principle on the one hand and Aristotle's immediately preceding discussion of Pythagorean monism and dualism, according to which the list of opposites of the Pythagorean dualists begins with 'limit'—'unlimited', on the other. If further we assume that he was in a position to adduce Theophrastus' analysis of the *archai* as posited by the pre-aristotelian philosophers, which sported a *non liquet* concerned with Xenophanes' one principle's being 'neither limited nor unlimited and neither moving nor at rest,'[45] we may see how the possibility of an interesting synthesis may have dawned upon his eirenic mind. The 'absence of clarity' singled out by Aristotle for severe condemnation would be most welcome in the context of a philosophical theology dealing with a *Hen*, or God, beyond a *systoichia* of opposites of which the first two are the Monad and the Unlimited Two that is equated with matter. Indeed, both pairs of opposites listed in Theophrastus' *non liquet* concerned with Xenophanes' principle actually occur in Aristotle's Pythagorean *systoichia*. As Ueberweg and Zeller cleverly noted long ago, the Greek of Theophrastus' formula is ambiguous and may mean both (*a*) "er setzt es weder als begrenzt noch als unbegrenzt . . ." and (*b*) "er setzt es als weder begrenzt noch unbegrenzt . . . ."[46] Eudorus was in a position to give it a metaphysical twist

---

[41] *Supra*, 100.

[42] *Supra*, 92.

[43] See my paper (*supra*, n. 5), 306 f.

[44] *Met.* A 5 986b24–5, τὸ ἓν εἶναί φησι τὸν θεόν.

[45] See further my paper (*supra*, n. 5).

[46] F. Ueberweg, Über den historischen Wert der Schrift de Melisso, Zenone, Gorgia, *Philologus* 8 (1853) 106; Zeller, *op. cit.* (*supra*, n. 6), 626 n. 3. That Zeller's (*b*) is possible is unnecessarily doubted on grammatical grounds by P. Moraux, *Der Aristotelismus bei den Griechen von*

and read it as 'he posits it as neither limited nor unlimited.' The negative verdict of Aristotle and Theophrastus that Xenophanes' One principle and God lies outside physics must have appealed to him as well; for this verdict was equally capable of a positive *interpretatio*.

The argument advanced up to now works both ways. The Pythagoreanization of Xenophanes at Simpl. *In Phys.* p. 29.12 ff. is best explained on the assumption that originally it was *Eudorus* who interpreted Xenophanes in this way. Conversely, the positioning by Eudorus of a *Hen* that is a most high *God* beyond the Pythagorean opposites is best explained on the assumption that his interpretation *of Xenophanes* played a decisive part.[47] Either way, we are still within the context of a close reading of *Met.* A 5 and of Theophrastus' further comments.[48]

Arguably, precedent, or inspiration, for a creative reinterpretation of this kind could be found in Plato's *Parmenides*, although what one may call the negative henology of the 1st hypothesis of the second part of this dialogue would afford little ground for the assumption that the One is God. However, it is plausible that *Parm.* was among Eudorus' sources of encouragement. The first two hypotheses, for instance, are even presented as alternatives[49] (*Parm.* 142b1−2). But there is more.

In the 1st hypothesis, at *Parm.* 137d−e, Plato argues that the 'One (ἕν) that is one,' which is not a whole containing parts, has neither beginning nor end nor middle since these would be parts. Therefore, it is 'unlimited' (ἄπειρον) and without shape. As Cornford has pointed out,[50] 'unlimited' here should not be thought of as a positive attribute, "for any sort of extent implies distinguishable parts, and so contradicts the definition." The counterpart of the

---

Andronikos bis Alexander von Aphrodisias, I: Die Renaissance des Aristotelismus im I. Jh. n. Chr., Berlin—New York 1972, 454 n. 16. His alternative suggestion, *ibid.*, 457, that Theophrastus originally may have written in terms of an "Entweder-Oder" for which the author of *MXG* (excerpted, according to Moraux, by Simplicius) would have substituted a "Weder-Nicht", is unfounded.

[47] H. Thesleff, *An Introduction to the Pythagorean Texts of the Hellenistic Period*, Act-AcAboensis, Hum. 24.3, Åbo 1961, 48, argues that (in his account of Pythagoreanism) Eudorus' "identification of the first ἕν with God is rather Peripatetic." Although there is no prima facie evidence either for (see, however, *infra* n. 59) or against the assumption that Eudorus was influenced by Aristotle's theology, one should recall that Aristotle's God, though neither limited nor unlimited (*Phys.* Θ 10.267b17 ff.), is an *Un*moved Mover and so not beyond rest (although being beyond natural rest, *Cael.* Γ 2, 300a27 ff.). One may also compare the theology of Ammonius the teacher of Plutarch at Plut., *De E* 393A−C, where the supreme divinity is τὸ ἕν. Whittaker, *Ammonius* (*supra*, n. 18), 185 ff., plausibly derives this from Eudorus; H. Diels *ap.* E. Norden, *Agnostos theos*, Berlin 1912, repr. Darmstadt 1974, 232, suggested that Plutarch/Ammonius had Xenophanes in mind. I believe Diels' suggestion is good as long as one thinks of Eudorus' Xenophanes.

[48] For a similar coupling of Pythagoreans and Eleatics cf. Simpl., *In Phys.* p. 7.1−3.

[49] Cf. *supra*, 100 f.

[50] F.M. Cornford, *Plato and Parmenides*, London 1939, repr. 1950, 118.

'One that is one,' viz. the 'One that is' of the 2nd hypothesis, is described at 144d–145b as being both limited (πεπερασμένον) because it has parts and as being unlimited for the same reason—presumably, because these parts would have to be infinitely many. Being limited, this 'One that is' has a beginning, a middle, and an end, and so must possess some sort of shape. It follows that the attribute 'unlimited' as predicated of the 'One that is one' indeed means, in Cornford's sense, 'beyond limit.' This entails that the 'One that is one' cannot be unlimited in the sense in which the 'One that is' is unlimited; it has to be neither determinably unlimited nor determinably limited.

Furthermore, at *Parm.* 138a–139b, Plato argues at some length that the 'One that is one' is neither at rest (ἑστάναι) nor in motion (κινεῖσθαι). If this withheld pair of opposites is made to perform a metaphysical turnabout, the 'One that is one' will as a result come to be beyond motion and rest. The result would be eminently applicable to Xenophanes' One (ἕν) provided the latter were to be interpreted as a First One beyond the opposites ἠρεμοῦν and κινούμενον of Aristotle's Pythagorean *systoichia*. In a similar way, the 'One that is one' in a sense that transcends limit could be equated with a Pythagorean One beyond the opposites 'limit'—'unlimited', and with Xenophanes' One God which, according to a creative misunderstanding of what Aristotle and Theophrastus really meant, may also be put beyond and on top of this polarity, thus coinciding with the Pythagorean *Hen*. Simplicius' remark[51] that the negated polar attributes he believes to have been positively predicated by Theophrastus upon Xenophanes' One God should be interpreted in the sense of [the negative henology] of the first hypothesis of *Parmenides* is explicit. I admit that one cannot be certain that the reference in Simplicius derives, ultimately, from Eudorus, but have argued that the interpretation of Xenophanes in Simplicius excellently fits the evidence pertaining to Eudorus.[52] Someone, at any rate, though not necessarily Simplicius himself who may have merely endorsed this view, must have noticed the connection.

The Eudorean reinterpretation of the Theophrastean-Aristotelian interpretation of Xenophanes I have postulated did not influence the doxographical vulgate concerned with the latter's ontology and theology.[53] We have acknowledged the fact that the only attributes in the vulgate which contradict the negated polar pairs are 'limited' or 'spherical', and 'unmoved'. The doxography in *MXG*, just as the much later account in Simplicius, combines these disparate data; if we follow Diels' date for *MXG*,[54] ps.-Aristotle wrote later than Eudorus. The hypothesis that ps.-Aristotle made up the combination of

---

[51] Quoted *supra*, 95.
[52] See *supra*, 97 ff.
[53] See *supra*, 93, and my paper (*supra*, n. 5).
[54] Cf. *supra*, n. 4, and text thereto.

his own accord is precluded by the far-reaching points of agreement with Simplicius' account. A common source, or tradition, must be postulated, and it would appear that Simplicius, though much later than ps.-Aristotle, reflects this source or tradition in a more accurate way;[55] to phrase it differently, unlike Simplicius the author of *MXG* seems to have brushed away such justification for the combination of the apparently disparate data as was available in his source in order the better to criticize Xenophanes' dogmatist views.

For the combination of data derived from the doxographical vulgate on the one hand and from the creatively misunderstood Theophrastus on the other several explanations are possible. The first is that someone to be dated in between Eudorus and ps.-Aristotle combined what was in the former with what was in the vulgate, and added the sophisticated arguments[56] to be found at the beginning of *MXG* 3 (and paralleled in Simplicius) either from a third source or from a version of the vulgate which was more complete than one of the sources of ps.-Plut., *Strom.* 4 (Plut. fr. *179 Sandbach, *Vorsokr.* 21 A 32).[57] The second explanation, which I prefer, is that Eudorus himself was responsible for the conflation. For Eudorus, as is proved by his treatment of Pythagoreanism, would have had an answer at his disposal if questioned about his procedure. He was in a position to justify his accomodation of at first sight conflicting data deriving from a plurality of traditions by arguing that all he did was to present things both according to a 'highest explanation' (or 'mode') and according to a 'second-best explanation.'[58] Under those circumstances, it would be perfectly responsible to attribute, following the second-best mode, at least some of the 'many appellatives' that may be listed in the left-hand, 'good' column of the open-ended Pythagorean *systoichia* to a *Hen*, or God, which according to the highest explanation is to be situated beyond polarity. Thus, monism and dualism are not two different systems; rather, they are two different ways of representing reality, albeit of unequal value. In the next section, I shall pursue this line of thought and attempt to find corroborating evidence for this assumption.[59]

---

[55] Also note that Simplicius lists 'limited', which is not in *MXG*.

[56] God cannot be born or give birth; God is the strongest, the ruler not the ruled.

[57] See further n. 40 in my paper cited *supra*, n. 5.

[58] See *supra*, 100 f.

[59] Dillon, *op. cit.* (*supra*, n. 13), 128, speculates that Eudorus, if he endorsed the Platonic Forms, will have placed these inside the Monad, or second One, which is opposed to the Unlimited Two, or Matter. Pursuing this suggestion, one cannot exclude that he placed the Forms inside the *Hen*, or first One, as well (cf. *supra*, 101, where I argue that the concept of a most high God leaves room for that of a less high one). Again, we should think of Xenophanes' One God as pythagoreanized by Eudorus. This God cogitates. *Vorsokr.* 21 B 24, "he sees, cogitates, hears as a whole" is only quoted by Sextus, *M.* IX 144, and anonymously at that, which is significant (attribution to Xenophanes certain because of passages in the doxographical vulgate dealing with divine cognition). The reverberations of this line in pagan and early Christian authors are many; see

5. The argument of the previous section, if acceptable, has shown that the pre-Middle Platonist theological system set out (or applied) by Eudorus in his account of Pythagoreanism is grounded in a systematical reinterpretation of traditions inherent to or concerned with Pythagoreanism and Platonism, and also of traditions regarding Xenophanes. This systematical structure much resembles the theology to be found in ch. 10 of Alkinoos'[60] *Didaskalikos*. There are, of course, significant differences. In *Did.* 10, Aristotle's First Unmoved Cogitating Mover has been incorporated;[61] Eudorus may have done so as well, but I have no real evidence that he did.[62] In *Did.* 10, the supreme God is an Intellect. The Forms are his Thoughts. The Second God, or Second Intellect, also always thinks all things (10;174.17−8 Hermann); the Forms thought by this Intellect are the paradigms of what is in nature (9;163.11−2 and 13−4). The First God is unmoved (ἀκίνητος) and everlastingly active toward the Second God, or Intellect of the World-Soul, who as a result is everlastingly active himself (14;169.31−5; 10;164.20−1). Structurally, this distinction between a First and a Second God recalls that made by Eudorus between the First *Hen*, or most high God, and the Second *Hen*, or Monad, although the essential difference of course is that Alkinoos does not speak of Ones, but of Intellects. The activity of the First Intellect toward the Second Intellect is described by

---

R.M. Grant, *The Early Christian Doctrine of God*, Charlottesville 1966, 107 ff.; R.M. Grant, *After the New Testament*, Philadelphia 1969, 103 ff.; W.R. Schoedel, ' "Topological" Theology and Some Monistic Tendencies in Gnosticism,' in: M. Krause (ed.), *Essays on the Nag Hammadi Texts in Honor of A. Böhlig*, Nag Hammadi Studies 3, Leiden 1972, 88 ff., esp. 92 ff.; W.R. Schoedel, The Early Christian Doctrine of God, in: W.R. Schoedel/R.L. Wilcken (eds.), *Early Christian Literature and the Classical Tradition. In honorem R.M. Grant*, Théologie historique 54, Paris 1979, 75 ff., esp. 78 ff.; R.M. Grant, Place de Basilide dans la théologie ancienne, *REAug* 25, 1979, esp. 211 ff.; cf. also *infra*, 112 f. Simpl., *In Phys.* p. 23.14 f., quotes *Vorsokr.* 21 B 25: 'and he says that he [God] thinks all things, saying: «but without conscious effort he sways all things with his mind».' Because Simplicius seems to have been unable to find a copy of Xenophanes' poems (see Diels, *Dox. gr.* 112), the quotation must have been lifted from a secondary source excerpted by him. Because it fits Simplicius' argument, it is a fair enough assumption that the quotation ultimately derives from the first person to propose this argument. I have argued that this person is Eudorus, or at any rate someone hard to distinguish from Eudorus. Consequently, Eudorus could have considered the (Xenophanean and Pythagorean) first One or *Hen* an Intellect cogitating the Forms which, at the level immediately below, are reproduced by the second One or Pythagorean Monad; we have noticed *supra*, 101 f., the existence of probably pre-eudorean Neopythagorean evidence regarding the conception of the Monad as God, and/or as an Intellect. That Eudorus endorsed the Forms does not follow from but is commensurate with his interpretation (see *supra*, n. 28 and text thereto) of Arist., *Met.* A 6.988a8 ff., according to which passage Plato's One (*Hen* not Monad) is the cause of 'whatness' for the Forms. If this is correct, Eudorus would also have been in a position to accomodate Aristotle's First Mover, an Intellect thinking itself.

[60] See *supra*, n. 2.

[61] Cf. R.E. Witt, *Albinus and the History of Middle Platonism*, Cambridge 1937, repr. Amsterdam 1971, 125 ff.; Donini, *op. cit.* (*supra*, n. 2), 107.

[62] However, see *supra*, n. 59.

means of two similes, the first of which (10, p. 164.22–3)[63] is based upon Aristotle's description (*Met.* Λ 7.1072b3) of the First Unmoved Mover as a cause of motion.

In what follows, Alkinoos first presents a description of the First Intellect, or First God (10.3–4), and next enumerates three ways of conceiving this First God (10.5–6). The chapter draws to a conclusion with a battery of arguments against corporealistic notions concerned with God (10.7–8), on which I shall not focus here.

The three ways of conceiving the First God (10;165.14–5 πρώτη ... νόησις; 165.17–8 δευτέρα ... νόησις; 165.24 τρίτη ... νόησις) are, respectively, the *via negationis*, the *via analogiae*, and the *via eminentiae*. Alkinoos' own term for the first of these ways is 'through abstraction' (165.15). It is illustrated by an example,[64] but there is an undeniable backward reference to the immediately preceding description of the First God (10.4, p. 165.4–14) by means of the withholding of several pairs of negated polar attributes (κατὰ ἀφαίρεσιν[65] τούτων). In other words, the *first* way of conceiving the First God pertains to the *last* part of Alkinoos' description, his famous negative theology. The second way (or *noēsis*) is illustrated by the example of the sun in relation to both sight and the things seen, which may be compared with the relation between the First Intellect and both the intelligizing activity of and the objects of thought in the (World)Soul (165.18 ff.). This corresponds with the first simile at 10.2 (164.21–2), where the relation between the First and the Second Intellect is described. It also occurs in the description of God at 10.3 (164.34–5): God is Truth because he is the source of all truth, as the sun is of all light; what follows (164.35–165.4) emphasizes the relation between the First God as 'Father' on the one hand and the Second Intellect, the World-Soul, and (by proxy) the world, on the other.

The third way (or *noēsis*) is illustrated by the method according to which one arrives at the notion of the supremely Good-and-Beautiful (165.24 ff., καλὸν and ἀγαθόν). Both these terms occur at the beginning of the description of God in 10.3. At 164.24 ff., it is argued that the First Intellect is κάλλιστος. That the First God is καλὸν is further explained 164.33 ff. That the First God is ἀγαθὸν is stated 164.30 and then explained 164.32–3.

---

[63] ὡς τὸ ὀρεκτὸν κινεῖ τὴν ὄρεξιν, ἀκίνητον ὑπάρχον.

[64] Cf. Whittaker, Neopythagoreanism ... (*supra*, n. 18). The reason why Alkinoos' illustration remains incomplete, i.e. does not go back beyond the mathematical point toward the One, is without doubt the fact that his First God is an Intellect, not a *Hen* (cf. also *infra*, n. 78). See further next n.

[65] Actually, the process of *aphairesis* (as appears from Alkinoos' illustration and from parallels such as Clem., *Strom.* V xi 71.2–3, where moreover the term is δι' ἀναλύσεως) is not necessarily concerned with the withholding of polar pairs of attributes. For clarity's sake, one should not put these different applications on a par; with this proviso, the parallels cited by Lilla, *op. cit.* (*supra*, n. 1), 221, may be adduced for comparison.

However, the description in 10.3 also anticipates the first *noēsis*, or *via negationis*, which as will be recalled is set out at some length in 10.4. For at 164.28 God, among other things, is called ἄρρητος. The first phrase of the negative theology (10.4;165.4–5) contains an undeniable backward reference to this (in its context unexpected) attribute: ἄρρητος δ᾿ ἐστὶ καὶ τῷ νῷ μόνῳ ληπτός, ὡς εἴρηται.

Clearly, in the description in 10.3 (164.24–165.4) notions conceived by means of each of the three distinct ways (*noēseis*) outlined in 10.5–6 (165.14–30) have been jumbled together. Actually, this appears to have been Alkinoos' explicit aim, for he declares (164.30–1): 'I present these qualifications not with the intention of separating them, but on the assumption that the object of thought they all relate to is one.'[66] Applying the principle of charity, I assume that Alkinoos, although presenting material that was the common property of a plurality of Middle Platonist traditions, knew what he was doing, and that the little chaos scholars have believed his theology to be[67] is merely apparent. The description of the three recipes for cognizing the divine is not there as an afterthought or a sort of obligatory item that has been inserted at random. Rather, the three ways have been made use of in the systematical theology itself, and their explicit distinction and description furthers the understanding of this systematical theology. The structure of the part of the chapter subsequent to the introduction is: (*a*) *Did.* 10.3–4, correct theology; (*b*) 10.5–6, justification of the correct theology by reference to the three modes of cognition; (*c*) 10.7–8, false theology.

Up to now, I have been talking of the three ways as 'first', 'second', 'third', as if Alkinoos had simply been listing them in an irrelevant numerical sequence. But as we have noted, the 'first' way to be enumerated is anticipated (by means of the epithet ἄρρητος) *after* themes linked up with the 'second' and 'third' ways have already been touched upon, and it is, moreover, the *last* to be applied in extenso in the descriptive section at 10.3–4. My assumption is that it comes last in the order of application because it is the most difficult and abstruse of the three, and so is *first in order of importance*. In other words, πρώτη should be understood as 'most important,' δευτέρα as 'second-best', and τρίτη as 'third-best'.[68] The first way clearly is the most abstract, the third being the most concrete; presumably, one may also recall Aristotle's well-known distinction between what is 'first according to nature' and so 'last in

---

[66] λέγω δὲ οὐχ ὡς χωρίζων ταῦτα, ἀλλ᾿ ὡς κατὰ πάντα ἑνὸς νοουμένου. Cf. the parallel in Clement quoted *infra*, 115.

[67] Cf. Festugière, *op. cit.* (*supra*, n. 1), 177 ff.; Dillon, *op. cit.* (*supra*, n. 13), who however prudently says: "certainly a jumble, but not entirely an incoherent one;" Donini, *op. cit.* (*supra*, n. 1), who speaks of "incongruenze".

[68] Of course, 'First' and (implied) 'Second' as predicated of Alkinoos' Gods pertain to an order of importance as well.

relation to ourselves' and what is 'last according to nature' and so 'first in relation to ourselves.' Following Alkinoos' first way, or applying his first or most
important cognitive mode, one withholds all the attributes that may be arranged in polar pairs. Applying the third mode, one predicates the positive
among those polar attributes in the most eminent way. Applying the second
mode, one is more positive and concrete than when applying the first but less
positive and concrete than when applying the third, for the notions one arrives
at express other-directed causal relations, not owned eminence.

Precedent for this interpretation is to be found in that of Eudorus' distinction between two 'modes' (tropoi), or 'accounts' (logoi), one of which, as I
have argued, is the 'highest' and the other the 'second-best' explanation.[69] I
have suggested above that to Eudorus these two modes are related and compatible, although not equivalent. Alkinoos goes farther. On the one hand, his
system is more refined than Eudorus' in that the via negationis and analogiae,
which in Eudorus 'highest' mode have not been separated from one another
(the Hen beyond the opposites being simultaneously the cause of all things),
are now being explicitly distinguished. This shows that Eudorus' analysis has
been further refined in the course of the one or two centuries that separate him
from Alkinoos. On the other hand, Eudorus' description of Pythagoreanism
avoids a commingling of the epithets belonging to each of his two modes. It
is only in the account of Xenophanes I have posited for him, in which the positive theology of the doxographical vulgate and Theophrastus' non liquet (creatively misunderstood) were combined, that such a blend of attributes is to be
found. In Alkinoos' descriptive theology, this mixture, which has puzzled the
learned,[70] is taken for granted. In view of the fact that (as is clear from
MXG's critique of Xenophanes' theology and from Simplicius justification
thereof)[71] such a mixture could be the target of criticism, Alkinoos—and
other Middle Platonists—must have had an argument to ward off the attack.
This, I wish to insist, was the argument of the alternative modes of cognition,
compatible albeit of unequal value, which suffices to explain the combination
of attributes and qualifications which to us (and to ancient scholars such as the
author of MXG) appear mutually exclusive.

For instance, according to Alkinoos' 'first', or 'most important,' mode of
cognition, viz. the negative theology, God is 'neither good nor bad nor indif-
ferent' (165.6−9), whereas according to the 'third-best' mode he is 'the Good
itself' (165.27) and indeed, in the descriptive section, is said to be 'good'
(164.30−3). In one and the same breath, Alkinoos allows himself to say that
God is 'eternal, ineffable, self-perfect i.e. needing nothing, ever-perfect i.e.

---

[69] Cf. supra, 106.
[70] Cf. supra, n. 1, and text thereto.
[71] Cf. supra, 93, 94 f.

always perfect, wholly-perfect i.e. everywhere perfect, Godness, Beingness, Truth, Symmetry, Good' (164.27–30), whereas to us the epithet 'ineffable' conflicts with all the others. In a similar way, the First Intellect, or First God, which according to the *via analogiae* is an *Un*moved *Mover* (164.21 ἀκίνητος, 164.22–3 κινεῖ ..., ἀκίνητον ὑπάρχον[72]), is described as being 'neither a cause of motion nor itself in motion' according to the negative theology (165.14, οὔτε κινεῖ οὔτε κινεῖται).[73] The contradiction *we* feel to be there need not be denied, or glossed over,[74] but can be explained both historically and systematically on the assumption that both descriptions, although of *different* value, are equally *valid*, and complement one another. Alkinoos is most conscientious in informing us about the three modes of cognition; other surviving Middle Platonist authors seem to take them for granted and provide us with a clutter of epithets without being very clear about the justification for their procedure, although hints are occasionally provided.

Among Alkinoos' positive qualifications according to the *via eminentiae* there are several which in my opinion are reverberations of a doxographical attribute of Xenophanes' God. viz. 'spherical'.[75] First, one of the epithets of his First God is 'Symmetry' (164.30), linked up with the attribute 'beautiful' by means of the explanation of the latter at 164.33–4: καλὸν δέ, ὅτι αὐτὸς τῇ ἑαυτοῦ φύσει τέλεόν ἐστὶ καὶ σύμμετρον. Furthermore, the epithet 'wholly-perfect' is explained as 'everywhere perfect,' 164.29: παντελὴς τουτέστι πάντη τέλειος. The notion of symmetry suggests that of *shape*, and 'perfect everywhere' or 'in every direction' (πάντη) strongly suggests that the symmetrical shape at issue is spherical. By focusing on what, from a theoretical point of view, is characteristic of the sphere as the most perfect shape and avoiding to speak of the figure itself, Alkinoos (or rather the tradition he is following) is able to keep an image at bay which perhaps too immediately would imply that God has parts [an idea which is refuted in the section dealing with the false theology, 165.30 ff. What is false cannot be reconciled with the theology according to the correct modes]. One cannot help thinking of the cat's smile in *Alice in Wonderland*. In an entirely similar way, as we have noticed,[76] Simplicius manages to desphericalize the sphere of Xenophanes (attributed by the doxographical vulgate and endorsed by Alexander of Aphrodisias as quoted by Simplicius) by explaining 'spherical' as 'everywhere (πανταχόθεν)

---

[72] Cf. also, in the final section of ch. 10, the account at 165.33 ff.

[73] Whittaker, Philological Comments ... (*supra*, n. 14), 158, points out that this is "a not unimportant revision of the argument at *Parm.* 139b3 that οὔτε ἔστηκεν οὔτε κινεῖται" (cf. *infra*, text to n. 77). A revision that is linked up with the aristotelian colouring of the First Principle.

[74] As is done by Invernizzi, *op. cit.* (*supra*, n. 2), 82.

[75] One may of course also think of occasional descriptions of the Stoic God (cf. *SVF* II p. 312.5.11), but the Early Middle Platonist account at D.L. III 72 provides a better parallel.

[76] *Supra*, 94.

homogeneous.' One may object that Alkinoos' would have to avoid even the slightest hint that God has some sort of shape because according to *Did.* 6; 159.3, whatever has shape possesses a quality,[77] whereas according to the negative theology (10;165.9–11) God is οὔτε ποιόν· . . . οὔτε ἄποιον. But this ensuing contradiction could have been resolved by appeal to the alternative and complementary ways of cognizing God.

Although Alkinoos' οὔτε κινεῖ οὔτε κινεῖται (p. 165.14) is by no means identical[78] with Plato's negation of motion and rest in respect of the 'One that is one' (*Parm.* 138a–139b), the negative theology of *Did.* 10.4 has been cogently linked with the spirit of the 1st hypothesis of Plato's dialogue.[79] However, I feel confident that Eudorus' contribution is even more tangible. The Eudorean schema of alternative and complementary approaches could be used to accomodate notions of various provenance, such as those of the theology of Arist., *Met.* Λ, or the epithets αὐτοτελὴς ἀειτελὴς παντελὴς for which Dillon has plausibly claimed a (Neo-)Pythagorean origin.[80] Yet the adage "qui trop embrasse mal étreint" cannot, as it would seem, be applied to Alkinoos. It would even seem that the annexation of Aristotle's First Unmoved *Cogitating* Mover rendered indiscernable any trace of Xenophanes' Cogitating God, or rather that the latter as reinterpreted by Eudorus provided a perfect pigeonhole for the overwhelming introduction of the former.

6. We may now turn to some passages in Irenaeus' *Adversus haereses*, composed ca. 185 CE, in which echoes of Xenophanes have been detected by scholars.[81]

At *Adv. haer.* I 12.2, a passage surviving in Greek, the 'Lord of all things' is in almost hymnical language described as follows:

> . . . ὅλος ἔννοια ὤν, [. . .], ὅλος νοῦς, ὅλος φῶς, ὅλος ὀφθαλμός, ὅλος ἀκοή, ὅλος πηγὴ πάντων τῶν ἀγαθῶν.

In ways both more and less extensive, this description recurs at II 13.3, 13.8, 28.4–5, and IV 11.2. We may quote part of II 13.3.66 ff., of which only the Latin translation survives:

---

[77] τὸ μετέχον σχήματος ποιόν ἐστι.

[78] Cf. *supra*, n. 72.

[79] See *supra*, n. 14, and cf. further the notes *ad loc.* in Invernizzi, *op. cit.* (*supra*, n. 2), vol. II: *Traduzione e commento del Didaskalikos*; Dillon, *op. cit.* (*supra*, n. 13), 284 f.; and esp. Whittaker, Philological Comments . . . (*supra*, n. 14), 156 ff., who, adducing Clem., *Strom.* V xii 81.5 f., proves that both this passage and *Did.* 165.4 ff. ultimately depend on the 1st hypothesis of *Parm.* But there are also important differences between these two texts (Whittaker, *ibid.*, 158 f.). Furthermore, nothing in *Did.* corresponds with *Strom.* V xii 81.6; again, Alkinoos (or the tradition he is following) avoids the One (cf. *supra*, n. 64).

[80] Dillon, *op. cit.* (*supra*, n. 13), 283. For αὐτοτελὴς see Thesleff, *PT* (*supra*, n. 37), pp. 52.13, 94.16 f., 127.13 f., 128.1.6.

[81] See *supra*, n. 59 (Grant, Schoedel).

... et simplex et non compositus et similimembrius et totus ipse sibimetipsi similis et aequalis est, totus cum sit sensus et totus spiritus [...] et totus auditus et totus oculus, etc.

The echo of Xenophanes, *Vorsokr.* 21 B 24[82], is undeniable.[83] As to the further attributes of the divine in these two passages (and in the equivalent texts in Irenaeus I have not transcribed), I trust it will not be necessary to provide a detailed list of parallels in the Xenophanes doxography and in Alkinoos. The Middle Platonist antecedents of Irenaeus' positive theology are manifest. In the context of the argument of the present paper the presence of a crypto-quotation of Xenophanes in this christianized Middle Platonist positive theology is of substantial importance. The more so, because without doubt Irenaeus was not aware of his debt to Xenophanes; the allusion has only been detected by the acumen of scholars.

But this is not all. At II 13.3, immediately after the Latin passage quoted above, Irenaeus argues that it is allowed that pious people speak of God in this (positively descriptive) way: *quemadmodum adest religiosis ac piis dicere de Deo*. For, he continues, there is also another way, according to which God 'is beyond these attributes and therefore ineffable' (*est autem et super haec, et propter hoc inenarrabilis*, II 13.4). God's Intellect and Light are totally different from those of man (*non similis hominum sensui; nihil simile ei quod est secundum nos lumini*). This latter point obviously echoes Xenophanes, *Vorsokr.* 21 B 23: 'one God, the absolutely greatest, neither in form similar to

---

[82] οὖλος ὁρᾷ, οὖλος δὲ νοεῖ, οὖλος δέ τ᾽ ἀκούει.

[83] A. Rousseau, in: *Irénée de Lyon: Contre les Hérésies, Livre II* t. 1, SC 293, Paris 1982, 240 ff., argues that because of the nouns (in Xenophanes, one has verbs) I Cor 12:18−20 may be more important in this context than *Vorsokr.* 21 B 24. However, Grant, *After the N.T.* (*supra*, n. 59), 104, already pointed out that passages such as Plin., *NH* II 14, *quisquis est deus, [...], totus est sensus, totus visus, totus auditus, totus animae, totus animi, totus sui*, echo Xenophanes "in nominal form." The Pliny passage is discussed by W. Theiler, *Die Vorbereitung des Neuplatonismus*, Berlin 1934, repr. Berlin—Zürich 1964, 82 ff., who suggests that Posidonius is the source and compares the whole context in Pliny to the Xenophanes doxography, referring to interesting parallels in Procl., *In Tim.* II, pp. 83.23 ff., 84.6 ff. (too long to quote). But *infinitus ac finito similis* (*NH* II.1, said of the *mundus*) is not to be compared with οὔτε ἄπειρον οὔτε πεπερασμένον (Theiler, *ibid.*, 84).
A remote influence (perhaps already upon Xenophanes himself) of two epic lines cannot be excluded: *Il.* Γ 277 ‿ *Od.* Λ 109 (also elsewhere in Homer), Ἥλιος θ᾽ ὃς πάντ᾽ ἐφορᾷς καὶ πάντ᾽ ἐπακούεις—verbal forms, and Hes., *Op.* 267, πάντα ἰδὼν Διὸς ὀφθαλμὸς καὶ πάντα νοήσας—verbal forms and a noun. On the second line, see the very informative note of M.L. West, *Hesiod: Works and Days*, Oxford 1978, 223 ff. N. Zeegers-Vandervorst, *Les citations des poètes grecs chez les Apologistes chrétiens du IIe siècle*, Univ. de Louvain, Rec. trav. hist. philol., 4e Série, Fasc. 47, Louvain 1972, 256, refers to the Homeric line a propos Theoph. *Ad Autol.* II 3, p. 24.25 Grant (printer's error: Zeegers-Vandervorst cites *Ad Autol.* II 30). Both lines together are quoted Macr., *Sat.* I 23.9, who presumably depends on Porphyry (see J. Flamant, *Macrobe et le Néo-platonisme latin à la fin du IVe siècle*, EPRO 58, Leiden 1977, 655 ff.), and at *Scholia in Aratum vetera* ed. J. Martin, Stuttgart 1974, p. 42.15−7 (cf. *ibid.*, p. 49.23 f. for *Op.* 267, and p. 50.8 f. for *Il.* Γ 277). I cannot pursue this question here.

humans nor in thought,'[84] a further echo of which may be discovered in the remark that God is beyond all such positive qualifications because of his greatness (*super haec secundum magnitudinem*—cf. B 23.2 μέγιστος). But the positive approach *rectissime dicitur*.

In a similar manner, Irenaeus argues that whoever [in the Xenophanean way] qualifies God as 'entirely vision and entirely hearing' *non peccat* but remains on a lower level of understanding: *minus quidem adhuc de Patre omnium sentiet* (II 13.8.171 ff.).

According to Irenaeus, therefore, the *via eminentiae*, although perfectly proper and acceptable, is inferior to the *via negationis*. Like Eudorus and, in part, Alkinoos (who has three 'modes of cognition'), he distinguishes between two forms of approaching God in a cognitive way. In this way, the *via analogiae* seems to have been combined with both others, so to speak, because according to Irenaeus' version of the *via eminentiae* God is the 'source of all good things,' and according to his *via negationis* the 'Father of all things,' i.e. a causal principle; or rather, what in Alkinoos constitutes the 'second-best' mode has not yet, in Irenaeus, been distinguished (or is no longer distinguished) from the 'most important' and the 'third-best' modes. We may safely assume that this theological epistemology is of Middle Platonist provenance,[85] and reflects a system that is somewhat cruder, so perhaps earlier, than Alkinoos'. The presence, in Irenaeus, both of unmistakable Xenophanean reminiscencies and of alternative but compatible ways of cognition of the divine corroborates the hypothesis argued in this paper, viz. the pivotal importance one should award to the reinterpretive tradition which incorporated the various strands of the Xenophanes doxography into a larger synthesis which also accommodated Pythagoreanism, Platonism, and, subsequently, Aristotelianism.

Finally, although here no verbal reminiscencies of Xenophanes are to be found, we may also adduce Clement of Alexandria, *Strom.* V xii 81.4–82.4. Whittaker has proved that the negative theology at 81.5–6 is a very close parallel to that at Alkinoos, *Did.* 10, p. 165.4 ff.[86] But one should also take the sequel in Clement into account. According to the negative theology, God

---

[84] εἷς θεὸς ἔν τε θεοῖσι καὶ ἀνθρώποισι μέγιστος,/ οὔτι δέμας θνητοῖσιν ὁμοίιος οὐδὲ νόημα.

[85] A.H. Armstrong/R.A. Markus, *Christian Faith and Greek Philosophy*, London 1960, 9 and n. 2, point out that Christians adopted the philosophical negative theology but "could not, ... and did not want to deny that the positive language of Scripture was a proper way, and the best possible human way, of speaking about God, but insisted that like all human language it was symbolical or analogical ...." But in my view the positive language of Scripture could be accommodated or at any rate defended against philosophical and other critics of Christian theology precisely because such a "human way of speaking about God" had been justified by the pagan philosophers themselves.

[86] Cf. *supra*, n. 79, and see further *infra*, n. 89.

is ἀνωνόμαστον.[87] But there is also an inferior, 'less proper' (οὐ κυρίως) way of knowing God,[88] 82.1–2:

[1] [. . .] κἂν ὀνομάζωμεν αὐτό ποτε, οὐ κυρίως καλοῦντες ἤτοι ἓν ἢ τἀγαθὸν ἢ αὐτὸ τὸ ὂν ἢ πατέρα ἢ θεὸν ἢ δημιουργὸν ἢ κύριον, οὐχ ὡς ὄνομα αὐτοῦ προφερόμενοι λέγομεν, ὑπὸ δὲ ἀπορίας ὀνόμασι καλοῖς προσχρώμεθα, ἵν᾽ ἔχῃ ἡ διάνοια, μὴ περὶ ἄλλα πλανωμένη, ἐπερείδεσθαι τούτοις.
[2] οὐ γὰρ τὸ καθ᾽ ἕκαστον μηνυτικὸν τοῦ θεοῦ, ἀλλὰ ἀθρόως ἅπαντα ἐνδεικτικὰ τῆς τοῦ παντοκράτορος δυνάμεως.

Note that Clement conflates, or rather does not distinguish, the *via analogiae* (e.g., 'Father') and the *via eminentiae* (e.g., 'good'). Otherwise, his epistemology as concerned with the divine is the same as that of Irenaeus and Alkinoos (but for the latter's finer distinction of three modes, again). The attributes to be found in his positive theology can be largely paralleled from Alkinoos and Irenaeus. But there is even more.[89] We have noticed above[90] that Alkinoos, 164.30–1, explicitly stated that he did not use the many attributes and names of the First God with the intention to distinguish them from one another, but did so with the proviso that the *object of thought denoted by all of them is identical*. Clement, as we now see, makes exactly the same point (81.2): 'for it is not the case that the individual appellation is revealing as to God; rather, they refer to the power of the Allmighty only *when all combined*' (my italics). This important parallel appears to have been overlooked by scholars. Clement clearly is familiar with the Middle Platonist argument in favour of a (to us) indiscriminate listing of names and attributes resulting in apparent contradiction, an argument also stated by Alkinoos. However, he does not proceed as far as Alkinoos, who even lists 'ineffable' among the attributes that have to be amalgamated.[91]

---

[87] For Middle Platonist and other parallels see Lilla, *op. cit.* (*supra*, n. 1), 220 f., and A. le Boulluec, *Clément d'Alexandrie. Les Stromates. Stromate V* t. II, *Commentaire*, SC 279, Paris 1981, 265.

[88] For a less explicit parallel in Max. Tyr. (*Or.* II 10; 28.12 ff. H.) partial parallels in Just. (*Apol. II* 6.1–4) and Theophil. (*Ad Autol.* I 3; 4.19–6.9 Grant, where the feasability of speaking about God in both ways is taken for granted), and other partial parallels see le Boulluec, *op. cit.* (*supra*, n. 87), 265 f., whose collection however, is not complete and whose analysis not sufficiently pertinent.

[89] For the very close parallel between 81.5 and *Did.* 165.5 ff. see O. Stählin/L. Früchtel/U. Treu (eds.), *Clemens Alexandrinus, 2. Bd, Stromata Buch I–VI*, GCS, Berlin ⁴1985, 535, addend. to p. 380.18–20, with reference to L. Früchtel, Clemens Alexandrinus und Albinus, *Ph. W.* 57 (1937) 591 f. However, rather than arguing that "die hier genannten Kategorien wörtlich aus Albinus stammen" (so Stählin/Früchtel/Treu) I would postulate a common source, or rather a common tradition, cf. Früchtel, *op. cit.* 592: "eine Verwandtschaft mindestens der Quellen beider [*sc.*, of Clement and Alkinoos] (ist) unverkennbar."

[90] *Supra*, 109.

[91] The parallels for the two 'modes' and their explicit distinction in Philo of Alexandria, excellently discussed by Runia (*supra*, n. 18), who has also noticed the parallel in Clement, and mentioned by Dillon, The Knowledge of God in Origen, this volume, 219 ff., should also be taken

7. The blend of positive and negative theology of a 'Xenophanean' stamp I have studied so far can be paralleled in Gnostic writings that have been clearly influenced by Middle Platonism.[92] In *Eugnostos the Blessed*, presumably composed at Alexandria in the 1st–2nd cent. CE,[93] the *ineffable* God is described (III 3.72.3–13) as a sphere (!) in rather veiled language that recalls Alkinoos' words about perfectly beautiful divine symmetry,[94] and as being 'all Mind' (73.9).[95] Even more interesting is a passage in the shorter version of the *Apocryphon of John* (*BG* 22.17–25.22), also a treatise which has connections with Alexandria and which should be dated, presumably, to the later 2nd cent. CE.[96] In a pythagoreanizing way,[97] God is here said to be a Monad which is a holy Spirit,[98] and in the rather full section containing a description according to the *via negationis* he is said, among other things (such as 'neither corporeal nor incorporeal, neither great nor small'), to be 'neither unlimited nor limited,'[99] the Greek word ἄπειρον being preserved in the Coptic text! I venture to add *Allogenes*, XI 3.63.1–4: 'he is neither boundless, nor bounded by another.'[100] The shorter *Apocryphon* and *Allogenes* have preserved a pair of

---

into account. Both these scholars argue that Philo did not invent the distinction. I should point out that the Philonic parallels further support the argument of the present paper that behind all this we have to assume the influence of Eudorus.

[92] One of the merits of Lilla's collection of parallels (see *supra*, n. 1) is that it includes Gnostic material.

[93] See now R. van den Broek, 'Jewish and Platonic Speculations in Early Alexandrian Theology: Eugnostus, Philo, Valentinus, and Origen,' in: B.A. Pearson/J.E. Goehring (eds.), *The Roots of Egyptian Christianity*, Studies in Antiquity and Christianity, Philadelphia 1986, 190 ff. He pointed out to me the passage cited in the text when he had read an earlier version of the present paper.

[94] Cf. *supra*, 111.

[95] Transl. in: J.M. Robinson (ed.), *The Nag Hammadi Library in English*, Leiden 1977, 209 f.; see van den Broek, this volume, *infra* 211 ff.

[96] See now R. van den Broek, *De taal van de Gnosis: Gnostische teksten uit Nag Hammadi*, Baarn 1986, 22 ff., transl. 38 ff. I owe this parallel (and its translation from the Coptic) to him as well.

[97] Cf. *supra*, 101 f.

[98] See W.C. Till/M.H. Schenke, *Die gnostischen Schriften des koptischen Papyrus Berolinensis 8502*, Berlin 1955, ²1972, 85 ff.

[99] This text is also quoted by Whittaker, Philological Comments ... (*supra*, n. 14), 166, who has not seen its full significance, and (without 'neither unlimited nor limited') by Lilla, *op. cit.* (*supra*, n. 1), 216, who puts it into the wrong context. In the descriptive theology in the longer version of the *Apocryphon*, which is virtually identical with that of the shorter version, this negated polar pair is missing, possibly by accident (for the translation see Robinson [*supra*, n. 95], 100, II 1.3.14 ff.). For 'neither unlimited nor limited' in *MXG* and Simplicius see *supra*, 92, 93 f.

[100] Translation: Robinson (*supra*, n. 95), 450. For 'not bounded by another' cf. *Apocr. John*, long version, II 1.3.7. ff. (I quote from Robinson, 100): 'He is [illimitable] because there is no one [prior to him to] limit him' ~ short version, *BG* 23.10 f.: 'He cannot be limited, because there was no one prior to him to limit him.' Note that, in at least the shorter version, the supreme God is both 'neither unlimited nor limited' and 'unlimited' (compatibility depending on mode of presentation again). The formula 'not bounded by another' in *Allogenes* is remarkably close to

negated polar attributes which is not found in the negative theology of Alkinoos or, to the best of my knowledge, in any other extant Middle Platonist,
although the polar attributes 'limit' and 'unlimited' are an important feature
of Eudorus' (and Aristotle's) Pythagorean[101] *systoichia*. We have, or so I
believe, sufficiently taken into account that in the doxography of Theophrastus
as well as in the accounts in Simplicius and *MXG* which (through Eudorus, as
I believe) have been influenced by Theophrastus' *non liquet*, this negated
polar pair is most prominent. Given the overall Middle Platonist theological
context in which the expression occurs in the above Gnostic sources, one may
safely submit that the authors of these tracts lifted this formula (together with
the context itself) from the standard Middle Platonist literature at their disposal which naturally they adapted to suit their convenience but still followed
very closely. That they took it from professional philosophical works, such as
Theophrastus' account of the *archai* of the pre-aristotelian philosophers or ps.-
Aristotle's *MXG*, may be discounted.

MXG 1 (the Melissus section), 974a11 f., εἰ γὰρ δύο ἢ πλείω εἴη, πέρατ' ἂν εἶναι ταῦτα πρὸς
ἄλληλα, and 3 (the Xenophanes section), 977b6 ff., περαίνειν δὲ πρὸς ἄλληλα, εἰ πλείω εἴη. [...]
ἓν γὰρ οὐχ ἔχει πρὸς ὅτι περανεῖ.
[101] See *supra*, 95, 97 f.

LA CONNAISSANCE DE DIEU ET LA HIÉRARCHIE DIVINE CHEZ ALBINOS

PAR

Pierluigi Donini (Torino)

L'interprétation de la théologie du *Didaskalikos* que je vais exposer* repose sur certaines prémisses qu'il faut que j'explique tout d'abord.[1] A mon avis ce traité parle au moins de deux divinités que j'appellerai respectivement le premier et le second dieu: la première expression est employée couramment par Albinos lui-même, la seconde n'apparaît pas dans ses pages, mais puisqu'elle est commode et familière aux spécialistes du moyen platonisme je prendrai la liberté d'en faire usage; par cette expression, j'entends indiquer ce qu'Albinos appelle dans la plupart des cas l'intellect du ciel ou l'intellect de l'âme du monde, mais une fois également «le dieu céleste».[2] Je ne crois pas cependant qu'il soit nécessaire, aux fins de ma discussion, de m'engager d'une façon trop nette sur le fameux problème soulevé par Loenen[3] à propos de la distinction effective entre l'intellect céleste et l'âme du monde. Que le «second dieu» soit uniquement l'intellect cosmique ou bien qu'il soit l'âme du monde avec son intellect, m'est indifférent.

Le premier problème que je voudrais examiner est bien connu aux lecteurs

---

* Je dois remercier ici Michelangelo Giusta qui, tout en sachant que mes vues au sujet du *Didaskalikos* n'étaient pas identiques aux siennes, a bien voulu mettre à ma disposition le texte dactylographié de son dernier travail et a discuté avec moi plusieurs passages du texte.

[1] Bien que je crois que M. Giusta, Ἀλβίνου Ἐπιτομή ὁ Ἀλκινόου Διδασκαλικός?, *Atti dell' Accademia delle Scienze di Torino* 95 (1960–61) 167–194, et J. Whittaker, Parisinus graecus 1962 and the Writings of Albinus, *Phoenix* 28 (1974) 320–54, 450–56, ont raison quand ils refusent l'attribution traditionnelle de l'œuvre au platonicien Albinos, élève de Gaius, et que, comme les manuscrits l'affirment, l'auteur est au contraire un certain Alkinoos, qui est d'ailleurs inconnu, dans mon exposition je continuerai toutefois à parler d'Albinos parce qu'il est pratique d'employer le nom largement connu de tous.—Les objections adressées à Giusta et à Whittaker par C. Mazzarelli, L'autore del Didaskalikos. L'Alcinoo dei manoscritti o il medioplatonico Albino?, *RFNS* 72 (1980) 603–39, sont très faibles. M. Giusta les infirme sans peine dans son dernier travail Due capitoli sui dossografi di fisica, dans le recueil *Storiografia e dossografia nella filosofia antica*, a cura di G. Cambiano, Torino 1986, 171–178.

[2] «L'intellect du ciel tout entier» 164,20.24 et cf. 36; «l'intellect de l'âme du monde» 165,2; 169,32; «le dieu céleste» 181,36. Avec J.H. Loenen, Albinus' Metaphysics: An Attempt at Rehabilitation, *Mnem.* S.IV, 9 (1956) 296–319, et 10 (1957) 35–56, je suppose que toutes ces expressions indiquent la même figure divine (voir Loenen, 310).

[3] Dans le travail cité ci-dessus, n. 2. Voir aussi H.J. Krämer, *Der Ursprung der Geistmetaphysik*, Amsterdam 1964, 101 ss. et J. Mansfeld, Three Notes on Albinus, *Theta-Pi* 1 (1971) 61 ss. *Contra*, J. Dillon, *The Middle Platonists*, London 1977, 284.

d'Albinos. On déclare plusieurs fois dans le texte que le premier dieu est *arrē-tos*, «ineffable» (trois fois au chapitre X, le plus important pour la théologie: 164,7. 28; 165,4); malgré cela, dans ce même chapitre, de nombreux attributs qui semblent en quelque sorte le définir, ou au moins le décrire, lui sont assignés. Au cours des études, à partir du vieux travail de Freudenthal,[4] en passant par Festugière[5] et surtout par Wolfson,[6] on a élaboré une explication qu'Invernizzi[7] a exposé récemment d'une manière complète dans son commentaire: d'après cette théorie, les attributs que le *Didaskalikos* confère au dieu suprême ne visent pas à définir l'essence de la divinité—en effet celle-ci est vraiment inexprimable et elle ne saurait être conçue qu'à travers la *via negationis*, c'est-à-dire en enlevant au dieu tout prédicat, comme l'auteur l'a fait justement à la p. 165,5 ss. Mais, puisque le dieu exerce une causalité et une activité sur le cosmos; puisqu'il y a dans le monde des œuvres et des activités qui dépendent de lui, les attributs du dieu servent donc tout simplement à décrire son rapport avec le cosmos, la dépendance de ce monde de lui comme de sa cause. Ces attributs peuvent être tirés en outre des deux autres voies conduisant à la connaissance du dieu que le chap. X adjoint à la *via negationis*: la *via analogiae* et la *via eminentiae*.

Je considère cette explication tout à fait inacceptable, pas tellement parce que je ne trouve pas dans le texte la trace d'une distinction explicite entre l'essence ineffable du dieu et les activités descriptibles: j'admets en effet qu'une telle distinction pourrait être simplement supposée sans être expliquée dans un manuel de caractère introductif comme le nôtre. Mais je n'accepte pas cette explication parce que je trouve que trop de données du texte la contredisent—en réalité, presque tout ce qu'on lit dans le texte, particulièrement au chapitre X.

Je traiterai tout d'abord de la deuxième partie de la thèse de Wolfson et d'Invernizzi, qui est la plus facile à réfuter. Il est vrai, évidemment, qu'on pourrait dégager des attributs positifs de la divinité des voies *analogiae* et *eminentiae*; cependant il n'est pas moins évident, je crois, que ce n'est pas le cas du *Didaskalikos*, vu la façon dont l'auteur expose les choses. En effet, si on commence par dire, comme le fait Albinos: «le dieu est ineffable et concevable par le *noûs* seulement» (165,4), pour continuer à dire ensuite, une fois la *via negationis* exposée, «voici donc la première voie pour s'en former une *noēsis*» (165,15) et puis, en annonçant les deux autres voies, «voici la deuxième forme de la *noēsis*» (165,18), «voilà la troisième forme de la *noēsis*» (165,24); il me semble absolument évident que toutes les trois voies ne sont ici en relation

[4] J. Freudenthal, *Der Platoniker Albinos und der falsche Alkinoos*, Berlin 1879, (*Hellenistische Studien*, 3), 286 s.
[5] A.J. Festugière, *La révélation d'Hermès Trismégiste*, IV: *Le dieu inconnu et la gnose*, Paris 1954, 137 s.
[6] H.A. Wolfson, Albinus and Plotinus on Divine Attributes, *HThR* 45 (1952) 115–130.
[7] G. Invernizzi, *Il Didaskalikos di Albino e il medioplatonismo*, Roma 1976.

qu'avec le caractère ineffable, indescriptible et inexprimable de la divinité. Le texte même empêche donc de penser que pour Albinos les voies *analogiae* et *eminentiae* ont une destination différente de la première, la *via negationis*, clairement présentée afin de rendre en quelque sorte concevable un dieu qui a été défini ineffable. Je remarque, en passant, que chez Celse la situation est exactement la même[8]: or, si chez les deux auteurs les *trois* voies sont toutes en relation avec le caractère ineffable du dieu, il est impossible que *deux* d'entre elles visent à établir des prédicats du dieu qui est indefinissable.

Qu'on m'entende bien: je ne nie pas qu'antérieurement, lorsque ces attributs ont été établis pour la première fois dans le platonisme, ils peuvent avoir été établis précisément de cette façon là, c'est-à-dire, par les voies *analogiae* et *eminentiae*. C'est-là une chose possible, voire très probable, du moins pour certains d'entre eux: le texte même du *Didaskalikos* 165,17–24 montre que l'attribut de «vérité» pourrait très bien ressortir de la *via analogiae*. Mais, chez Celse et chez Albinos, et—on peut le supposer—chez la source de celui-ci, toutes les trois voies ont été réunies autour du concept d'un dieu indéfinissable: dès lors, les voies *analogiae* et *eminentiae* ne pouvaient plus viser à produire des prédicats, mais seulement à suggérer une intuition: cf. p. 165,28. Les prédicats, devenus traditionnels, détachés des procédés qui anciennement en expliquaient très bien l'origine, demeurent maintenant juxtaposés à la notion du dieu *arrētos*. Ajoutons que, comme l'avait vu Festugière,[9] les voies *analogiae* et *eminentiae* «mènent à une Cause et à une Excellence»: mais le dieu *arrētos* n'est plus (on le verra) à proprement parler une cause. En tant que capable de produire des prédicats qui ont une signification causale, une voie qui mènerait à la connaissance du dieu deviendrait ainsi tout à fait inutile.[10]

Venons-en maintenant au point le plus important, les attributs divins. J'ai déjà dit que ce ne serait ni grave ni décisif si le texte n'expliciterait pas la distinction entre l'essence ineffable et les attributs destinés (si vraiment ils le sont) à décrire l'influence et les activités du dieu sur le cosmos; de toute façon il s'agit, c'est bien connu,[11] d'une distinction diffusée dans les textes philosophiques et

---

[8] Voir Orig. C. *Celsum* VII 42: ἐπειδὴ δὲ τούτου χάριν ἐξηύρηται σοφοῖς ἀνδράσιν, ὡς ἄν τοῦ ἀκατονομάστου καὶ πρώτου λάβοιμέν τινα ἐπίνοιαν διαδηλοῦσαν αὐτὸν ἢ συνθέσει τῇ ἐπὶ τὰ ἄλλα, ἢ ἀναλύσει ἀπ' αὐτῶν, ἢ ἀναλογίᾳ, τὸ ἄλλως ἄρρητον θέλων διδάξαι θαυμάσαιμι δὲ ἂν εἰ ἀκολουθῆσαι δυνήσεσθε κτλ.

[9] *Op.l.*, 137.

[10] Ici je ne peux que remarquer brièvement qu'en reconnaissant l'unité du bloc des paragraphes 4–6 du chap. X au sujet du concept de l'ineffabilité du dieu suprême, on gagne la possibilité de résoudre un certain nombre de questions débattues à propos de la constitution et de l'agencement du texte. Un texte qui coule, à mon avis, avec une continuité acceptable jusqu'à la fin du § 6, p. 165,30; le passage suivant, par contre, n'est que mal accroché aux précédents et doit provenir soit d'une source différente de celle qui a été suivie jusque-là et qui nous est inconnue, soit d'un très mauvais travail d'abrégé de la même source. Les prédicats de ce passage n'ont rien à voir avec la *via negationis* du § 4.

[11] Voir le travail de Wolfson cité ci-dessus, n. 6, et R. van den Broek, Apuleius on the Nature

non philosophiques de l'époque du moyen platonisme et si grâce à elle tout tombait juste chez Albinos, nous serions simplement sages en acceptant de l'assumer comme la base de l'interprétation de cet auteur. Mais l'ennui c'est que, au contraire, dans le texte d'Albinos la grande majorité des données arrivent même à la contredire. Considérons donc directement les attributs que le texte assigne au premier dieu, en excluant cependant tout de suite la deuxième série d'entre eux (p. 165,30 ss.): «privé de parties», «immobile», «incorporel», qui personne en réalité n'a jamais sérieusement proposé de comprendre dans le sens causal.

Or, dans la série principale des attributs (au § 3; 164,28−35), le seul fait que l'ineffabilité même du dieu ait été citée avec les autres prédicats nous rend déjà suspecte une interprétation, comme celle de Wolfson et de Invernizzi, où les attributs énumérés devraient tous sans distinction se référer non à l'essence divine, mais à sa fonction causale par rapport au cosmos. De toute façon, il est vrai que *trois* parmi les *onze* attributs énumérés sans ordre dans le § 3 semblent être expliqués dans le sens causal: il s'agit de «bien», de «vérité» et de «père», dont je dirai ensuite quelque chose de plus précis. Mais, vu la présence de ces trois attributs, est-il juste d'induire comme le fait Invernizzi[12] que tous les autres aussi doivent être compris de la même façon? Il est même trop évident que ceci entraînerait une interprétation forcée du texte absolument intolérable et c'est pour cette raison qu'Invernizzi finit lui-même avec sagesse par passer complètement sous silence les attributs d'«éternel», de «proportion», de «divinité» et de «substantialité», en renonçant tout à fait à nous expliquer comment ils pourraient se référer non à l'essence du dieu, mais à son rapport causal avec le cosmos.

Pour trois autres attributs (*autotelēs*, équivalent à «sans besoins»; *aeitelēs*, «éternellement parfait»; *pantelēs*, «entièrement parfait»), même s'il reconnaît honnêtement[13] qu'une interprétation dans le sens causal est plutôt difficile, Invernizzi suggère toutefois que la signification pourrait être la suivante: «on peut dire que dieu est la plus grande perfection parce qu'il est la cause de toute perfection de l'univers», affirmation que nous ne pourrions accepter qu'en accomplissant un acte de foi envers la validité complexive de la théorie de la signification causale. Mais enfin, devant l'attribut «beau», même Invernizzi est obligé de reconnaître qu'«il semble se rapporter à l'essence du dieu»;[14] il

---

of God (*De Plat.*, 190−91), in: *Actus, Studies in Honour of H.L.W. Nelson*, Utrecht 1982, 57−72.

[12] *Op.l.* II 128, n. 32. Je dois discuter ici avant tout l'interprétation d'Invernizzi, puisqu'elle est la plus analytique, comme il est naturel que cela arrive dans un commentaire continu. Wolfson, tout en étant le vrai responsable de la théorie, se contente d'explications générales.

[13] *Op.l.*, I 76.

[14] *Op.l.*, II 128, n. 32.

suppose alors que le texte est altéré.[15] Il me semble qu'on puisse dire sans ex-
agérer qu'à l'épreuve des textes dans huit cas sur onze la théorie de Wolfson-
Invernizzi se révèle un échec.

Il reste trois prédicats pour lesquels l'explication causale se trouve effectivement écrite dans le texte: le premier dieu est «bien, parce qu'autant qu'il le peut
il répand ses bienfaits sur toutes choses en étant la cause de tout bien»; il est
«vérité, parce que principe de toute vérité comme le soleil de toute lumière»;
«père, parce qu'il est la cause de toute chose et parce qu'il met en ordre l'intellect du ciel et l'âme du monde etc». (164,32–36). Or mon intention n'est pas
pour le moment de préciser jusqu'à quel point et sur quels objets s'exercerait,
d'après ces trois prédicats, la fonction causale du premier dieu; j'admets pour
le moment qu'ils expriment une fonction causale. Toutefois, j'observe que
trois seuls prédicats exprimant une telle fonction sur huit qui l'excluent, c'est
vraiment peu: c'est si peu, qu'il me semble raisonnable, à ce point-ci, que nous
nous interrogeons sérieusement sur les limites et sur la consistance effective de
la prétendue fonction causale du premier dieu par rapport au cosmos. Est-ce
qu'une pareille fonction existe donc vraiment dans le *Didaskalikos*?

Aussitôt cette question posée, on s'aperçoit qu'il y a une contradiction
remarquable dans les études plus récentes. D'une part, on prétend que le dieu
suprême n'a dans le *Didaskalikos* qu'*une* fonction de la causalité—c'est-à-dire
la fonction de la causalité finale, propre à un dieu qui est issu du moteur immobile aristotélicien.[16] D'autre part, la grande majorité des spécialistes estime
toujours qu'Albinos enseigne que le premier dieu est aussi le démiurge.[17] En
faveur de cette identification du premier dieu avec le démiurge du *Timée* il y
a évidemment l'appellation de «père» qui revient à la page 164,35 citée plus
haut, tout comme la conviction très diffuse que Loenen[18] exprima un jour
sous forme dogmatique, à savoir que partout ailleurs où le texte parle simple-

---

[15] Il y a en effet quelque chose qui nous gêne dans l'édition de Hermann à la ligne 33, p. 164:
précisément la conjecture σχῆμα, du même Hermann. Voir l'édition de P. Louis, et Festugière,
op.l., 98 n. 4. Invernizzi était très probablement sous l'influence de la conjecture de Freudenthal,
op.l., 319 s. ὅτι αὐτὸς τῆς τοῦ ⟨καλοῦ⟩ φύσεως αἴτιον.

[16] On peut songer aux remarques de P. Moraux, *Der Aristotelismus bei den Griechen* II,
Berlin—New York 1984, 462 ss., ainsi qu'à Invernizzi, *op.l.*, I 72 s.

[17] A ce point-ci de mon exposé je dois écarter la question de l'interprétation non-littérale du
Timée que donne Albinos. Peut-être est-il vrai—comme on l'a dit quelques fois—qu'avec une
pareille interprétation il n'est aucunement besoin d'un démiurge et que tout ce qui concerne le
démiurge est, dès lors, du domaine du mythe (Festugière, *op.l.* II, *Le dieu cosmique*, Paris 1949,
149). Mais, puisqu'Albinos expose le mythe du démiurge et parle de celui-ci comme d'un dieu,
nous sommes de toute façon obligés de nous interroger au sujet de ce dieu qui est démiurge.—La
thèse de l'identité entre le démiurge et le premier dieu est partagée par Freudenthal, *op.l.*, 291; R.E.
Witt, *Albinus and the History of middle Platonism*, Cambridge 1937, 124–26; Festugière, *op.l.*,
II 149; C.J. De Vogel *Der sog. Mittelplatonismus, überwiegend eine Philosophie der Diesseitig-
keit?*, in: *Platonismus und Christentum, Festschr. H. Dörrie*, Münster 1983, 300; Moraux, *op.l.*,
461; et Giusta, *Due capitoli sui dossografi di fisica*, 185 s.

[18] *Op.l.*, 310: «for simple *theos* always means the *prōtos theos*».

ment de «dieu» (*theos, ho theos*), il s'agit alors toujours du premier dieu. Lorsqu'on a une pareille conviction en tête, le passage fondamental du chap. XII 1, p. 167,5 ss., qui décrit précisément la génération du cosmos, devient une preuve définitive de l'identité entre le premier dieu et le démiurge.[19] A cette interprétation toutefois je peux objecter immédiatement qu'elle ignore la deuxième partie de l'explication qu'Albinos donne de l'attribut de «père»: «père»—dit Albinos—«parce que cause de toute chose et parce qu'il met en ordre l'intellect céleste et l'âme du monde en les tournant vers lui et vers ses *noēseis* (c'est-à-dire, vers les idées) ... il est la cause de l'intellect de l'âme du monde, intellect qui, *mis en ordre par le père, ordonne la nature toute entière en ce monde-ci*». Donc, d'après ce passage, la causalité du premier dieu ne s'exercerait directement que sur le second dieu, qui, à son tour, serait celui qui entre vraiment en rapport avec le cosmos. C'est substantiellement sur ce passage que se fonde, je suppose, le groupe très restreint de spécialistes modernes qui identifie le second dieu avec le démiurge.[20] Naturellement, cette interprétation a elle aussi ses points faibles qui, aujourd'hui, ne me semblent pas tellement se trouver dans l'appellation de «père» attribuée au premier dieu (puisqu'en étant la cause de l'activité du second, il demeure vraiment dans un sens le père de toute chose); ce qui est grave, c'est plutôt de n'avoir pas su confuter le dogme de Loenen et de n'avoir pas su par conséquent expliquer des passages fondamentaux comme celui du chapitre XII, qui resterait ainsi une très forte preuve en faveur de l'identité entre le démiurge et le premier dieu.

Maintenant on pourrait peut-être citer les solutions de compromis comme celle d'Invernizzi, qui, à vrai dire, est bien raisonnée;[21] mais il vaut mieux affronter une fois pour toutes le problème du chapitre XII, qui est certainement décisif à propos de la question du démiurge. Comme nous le savons, le premier paragraphe de ce chapitre est presque littéralement identique à un fragment de la doxographie d'Arius Didyme.[22] L'identité presque complète du texte d'Albinos avec le fragment doxographique constitue depuis longtemps la pièce de résistance de la thèse selon laquelle le *Didaskalikos* dépend très fortement ou même totalement d'Arius Didyme, une thèse énoncée par Diels, élaborée par Witt et portée à ses extrêmes conséquences par Giusta.[23] Or, Loenen déjà

---

[19] On le voit très bien chez De Vogel, *op.l.*, 300, qui ne cite que ce passage en faveur de l'identification entre le démiurge et le premier dieu.

[20] Je ne connais que deux auteurs qui soutiennent cette identification d'une manière explicite: M. Isnardi Parente, *Introduzione a Plotino*, Bari 1984, 42; et moi-même, dans un de mes livres précédents, *Le scuole l'anima l'impero. La filosofia antica da Antioco a Plotino*, Torino 1982, 108. Peut-être il faut ranger dans ce groupe J. Mansfeld aussi, qui dans son travail cité plus haut (n. 3) écrit: «the nature of the superior principle is not adequately expressed by the word αἴτιος, which only reveals its relation to the active intellect» (p. 63).

[21] Voir l'*op.l.*, I 70.73.

[22] Fr.1 Diels. A la p. 447 des *Doxographi graeci* tout le matériel est largement présenté.

[23] Voir Diels, *Dox. Gr.* 76; Witt, *op.l.*, 95–103; M. Giusta, *I dossografi di etica* I–II, Torino

avait protesté—à bon droit—contre elle, en remarquant que chez Albinos le texte reparaissait riche en détails (l'allusion à la bonté du dieu tirée du *Timée*, par exemple) et qu'il était présenté en meilleure forme du point de vue logique et syntaxique aussi. Loenen avait raison, je pense, de revendiquer l'autonomie de son auteur; mais, on a peine à le croire, le point le plus important lui échappa. A la page 167,7 le *Didaskalikos* ajoute en effet une brève incise au texte d'Arius: le cosmos, dit Albinos, fut construit «*par le dieu ... en regardant (apoble-pontos) une idée du monde*». Quel peut être le sens de cet ajout?

A ce point-ci on pourrait se demander si cette incise n'aurait vraiment pu se trouver déjà dans le texte d'Arius—ce qui serait très invraisemblable à mon avis;[24] ou bien si Albinos ne visait, par ces mots, qu'à reproduire quelque passage du *Timée*: et il est évident que chez Platon on lit plusieurs expressions semblables, mais aucune qui soit identique à celle employée par Albinos.[25] Mais toutes ces questions-là n'ont que très peu d'importance: la chose fondamentale est que, heureusement, nous pouvons dire avec certitude quel était le sens de ces deux ou trois mots aux yeux d'Albinos, les eût-il recopiés d'après Arius, ou d'après Platon, ou bien imaginés lui-même.

En fait, le verbe *apoblepein* avec *pros* + accusatif est employé une deuxième fois par Albinos à la p. 169,33 à propos de l'intuition des idées (qui, ne l'oublions pas, sont incluses dans l'esprit du premier dieu) de la part de l'intelligence de l'âme du monde. Il est évident qu'Albinos emploie ici cette expression dans le sens très littéral de «regarder quelque chose de l'extérieur», car le dieu inférieur n'a pas dans son esprit les *noēta*, qui sont les pensées du premier dieu: le verbe *blepein*, d'autant plus qu'il est uni au préverbe *apo*-souligne bien cette extériorité de l'observateur par rapport au *paradeigma* inclus dans l'esprit du dieu transcendant et suprême. Par contre, on ne pourrait pas dire, à propos du premier dieu, qu'il *(apo)blepei* les idées, parce qu'il les possède dans son esprit et les *pense*: il *noei* et non *apoblepei*, comme en fait Albinos écrit à la p. 164,27. Le fait d'*apoblepein* les idées est donc du domaine du dieu inférieur: une autre preuve en est qu'un verbe fort semblable (*prosblepein*) apparaît encore à la p. 164,22[26] et toujours à propos du second dieu s'adressant au premier. De tout ceci s'ensuit que, puisque le démiurge du chap. XII n'est pas un dieu qui *noei*

1964–67, *passim* (voir l'index *s.v.* Alcinoo, t.II, 553 s.). On peut lire les remarques de Loenen dans l'*op.l.*, 41 s.

[24] Le texte d'Arius nous a été transmis par deux autres témoins, Stobée et Eusèbe: tous les deux ne gardent aucune trace des mots qu'on lit chez Albinos. Voir Diels, *DG* 447.

[25] Cf. *Tim*. 28a6: ὁ δημιουργὸς πρὸς τὸ κατὰ ταὐτὰ ἔχον βλέπων ἀεί, 29a3 ὅ τε δημιουργός ... δῆλον ὡς πρὸς τὸ ἀίδιον ἔβλεπεν, 39e9 νοῦς ἐνούσας ἰδέας τῷ ὅ ἔστιν ζῷον ... καθορᾷ.

[26] Dont je tiens le texte pour authentique, contrairement à Giusta, *Due capitoli ...*, 199 n. 94. Je crois qu'on peut garder le texte des manuscripts en plaçant entre parenthèses les mots ὡς—ὅρασιν et en donnant a προσβλέπῃ comme sujet οὗτος, qu'on peut tirer de τοῦτον de la ligne 21 et qui est évidemment le νοῦς τοῦ σύμπαντος οὐρανοῦ.

l'idée du cosmos, mais un qui *apoblepei pros idean kosmou*, il ne peut pas être le dieu suprême de la hiérarchie supposée par Albinos: contrairement à ce que croyaient Loenen et tous ceux qui le suivirent, ce dieu, qui est inéquivocablement le démiurge du *Didaskalikos*, ne peut être que le second dieu et à juste titre Albinos a retenu important de préciser ce fait par un ajout au texte d'Arius, dont la transcription lui avait semblé jusque-là si commode.

Notre passage de 167,7 n'est donc pas un redoublement inutile de la notion déjà clairement exprimée chez Arius (447,24–26 Diels, *DG*) et reprise ensuite par Albinos aussi (167,8–9) que le démiurge disposait d'un modèle idéal: c'est un éclaircissement nouveau et fondamental. Nous pouvons en donner un autre indice. Que l'on songe à un texte du même caractère que celui d'Albinos, puisqu'il s'agit d'un texte doxographique, qui pourrait, en outre, dépendre lui aussi de l'oeuvre d'Arius[27]: je veux dire le texte d'Hippolyte.[28] Or, chez Hippolyte il est clair dès l'abord qu'il n'y a qu'un dieu-démiurge qui a dans son esprit les idées et le *paradeigma*; ainsi, son langage est très différent de celui qu'emploie Albinos: le dieu-démiurge ne «regarde» pas son *paradeigma*, mais il «se concentre sur son âme» (*prosechōn en tēi psychēi*). Tous le deux auteurs emploient les mots convenables, chacun d'entre eux en envisageant sa propre conception.

Maintenant que nous avons expliqué le sens de l'ajout fait par Albinos au texte d'Arius, p. 167,7, il est raisonnable de poser une question semblable au sujet de l'addition qui se trouve à la page 167,11 aussi: ici, en fait, Albinos ajoute au texte d'Arius une explication qu'il tire du *Timée* 29e, en disant que «le dieu» s'adonna à la démiurgie «parce qu'il était bon». Loenen jugeait cet ajout important,[29] mais il n'expliqua pas pourquoi. Or, il est évident que, s'il s'agit tout simplement de quelques mots qu'Albinos a tiré du texte du *Timée* pour donner une tournure plus platonicienne à son exposition, l'importance de l'addition n'est pas très grande. Toutefois, nous savons désormais—d'après l'interprétation que nous avons donnée de l'ajout de la ligne 167,7—que le démiurge dont parle Albinos n'est pas le premier dieu. Le premier dieu est (le) «bien» (164,30), mais *n'est pas* «bon» (165,7) parce qu'il est inconcevable qu'il participe à la bonté qui serait par là-même supérieure à lui (*ibid.*), de sorte qu'il n'a pas même part à l'*aretē* et ainsi est meilleur que l'*aretē*.[30] Or, en lisant à la p. 167,11 que le démiurge «était bon» on peut soupçonner que par cette nouvelle addition au texte d'Arius Albinos visait à faire ressortir une fois encore que le démiurge dont il parlait était le dieu inférieur et non pas le dieu suprême et que cette identification était justifiée par le texte même de Platon.

---

[27] Voir Giusta, Due capitoli ..., 179 s., 182 ss. et *I dossografi* ..., I 346; II 49 s., 54 s., 61 ss.

[28] P. 567,12–14 Diels: τὸ δὲ παράδειγμα τὴν διάνοιαν τοῦ θεοῦ εἶναι, ὃ καὶ ἰδέαν καλεῖ οἶον εἰκονισμά τι, ᾧ προσέχων ἐν τῇ ψυχῇ ὁ θεὸς τὰ πάντα ἐδημιούργει.

[29] *Op.l.*, 42.

[30] Voir aussi Krämer, *op.l.*, 109 et n. 296.

Je ne peux m'empêcher d'ajouter encore quelques considérations avant de revenir au problème des attributs divins. Comme l'indique le fr. 1 d'Arius, le platonisme du premier siècle av. J.C. n'a dû connaître qu'un seul dieu: le dieu cosmique évidemment, comme le confirment les autres témoignages qu'on peut rapporter à cette phase de la tradition platonicienne, c'est-à-dire Aet. *Plac.* I 3,21 = Diels *DG* 287,17 et Varron, ap. Aug. *de civ.dei* VII 28. La comparaison entre Albinos et Arius est très importante parce qu'elle permet justement de confirmer avec certitude que le *Didaskalikos* n'est pas une simple transcription, dans cette partie du moins, de la doxographie d'Arius, mais qu'il tient compte des développements successifs du moyen platonisme et en particulier de la tendance à multiplier les figures divines. C'est exactement au même résultat qu'aboutit la comparaison d'un autre texte d'Albinos, p. 181,36, où apparaît la plus claire distinction entre les deux dieux que l'on puisse rencontrer dans le traité, à un autre texte d'Arius chez Stobée (II 49, 16—18 W.) comparé récemment par Giusta au passage d'Albinos.[31] Dans ce texte préservé par Stobée, on remarquera qu'il n'y a pas d'article devant *horatōi* et *noētōi*: ce fait nous porte à croire qu'Arius distinguait tout simplement les *deux* aspects d'*une* divinité, le dieu cosmique qui est en fait nommé dans la même page à la ligne 12 et qui est à la fois visible et intelligible.[32] Le sens du passage est donc que «l'on doit suivre dieu, mais évidemment non en tant qu'il est visible et ...,[33] mais en tant qu'il est intelligible et qu'il harmonise l'ordre du monde». Bien au contraire, dans le passage du *Didaskalikos* p. 181,36 la distinction est désormais très clairement posée entre deux dieux.

Mais revenons aux attributs du premier dieu. La raison pour laquelle la grande majorité d'entre eux n'a rien à voir avec une prétendue fonction causale du dieu même paraît à ce point tout à fait claire: c'est parce que en réalité une telle fonction n'est prévue par la théologie et la cosmologie du *Didaskalikos* qu'en très faible mesure, vu que la fonction démiurgique est attribuée au second dieu et que l'influence du dieu suprême sur le cosmos résulte seulement indirecte, réalisée par l'intermédiaire de l'intellect céleste. Désormais, nous pouvons ajouter que même les trois attributs qui semblaient établir, eux au moins, la fonction causale du dieu suprême expriment en réalité bien moins que tout ceci. D'abord, leur présence est imposée par le souvenir des textes platoniciens qui sont à l'origine de la spéculation d'Albinos: «père» dérive bien sûr du *Timée*, tandis que «bien» et «vérité» présupposent *Rep.*508e—509b. Mais eux non plus n'établissent pas un lien direct entre le cosmos et le dieu suprême:

---

[31] Giusta, Due capitoli ..., 199 n. 98. Voici le texte de Stobée: Πλάτων ταὐτὰ τῷ Πυθαγόρᾳ, τέλος ὁμοίωσιν θεῷ ... Πυθαγόραν δὲ παρ' αὐτὸν εἰπεῖν· ἕπου θεῷ· δῆλον ὡς οὐχ ὁρατῷ καὶ προηγουμένως, νοητῷ δὲ καὶ τῆς κοσμικῆς εὐταξίας ἁρμονικῷ.

[32] Festugière a très bien expliqué cette conception, *op.l.*, II 153 s.

[33] Le mot προηγουμένῳ demeure inexplicable.

Albinos évite attentivement une pareille conclusion. Comme nous l'avons déjà vu, précisément après avoir parlé du «père» il se soucie d'expliquer (164,36–165,4) que c'est réellement le dieu inférieur qui intervient sur le cosmos. Et de plus, que le dieu en tant que bien est la cause de tout bien, ceci s'explique de la même façon que le cas précédent: en effet, dans le *Didaskalikos* il manque toute allusion à des interventions providentielles de la part du premier dieu et l'allusion du chapitre XII, p. 167,10, où l'on parle justement de *pronoia*, doit être désormais rapportée au second dieu. Enfin, en disant que le dieu est «principe de toute vérité», l'auteur établit sans aucun doute un lien de dépendance entre les multiples vérités et le dieu: mais il s'agit évidemment de la plus abstraite des formes pensables de causalité et de toute façon, cette fois encore, le dieu n'entre pas en relation directe avec le cosmos, ni avec la démiurgie, mais simplement avec l'intelligence (et peut-être s'agirait-il alors de la seule intelligence céleste, bref, du dieu inférieur. La théorie gnoséologique développée au chap. IV ne souffle mot de l'intervention d'un pareil *noûs poiētikos* dans la formation de la connaissance humaine).

C'est pour cela que ma conclusion à propos des attributs du premier dieu dans le *Didaskalikos* est absolument opposée à celle de Wolfson et d'Invernizzi: je dirais en effet que, chez eux, il n'y a plus aucune trace de la fonction démiurgique et du rapport causal du dieu avec le cosmos; ce qu'ils semblent exprimer c'est plutôt la notion d'un dieu lointain, transcendant et parfait, dont le rapport avec le cosmos est extrêmement mince et indirect, toujours effectué par l'intervention du second dieu. Il y a une cohérence en tout ceci: en effet, le caractère des attributs divins est cohérent avec la présentation du dieu inférieur comme le démiurge authentique.

S'il en est ainsi, on peut se demander si la brève remarque qu'on lit p. 164,30 s., à la suite de la liste principale des attributs du dieu («je n'énumère pas ces termes pour les séparer,[34] mais pour faire concevoir, par leur réunion, un tout unique») ne viserait pas précisément à mettre en garde les lecteurs contre une interprétation des attributs semblable à celle qui a été proposée par Wolfson et Invernizzi: car celui qui ne veut voir en *chaque* attribut que la description d'*une* activité du dieu par là-même «sépare» les attributs, soit entre eux, soit de l'essence divine. On voit bien que, si l'on abandonne l'explication causale des attributs et l'identification du démiurge avec le dieu suprême, la théologie d'Albinos y gagne en cohérence et le texte du chapitre X en clarté.

Faut-il croire que cette systématisation, somme toute assez cohérente, est entièrement l'œuvre d'Albinos et que, de même qu'il avait modifié le texte d'Arius à propos de la démiurgie, il a travaillé ici d'après une liste de prédicats

---

[34] Il faut évidemment lire avec Louis χωρίζων au lieu de ὁρίζων (Hermann).

traditionnels[35] en effaçant ou en modifiant tous ceux qui faisaient référence à la fonction causale du dieu suprême (comme nous l'avons vu à propos de l'attribut de «père»)? Evidemment, nous ne pouvons pas donner une réponse: nous n'avons pas, dans ce cas, un texte qui pourrait être censé être la «source» suivie par Albinos dans le chapitre X.[36] Bornons-nous à dire que ou bien cette systématisation est l'œuvre d'Albinos lui-même, ou bien elle était propre à une tradition assez cohérente du moyen platonisme qui est résumée dans le *Didaskalikos*.

Naturellement, je sais aussi que dans le *Didaskalikos* la cohérence n'atteint qu'un certain point. La contradiction entre la prétendue ineffabilité du dieu et les attributs qui le décrivent paraît réelle;[37] de plus, il est vrai que le chapitre théologique est mal construit, je l'ai déjà dit, et qu'il est difficile de comprendre pourquoi certains attributs du dieu (p.ex. «bien») affirment à son sujet précisément ce que l'*aphairesis* qui suit lui nie («il n'est pas bon», 165,7). Enfin, on ne peut pas oublier non plus que la cohérence dans la division des compétences entre les deux divinités ne s'étend pas beaucoup au-delà des chapitres X et XII; l'auteur n'a pas montré ailleurs un pareil bon sens et les lieux dans lesquels il ne serait pas facile de dire à quelle divinité il pense ne sont pas rares (comme aux chap. XV et XVI). Je n'ai nullement l'intention de faire d'Albinos un génie philosophique.

Mais il y a peut-être encore un texte où Albinos a gardé un souvenir affaibli de cette division des compétences entre les deux dieux que nous avons rencontré aux chapitres X et XII. On s'aperçoit de ça lorsqu'on pose une question qui, à ma connaissance, n'a jamais été soulevée: nous autres hommes, comment parvenons-nous à connaître le dieu inférieur, son existence ou ses propriétés, ou au moins ses fonctions? Je suggèrerais de ne pas répondre en toute vitesse qu'il n'y a pas d'indications dans le texte. En effet, il y a une caractéristique de ce dieu sur laquelle Albinos insiste constamment, je veux dire son lien avec le ciel: il parle de «l'intellect du ciel entier» (164,20.24), d'un «intellect céleste» (164,36), d'un «dieu céleste» (181,36). Rien ne nous fait jamais penser que ce dieu ou que cet intellect céleste ait un aspect visible ou bien qu'il ait pris place dans un corps céleste visible, bien entendu. Mais le lien avec le ciel, marqué comme il est, ne peut pas manquer de nous frapper.

Or, le *Didaskalikos* consacre un chapitre aux sciences mathématiques, le septième. Les spécialistes modernes ont reconnu facilement qu'il dépend en large

---

[35] Qu'il s'agit de prédicats traditionnels est ce qui ressort des remarques de Dillon, *op.l.*, 283, ainsi que de C. Moreschini, *Apuleio e il platonismo*, Firenze 1978, 71–73.

[36] Mais n'oublions pas que le mauvais état du texte entre les paragraphes 6 et 7 pourrait être l'indice qu'il y a eu contamination entre deux sources.

[37] A moins qu'on n'accepte la brillante hypothèse de J. Mansfeld exposée dans ce livre même, pp. 92 ss.

partie du passage correspondant de Platon dans la *République*.[38] On rencontre dans ce chapitre un texte curieux, relatif à l'astronomie, à la p. 161,22–27: «l'astronomie aussi est utile, comme quatrième discipline» [après l'arithmétique, la géométrie et la stéréométrie, comme dans la *République*], «grâce à laquelle nous contemplerons dans le ciel les mouvements des astres et de la voûte céleste ainsi que le démiurge de la nuit et du jour, des mois et de l'année; d'où, en suivant une route appropriée, nous rechercherons aussi le démiurge du tout, en nous efforçant de l'atteindre à partir de ces connaissances comme à partir d'une base et des éléments». Ce qui saute immédiatement aux yeux, dans ce passage, c'est que deux démiurges y sont mentionnés: Platon (*Rep.* 530a) nommait seulement un «démiurge du ciel». Pourquoi y a-t-il ce dédoublement chez Albinos?

D'après la seule interprétation explicite du passage que je connaisse, celle de Festugière,[39] le «démiurge de la nuit et du jour, des mois et de l'année» serait le soleil et l'astronomie viserait à promouvoir l'accès à la connaissance du dieu par l'étude préliminaire des phénomènes célestes. Je crois cependant qu'il y ait plusieurs objections à faire à Festugière: la première et la plus évidente est que le soleil ne saurait être défini, entre autres choses, un «démiurge des mois», à moins de vouloir attribuer à Albinos une stupidité exceptionnelle. Outre cela, une telle stupidité serait extrêmement improbable, vu qu'ailleurs (170,27) l'auteur montre de très bien savoir que le cycle des mois dépend de la lune et non du soleil. On ne saurait pas prétendre non plus que la référence au soleil soit imposée par quelques passages de la *République*: à la p. 530ab le soleil n'est pas mentionné.[40] Enfin, puisque Festugière est un des spécialistes qui admettent (très justement) l'existence de deux dieux dans le *Didaskalikos*, on devrait lui objecter que son interprétation est au moins incomplète: en effet, il n'a pas expliqué à la connaissance de quel degré du divin l'astronomie nous préparerait éventuellement. Mais une alternative raisonnable à cette interprétation peu plausible est sans doute également possible.

En premier lieu, il n'est absolument pas nécessaire de supposer que par l'expression «le démiurge de la nuit et du jour, des mois et de l'année» le *Didaskalikos* fasse allusion à un corps céleste visible: en effet, le verbe *theasthai* de 161,24 (que j'ai traduit par le verbe ambigu «contempler») peut très bien impliquer une considération rien qu'intellectuelle des phénomènes, une activité uniquement de l'esprit: cette signification est fréquente chez les philosophes.[41] Et ce n'est pas tout: le fait évident que le septième chapitre d'Albinos suit de

---

[38] Voir Witt, *op.l.*, 67; Invernizzi, *op.l.*, notes du chap. VII.
[39] *Op.l.*, II 504 s. Invernizzi est parfaitement muet sur le problème.
[40] Le soleil *et la lune* peuvent être sous-entendus par ταῦτα, 530b 1.
[41] Cf. Plat. *Symp.* 210c3, 211d2, *Rep.* 511c8, *Phaedr.* 247d4, 249e6; Arist. *Metaph.* 1086a31, *EN* 1097a10, 1180b17; Plot. I 6,9,33.

très près la *République*, ce fait même conseillerait d'attribuer à *theasthai* la signification d'une pure activité intellectuelle. En effet, c'est Platon même qui, dans le texte résumé par Albinos, invite à pratiquer l'astronomie comme un exercice exclusivement intellectuel: il place avec indignation la considération des phénomènes visibles du ciel sur le même plan que l'observation d'un phénomène sensible quelconque: celui qui pratique l'astronomie de cette façon, dit-il, continue en vérité à «regarder vers le bas» tout en levant les yeux au ciel. Or, Albinos sait très bien tout cela et il l'approuve, d'où la version diligente qu'il donne dans les lignes qui suivent immédiatement (p. 161,28–162,7) celles que l'on a traduites, quand il relie le problème de l'astronomie à celui de la musique. Donc, le démiurge de la nuit et du jour, des mois et de l'année ne peut et ne doit être ni le soleil, ni tout autre corps céleste visible. Reste-t-il peut-être une autre possibilité raisonnable si ce n'est celle qu'il est identique à l'intellect du ciel, à notre second dieu? Les démiurges aussi, après tout, *non sunt multiplicandi praeter necessitatem*. Dans ce cas, la voie exacte pour connaître le second dieu serait indiquée par Albinos dans l'astronomie, platoniquement entendue comme étude des mouvements et des liens intelligibles et non comme observation des phénomènes célestes visibles. Ainsi tout le système théologique du *Didaskalikos* reposerait sur une série de correspondances précises: aux deux intellects correspondent les deux dieux, qui sont également les deux démiurges de la p. 161.

De cette façon aussi, la cohérence ne serait toutefois pas vraiment parfaite et le cadre conceptuel de la p. 161 ne se concilierait pas jusqu'au bout avec la théologie et la cosmologie des chapitres X et XII. La présentation des fonctions du second dieu serait ici plutôt modeste par rapport aux larges devoirs attribués à cette divinité aux chapitres déjà cités. On pourrait cependant trouver une justification dans le fait que cette présentation est conditionnée par la référence nécessaire aux contenus de l'astronomie (je ne verrais par contre aucune difficulté particulière dans le nom de «démiurge du tout» qui, d'après l'interprétation que j'ai proposée, reviendrait alors au premier dieu. Celui-ci en effet pourrait très bien être défini ainsi de la même façon qu'on le définit ailleurs, nous l'avons vu, «cause de tout»: on sous-entend toujours que sa causalité universelle s'exerce seulement à travers la médiation du dieu inférieur). Enfin, je ne trouve pas qu'il soit facile de comprendre quelle pourrait être la «route appropriée» qui des mathématiques devrait nous conduire à la connaissance du dieu suprême; aucune des voies illustrées au chapitre X ne semble admettre une référence facile aux mathématiques du septième chapitre.[42]

En conclusion, j'observerais que d'après l'interprétation que j'ai proposée

---

[42] Krämer, *op.l.*, 108 n. 288, a affirmé mais n'a pas démontré qu'il y a un lien avec la *via negationis* du chap. X.

il est possible de reconnaître dans la théologie du *Didaskalikos* la présence de nombreuses structures de pensée typiques de cette aire-ci du moyen platonisme ou de celle-là: hiérarchie des figures divines (comme chez Numénius, chez Apulée, chez Plutarque); transcendance absolue du premier dieu (Numénius, Celse); identification du démiurge avec le dieu inférieur (Numénius encore). Le crédit dont Albinos a joui en tant que représentant typique du moyen platonisme apparaît donc encore justifié.

THE WAY OF THE MOST HIGH
AND THE INJUSTICE OF GOD IN 4 EZRA

BY

Michael Edward Stone (Jerusalem)

It has been claimed that it was the crisis of Jewish apocalypticism engendered by the destruction of the Temple that begot Gnosticism, a religious movement at whose very centre lay an idea of knowledge of God.[1] Others dispute this, but in any case there is obviously a good deal to be learned germane to the theme "The Knowledge of God in Religion and Philosophy" from the examination of a Jewish book, written in reaction to the destruction of the Temple and much concerned with knowing God. Most of the paper will be devoted to an exposition of the text of the work under discussion, but from that exposition some more general observations flow.

The Fourth Book of Ezra (4 Ezra) is a Jewish apocalypse written in the aftermath of the destruction of Jerusalem by the Romans in 70 C.E. It was composed in Hebrew, in the last decade of the first century and was translated from Hebrew into Greek. The Greek translation perished and today all that survives is a flock of daughter versions made from the Greek.[2] The book is extremely interesting for its theological daring and conceptual power and has had extensive influence on Latin and Oriental Christianity.

The first of the seven visions of which 4 Ezra is composed has recently been the subject of lively discussion relating to two issues in particular: the exact

---

[1] See e.g. R.M. Grant, *Gnosticism and Early Christianity*, New York: Harper, 1966, 27 ff. See comments of B.A. Pearson, "Friedlaender Revisited; Alexandrian Judaism and Gnostic Origins," *Studia Philonica* 2 (1973) 35.

[2] See most recent introduction in: M.E. Stone, *Jewish Writings of the Second Temple Period* (Compendia Rerum Iudaicarum ad N.T. 2.2), Assen and Philadelphia: v. Gorcum and Fortress, 1984, 412–414; and most recent English translation by B. Metzger in J.H. Charlesworth, *The Old Testament Pseudepigrapha*, Vol 1, Garden City: Doubleday, 1983, 517–559. The Latin version includes two additional compositions with the Jewish apocalypse and these are numbered as chapters 1–2 and 15–16 of the book. So the Jewish apocalypse commences with 3:1.

Throughout this paper we have used the name "Ezra" for the *persona* of the seer. We have, somewhat ingenuously, talked as if the dialogue and dispute actually represent the views of two different protagonists, Ezra and the angel. We are, of course, conscious that an author composed the work and is responsible for presentation of the views of both these characters. Nonetheless, since we are convinced that the dynamic of the discussions is deliberate, and since our presentation here does not cover the whole book, we have abided by the author's literary conventions. At a more general level of analysis, which must be based upon such detailed exegetical forays as that presented here, the broader patterns and structures of the work, surpassing the individual characters, may become evident. The coherence of our analysis is its own best defence.

nature of the address that Ezra directs to God at the opening of the vision and, arising from this, what is the knowledge of the "way of the Most High" which forms a chief motif of the first vision and a minor but significant one in the second?[3]

In 3:1−3 the background is sketched and the central concern is articulated, the sufferings of Zion. A recital of the *magnalia dei* in the history of Israel follows (3:4−27). In the Hebrew Bible such recitals are found first and foremost in covenant contexts in which they serve as testimonies of God's goodness to Israel. Moreover, and of particular interest here, in biblical literature the recital of God's mighty acts may also be part of the proem to a legal indictment of Israel. In such contexts it serves to support charges, made by God or his spokesman, of transgression of the covenant.[4]

What then is the role of this recital in 4 Ezra? Its contents and literary form may provide clues. Some of its chief points are that God created human beings and punished them (3:4−10); that God let Noah survive, elected Abraham, gave the Torah, raised up David who built the city and offered oblations, and punished Israel (3:10−27); and that the evil heart was in Adam from the beginning so that even the gift of the Torah could not prevail against it (note especially 3:20). By formulating the historical recital as an address to God, the author is able to lay particular stress on God's role in this series of events, which is further highlighted by the powerful reiteration of "thou" and "thou alone" throughout. The purpose of this narrative is neither the celebration of God's gracious acts towards Israel, nor the enumeration of Israel's sins (though elements of both are present). It is primarily the attempt to establish God's twofold responsibility for the state of the world and, by direct implication, for the destruction of Zion. For, not only did God create human beings with a weakness which led to sin, but having done this, he then proceeded to punish mankind and Israel for sinning. The destruction of Zion is thus the direct result of a chain of events, the ultimate responsibility for which lies with God.

How boldly the author inverts the traditional role of the historical recital and uses it to indict not Israel, but God! God is summoned before the bar of His own justice: the human being is the plaintiff not the accused. The case is argued using the same techniques and literary forms which elsewhere constitute part of the indictment of Israel before the divine court. Even the specific charges

---

[3] See the articles by P. de Villiers, Understanding the Way of God: Form, Function and Message of the Historical Review in 4 Ezra 3:4−27, *SBL Seminar Papers*, Chico: Scholars, 1983; K. Koch, Esras erste Vision. Weltzeiten und Weg des Höchsten, *Biblische Zeitschrift* NF 22 (1978) 46−75.

[4] See, e.g., Ezekiel 20; this is also one element in Joshua 24 and Nehemiah 9. It is particularly part of the *rib* form, see G.E. Wright, The Lawsuit of God: a Form-Critical Study of Deuteronomy 32, *Israel's Prophetic Heritage: Muilenberg Festschrift* (ed. B.W. Anderson and W. Harrelson) New York: Harper, 1962, 26−67.

that follow the general indictment are set forth (3:28–33).[5]

In spite of the title sometimes given to it, this is no prayer to God; it is a challenge to God's justice. Such argumentative addresses to God, presenting the seer's inspired plaint against Him, are uncommon in the apocalypses. Somewhat similar, however, are *Second Apocalypse of Baruch* 14:4–9, 21:4–26, 48:1–24; *Third Apocalypse of Baruch* 1:2.[6] The prayer of the oppressed souls in *First Book of Enoch* 9:4–11 is definitely in a legal context and provokes divine action. It too casts the responsibility back upon God. A similar demand is laid upon divine justice by Taxo's words in *Testament of Moses* 9:7.[7] Uniquely, however, 4 Ezra reapplies the telling of God's gracious acts to God himself so that it becomes the summons calling Him to account before the bar of His own justice. This striking inversion of the matrix and point of the literary form emphasizes the author's theological daring: he is questioning the central axiom, the justice of God.

It is this that makes Ezra's request for knowledge of the way of the Most High, first raised in 3:31 and taken up in 4:2–3, 4:11, 4:23, 5:34, etc, so urgent. The "way" is, it seems, God's way of conducting the world; knowledge of it may explain God's injustice towards mankind.[8] However, the angel answers Ezra's request by asserting strongly that "the way of the Most High" cannot be understood by human beings.[9]

Indeed, all of 4:1–25 is held together by the motif of understanding. Taking the whole of Ezra's plaint in chap. 3 as a question, the angel picks up the theme of 3:31 "(thou) hast not shown to any one how thy way is to be comprehended," and chides Ezra for his presumption that he can understand the way

---

[5] C. Westermann, Struktur und Geschichte der Klage im AT, *Zeitschrift für die A.T. Wissenschaft* 66 (1954) 77–8 wishes to analyse this and certain other addresses in 4 Ezra in terms of the "communal lament" form found in Psalms and Lamentations. This is not appropriate here, for the recital of the *magnalia dei* is not at home in the "communal lament." The lament may have exerted some influence on the questions in 3:27–36, but even that is far from certain.

[6] It is likely, however, that *Second Apocalypse of Baruch* is dependent on 4 Ezra. Perhaps *Third Apocalypse of Baruch* also depends on the same tradition.

[7] See J. Licht, Taxo or the Apocalyptic Doctrine of Vengeance, *Journal of Jewish Studies* 12 (1961) 95–103. The indictment of God by an individual may be found, of course, in biblical Job. Similar in some respects is Abraham's reproach of God in Genesis 18:25.

[8] "Way of God" in this sense occurs elsewhere, e.g. 1QH 7:31–32, Romans 11:33, *Second Apocalypse of Baruch* 14:8, 20:4; in 4 Ezra 5:34, *Second Apocalypse of Baruch* 44:6 "way" stands parallel to "judgment", cf. Isaiah 40:14, *Second Apocalypse of Baruch* 15:4. The problem of understanding God's way in the destruction of the Temple is also to the fore in *b Berakot* 3b.

[9] The inaccessibility of knowledge of God's action is already highlighted by texts like Isaiah 40:13 and Job 9:10; cf. in general *Odes of Solomon* 7:8: "He who created wisdom is wiser than his works." The language of understanding used by 4 Ezra connects with wisdom terminology which, although present in Vision 1, is much more prominent in Vision 2. Observe the following uses in our text: "spirit of understanding" (5:22); the form of address (5:32); language of learning such as "strive to understand" and "search out" (5:34 and 37); "I am without wisdom" (5:39); and "discover" (5:40). Naturally the riddle questioning itself, which is discussed below, may be explained in sapiential terms.

of God, the working of His providence. In 4:5−8 (and in 5:36−7) the angel uses lists of riddle questions to demonstrate that human beings cannot know such things.[10] The immediate sources of this type of interrogative list are to be sought in the wisdom literature, particularly in Job 37:14−39:30, an extensive enumeration of questions designed to show human inability alongside God's power and knowledge.[11] Series of questions designed to show that humans cannot know the wonders of nature, and *a fortiori* of the heavenly realm, recur in apocalyptic texts like *First Book of Enoch* 93:11−14.[12] Closest to our passage in specific details, however, is the list in *Second Apocalypse of Baruch*, 59:5−11 which is not composed of questions expecting a negative answer, but is an enumeration of things revealed. Indeed, a distinct and widespread literary form, the list of revealed things, has been discerned in apocalyptic literature.[13] Some chief instances of these lists are *Second Apocalypse of Baruch* 59:5−11, *First Book of Enoch* 60:11−13, 14−22, 41:1−7, 43:1−2, *Second Book of Enoch* 23:1.[14]

In 4 Ezra 4:5−8 and 5:36−7 such a list of revealed things has been deliberately combined with the interrogative type of list found in Job 37−39, Wisdom

---

[10] The word "ways" in 4:3, clearly denoting the "riddles" with which it is parallel, is difficult. It is particularly intriguing since in 4:2, 4, 11, etc. the word is used with a specific and clear sense which is central to the whole vision. Wellhausen, *Skizzen und Vorarbeiten*, Berlin: Reimer, 1899, 6.240 suggested a Hebrew *drk* meaning "fashion". Greek *tropon* is apparently rendered by Armenian *aṙak* "proverb" in *Paenitentia Adam* 36(9): see M.E. Stone, *The Penitence of Adam* (CSCO 429), Louvain: Peeters, 1981. The polyvalency of the word "way" is at play in the discussion, see 4:23 and cf. 4:8: compare with 4:2 and 4:4. As is abundantly clear from 4:22−25, the meaning of the "way" is not exhausted by something like "the reason for the existence of the evil heart." Indeed, the author refers again only rarely in such terms to the way of the Most High.

[11] Certain of the specific questions there and also in Wisdom of ben Sira 1:2−3 recur in the two passages in 4 Ezra.

[12] There are other lists of questions about nature designed to show God's presence in all of the cosmos or associated with the sapiential themes of the search for wisdom or her presence in creation. See, e.g. Psalms 139:7−11, Proverbs 30:4, Job 28, Wisdom of ben Sira 24, Book of Baruch 4:29−34, with which cf. Deuteronomy 30:11−14. See also G.W.E. Nickelsburg and M.E. Stone, *Faith and Piety in Early Judaism: Texts and Documents*, Philadelphia: Fortress, 1983, 203−225. Compare the lists of natural phenomena discussed by G. von Rad, Hiob und altägyptische Weisheit, *Gesammelte Studien zum Alten Testament*, Munich: 1958, 262−272. John 3:12−13 is not the same, despite some similarities of wording. The structure of *Second Apocalypse of Baruch* 22−23:2 resembles 4 Ezra here in some ways, but the questions asked there are not analogous to the cosmological lists.

[13] For a full analysis of the form with numerous examples and extensive discussion, see M.E. Stone, Lists of Revealed Things in Apocalyptic Literature in *Magnalia Dei* (*G.E. Wright Memorial* ed. F.M. Cross *et al.*) Doubleday: Garden City, 1976, 414−452; see also M.E. Stone, Paradise in 4 Ezra iv.8 and vii.36, viii.52, *Journal of Jewish Studies* 17 (1966) 85−88.

[14] Furthermore, some of the apocalypses actually describe how these actions, such as the weighing of the winds, took place; see, e.g. *Second Book of Enoch* 40:2−3. It seems evident that *Biblical Antiquities* 19:10 also belongs with the lists of revealed things. Even though that work is not an apocalypse, the context in which the list occurs is clearly analogous. In Wisdom of Solomon 7:17−21, however, the rather different range of revealed information catalogued is a function of Solomon's well-known role as magician.

of ben Sira 1:2–3, etc. By this means, "the writer wishes to emphasize the limits of human knowledge, to deny the possibility of such revelations. To do this he does not simply have the angel ask the seer some riddles, to show him how limited his knowledge is. He chooses those riddles and adduces other elements of knowledge from a complex of ideas, a catalogue of those very subjects which in the 'normal' run of events apocalypticists considered as central to their revelatory experiences. When seen in this light, the passage receives its full dramatic dimension. It is a denial, daring, perhaps even polemical, of the availability of certain types of special knowledge, a denial therefore of a specific part of apocalyptic tradition."[15] In their inversion of the intent of a literary form then, these riddle questions strikingly make their point, just as the inversion of the indictment form did in the address with which the vision opened. In the context of the argument of the book, the riddle questions demonstrate that Ezra cannot even understand the wonders of nature, how much less Divine providence.

The angel employs a second means of making the same point, the parable of the trees and the sand which teaches that "those who dwell on earth can understand only what is on the earth, and he who is above the heavens can understand what is above the height of the heavens" (4:21).[16] Ezra who is corruptible (and therefore a fragile vessel) is incapable of grasping the way of Him who is incorruptible (4:11).[17]

In his remarks on the riddles and on the parable the angel dealt with the fate of Israel only by implication: Ezra cannot know the way of the Most High. Consequently, in 4:23–25 Ezra observes that this response is beside the point. He did not ask about heavenly matters, but about the earthly suffering of Israel. He will not accept the view that Israel's fate is incomprehensible and he

---

[15] Stone, Lists, 420.

[16] The gap between earthly and heavenly knowledge is a common theme. Compare Wisdom of Solomon 9:16–17 for another solution:

    16c but who has traced out what is in the heavens?

    17 who has learned thy counsel,

          Unless thou hast given wisdom

          and send thy holy spirit from on high?

Divergent attitudes to this question may provide one key for differentiating theories of knowledge and revelation: see Stone, Lists, 438–439; cf. also Isaiah 55:8–9, John 1:12–13. See the acute observations of S. Loewenstamm, The Death of Moses, *Studies on the Testament of Abraham* (ed. G.W.E. Nickelsburg, SCS 6), Missoula: Scholars Press, 1976, 198.

[17] The terms "corruptible" and "incorruptible" occur throughout the book. They do not have any obvious biblical parallels. "Corruptible" or "corruptibility" is typical of this world, e.g. 7:15, 7:111, 8:34 and 14:13. It signifies death and is brought about by the evil heart (7:48). It is said to be overcome at the end or in the eschatological state (6:28, 7:31, 7:96, 7:113, 8:3, 8:53). Thus the incorruptible is typical of the heavenly (4:11) or of the eschatological (7:13). The Greek was probably *phthartos*, etc. but the Hebrew remains enigmatic. Licht suggests *klh* which occurs in this sense in the Dead Sea Scrolls (J. Licht, *Sefer Hazon 'Ezra*, Jerusalem: Mosad Bialik, 1968, 24–25). On nature parables, see M.E. Stone, The Paradigmatic Use of Natural Phenomena in the Second Temple Age, *Gilgul: Essays on Transformation, Revolution and Permanence in the History of Religions* (R.J.Z. Werblowsky FS, ed. S. Shaked et al; SHR 50), Leiden: E.J. Brill, 1987, 304–308.

buttresses his refusal by pointing out God's special relation to Israel and the Torah. Israel is called by His name. This reformulation returns the discussion to the point at which it stood at the end of chap. 3 and these issues are taken up again in a different form at the start of the dispute section of Vision 2 (5:33).

The emphasis on understanding is the more telling because of the limits 4 Ezra has placed on the role and range of revealed knowledge. The rejection of cosmographical and uranographical speculations in 4:5–9 makes the cry of despair in 4:12 with its implicit questions the more piercing, and the questions in 4:22–25 the more acute. Ezra's understanding, the angel asserts, is human, limited and corruptible (4:11,20) and he cannot comprehend the heavenly realm. Ezra does not deny this, but he claims that what he wishes to know is within the human range. The search for understanding of the way of the Most High lies for him at the heart of purposeful human existence. It is better, he claims, to die than to suffer and not understand why (4:12). Else why, he asks, were we given the "power of understanding?"[18] The seer and the angel both reject knowledge of heavenly secrets. Ezra has neither sought it nor has he been granted it. The proper concern for the mind then is the fate of Israel.

Indeed, the seer's pain over his lack of understanding bursts forth in two striking laments over the mind. The first is in chap. 4 with two cries of woe, one following each angelic demonstration of Ezra's innate inability to comprehend the way of the Most High:

> It would be better for us not to be here
> than to come here and to live in ungodliness
> and to suffer and not understand why we suffer. (4:12)

and again:

> I beseech you, my lord, why have I been endowed with the power of understanding ...? (4:22)

In 7:63–75 there is another extensive lament over the mind. Ezra has been informed that in the final judgment there will be no mercy for the sinners. He then addresses the earth, reproaching it with having produced a mind from the dust, "for it would have been better if the dust itself had not been born, so that the mind might not have been made from it" (7:63). The mind grows with humans who are tortured by the very knowledge that they will perish in final judgment (7:65). The beasts, who have neither torment nor salvation are much happier (7:65–69).[19]

---

[18] In this passage: (1) heart = mind = power of understanding (3:30); (2) it is human and limited; (3) its satisfaction is central to purposeful human existence. This accords with the use of the term in 3:1, 5:21, 9:27 and 14:40.

[19] The "heart" which has received the law will perish along with human beings who have not observed it (9:36–7).

The angel replies that God created all that pertains to judgment when he created Adam, "for this reason ... those who dwell on earth shall be tormented, because though they had understanding they committed iniquity, and though they received the commandments they did not keep them ..."(7:72). They will have nothing to say in judgment which is only delayed because God foreordained the times (7:73−4).

Consequently, mind, being consciousness so it seems, is that part of humans which makes them liable for judgment at all. Although this apparently contradicts the point of chap. 4, that humans cannot understand the way of the Most High, the anomaly is readily resolved if the contexts of the two passages are borne in mind. In chap. 4 the discussion turns on the incomprehensibility of the working of divine justice when the fate of Israel is compared with the abundance of Babylon (i.e. Rome). It is this that human beings cannot understand. On the other hand, 7:62−72 discusses the actions of humans in general; in that context it is precisely the power of thought or consciousness that distinguishes humans from beasts and makes humans liable to be judged.

At this juncture in chap. 4, a cryptic statement by the angel ensues about sowing and harvest, about the future—Ezra must await future vindication of the righteous in order to see the resolution of his problems (4:26−4:31). This forms the transition to the second part of the dialogue, for following it dispute is abandoned for a series of requests for eschatological information which the angel answers. In each answer he stresses the predetermination of the times (4:36−37, 4:40, 4:44−46). Yet this emphasis is paralleled by and in tension with a growing sense of urgency and haste.[20] This tension is inherent to the author's thought.

The second vision opens with a speech which sets the tone and introduces the themes that characterize the first part of the ensuing dialogue. The issues it raises resemble those highlighted in the address and dispute sections of Vision 1 but it reproves God less pressingly and differs in its focus.

In the address in Vision 1 Ezra had summoned God to court to answer the questions arising from Israel's suffering. In the course of the predictions in the latter part of that vision, however, Ezra's views modify and by its end he accepts the idea that history's process is predetermined. Although this acceptance does not diminish his distress or alleviate his pain, it does lead him to pose his questions about the destruction of Zion from a different perspective. No longer is the reason for the actual punishment of Israel central, but the question, "Why is Israel, the faithful and elect people, punished *by the Gentiles*, the hated Romans?" This minor theme of Vision 1 now becomes dominant. "If thou dost really hate thy people," he cries out, "they should have been

---

[20] This is clear from 4:26, from the image of 4:42, and from the parable of the third question.

punished at thy own hands" (5:30).[21] How anomalous is Israel's fate when viewed in light of Israel's election and God's love! So God's punishment of Israel is called "hate" (5:30).[22]

Since the address focuses on election and love, the angel's opening question in the dispute that follows is not, why does Ezra search to understand the ways of providence, but whether he loves Israel more than God (5:33). The changed emphasis is clear, and it is well illustrated by contrasting the following verses:

> I also will show you *the way* you desire to see, and will teach you *why the heart is evil* (4:4).

So Vision 1, while in Vision 2 we read:

> and then I will explain to you *the travail you seek to understand* (5:37).

Of course, at the root of Ezra's concern is the fate of Israel: here he poses the question to God in terms of God's love of Israel while in Vision 1 it was formulated in terms of divine providence and God's conduct of the world. The changed formulation raises a less acute theological issue, although emotionally a no less distressing one. Ezra seems to have moved from his doubt about the justice lying at the basis of God's conduct of the world to bewilderment at His actions. He has, in spite of it all, advanced in "knowledge of the way of the Most High."

Following the address is a disputatious passage corresponding to that in the first Vision (5:33–40). Its terminology differs from that in Vision 1 and the stress on comprehension of the way of the Most High is markedly less. First the angel reproaches Ezra with his distress (5:33), to which Ezra responds that he is deeply upset all the time when he seeks to comprehend the way of the Most High (the only instance of the expression in this passage, contrast Vision 1). The angel again poses riddle questions to which Ezra responds that only the superhuman can know these things, but that he is "without wisdom." The angel assents, saying that Ezra cannot know God's judgment.

The dispute passages of both visions do not present the actual existence of the problematic and painful situation as that which lies at the very heart of Ezra's concern, but rather his drive to comprehend these situations. After the discussion with the angel in Vision 1, Ezra asserted that his mind, his ability

---

[21] It is foreshadowed in 4:23 in a passage that presages many of the themes of Vision 2.

[22] Interestingly, God's punishment of Israel is not described in legal terms by the seer in his speech (5:28–30), even though in 5:34 and 5:40 the "way of the Most High" (also absent from the speech) is described as "judgment". *Second Apocalypse of Baruch* 44:6 speaks of the making known of God's "judgment" and "ways". A most striking parallel in *Second Apocalypse of Baruch* 20:4 which says that in the events of the eschaton:

I will show the *judgment* of my might,
And my *ways* which are unsearchable.

to know is properly to be applied to the subject matter of his questions, i.e. the way of the Most High (4:22–25). The dynamic of the book is evident when at the end of the dispute in the second Vision (5:31–40) Ezra no longer repeats this demand for understanding. Instead he seems to accept the limitations of his wisdom and abilities.[23] So he simply proceeds on with his questioning.

It is notable here that while understanding is referred to as knowledge and wisdom, understanding the way of the Most High is described as "discovering his judgment."[24] Indeed a second chief theme of the dispute is God's judgment. In 4 Ezra judgement is often, but not always, eschatological in character and in this section judgment is the object of Ezra's search (5:34), that which the angel says he cannot discover (5:40) and, in fact, the chief point of the oracle in 5:42–44. Both from a literary and a conceptual perspective it complements the theme of love. Judgment, because of its double reference, both present and eschatological, serves as a sort of key. The author is very subtle. Ezra's ability to discover "divine judgment" is denied in 5:40. Yet in the same verse 5:40 Ezra takes up the theme of judgment and asks his questions in a specific way about the eschaton, implying a different sense of "judgment". Ezra vainly seeks to understand (this worldly) judgment but is answered about (eschatological) judgment in 5:42 ff.

It is worth observing that there is here no further questioning of the basic axiom of divine righteousness. Indeed, this is another indication of the change from Vision 1. God is not indicted here, he is simply not understood; he is admonished only in the last verse of the address (5:30). The angel responds that Ezra cannot love Israel like God or understand God's judgment or the end of his love. This implies both the justice and the mercy of God.

It is this implication that opens the way for the continuation into dialogic revelation which is in fact paradoxical. Ezra's admission that he cannot know the way of God's love seems to pave the way into his further revelatory questions. The seer has understood the first part of the dialogue to lead to the conclusion that God loves Israel and that his love, contrary to appearances (5:30) has a goal, an end (5:40). God's ways are unknowable by Ezra (5:38) but the angel/God has, in 5:40, made a response pregnant with promise.

Let us now try to draw out, in a more general way, some of the implications of our analysis of the text. In broadest terms it presents the seer distressed by the destruction and pushed by this distress to question what had always been a basic axiom of Israelite and Jewish thought, that God's action towards

---

[23] Yet, in spite of this, in 12:4 he can still speak of the search for understanding as the motive of his receiving of visions.

[24] See note 22. Observe that in Latin *mens* serves in 5:33 where "heart" served in chaps. 3–4; and that "reins" also plays the same role in 5:34.

mankind and towards Israel is just. In order to test (and perhaps to mitigate) the conclusion that seems to impose itself from his consideration of the situation of Israel, Ezra wishes to understand the "way of the Most High," the nature of God's action in the world. In the course of attempting to do this the seer, like his angelic interlocutor, rejects as irrelevant and inaccessible the idea of special knowledge, of revealed information about heavenly secrets— theosophical, cosmological, uranological or other. The ascent to heaven and other modes of revelation of supernal secrets are dismissed. Such matters are, by their very nature, beyond human ken.

In taking this stance, the author is deliberately engaging and rejecting the dominant stream of apocalyptic tradition. His position appears more conservative, more "old fashioned," more like central strands of biblical thought. In fact, as is clearly evidenced in his inversion of the lists of revealed things and turning them into lists of what cannot be known, he is deeply rooted in apocalyptic tradition, but goes on to reject certain aspects of it.

The seer, then, seeks to understand the way of the Most High, God's action in the world, from a strongly demythologized perspective. Moreover, he believes that special revelation and knowledge of God in the heavenly dimension cannot be gained by human beings. He wishes to know God, not in a mystical or gnostic sense, but as He acts in the arena of history. This forces the question of theodicy into a more acute formulation and, *mutatis mutandis* the issue of theodicy is dominant throughout the first three visions.

In the course of the first dialogical vision, as we have seen, the seer comes to accept of the role of determinism in the divine conduct of the world. This opens up the direction he takes in the second vision: the injustice of God is no longer to the fore but instead, the anomalies arising from the condition of the world when compared with God's relationship with Israel are formulated in terms of God's love and hate. It is, of course, the same issue as in the first vision, but the questioning of the basic underlying axioms about the justice of God has been left behind. This time the issue is put in the language of election and love, while God's way in the world is called his "judgment".

It is impossible here to lay out the further development of these themes in the book, in which they are prominent. We have claimed elsewhere that the resolution of the tensions engendered in the course of the first three visions is to be found in the conversion experience described in the fourth vision.[25] But, for the present what is significant is the development from the first to the second vision and the correlations between them. In the one the seer cannot understand the justice of God and way of the Most High; in the other he is unable to grasp the working of God's love and election or to know his judgements.

---

[25] M.E. Stone, Reactions to Destructions of the Second Temple, *Journal of the Study of Judaism* 12 (1982) 202–204.

In neither case is it an issue of the knowledge of God himself, either in philosophical or mystical terms. It is knowledge of the working of God in the history of the world and Israel. In this insistence on history 4 Ezra takes a position in many ways conservative when compared to much more ancient works, such as *First Book of Enoch* in which, half a millenium or so before, the revelation of heavenly secrets and, indeed, the very vision of God on his throne, stand at the centre of the stage. However, 4 Ezra represents not a stage before this idea, but a development which has abandoned it. The author deliberately rejects such knowledge of God and the heavenly realm. He longs to understand his ways, his working in the world, and from this his justice. He comes not to deny, but to accept, in spite of circumstances.[26]

---

[26] Two major works dealing with 4 Ezra have not been addressed in the course of the present paper. We are in basic disagreement with the presuppositions made by their authors about the nature of 4 Ezra and the methods to be used to analyze it. We refer to W. Harnisch, *Verhängnis und Verheißung der Geschichte* (Forschungen zur Religion und Literatur des Alten und Neuen Testaments 97), Göttingen: Vandenhoeck und Ruprecht, 1969 and E. Brandenburger, *Die Verborgenheit Gottes im Weltgeschehen*, Zürich: Theologischer Verlag, 1981. The significant views of these authors will be discussed in the detail they deserve in our forthcoming Commentary on 4 Ezra (Hermeneia), Philadelphia: Fortress Press.

MAN'S BEHAVIOUR AND GOD'S JUSTICE IN EARLY JEWISH TRADITION. SOME OBSERVATIONS

BY

P.W. van Boxel*

Introduction

In the tradition attributed to Moses—the *Torah she-bi-Khetav* and the *Torah-she-be-al Peh*—one finds an interrelation between man's behaviour as imposed upon him by God and God's answer to it by means of blessings. If man behaves according to God's directives and instructions he will certainly enjoy all the benefits God has promised to give him. So it is said in Deut 28:

> "And if you obey the voice of the Lord your God, being careful to do all his commandments which I command you this day, the Lord your God will set you high above all the nations of the earth. And all these blessings shall come upon you and overtake you, if you obey the voice of the lord your God. Blessed shall you be in the city, and blessed shall you be in the field. Blessed shall be the fruit of your body, and the fruit of your ground, and the fruit of your beasts, the increase of your cattle, and the young of your flock. Blessed shall be your basket and your kneading-trough. Blessed shall you be when you come in, and blessed shall you be when you go out. (1–6) .... The Lord will open to you his good treasury the heavens, to give the rain of your land in its season and to bless all the works of your hands (12) .... But if you will not obey the voice of the Lord your God or be careful to do all his commandments and his statutes which I command you this day, then all these curses shall come upon you and overtake you. Cursed shall you be in the city and cursed shall you be in the field. Cursed shall be your basket and your kneading-trough. Cursed shall be the fruit of your body, and the fruit of your ground, the increase of your cattle, and the young of your flock (15–18)."[1]

This biblical pattern has been questioned in the course of Israel's history. First indications of the dissolution of this selfevident link between man's action and God's reaction we find already in the Bible itself. Illustrative is Kohelet 7:15 "In my vain life I have seen everything; there is a righteous man who perishes in his righteousness, and there is a wicked man who prolongs his life in his evildoing."[2] Human experience contradicts here the original divine regulation as

---

* Bible quotations are from the Revised Standard Version (London 1973), Mishnah quotations from H. Danby, The Mishnah (Oxford 1933) and Babylonian Talmud quotations from I. Epstein, The Babylonian Talmud (London 1952).

[1] Cfr. the blessings of obedience and the results of disobedience in Lev 26 and Deut 11.

[2] Cfr. Eccles. 2,14 f. 3,16 4,1 5,7 8,14 9,2 f. Cfr. also Jer. 12.1–2; Ps. 73,3–12 and Job 21. See further A. Lauha, *Kohelet* (BKAT), Neukirchen 1978, espec. 135–136.

formulated in texts as Deuteronomy 28. The same tension between human experience and the presupposed divine reaction to man's behaviour we find in a much stronger way expressed in the apocryphal partly apocalyptic literature. As an example I quote from the Psalms of Solomon:

> "I cried unto the Lord when I was in distress, unto God when sinners assailed. Suddenly the alarm of war was heard before me; (I said), He wil hearken to me, for I am full of righteousness. I thought in my heart that I was full of righteousness, because I was well of and had become rich in children. Their wealth spread to the whole of the earth. They were exalted unto the stars; they said they would never fall (Psalm 1,1−5)."

Sanders comments on this Psalm as follows: "The author of Ps. 1 ... had counted himself righteous because of his prosperity, so that when war threatened he thought that God would protect him (1.2 f.). But he has to grant that the prosperity of his enemies (probably the Romans, though possibly the Hasmoneans) exceeded anything he had imagined ... If prosperity is a test of righteousness, the Romans (or Hasmoneans) must have been really righteous! But they became insolent; their sins were in secret (1.6 f.)—that is, they were not punished for them and still appeared prosperous and consequently righteous. In this situation the view seems to have developed that it is the special characteristic of the pious to be chastened. This combines the old view with the new situation. The sign of righteousness is to be chastened for one's sins rather than to be prosperous, for the wicked may be prosperous; but not to be destroyed, for the wicked will ultimately be destroyed. The final salvation of the righteous after their chastening and the destruction of the wicked are repeated themes."[3]

Two attributes of God

In a way comparable with the apocryphal literature one has dealt with the problem of the obvious abolition of the biblical pattern concerning man's behaviour and the consequent blessing or punishment by God in pharisaic and early rabbinic Judaism. Illustrative in this context is the rabbinic conception of justice and mercy or goodness as attributes of God. We will first give a general outline of these two hardly compatible attributes and then discuss one particular rabbinic text in view of the biblical pattern concerning man's behaviour and God's reaction to it.

---

[3] E.P. Sanders, *Paul and Palestinian Judaism. A Comparison of Patterns of Religion*, London 1978, 390−391. For a detailed discussion of the position of the righteous and God's justice see G.W.E. Nickelsburg, Resurrection, Immortality and Eternal Life in Intertestamental Judaism, *Harvard Theological Studies* 26 (1972) 112−130.

A classical study in this field is A. Marmorstein's *The Old Rabbinic Doctrine of God. The Names and Attributes of God*.[4] Dealing with God's justice Marmorstein shows that rabbinic Judaism at least partly sticks to the interrelation between man's behaviour and his actual situation as caused by God's righteous answer. As an example serves the discussion between the emperor and R. Joshua b. Hananja. The emperor asked him: 'Where is your God's sense of justice? Why are children born deaf and dump, blind and lame? Why should they suffer? They are innocent.' Rabbi Joshua replied: 'God knows the deeds of man long before he was born, whether he is going to be good or bad.' The emperor: 'Let him repent, and God shall open his eyes!' Thereupon rabbi Joshua tests the case of a blind man, who turns out to be a greedy, faithless man, and convinces the emperor of God's justice."[5] Although human experience seems to contradict it, God's justice cannot be denied.

On the other hand, however, there is the experience that the good and the righteous suffer in this world. Why should they suffer? With regard to this question Marmorstein refers to the distinction between God's justice exercised in this world and His justice which He will show in the world to come, a solution which is very similar to the answer given in the apocryphal literature. "Rabbi Akiba was the first to emphasize the teaching that God makes the righteous pay in this world for the few 'evil deeds' which they have committed, in order to bestow upon them hapiness and give them a good reward in the world to come."[6] Just the opposite is the case with the reward and the punishment of the wicked. So daily life and common happenings are reconciled with God's justice and they are even signs of God's love towards the righteous as it said in *Sifre* to Deuteronomy par. 32: "Man should welcome suffering more than happiness, for if man is happy he cannot acquire forgiveness of sin; how does he acquire it? By suffering!"[7]

In a subsequent chapter Marmorstein discusses the attribute of goodness. A characteristic feature of this attribute is the universal dimension of God's love and his care for humankind. (An undertone of protest against the claim that only the God of the christians shows this feature can hardly be denied). The God of the Jews, Marmorstein states, "deals mercifully with his creatures. He feeds and sustains all. This act of lovingkindness is shown not only to those who are just and righteous, but even to the wicked." [8] Then he refers to God's providence as formulated by R. Gamaliel II or R. Zadok, a providence "in which all creatures share equally . . . : God, who created the world, causes wind

---

[4] New York 1968[2]
[5] Marmorstein, *o.c.*, 183.
[6] Marmorstein, *o.c.*, 186.
[7] Marmorstein, *o.c.*, 187.
[8] Marmorstein, *o.c.*, 197.

to blow, sun to shine, rain and dew to descend, plants to grow, and decks a ready table to all!''[9] The love and the goodness of God, which are indisputable in early Judaism, are however not only an aspect of God which man can experience, but are also an appeal to him. Man is expected to act according to God's attitude towards mankind, but at the same time his attitude is dependent on man's behaviour. Marmorstein illustrates this interrelationship with statements from R. Akiba and R. Aha: "Rabbi Akiba said: He who shows no love to his fellow-men can expect no love from Heaven. Rabbi Aha said: When drought comes, and the creatures are merciful to each other, God is also filled with mercy to you!''[10] Actually it concerns here ways of imitatio Dei as R. Levi said: "God is good to all, and the greatest good is that His creatures learn of Him to be merciful to each other.''[11] How could a New Testament student resist the temptation to quote from the gospel of Luke: "Be merciful, even as your Father is merciful (Lk 6:36).

The preceding quotations are theological convictions and ethical admonitions taken from the aggadah. Also in a halakhic context, however, God's goodness is mentioned and man must gratefully bless Him for this goodness. In *Berakhot* 9:2 it is said: "Rabbi Judah says: If a man saw the Great Sea he should say, 'Blessed is he that made the Great Sea,' but only if he sees it at intervals of time. For rain and good tidings he should say, 'Blessed is he, the good and the doer of good.'" Rabbi Juda,—third generation of the Tannaim—, is the main representative of his generation and is mentioned in the Mishnah more than 600 times. His conviction is that rain depends on God's goodness, a conviction held also by many of his contemporaries.

According to Marmorstein's presentation the rabbis kept to the biblical pattern of interrelation between man's behaviour and God's justice, though partly postponed till the world to come. On the other hand God is described in early rabbinic Judaism as merciful even with regard to the wicked. This attribute of God seems to be connected with nature and natural phenomena. Although Marmorstein does not discuss the incompatibility of justice and mercy or goodness, he suggests that these two attributes of God have their own domain in early rabbinic Judaism.

A similar presentation we find in more recent studies. Sanders—referring to Urbach—emphasizes that the theme of reward and punishment is current in the tannaitic literature: "God rewards successful fulfilment of commandments and punishes transgression" in this world or in the next.[12] With a note of warning against a common christian misunderstanding—that the world to

---

[9] *Ibid.*
[10] Marmorstein, *o.c.*, 204.
[11] Marmorstein, *o.c.*, 203.
[12] Sanders, *o.c.*, 117.

come is earned by the performance of a certain number of commandments—Sanders summarizes the rabbinic view of the justice of God as meaning "that God appropriately rewards and punishes for obedience and disobedience. When this was seen not to be the case in this world, the exercise of God's justice was postponed to the next."[13]

Holding to the justice of God the rabbis do not overlook his mercy. That God is merciful becomes even a major theme in the tannaitic literature. Rabbinic thought is dominated by the idea of God's love rather than by the idea of his justice.[14] The question of how the two attributes are to be reconciled cannot be answered—Sanders states—in a general way. Justice and mercy do not fit in "a doctrinal sytem in which every statement has a logical place. One thing or the other would be said depending on the particular needs of the instance. But there should be no doubt that the latter type of statement—that mercy outweighs justice—reflects the Rabbinic attitude towards God at its most basic level."[15]

Both, Marmorstein and Sanders come to the conclusion that God's justice, though not denied or overlooked, must share its place with the attribute of mercy or goodness in early rabbinic Judaism, Marmorstein—in view of the examples he gives—suggesting that both attributes have their own domain, whereas Sanders explicitly points at the particular needs which call for either justice or mercy.

Mishnah

In the following pages I will examine a particular mishnaic text that raises the matter of the relation between man's fulfilment of God's commandments and the consequent blessing which God has promised, a relationship as formulated in Deut 28. The text seems to me a *terminus a quo* for the precedence of Gods mercy and goodness over his justice because of the special situation (Sanders) in a particular field (Marmorstein). The mishnah is from the tractate concerning the tithes, *Ma'aser sheni*, and based on Deut 26,12—15:

> "When you have finished paying all the tithe of your produce in the third year, which is the year of tithing, giving it to the Levite, the sojourner, the fatherless, and the widow, that they may eat within your towns and be filled, then you shall say before the Lord your God, 'I have removed the sacred portion out of my house, and moreover I have given it to the Levite, the sojourner, the fatherless, and the widow, according to all thy commandment which thou hast commanded me; I have not transgressed any of thy commandments, neither have I forgotten them;

---

[13] Sanders, *o.c.*, 126.

[14] Sanders, *o.c.*, 124, with reference to M. Kadushin, *The Rabbinic Mind*. New York 1972[3], 219.

[15] Sanders, *o.c.*, 124.

I have not eaten of the tithe while I was mourning, or removed any of it while I was unclean, or offered any of it to the dead; I have obeyed the voice of the Lord my God, I have done according to all that thou hast commanded me. Look down from thy holy habitation, from heaven, and bless they people Israel and the ground which thou hast given us, as thou didst to our fathers, a land flowing with milk and honey."

After a detailed description of the actual obligations one is supposed to have fulfilled when making the avowal (*Ma'aser Sheni* 5:10–12) the text of the Mishnah continues as follows:

13. *Look down from thy holy habitation from heaven*—we have done what thou hast decreed concerning us: do thou also what thou hast promised to us; *Look down from thy holy habitation from heaven and bless thy people Israel*—with sons and daughters; *and the ground which thou hast given us*—with dew and wine and with the young of cattle; *as thou swarest unto our fathers, a land flowing with milk and honey*—that thou mayest give flavour to the fruits.

Here the Mishnah adopts clearly and strengthens even the biblical pattern of obedience and consequent blessing, which is specified as the various blessings of nature.

In the last mishnah of *Ma'aser Sheni*, however, it is recorded that the biblical obligation of making the avowal was annuled:

15. Johanan the High Priest did away with the Avowal concerning the Tithe. He too made an end also of the 'Awakeners' and the 'Stunners'. Until his days the hammer used to smite in Jerusalem. And in his days none needed to inquire concerning *demai*-produce.

We will first examine the tradition of the abolition of the confession as to the question why the highpriest took this decision. Then we will confront the reconstructed reason of the annulment with some early aggadic traditions which should support our position. Finally we will see whether the current halakhah in early Judaism and the tradition in the New Testament confirm our conclusions.

The Babylonian Talmud

The tradition of the annulment is also recorded in *Sotah* 9:10 and commented on in *Sotah* 47ᵇ–48ᵃ of the Babylonian Talmud.

In *Sotah* 47b it is asked *why* Johanan the high priest "brought to an end the confession made at the presentation of the tithe." The question is answered by R. Jose b. Hanina. He said: "Because people were not presenting it according to the regulation; for the All-Mercifull said that they should give it to the Levites whereas we present it to the priests." According to R. Jose b. Hanina (belonging to the second generation of Amoraim: 257–320) there was "only" a formal reason which brought the high priest to the decision. The actual recipients—the priests—were according to the confession not supposed to receive the tithe.

The explanation given by Jose b. Hanina is obviously dependent on an older discussion recorded in *Yebamot* 86ᵃ⁻ᵇ where the question is discussed as to whom the first tithe belongs. According to R. Akiba it belongs to the Levite. But R. Eleazar b. Azariah said: to the priest (He himself was an influential and rich priest!), which should be understood as "to the priest also." Both defend their position by referring to Scripture. R. Akiba sees his interpretation supported by Numbers 18:26, where it is said with regard to the tithe: "Moreover thou shalt speak unto the Levites, and say unto them." R. Eleazar refers to the fact "that in 24 passages (in Scripture) the priests were described as Levites and the following is one of them: But the priests the Levites, the sons of Zadok (Ez 44:15)." Then the discussion turns to the question, why the Levites were penalized (by being deprived of the) tithe. The answer is "that the penalization was due to their not going up in the days of Ezra ... Whence is it deduced that they did not go up in the days of Ezra?—It is written, And I gathered them together to the river that runneth to Ahava; and there we encamped three days; and I viewed the people and the priests, and found there none of the sons of Levi (Ezra 8:15)."

When we compare the two texts from the Talmud we may conclude that the actual recipients of the tithe were (the levites and) the priests (= *Sotah*), a practice defended with arguments from Scripture by R. Eleazar (= *Yebamot*). From that point of view there was no need whatsoever to abolish the confession made at the presentation of the tithe. The practice was not necessarily in contradiction with the confession, because the levites could be understood as the priests (also). It is therefore not surprising at all that in the earlier discussion as recorded in *Yebamot* the abolition of the confession is not even mentioned. It is remarkable, however, that the question of the levites as presented by R. Jose has become an accepted reason to explain the historical decision of the high priest.[16] The text of *Sotah* shows that the answer of Jose b. Hanina was not the final say in the matter, for it continues to discuss the issue connecting it with *demai*, the produce not certainly tithed, which connection is presented as a baraita: "But surely it has been taught: He also annulled the confession and decreed in respect of *demai*; because he sent (inspectors) throughout the Israelite territory and discovered that they only separated the great *terumah* but as for the first and second tithes some fulfilled the law while others did not. So he said to (the people), 'My sons, come, I will tell you this. Just as in (the

---

[16] Cfr. the explanation in the various editions and translations of *Maʿaser Sheni* as W. Bunte, *Die Mischna, Maaserot/Maaser Scheni*, Berlin 1962, *Mischnajot, Maaser Scheni* (Basel, 1968), *The Babylonian Talmud, Maʿaser Sheni* (ed. by I. Epstein, London 1948), *The Mishnah* (transl. by H. Danby) Oxford 1933, 73–82.

neglect) of the "great *terumah*" there is mortal sin, so with (the neglect) to present to *terumah* of the tithe and with the use of untithed produce there is mortal sin.' He thus arose and decreed for them that whoever purchases fruits from an ʿ*Am ha-arez* must separate the first and second tithes therefrom. From the first tithe he separates the *terumah* of the tithe and gives it to a priest, and as for the second tithe he should go up and eat it in Jerusalem. With regard to the first tithe and the tithe of the poor whoever demands them from his neighbour has the onus of proving (that they had not been already apportioned)!''

If one tries to reconstruct the historical reason that led the high priest Johanan to his decision the baraita is besides the fact that it preserves an old accepted tradition, a far better explanation than the one given by R. Jose b. Hanina. The baraita suggests an interrelation between the abolition of the obligation to make the confession regarding the tithes and the fact that many people did not fulfill this biblical commandment of paying them. The suggestion of interrelation is due to the iuxtaposition of the two items, a iuxtaposition which does not occur in the Mishnah.[17] That an actual situation especially due to transgressors of the law influences halakhic decisions is a well known fact in early Judaism. A good example thereof is the discussion in *Shabbat* 40ᵃ regarding the allowance of taking a steam bath on Sabbath, where the halakha continuously is changed because of the transgressors: "When transgressors grew in number, they began forbidding it," and then after a series of restrictions having made the Sages "forbade the hot springs of Tiberias but permitted cold water. But when they saw that this (series of restriction) could not stand, they permitted the hot springs of Tiberias, whilst sweating remained in statu quo." Because of the transgressors halakhic decisions are abolished, which does not only apply to Rabbinical enactments but also to biblical commandments. The institution of the *prosbul* by Hillel is perhaps the clearest proof of this kind of abolition.[18]

Taking into account that the baraita does not explicitly give any reason why the high priest abolished the confession and on the other hand connects the annulment with the question of *demai*, taking into account also the possible role of transgressors as influencing the halakhah, I would propose to interpret the connection as a causative one. The baraita is then the oldest answer to the question why the high priest brought to an end the confession made at the presentation of the tithe: because the majority of the people did not keep to the commandment of tithing.

---

[17] In the Mishnah *Demai* is the last question that is delt with. *Sotah* 48ᵃ knows of the sequence of the Mishnah, but anticipates the explanation of *Demai*.

[18] See *Sheviʿit* 10:3. With regard to the uprooting of biblical commandments see E. Berkovits, *Not in Heaven*, New York 1983, 57–64.

The consequences of the transgression of the Law

When presupposing the biblical pattern of interrelation between man's behaviour according to the commandments and God's answer by means of prosperity as formulated in *Ma'aser sheni* 5:12 ff. in conformity with Deuteronomy we may expect the cessation of God's blessings as asked for in Deut 26:13 ff. which would have caused an appeal to the people to repent and keep again God's ordinances. This however will be seen not to be the case. Taking as an example of the blessings of nature the blessing of dew and rain I will examine some early aggadic texts in view of the abolition of the confession. The decision was made between 135–104 B.C.E. being the reign of Johanan Hyrcanus the ethnarch of Judea and the high priest, the aggadic traditions are related to famous rabbis from the beginning of the first century B.C.

The aggadah

When dealing with the question why and when God gives rain to the land the story of Honi the circle drawer seems to me essential. Honi was a renowned miracle worker in the period of the Second Temple (first Century B.C.E.). The story starts with the problem that the greater part of the month of Adar had gone and yet no rain had fallen. The people came to Honi and asked him to pray that rain may fall. He prayed and exclaimed: "Master of the universe, Thy children have turned to me because (they believe) me to be a member of Thy house. I swear by Thy great name that I will not move from here (i.e. from the circle he had drawn) until Thou hast mercy upon Thy children!" Thereupon it began to rain and through his prayer Honi controled the quantity of rainfall. In this story there is obviously no relation between human behaviour and the blessing of rain. The only one who causes the rain to fall is Honi, not because he merits the rain but because he is believed to be a member of God's house, which means that he is capable of influencing and changing God's decisions. The continuation of the story emphasizes this peculiar power of Honi in two ways. First it is told that Simeon b. Setah sent this message to him: "Were it not that you are Honi I would have placed you under the ban; for were the years like the years of Elijah would not the name of Heaven be profaned through you?[19] But what shall I do unto you who actest petulantly before the Omnipresent and He grants your desire, as a son who acts petulantly before his

---

[19] Simeon b. Setah refers to the time that the heavens were closed and rain did not fall because Ahab and his father's house had forsaken the commandments of the Lord, see 1 Kings 17,1 ff., esp. v 18. Only after the people had seized the prophets of Ba'al and Elijah had killed them, and after they had said: 'The Lord, he is God; the Lord, he is God' the heavens opened again and there was a great rain, see 1 Kings 17,39–40.45.

father and he grants his desires . . . ." By referring to Elijah Simeon b. Setah characterizes implicitly the actual situation as sinful, which must have caused the lack of rain. But he accepts that the biblical pattern that functioned in the time of Elijah is broken down by Honi the circle drawer, who does not ask the people to repent or to confess their sins as Elijah did.[20]

Secondly the response of the Sanhedrin, which at that time according to the anonymous sages was presided by Simeon ben Setah, is recorded. The response is based on Job 22:28–30: "You will decide on a matter, and it will be established for you, and light will shine on your ways. When they cast you down, you shall say: There is lifting up, for He saves the humble person, He delivers him that is not innocent, yea, he shall be delivered through the cleanness of your hands." Applying the text to Honi the Sanhedrin says of him:

> "You have decreed (on earth) below and the Holy One, Blessed be He, fulfils your word (in heaven) above. You have illumined with your prayer a generation in darkness. You have raised with your prayer a generation that has sunk low. You have saved by your prayer a generation that is humiliated with sin. You have delivered by your prayer a generation that is not innocent. You have delivered it through the work of your clean hands."[21]

By interpreting the text of Job in such a way the Sanhedrin points explicitly to the sinful situation that obviously has caused the drought, from which the people however are saved through the prayer of Honi. It is not the fulfilment of commandments neither repentance but prayer that gives rain to the land. It is therefore not God's justice which is called upon, but his mercy!

The position of Honi the circle drawer is not an exception, but introduces a kind of family-tradition. Of Honi's grandson Abba Hilkiah it is told that whenever the world was in need of rain the Rabbis sent a message to him and he prayed and rain fell. It is remarkable that there is no sin or transgression mentioned here, but just the situation of drought which is solved through the prayer of Honi's grandson. The same power is ascribed to the son of the daughther of Honi the circle drawer:

> "When the world was in need of rain the Rabbis would send to him school children and they would take hold of the hem of his garment and say to him: Father, Father, give us rain. Thereupon he would plead with the Holy One, Blessed be He, (thus): Master of the Universe, do it for the sake of these who are unable to distinguish between the Father who gives rain and the Father who does not."[22]

---

[20] The actual uprooting of the biblical pattern must have been hard to accept for Simeon b. Setah because of his persistent endeavour to urge obedience to the Torah. In the Talmud he is referred to as "restoring the Torah to its former glory" (*Taʿanit* 23ᵃ). This restoration concerns first of all the pharisaic conception of Torah in opposition to the position of the sadducees, which, however, certainly includes concern with regard to the Torah she-bi-ktav, see *Kiddushin* 66ᵃ.

[21] *Taʿanit* 23ᵃ.

[22] *Taʿanit* 23ᵇ.

Children who are not able to distinguish with regard to rain means that they are not aware of the interrelation between human behaviour and God's answer to it. Therefore God is asked not to keep to his justice on which rain depended.

Having pointed at the story of Honi the circle drawer as an essential—even by the Sanhedrin accepted—change regarding the interrelation between human behaviour and the heavenly blessing of rain I will add some observations about the expression *rain . . . in its season* as found in Lev 24:6 and Deut 11:14, which confirm the conclusion drawn from the story of Honi. In Lev 26:3 f. it is said: "If you walk in my statutes and observe my commandments and do them, then I will give you rains in their season, and the land shall yield its increase, and the trees of the field shall yield their fruit." The expression is commented on in *Sifra, Sifre* and *Vayyikra Rabbah*.

In *Sifre* on Deuteronomy 11:14 R. Natan says: "In its season: that means regular during the Shabbat nights as in the days of queen Salome. Why did it happen like this? Rabbi says: So that those who come into the world cannot open their mouth and say: Look that is the reward for keeping all the commandments, but much more (that they should realize): If you walk in my statutes and observe my commandments then I will give you rain in its season (Lev 26:3)." If rain troubles people by hindering them from working one could possibly see it as a curse instead of a blessing. But rain during the Sabbath nights is the culmination of blessing, since it bothers nobody, everybody taking his Sabbath rest at home.

The same tradition of rain falling during the Sabbath nights we find in *Vayyikra Rabbah* XXXV,10. It is noteworthy that the days of queen Salome mentioned in the previous midrash are here also called the days of Simeon ben Setah, who was her brother. In the story of Honi the circle drawer he opposed to Honi's action because it broke down the biblical pattern of behaviour and reward. It is exactly this biblical pattern that underlies the interpretation of *in its season* and which is connected with queen Salome and her brother Simeon ben Setah. We may therefore conclude that in opposition to the family tradition of Honi the circle drawer Simeon ben Setah's family still kept to the biblical pattern of behaviour and reward. But according to the midrashim this biblical pattern belongs to the past: it *happened* in the days of queen Salome and Simeon ben Setah, who as the president of the Sanhedrin finally did not protest against Honi's appeal for God's mercy.

The halakhah

Having proposed that already at the beginning of the first century B.C.E. God's justice was not a criterion with regard to the blessings of nature we now turn to the halakhah concerning the natural phenomena. I have limited my investigation to the words *geshem* (heavy rain), *mathar* (rain) and *thal* (dew) as far as they occur in the Mishnah.

First it should be noted that dew and rain are mainly used as halakhic categories. We find rain and dew as liquids on which uncleanness yes or not depend. So in *Makshirin* 2:4 "If a man was plastering his roof (with dirty water and clay) or washing his raiment, and rain came down (on the dirty water), if the greater part was from the unclean (water) the whole is unclean; if the greater part was from the clean, the whole is clean; if they were equal the whole is unclean. R. Judah says: If the rain continued falling (the whole is clean)."[23]

In a number of cases rain is used as a term of time regarding the allowance of action. So in *Shevi'it* 3:8 "In the sixth year, after the rains have ceased, steps may not be built up the sides of ravines (from which water can be drawn for the field during the rainy season), since this would be to make them ready for the Seventh year; but they may be built in the Seventh year after the rains have ceased, since this is to make them ready for the eight year."[24]

Only in a limited number of texts rain and dew are not used as halakhic categories. Those texts deserve our attention.

Massekhet Ta'anit opens with the question: "From what time do they make mention of 'the Power of rain'?" The question is answered as follows: "R. Eliezer says: From the first Festival-day of the Feast (of Tabernacles). R. Joshua says: From the last Festival-day of the Feast. R. Joshua said to him: Since rain is but a sign of curse at the Feast, why should they make mention of it? R. Eliezer answered: I did not, indeed, say 'pray for,' but 'make mention of' (the rain): 'Who maketh the winds to blow and sendeth down the rain'—in its due season. He said to him: If so a man make mention thereof at all times." (1:1). Remarkable is the distinction made by R. Eliezer between 'making mention of rain' and 'praying for it.' To make mention of rain is connected by him with the confession that God is the one "who maketh the winds to blow and sendeth down the rain." This confession is also reflected in the expression 'the Power of rain.' God has the power with regard to rain and the confession of it leads man to pray for rain. It should be noted that this kind of confession—to be dated at the end of the first century C.E.—directing to prayer is remarkably different from the confession formerly made at the presentation of the tithe which was meant to remind God of his promises to bless the ground with dew and rain because of man's behaviour.

The mention of the Power of rain and the prayer for rain are actually part of the *Shemoneh Esreh*, the eighteen benedictions or the *Amida* prayer. The power of rain is mentioned in the second benediction. The prayer for rain in the 9th:

> "Bless for us, O Lord our God, this year and all kinds of its yield for (our) good; and shower down dew and rain for a blessing upon the face of the earth: fulfil us of Thy bounty and bless this our year that it be as the good years. Blessed be Thou, O Lord, who blessest the years."

---

[23] Other texts are *Para* 9:1 11:1 *Makshirin* 2:3 3:5.6 4:2.10 5:7 6:1.4.8.
[24] Other texts are *Shevi'it* 9:7 *Sukkah* 2:9 *Nedarim* 4:4 8:5.

According to the Mishnah rain is in the powerful hand of God and rainfall depends on prayer. Nothing is said about human behaviour, which would influence the rainfall, except in one text: *Yadaim* 4:3. This mishnah deals with the question what tithes must be payed by Israelites living in Ammon and Moab in the Seventh Year when no harvest is reaped in the land of Israel, and what grows is ownerless property and exempt from tithes; but what Israelites grow outside the land of Israel is not subject to the same rules. With regard to this question R. Tarfon decreed: (They must give) Poorman's tithe. And R. Eleazar b. Azariah decreed: (They must give) second tithe. By comparing Ammon and Moab with other countries both give their arguments which are meant to legitimate their decision. "R. Tarfon said, On Egypt, because it is near, have they imposed Poorman's Tithe that the poor of Israel might be stayed thereby in the Seventh Year; so, too, on Ammon and Moab, which are near, have they imposed Poorman's Tithe, that the poor of Israel might be stayed thereby in the Seventh Year. R. Eleazar b. Azariah answered, Lo, thou art as one that would bestow on them wordly gain, yet thou art but as one that would suffer souls to perish; thou wouldest rob the heavens so that they send down neither dew nor rain, for it is written, *Will a man rob God? yet you rob me. But ye say, Wherein have we robbed thee? In tithes and heave offerings* (Mal 3:8)."

The second tithe—to be eaten in Jerusalem and only in the third and the sixth year changed into Poorman's tithe—is according to rabbi Eleazar b. Azariah more important because it is holy (a typically priestly position!) and he points at dew and rain as dependent on the fulfillment of this commandment. But the question of dew and rain does not influence the halakhic discussion at all. The final decision is made through a hermeneutical rule in favour of the Poorman's tithe. This decision is then communicated to R. Eliezer, who, because of heresy, was under a ban and so forbidden to have any part in the Court's discussions and decisions. The decision already made was however—obviously because it was based on a rabbinical argumentation—not completely easing. Otherwise one cannot explain R. Eliezer's answer to R. Jose, who told him what they had decided. R. Eliezer said: "Go and tell them, Be not anxious by reason of your voting, for I have received a tradition from Rabban Johanan b. Zakkai, who heard it from his teacher, and his teacher from his teacher, as a Halakhah given to Moses from Sinai, that Ammon and Moab should give Poorman's tithe in the Seventh Year." By using the fixed formula 'be not anxious' R. Eliezer takes away any possible doubt as to the legitimacy of the decision already made.[25]

The mishnah *Yadaim* 4:3 makes clear that in the Court's discussion one was confronted with the biblical interdependence of correctly keeping the com-

---

[25] As to the expression 'not to be anxious' with regard to halakhic decisions cfr. *Bava Mezia* 5:5 and *Hullin* 8:2.

mandments and God's blessing of rain which, however, was not discussed as
a real argument in establishing the halakhah. The discussion afterwards between R. Eliezer and R. Jose shows that the Court did not find it easy to ignore
this biblical pattern of interdependence.

The tradition of rain in the New Testament

After having confronted the current halakhah with the supposed early change
from justice to mercy as God's preferable attribute regarding the blessings of
nature we will now turn to some aggadic traditions in the New Testament which
confirm once more the conclusion that justice did not play a part in this "field"
in the first century C.E. and onwards.

James 5:17

In James 5:17 the efficacy of human prayer is emphasized by referring to
Elijah: "Elijah was a man of like nature with ourselves and he prayed fervently
that it might not rain, and for three years and six months it did not rain on the
earth." Actually we do not find this efficacy of Elija's prayer in the story as
it is told in 1 Kings 17–18. There it is—as we said before—because of the sins
of Ahab and his father's house that rain did not fall and because of repentance
that the heavens opened again. It is much more according to jewish tradition
that Elijah is presented in the letter of James. One could refer to 4 Ezra 7:109
where Elijah is mentioned among the intercessors who have prayed for others.
He, Elijah, prayed "for those who received the rain, and for the dead that he
might live." When asking for the origin of this in the first century C.E. established tradition one could possibly refer to the story of Honi the circle drawer.
It is there that Elijah is presented by Simeon b. Setah as the opponent of Honi
who does not stick anymore to the pattern of human behaviour and justice as
far as rain is concerned. But the same Simeon b. Setah confesses that he does
not live in the days of Elijah anymore. Honi the circle drawer seems the
turningpoint from justice to (praying for) mercy according to which then also
Elijah is shaped.

Matthew 5:43–48

A God who does good to the world without taking into account man's behaviour seems also to be the obvious framework for the interpretation of Mat
5:43–48.

In Mat 5:45 it is said: "He (God) makes his sun rise on the evil and on the
good, and sends rain on the just and on the unjust." With this reference to
God's activity the Matthean Jesus wants to stress the commandment "to love

your enemies and to pray for those who persecute you'' (5:44). One should not only love his friends, since God does not limit his sun and rain only to the righteous. It is clear that Matthew follows the established tradition, in which the principle of justice with regard to the blessings of nature does not work anymore. Also for the Matthean Jesus God has the power of giving sun or rain and when he gives it he does it without distinction.

In context of the statement in Mat 5:45 one should ask what kind of God the Matthean Jesus wants his disciples to know. Obviously He is here not a God of justice, but it seems that He is not a God of mercy and goodness either. There is in any case no mention of these qualities in our greek text. The only attribute God is called with is his perfection in Matt 5:48: "You therefore, must be perfect (teleios) as your heavenly father is perfect.'' At first sight, however, there is no relation between God's perfection and the distribution of rain—we did not come across this quality in the analysis of the rabbinic texts—and in the various interpretations Matt 5:48 is not connected with the preceding verses and not understood as referring to them. In illustration I mention the recent commentary on the Gospel of Matthew by Ulrich Luz.[26] With regard to v. 48 Luz says that Matthew reformulated this tradition from Q in such a way that it became a fitting conclusion of the whole series of antitheses. "Damit er zugleich die ganze Antithesereihe abschliessen und einen Rückverweis auf V 20 geben kann. Im einzelnen bleibt manches unsicher.'' Further he states that this qualification of God serves as a transition to Matt 6:1−18 "wo diese Gottesbezeichnis zum Zentrum wird.''[27] Not seeing any connection with the preceeding verses the commentaries deal with Mat 5:48 separately, looking for the background of the interrelationship "you therefore must be ... as your heavenly father is'' and for the meaning of teleios in context of this interrelationship.

J. Dupont states that the background of Mat 5:48 is so evidently biblical that there is no need to suppose that the writer wanted to introduce a completely new concept.[28] He then refers for this biblical background a.o. to Lev 19:2 and Deut 18:13. I mention Dupont's position because it presents a rather common interpretation. As far as the interrelationship between God and man is concerned one certainly can refer to Lev 19:2. In "You shall be holy; for I the Lord your God am holy'' a comparison is made between God and man by urging man to be like God with regard to his holiness. As to the perfection of man Deut 18:13 could be called upon: "You shall be perfect with the Lord your God.'' Here, however, the interrelationship between God and man is not very

---

[26] *Das Evangelium nach Matthäus* (Evangelisch-katholischer Kommentar zum neuen Testament I) Zürich 1985.
[27] *o.c.* 306.
[28] J. Dupont, *Les Beatitudes*, I Louvain 1969 153.

clear. The obscurity of the hebrew "tamim tihejeh *im adonai* elohekha" is solved in the various versions. The Septuagint translates: "You shall be perfect *before the Lord* (enantion Kuriou) your God." In Onkelos and Pseudo-Jonathan we read: "You shall be perfect (selim) *in the fear of the Lord* (bedak-halta de-adonai) your God." Neofiti is quite close to the hebrew: "My people, children of Israel, you shall be perfect in good work *with the Lord* your God," but in margine it is said: "you shall be perfect in good work *before the Lord* your God." So the various translations do not understand the obscure hebrew "with the Lord your God" as indicating an interrelationship between God and man with regard to perfection.

Being perfect (*tam*) is also a motive in the dead sea scrolls, to which regularly is referred in the commentaries with regard to the tradition used in Mat 5:48. That a member of the Qumran community must be perfect is said in a number of texts. The members of the community must walk perfectly together in all that has been revealed to them (1QS 9:19) (cfr. 1QS 1:8 2:2 4:22 5:24 9:6).[29] The Qumran tradition is very close to the marginal interpretation in targum Neofiti. But also here human perfection is not connected with Gods' perfection. For Mat 5:48 one cannot refer to a tradition that connects perfection with man's imitation of God and it is a question whether this imitation is meant.

Interpreting Mat 5:48 one should first of all take into account the preceding verse as Matthew Black has indicated.[30] Black sees the perfection mentioned in 5:48 linked up with the behaviour of the Gentiles as described in 5:47 which should be exceeded by the disciples: "And if you salute only your brethren, what more are you doing than others? Do not even the Gentiles do the same?" He calls this link one of the more interesting examples of paronomasia, where the regular semitic expression for 'to greet' is 'to ask for peace or welfare' *shaleem* and the semitic equivalent for *teleois* is *shelim*.[31] This linking of verses through a play upon the word *shaleem* leads to the interpretation of Mat 5:48 in its context. It does, however, not give a satisfactory explanation for the use of the greek *teleios*, especially because the context speaks of God as giving sun and rain to everybody, whether he is good or wicked. For a contextual interpretation of Mat 5:48 we should therefore consider the meaning of the word *shelim* being 'peaceful' or 'friendly'. This meaning fits very well in the context of the last antithesis and is a more understandable appeal for imitation of God comparable with the appeal to be merciful as we find this in Luke 6:36 and in the early rabbinic tradition, where man's love to his fellowman is related to God's love for mankind.

---

[29] Cfr. W. Grundmann, *Das Evangelium nach Matthäus* (Theologischer Handkommentar zum neuen Testament I) Berlin 1968, 180; H. Braun, *Spät-jüdisch-häretischer und frühchristlicher Radikalismus: Jesus von Nazareth und die essenische Qumransekte.* Tübingen 1957, II 43 note 2.

[30] *An aramaic Approach to the Gospels and Acts*, Oxford 1967³.

[31] *o.c.*, 181.

When taking the aramaic shelim as indicating the attribute of God's friendly attitude towards man which attitude expresses itself in giving rain to everybody one should however not exclude the meaning of 'being perfect' as indicated by the greek teleios. It is here that we should assume the paronomasia Black speaks of with regard to Mat 5:47–48. Shaleem as being perfect is well attested in mishnaic hebrew and palestinian aramaic. We mentioned already the Targum version of Deut 18:13 in Neofiti. Other examples can be added. So in Neof on Gen 6:9 it is said: "This is the descend of the generations of Noah: Noah was a just man, *perfect in good work* he was in his generation; *before the Lord Noah served in truth.*" And in Neof on Gen 17:1 God says to Abraham: "I am the Lord of the heavens. Serve before me in truth and be *perfect in good work.*" This is said to Abraham immediately before he circumcises himself. The connection between being perfect in good work and circumcision is attested in *Nedarim* 3:11; "Rabbi says: Great is circumcision for despite all the mizwot which Abraham our father fulfilled, he was not called perfect until he was circumcised as it is written: Walk before me and be thou perfect."

In Mat 5:48 man is also asked to be perfect, which perfection consists in the imitation of a friendly God. This friendliness exceeds even the commandment of love in which the enemy is not included. This does not mean, however, the abolition of the commandments. The perfection that is asked for is—as in jewish tradition—essentially linked with the commandments. This connection of keeping the commandments and perfection we find once more in Mat 19,16–21. "If one would enter life—Jesus says—keep the commandments." And the young man who had asked the question says: 'All these I have observed; what do I still lack? Jesus said to him: 'If you would be perfect, go, sell what you possess and give to the poor, and you will have treasure in heaven." It is remarkable that the word 'perfect' does not occur in the parallel stories in Marc and Luke and that in Matthew no comparison is made with God as to the perfection one is asked to pursue.

My conclusion is that with regard to natural phenomena already at the end of the second century B.C. God's justice did not pay a role anymore, which explains the absence of this attribute of God when a phenomenon as rain is discussed in a halakhic setting. Also in the New Testament the biblical pattern of behaviour and natural blessings is not used. God's power, which is supposed to manifest as goodness and mercy, seems to be the generally accepted image of God with regard to nature during the whole period of halakhic development and of the growth of the New Testament.

GÉNÉRATIONS ANTÉDILUVIENNES ET CHUTE DES ÉONS DANS L'HERMÉTISME ET DANS LA GNOSE

PAR

JEAN-PIERRE MAHÉ (PARIS)

Au début de son traité *Contre les gnostiques* (*Enn.* II,9,6), Plotin[1] accuse ses adversaires d'avoir détourné les concepts platoniciens «précis et sans enflure» (σαφῶς καὶ ἀτύφως) pour multiplier les hypostases et les représentations mythologiques qui dénaturent (πρὸς τὸ χεῖρον ἕλκουσι) les doctrines du philosophe. Le lecteur moderne serait quelquefois tenté d'adresser des reproches analogues à certains écrits d'Hermès Trismégiste, où l'une des premières difficultés d'interprétation consiste précisément dans le travestissement, sous un langage apparemment philosophique, de notions qui sont, en réalité, purement mythologiques.

L'idée que l'homme est double, à la fois terrestre et supérieur aux dieux astraux, fait partie d'un vieux fonds de gnomologie hermétique attesté, par exemple, en *DH* I,5 «L'homme est mortel, tout en étant toujours vivant», *DH* VI,6 «L'homme a les deux natures, à la fois la mortelle et l'immortelle», *DH* VIII,6.7 etc. Dans *CH* I,15.24 et dans *Ascl.* 7–8.22, cette double nature de l'homme est caractérisée dans un langage apparemment philosophique par l'opposition entre l'homme «essentiel» (οὐσιώδης), qui est simple, et son revêtement «matériel» (ὑλικόν), qui est quadruple, tiré des quatre éléments.

Cependent nous aurions bien tort de chercher la signification profonde de cette opposition dans l'analyse philosophique des termes ὕλη et οὐσία. L'origine de cette interprétation est évidemment tout autre. Elle résulte d'un rapprochement des sentences hermétiques avec le récit mythique de la double création de l'homme en *Gen.* 1,26–27. 2,7. En effet, tandis qu'*Ascl.* 7 identifie l'οὐσιώδης, *divinae similitudinis formam*, à l'homme de *Gen.* 1,26, κατ' εἰκόνα ... καὶ καθ᾽ ὁμοίωσιν (cf. *CH* I,12: τὴν τοῦ πατρὸς εἰκόνα ἔχων), *Ascl.* 22 (= *NH* VI,66,35–67,4) identifie bien l'homme tiré de l'élément matériel (ϩⲛ ⲧⲙⲉⲣⲓⲥ ⲛⲑⲩⲗⲏ) à celui qui reçoit le souffle de Dieu (ⲛⲓϥⲉ) en *Gen.* 2,7: καὶ ἐνεφύσησεν εἰς τὸ πρόσωπον αὐτοῦ πνοὴν ζωῆς. Considérant que l'homme matériel de *Gen.* 2,6 avait reçu l'eau en même temps que la terre, explicitement nommée dans le texte biblique, et le feu en même temps que le

---

[1] Plotin, *Ennéades* II,9,1 (Bréhier 1956, 111), cf. Puech 1978, 83 s. (reprise d'une conférence sur «Plotin et les gnostiques» à la Fondation Hardt en 1957).

souffle divin,[2] l'auteur hermétique se croit fondé à opposer une première création de l'homme dans l'essence de Celui-qui-est (*FH* 3 A),[3] à une seconde création dans les quatre éléments.

Il est notoire que, sur ce point, Hermès Trismégiste rejoint l'opposition philonienne de l'homme selon l'image et de l'homme modelé: non qu'Hermès s'inspire directement de Philon, qui n'est pas l'inventeur de cette exégèse,[4] mais très probablement tous deux dépendent de sources ou de traditions exégétiques antérieures.[5] Cependant, comme le *Poimandrès* (*CH* I,1−19) commente la *Genèse* depuis le récit de la création des six jours, jusqu'à l'épisode du Déluge inclusivement (*Gen.* 1,1−10,1, en comparant les γενέσεις de *CH* I,19 aux descendances de Noé), et que la *Paraphrase de Sem* (*NH* VII[1]), qui présente de remarquables convergences avec *CH* I, *CH* XIII et d'autres écrits hermétiques,[6] poursuit le commentaire jusqu'à Abraham et la destruction de Sodome et Gomorrhe, on peut s'attendre à trouver d'autres analogies entre les exégèses de Philon et celles de Trismégiste.

Observons notamment un point essentiel: de même que le double récit de la création de l'homme (*Gen.* 1, 26−27. 2,7) a été interprété, chez Philon et dans l'hermétisme, comme la création d'un homme spirituel puis matériel, de même la répétition en *Gen.* 9,1.7, de la bénédiction divine «Croissez et multipliez» de *Gen.* 1,22.28 a été interprétée dans les mêmes sources comme le début d'une seconde création, l'avènement d'un nouvel âge, qui s'oppose au précédent comme celui des générations humaines divisées en deux sexes et non plus celui des éons infinis, mâles et femelles à la fois.

Dans *QG* II,56 (p. 289), Philon rapproche *Gen.* 9,1−2 de *Gen.* 1,28 pour en déduire que «Noé, qui a été à l'origine de cette seconde création des hommes, fut estimé égal en honneur à celui qui avait été créé en premier lieu à l'image (de Dieu)», c'est-à-dire non pas à l'homme matériel de *Gen.* 2,7, mais à l'homme spirituel de *Gen.* 1,26−27. Cependant, en *QG* II,66 (p. 311), le rapprochement de *Gen.* 20 avec *Gen.* 3,26, sur le travail de la terre, permet d'ajouter que Noé est également semblable au «premier homme modelé du sol.»

A vrai dire, de grandes différences opposent l'ère que vit ce patriarche, à la

---

[2] Une exégèse analogue à celle des *Hermetica* est donnée dans la *Caverne des trésors* (Bezold 1888, 3), où les quatre éléments sont indiqués dans l'ordre: poussière, eau, air, feu.

[3] Sur le nom divin ὁ ὤν dans les *Hermetica* et en *Ex.* 3, 13−15, cf. Mahé 1984, 54. 59 et 63 et notes 24 et 64 de ce même article.

[4] D'après *QG* I,8 (Mercier, 71), la théorie de la double création de l'homme est antérieure à Philon (cf. Tobin 1983, 102). Sur cette théorie dans les *Hermetica*, cf. Mahé 1986 b, 35−36. 41−43.

[5] Cf. *HHE*, tome 2, 316−318.

[6] On nous permettra de renvoyer à notre article sous presse «La *Paraphrase de Sem* et les *Hermetica*» (dans les *Cahiers de la Bibliothèque Copte* 4, Louvain—Paris 1987) et à la publication de la *Paraphrase de Sem* par M. Roberge dans BCNH (en préparation).

sortie de l'arche, à celle que connut Adam, expulsé du paradis. *QG* II,45 (p. 263–267) nous apprend, d'après *Gen.* 8,13, que, la 601ème année de la vie de Noé, Dieu établit une Limite (*sahman*/ὅρος) entre deux âges (*azgac^c ew daruc^c*/αἰῶνες), celui qui s'achevait et celui qui commençait, et que le premier de cette nouvelle génération ou, plus exactement peut-être, de cette régénération des hommes (*verstin cnund*/ἀναγέννησις ou παλιγγενεσία), «n'est pas délivré des nécessités corporelles; en effet, quoiqu'il ne soit pas assujetti, mais souverain, néanmoins, étant mort, il a été mélangé à la mort».

Avant même le Déluge, en effet, en *Gen.* 6,2, la vie des hommes a été limitée à 120 ans, quoique la miséricorde divine ait accordé un délai pour la pénitence à la dernière génération avant la catastrophe (*QG* I,91). De plus, un commentaire considéré par Aucher comme une glose, parce qu'il figure, sur les manuscrits arméniens, tantôt en marge et tantôt dans le texte, tantôt en *QG* I,87 (p. 162 n. 1) et tantôt en *QG* I,89 (p. 163 n. 6), témoigne d'une exégèse intéressante: «Certains disaient que les éons infinis (*anbaw dars*/ἄπειροι αἰῶνες, cf. Irénée, *Haer.* I,1,1), s'étendent depuis Adam jusqu'à Noé; d'autres disaient que Noé est le premier principe».

Marquée par la catastrophe du Déluge, la génération de Noé apparaît donc bien comme une limite et une rupture, le moment où commence une nouvelle humanité, égale, certes, en honneur à la précédente, mais plus étroitement mélangée à la mort, où elle a été engloutie par les eaux du Déluge. Avant Noé s'étendent les éons infinis; après lui commencent les générations humaines. Une Limite d'eau sépare ces deux époques, comme la barrière de feu qui séparait Adam du paradis (*Gen.* 3,24).

L'épisode du Déluge figure aussi, sous une forme allusive, dans le *Poimandrès*, grâce à la citation de *Gen.* 9,1 en *CH* I,18. C'est à la fois la fin d'un âge (τῆς περιόδου πεπληρωμένης) et l'annonce d'une rupture, brisant le lien de toutes choses (ἐλύθη ὁ πάντων σύνδεσμος). Désormais, l'homme et tous les êtres vivants, jusqu'alors pourvus des deux sexes à la fois, deviennent mâles et femelles séparément. Au-delà de l'allusion au texte biblique, qui oppose l'unité primordiale (*Gen.* 1,27. 2,24) à la dualité introduite par le Déluge (*Gen.* 7,2 s.: δύο δύο, ἄρσεν καὶ θῆλυ; *Gen.* 7,9 etc.), la séparation des sexes implique pour les hommes dotés de l'intellect un bouleversement radical de leur condition antérieure, de leurs rapports avec la vie et avec la mort. Désormais, l'immortalité n'est plus de règle, comme dans la période antérieure. Elle est réservée à ceux qui, dans l'intellect, se reconnaissent eux-mêmes comme immortels; tandis que la division des sexes, assujettissant l'homme à l'amour et à la mort, met en route le cycle des générations, la vie délimitée, pour «toute âme dans la chair, par la course des dieux cycliques» (*CH* III,3; cf. *CH* I,15.18).

Or, on n'a peut-être pas assez remarqué que l'exposé de ce changement radical dans l'histoire mythique de l'humanité s'accompagne, chez Philon comme dans l'hermétisme, de spéculations sur la Décade qui, malgré des différences avérées, sont plus ou moins convergentes: «Observe bien, écrit Philon en *QG* I,87 (p. 163), que Noé est le dixième à partir de celui qui est né de la terre». Ce nombre dix est conforme au βίβλος γενέσεως ἀνθρώπων de *Gen.* 5, à ceci près que, s'appuyant sans doute sur le fait que *Gen.* 5,2 mentionne le nom d'Adam, Philon compte à partir de l'homme terrestre et non pas à partir de l'homme selon l'image mentionné dans le même verset. Dans ce cas, la Décade est envisagée dans le sens descendant, de l'unité originelle jusqu'à la dixième génération. Dans la prétendue glose de *QG* I,87 (p. 162 n. 1), la Décade est envisagée dans le sens ascendant: «a Noe (usque) ad Adam decimus est neque amplius», écrit Ch. Mercier corrigeant une faute de la traduction d'Aucher.[7]

C'est également dans le sens ascendant qu'apparaît la Décade en *CH* I, 24–26. Une fois dissous le corps matériel, abandonnant vices et passions aux sept sphères planétaires, l'homme «entre dans la nature ogdoadique, ne possédant que sa puissance propre». Puis «il entend certaines puissances qui siègent au-dessus de la nature ogdoadique», c'est-à-dire, sans doute, dans l'Ennéade, et enfin, devenu puissance à son tour, il entre en Dieu. Il en résulte que Dieu est inclus dans la Décade et que, si nous voulons considérer celle-ci dans le sens descendant, de la création de l'homme à l'humanité post-diluvienne, il nous faudra, à la différence de Philon, partir, non pas de l'homme matériel—que l'auteur hermétique rejette en-dessous de l'Hebdomade planétaire—, mais de Dieu lui-même, qui se manifeste successivement par l'homme primordial créé à son image et par les huit autres prototypes humains qui constituent le premier âge, antérieur à la rupture de l'androgynie des origines.

Si l'on considère la vision et l'anthropogonie du *Poimandrès* (*CH* I,1–18), on distinguera:

(I) la divinité qui se fait connaître au visionnaire (*CH* I,6)

(II) un Homme primordial à l'image du Père (*CH* I,12)

(III) un Homme devenu double après l'union avec Nature (*CH* I,15)

(IV–X) sept Hommes androgynes correspondant à la nature des Sept Gouverneurs planétaires (*CH* I,16).

Après quoi, commence l'humanité historique, divisée en deux sexes distincts (*CH* I,18), érigée en espèce, et non plus constituée de prototypes (*CH* I,17).

Essayons de comprendre comment ces diverses entités se situent par rapport à *Gen.* 1–10. Tout d'abord, la divinité qui se révèle au visionnaire déclare: «C'est moi, Intellect, ton Dieu». Cela semble être une allusion à la théophanie d'*Ex.* 3,6 (c. *Dt.* 5,6) et une façon de laisser entendre que le visionnaire est une

---

[7] Cf. Mercier 1979: traduction de *QG* II,87 (Mercier, 162–163, note 1).

sorte de Moïse, mais, nous allons le voir, un Moïse qui se réclame d'une tradition plus ancienne et se juge bien mieux renseigné que l'auteur supposé du *Pentateuque*.

On sait en effet qu'Artapanus, qui était probablement Juif et vivait en Egypte, assimilait l'Hermès égyptien à Moïse.[8] Mais cette identification n'est valable que pour Hermès Trismégiste, supposé postérieur au Déluge.[9] Hermès-Thot, le premier Hermès, est bien antérieur et assimilé à Adam (*FH* 21). Or, selon la tradition hermétique, Trismégiste est non seulement le descendant, mais la troisième réincarnation de Thot.[10] C'est en cette qualité qu'il reçoit la révélation de Poimandrès, Intellect de la Souveraineté (αὐθεντία, *CH* I,3; *CH* XIII,15). Il est donc autorisé à corriger Moïse, pour rétablir le texte «authentique» de la révélation.

Or, le dieu manifesté par Poimandrès, tout en revendiquant son identité avec le dieu de Moïse, se fait connaître comme mâle-et-femelle (*CH* I,9) et paraît constitué d'une triple syzygie:

mâle	*femelle*
1. Préprincipe	: Souveraineté absolue
CH I,8	*CH* I,2
(mais le mot est de genre neutre)	
2. Intellect, Père et Lumière	: Vie
CH I,6.9	*CH* I,9
3. Verbe du Seigneur	: Volonté de Dieu
CH I,6	*CH* I,8

Cette interprétation de *CH* I peut sembler tout d'abord comporter une large part de conjecture, étant donné le peu de renseignements que nous avons sur ces entités. Nous verrons en fait qu'elle se confirme à la fois par des arguments de cohérence interne et par la comparaison avec *Eugnoste* et les sources hermétiques de Jamblique, que nous étudierons ci-dessous.

Le «Verbe du Seigneur», appelé «Verbe pneumatique» en *CH* I,5, est «porté au-dessus» des eaux comme l'Esprit de Dieu en *Gen.* 1,2 (ἐπιφερόμενον/ ἐπεφέρετο). En tant que «Verbe saint», en *CH* I,5, il «vient couvrir» la Nature, comme l'Esprit Saint de *Luc* 1,35 «survient» sur Marie, d'après la parole de l'Ange (ἐπέβη/ἐπελεύσεται).[11] Quant à l'Intellect-Lumière, l'auteur hermé-

---

[8] Cf. Mussies 1982, 91 s.

[9] Cf. NF, tome 3, CLXIII, note 3 (commentaire du témoignage du Pseudo-Manéthon sur la généalogie d'Hermès Trismégiste).

[10] Cf. NF, tome 4, 148, note 3, sur un témoignage hermétique de Hermias et de Cyrille, commenté par Puech 1978, 117–118 (reprise d'un article dans la *REG* 49/50, (1946/47) XI–XIII).

[11] Si, comme on l'admet ordinairement, *CH* I a été composé au début du IIe siècle, rien n'empêche que l'auteur ait connu le NT. Toutefois, Dodd 1975, 54–55, après avoir cité l'ensemble des parallèles entre *Jn* et *CH* I, conclut que ces ressemblances sont plutôt dues à des sources communes qu'à une influence de l'un sur l'autre. Sur les analogies entre Paul et *CH* I, cf. G. Quispel (sous-presse, exemplaire dactylographié, spécialement 119 s.).

tique explique qu'il existe «avant la Nature humide apparue hors de l'obscurité» (*CH* I,6), C'est une façon de dire qu'il est antérieur au tohu-bohu primordial (*Gen.* 1,2) et au *Fiat lux* de *Gen.* 1,3 (cf. *FH* 23). Le préprincipe enfin ne peut être compris que comme antérieur au Principe de *Gen.* 1,1. Cependant cette triade se présente comme l'unique Dieu d'Israël, le Dieu saint, à qui sont dues, sous une forme quelque peu épurée, les *Bénédictions* de la Synagogue (*CH* I,31).[12]

Après ce Dieu, vient l'Homme primordial, qui possède l'«image du Père», c'est-à-dire de l'Intellect, comme l'Homme de *Gen.* 1,27 «selon l'image de Dieu».[13] Son créateur lui «livre toutes ses œuvres» (*CH* I,12), comme Dieu en *Gen.* 1,29. Il est Intellect comme son Père, mais possède sans doute en lui une participation au Verbe, comme l'interlocuteur de Poimandrès (*CH* I,6).

L'Homme double,[14] qui apparaît en *CH* I,15, pourrait rappeler l'homme matériel de *Gen.* 2,7. Mais l'exégèse de l'auteur hermétique est plus complexe. En effet, l'Homme est devenu double, non parce qu'il a été façonné dans les éléments—comme cela nous est rapporté par la suite pour les Sept premiers Hommes, *CH* I,17—, mais parce que, à la suite d'une chute, il s'est uni à Nature (cf. *Gen.* 4,1), en qui il avait cru préalablement reconnaître «une forme semblable à lui» (*CH* I,14, cf. *Gen.* 2,20.23). En fait, l'Homme double de *CH* I,14−15 occupe tout l'espace qui va de la création de l'homme matériel, en *Gen.* 2,6, à la naissance de Seth, en *Gen.* 4,25. En effet, il précède immédiatement les Sept Hommes androgynes, comparables aux générations antédiluviennes de *Gen.* 5,6−28, d'Enoch à Lamech.[15] A la différence des descendants de Caïn, en *Gen.* 4,17−24, ces sept patriarches descendant de Seth n'ont aucune conjointe désignée dans le texte biblique: on peut donc supposer qu'il s'agit d'êtres androgynes et qui ont un caractère gigantesque ou cosmique, étant donné la longueur de leur vie. Or, ils précèdent Noé, dont l'épouse est explicitement mentionnée en *Gen.* 6,18. De même, en *Gen.* 1,18, après les Sept Hommes androgynes, les hommes deviennent «mâles d'une part et femelles de l'autre», recevant en outre la même bénédiction que Noé et ses fils en *Gen.* 9,1.

---

[12] Cf. *HHE*, tome 2, 433−434.

[13] G. Quispel cite également à propos de ce texte *Ez.* 1,26, où Dieu apparaît au prophète sous la forme d'un «Homme». A propos de la pierre de saphir mentionée dans ce dernier verset, cf. *NH* VI, 62,14.

[14] On pourrait objecter que cet Homme double n'est pas une personne distincte de l'Homme primordial cité précédemment. En fait, comme l'observe G. Quispel (sous-presse, exemplaire dactylographié, 163), le mythe a surtout pour but d'expliquer comment, d'après la formule de *CH* I,17, Nature «a produit un corps selon la forme de l'Homme». Ainsi, d'une certaine façon, l'Homme céleste et l'Homme terrestre coexistent; l'Homme est à la fois déchu et glorieux. G. Quispel (*ibid.*, 47) cite à ce sujet l'Homme céleste des Mandéens qui, tout en vivant dans les corps des hommes, est en même temps une hypostase distincte.

[15] Toutefois, à la différence des générations bibliques, ces Sept Hommes semblent naître simultanément, ce qui nous paraît dû à l'interprétation astrologique du texte: chacun d'eux représente un tempérament planétaire.

Comparons maintenant cette préhistoire de l'humanité en dix étapes aux dix niveaux ontologiques qui, dans *Ogd.Enn.* (*NH* VI,63,15−24), vont du plus haut degré de la divinité jusqu'aux quatre éléments matériels[16]:

(I) Inengendré

(II) Autogène

(III) Engendré

(IV−X) Sept Ousiarques contenant l'Esprit démiurgique. Viennent ensuite le ciel, la terre, le feu et l'eau.

Si l'on compare les trois premiers degrés de cette hiérarchie avec *NH* VI,60, 17−25 on se convaincra des équivalences suivantes entre *Ogd.Enn.* et la triade divine de *CH* I:

	Ogd.Enn.	*CH* I
(I) Inengendré/ Principe du principe		: Préprincipe
(II) Autogène/ Lumière et Vérité		: Intellect−Lumière
(III) Engendré/ Verbe		: Verbe

En *NH* VI,60, 22−23, la relation d'origine des deux entités inférieures au Principe du principe est spécifiée par deux noms d'agent qui doivent être interprétés par opposition de l'un à l'autre: ⲣⲉϥϫⲡⲟ et ⲣⲉϥⲥⲓⲧⲉ. L'un et l'autre peuvent s'appliquer à la génération ou à la procréation, mais il est clair que le premier «Celui qui fait venir à l'être» a un sens moins matériel que le second «Celui qui sème». Le premier pourrait donc définir le mode de procession propre à l'Autogène, tandis que le second indiquerait une procréation séminale caractéristique du Verbe, qui est «Fils de Dieu» (*CH* I,6) et donc Engendré à proprement parler, servant en outre de semence aux éléments de la Nature (*CH* I,8).

Mais si les trois termes, Inengendré, Autogène, Engendré, s'appliquent à la triade divine, les deux derniers s'appliquent aussi nécessairement aux prototypes de l'humanité qui portent en eux l'image de l'Intellect et du Verbe. D'une certaine façon, l'Homme primordial de *CH* I,12, «enfanté» par l'Intellect paternel (qui est androgyne) et non pas, comme l'humanité actuelle, issu de l'union de deux parents de sexes différents, est une image de l'Autogène ou, si l'on veut, un Autogénéré.[17] Cela s'applique aussi bien à l'Homme de *Gen.* 1,27 qu'à l'Adam de *Gen.* 5,1. En revanche, d'après *Gen.* 5,3, le premier Homme engendré est Seth. Mais nous avons montré que l'Homme double de *CH* I,15 emplit tout l'intervalle de *Gen.* 2,7 à *Gen.* 5,6. Il doit donc avoir quelque rapport avec la génération de Seth, quoique, d'après *CH* I,18−19, la génération sexuée soit beaucoup plus tardive et ne commence qu'après le Déluge. Quant aux Sept Ousiarques, ils reflètent à la fois, d'après *Ascl.* 19, les Sept

---

[16] Nous précisons ici nos précédentes observations (Mahé 1986 a, 138−144).

[17] G. Quispel (sous-presse, exemplaire dactylographié, 89) mentionne à ce propos l'Archanthropos autogène des Naassènes.

Gouverneurs planétaires de *CH* I,9 et les prototypes humains engendrés à leur image en *CH* I,16, en qui nous avons reconnu les générations antédiluviennes.[18]

Que les catégories de l'Autogène et de l'Engendré puissent s'appliquer à la génération de l'Homme se confirme grâce au mystère de régénération décrit dans *Ogd.Enn.* Hermès s'identifie à l'Intellect (*NH* VI,58, 15.21.27.28), c'est-à-dire à l'Autogène. On peut rappeler à ce propos *FH* 21, où le «Fils de Dieu», «devenu homme passible» (cf. *CH* XIII,4), «fait monter l'intellect de chacun vers la région bienheureuse où il se trouvait déjà avant qu'il ne fût corporel» et le «guide vers la lumière d'en-haut». Or, cet Hermès-Thot, «opérateur dans l'œuvre de la régénération» (*CH* XIII,4), est comparé dans le même fragment, au premier Homme qui, comme Adam (*Gen.* 2,19), a nommé tous les êtres.[19] Quant aux initiés, Hermès-Intellect déclare les avoir «engendrés comme des fils» (*NH* VI,53, 14–15), ce qui implique peut-être «matrice», «semence» et «ensemenceur» comme en *CH* XIII,2. En *NH* VI,63,1, nous apprenons que Dieu—en l'occurrence l'Intellect—est l'auteur de cet engendrement.

On peut résumer l'isomorphisme des systèmes de *CH* I et d'*Ogd.Enn.* par le schéma suivant, où nous proposons deux lectures, descendante puis ascendante, de la Décade.

Lecture descendante				Lecture ascendante	
Ogd.Enn.	*CH* I		*Gen.* 5	*Ogd.Enn.*	*CH* I
Inengendré	: Préprincipe		Dieu	Terme et principe	Dieu
Autogène	: Intellect			Ennéade	Au-dessus de l'Og-
	Homme primordial		Adam		doade
Engendré	: Verbe			Ogdoade	Ogdoade
	Homme double		Seth		
-X) Sept Ousiarques	: Sept Gouverneurs		Sept généra-	Hebdomade	Armature des sphères
			tions anté-	(Loi)	
			diluviennes		

	Noé	
(8ème)		(1er)

Hommes actuels sous les éléments	Hommes actuels sous les éléments

Un indice supplémentaire nous permet de comparer les Sept Ousiarques d'*Ogd. Enn.* aux Sept générations antédiluviennes après Seth: c'est le lien suggéré par l'en semble du traité entre Ogdoade et régénération. L'Ogdoade, c'est

---

[18] Pour une confrontation systématique de *Gen.* 1–10 et de *CH* I, 1–19, cf. Mahé 1986 b, 36–43.

[19] *FH* 21 est tiré de Zosime, *Sur la lettre Ω*, dont A.-J. Festugière donne une traduction annotée dans *RHT*, tome 1, p. 263–273. L'auteur y décrit (270 s.) un homme spirituel dont le nom propre est inconnu et dont le nom commun est phôs, avec le même jeu de mots «Homme/Lumière» qu'en *CH* I,12. 17.

évidemment, comme pour *CH* XIII,15 et *CH* I,26, la zone qui domine les sept sphères, donc aussi bien les Sept Ousiarques qui résident dans chacune d'entre elles; c'est l'endroit où, débarrassé du corps matériel et des affections planétaires, l'Homme se retrouve dans son état originel, revêtu de sa seule puissance.

Mais, d'un autre côté, l'association de l'Ogdoade à l'idée de repos (*CH* XIII,20, *NH* VI 60,9) nous renvoie au symbole de Noé, qui unit ces deux idées. Huit âmes furent sauvées dans l'arche, nous apprend *I Pet.* 3,20, en sorte que, d'après *II Pet.* 2,5, Dieu n'épargna pas l'ancien monde à l'exception de Noé, le huitième, qui était le héraut de la justice. Plus explicitement encore, les *Recognitiones Clementinae* (I,29) situent la perversion qui précéda le Déluge à la «huitième génération» après Seth, où il ne resta plus qu'un seul juste, Noé, qui fut sauvé dans l'arche avec son épouse, ses trois fils et ses trois belles-filles. Or, *Gen.* 5,29 nous enseigne que Noé est celui qui «fait reposer des travaux et des tristesses de la terre qu'a maudite le Seigneur Dieu».

Dixième depuis Adam, comme l'enseignait Philon, mais huitième depuis Seth, selon une tradition connue des *Recognitiones* et probablement aussi de notre traité *Ogd.Enn.*, Noé est en même temps le premier de la nouvelle génération des hommes. Le double sens du préfixe ἀνα—(«de bas en haut» ou «à nouveau»), que l'on trouve dans ἀνά-παυσις ou dans ἀνα-γέννησις, autorise, à partir de Noé, à relire dans le sens ascendant les généalogies de *Gen.* 5. Il nous permet de comprendre comment l'ascension à travers les sphères peut être, dans la tradition hermétique, en même temps une remontée vers l'origine.

L'Ogdoade n'est pas seulement la huitième sphère, mais aussi le premier Homme Engendré, grâce auquel on accède à l'Autogène dans l'Ennéade et à la connaissance du Dieu suprême qui réside au sommet de l'Aἰών, un et dix à la fois. Seule l'hypothèse d'une lecture allégorique de *Gen.* 5,1–30, permet d'interpréter la tradition hermétique sur la position actuelle de l'homme en dessous de la Décade et sur les voies de la remontée.[20]

---

[20] La Décade décrite en *CH* XIII, 9–10 fait intervenir des entités uniquement féminines, c'est-à-dire l'aspect perceptible à l'âme des syzygies intelligibles. En se fondant sur les indications de *CH* XIII, 2. 12. 18–19, on peut essayer de reconstituer le système suivant, superposable à celui de *CH* I et de l'*Ogd.Enn.* où les syzygies IV–X ne sont connues que sous leur aspect féminin:

I	Bien-Un-Esprit et Silence
II	Intellect et Sagesse intelligente/ Genesiurgos (*CH* XIII,4)
III	Engendré/Verbe (*CH* XIII,19)/ Homme régénéré
IV	Vérité
V	Koinônia
VI	Justice
VII	Endurance
VIII	Continence
IX	Joie
X	Connaissance

Primordialement, Inengendré, Autogène et Engendré ne forment qu'un seul Dieu, «le Nom» par excellence (*NH* VI,62,13; 63,36), à qui est due la prière juive du Shema, ou du moins les paroles de *Dt.* 6,5 citées en *NH* VI,55,10−14 et 57,21−23.[21]

Mais en outre l'Autogène et l'Engendré se reflètent, en dehors de la divinité, dans deux prototypes humains successifs, que l'on peut comparer à Adam et à Seth. Cette liaison au texte biblique, que, sur la base des exégèses très allusives du *Poimandrès*, on avance sur un mode presque hypothétique, devient une certitude quand on compare le système hermétique à celui, beaucoup plus explicite et quasiment isomorphe, de deux traités de Nag Hammadi, *Eugnoste* et son dérivé *Sophia Jesu Christi*.[22]

En effet, ces textes représentent le monde supérieur comme l'emboîtement de deux triades: Inengendré, Autogéniteur, Engendré, correspondant aux entités presque homonymes d'*Ogd.Enn.* et à leurs homologues dans *CH* I, puis, incluses dans l'Engendré, une seconde triade, Homme immortel, Fils de l'Homme et Grande Lumière, à quoi viennent s'ajouter six êtres spirituels androgynes, dont les éléments mâles et femelles se multiplient par six et ensuite par cinq, pour devenir successivement 72 et 360, à l'image de l'année et des cieux.

Ce système est superposable à celui de *CH* I et d'*Ogd.Enn.* selon le schéma suivant:

	Eug.	*Ogd.Enn.*	*CH* I
(I)	Inengendré	Inengendré	Préprincipe
(II)	Autogéniteur	Autogène	Intellect
	(Adam) Homme immortel		Homme primordial
(III)	Engendré	Engendré	Verbe
	(Seth) Fils de l'Homme		Homme double
(IV)	(Enoch) Grande Lumière	Ousiarque	Homme androgyne
(V−X)	Six puissances androgynes	Six Ousiarques	Six hommes androgynes
	(× 2 × 6 × 5 = 360)		

Humanité actuelle

De même que l'Homme primordial de *CH* I est l'image de l'Intellect autogène, l'Homme immortel d'*Eugnoste*, qui est αὐτοφυής et αὐτόκτιστος est l'image de l'Αὐτογενέτωρ divin. De plus, l'Homme immortel d'*Eugnoste*, qui s'est créé lui-même, est identifié à l'Adam Lumière[23] (*NH* III,81,10−12); sa similitude est une grande Puissance (*NH* III,76, 20−21); avec lui commencent la divinité et la royauté (*NH* III,77, 24−78,1). Il est donc effectivement semblable

---

[21] Cf. *HHE*, tome 2, 473−474.

[22] Traductions française (Tardieu 1984, 176−186), que nous avons utilisée, en recourant aussi à l'édition photographique des codices III et V de Nag Hammadi. G. Quispel (sous-presse, exemplaire dactylographié, 83) esquisse une comparaison entre *Eugnoste* et *CH* I.

[23] Cf. *supra* notes 13.14.17.19.

à l'Autogène hermétique, qui est un Adam Lumière, Ζωὴ καὶ φῶς d'après *CH* I, 12.17, régnant sur les Puissances d'après *NH* VI,55,25–26. 59,31–32. De même, d'après *NH* III,81,1–3, le Fils de l'Homme d'*Eugnoste* est le créateur des anges: il ressemble en cela à l'Engendré de l'Ogdoade hermétique où résident les anges et les âmes (*NH* VI,56,1–2; 58,19; 59,29–30). Nous pouvons ainsi confirmer indirectement par le mythe d'*Eugnoste* la relation d'exemplarité existant entre l'Autogène divin et Adam le premier Homme, puis entre l'Engendré et le Fils de cet Homme, c'est-à-dire Seth, d'après *Gen.* 5,3.

L'influence directe d'une source hermétique sur *Eugnoste* (+ *SJC*) nous paraît assez probable[24] en raison du parallèle qu'on découvre non seulement avec *Ogd.Enn.*, mais aussi avec la source hermétique de Jamblique (*Myst.* VIII).[25] Tout comme *Eugnoste*, l'auteur de ce dernier document énonce deux triades successives, l'une philosophique, l'autre mythologique. Simplement, dans *Myst.* VIII, l'élément mythologique est emprunté non pas au judaïsme mais à l'Egypte. L'isomorphisme foncier des deux systèmes peut être représenté comme il suit:

	Eug.	*Myst.* VIII
(I)	Inengendré	Dieu Un, Tout-Premier
(II)	Autogéniteur	Ἀυτοπάτωρ
	Homme immortel	Iktôn, le premier Intellect
(III)	Engendré	Οὐσία
	Fils de l'Homme	Emeph (Kmeph?), le premier
(IV)		
	Grande Lumière	⟨ . . . . . ⟩
	Puissances	Chefs préposés à la création

Cependant l'exposé le plus classique de la procession et de la chute des éons est la grande notice d'Irénée sur la doctrine du valentinien Ptolémée, que F.M. Sagnard complète par Epiphane, Origène et Clément d'Alexandrie.[26] Or, l'Ogdoade du valentinisme présente une sémantique complexe qui rejoint l'exégèse hermétique de *Gen.* 5.

En effet, dans *Théodote 63–64*, l'Ogdoade inférieure du mythe valentinien est, comme l'Ogdoade hermétique, à la fois un lieu, un âge et un symbole de repos pour les âmes.[27] Située au-dessus des sept sphères planétaires, elle

---

[24] M. Tardieu (1984, 357) écrit que «le fragment hermétique 26 est la source littéraire d'où l'ancêtre d'*Eugnoste* a tiré sa spéculation sur l'Aiôn»; mais il ne mentionne pas les *Hermetica* à propos de la triade Inengendré-Autogène-Engendré.

[25] Jamblique (éd. 1966, 195–197) et les remarques d' E. Desplaces (*ibidem*, 13–14) sur l'interprétation hermétique de l'auteur.

[26] Cf. Sagnard 1947. Nous nous garderons bien d'attribuer à Valentin lui-même la doctrine rapportée par Irénée. La découverte des textes de Nag Hammadi, inaccessibles à F. Sagnard, a permis de constater que les sources connues d'Irénée ne représentent qu'une certaine variété de valentinisme: mais l'analyse qui en était donnée en 1947 garde, en elle-même, toute sa valeur.

[27] Cf. Clément d'Alexandrie, éd. 1948, 184–187 et les notes de F. Sagnard sur ces deux fragments de Théodote.

s'appelle aussi Κυριακή, «Jour du Seigneur». Autrement dit, elle symbolise le huitième âge, c'est-à-dire à celui du renouvellement qui fait suite à la Loi du Sabbat, instituée le septième jour. Or ce renouvellement renvoie synonymement à la naissance de Noé, au huitième âge, où ce personnage préfigure la nouvelle génération des hommes, tout autant qu'au dernier âge, marqué par l'avènement du Sauveur et le dépassement de la Loi dans la consommation finale, quand toutes les âmes se retrouveront dans l'Ogdoade, tandis que les pneumatiques, réunis à leurs anges, franchiront la Limite du Plérôme, participeront à l'Intellect et remonteront jusqu'au Père.

Mais l'Ogdoade hermétique est aussi tout cela. Elle est, tout à la fois, remontée dans le temps au-dessus des Sept Hommes androgynes (*CH* I,16−17) et remontée dans l'espace au-dessus des sept sphères (*CH* I,26); elle est au-delà de la Loi qui réside dans l'Hebdomade, avec l'obligation du repos sabbatique (*NH* VI, 56, 25−31); elle est Limite, non seulement comme dit Philon (*QG* I,87−p. 162 n. 1), parce qu'elle est l'endroit où s'achèvent les éons infinis, mais aussi parce qu'elle marque, dans «l'ordre de la tradition» (*NH* VI, 52, 6−7), la rupture entre l'humain (*NH* VI,52, 9−10: ⲕⲁⲧⲁ ⲧⲙⲛⲧⲣⲱⲙⲉ) et le divin, entre l'enseignement et la réminiscence de la grâce (*CH* XIII,2), entre la Loi et la miséricorde divine (ἔλεος θεοῦ *CH* XIII,3.8.10)[28]; l'Ogdoade est hymen au sens propre, puisque, d'après *CH* X,11, elle est la membrane ὑμήν[29] qui sépare le hylique du noétique, mais elle l'est aussi au sens figuré qu'entendent les valentiniens, puisqu'elle est le lieu où les âmes rencontrent les anges (*NH* VI,58,19; 59,29−30); elle est le lieu du repos et de la régénération (*CH* XIII,20. 22; *Théodote* 63,1; 8,1).

Cependant, d'après Irénée (*Haer.* I,5,2), l'Ogdoade inférieure d'Achamoth «présente aussi le nombre de la fondamentale et primitive Ogdoade, celle du Plérôme.» Avec ses trente éons, le Plérôme valentinien paraît beaucoup plus compliqué que l'Ogdoade et la Décade hermétiques. Une part de cette complication résulte sans doute, comme l'a bien observé F.M. Sagnard, de spéculations arithmologiques, auxquelles la Décade ne nous paraît pas étrangère.[30] Pour nous limiter à l'essentiel, il nous suffira d'observer que l'Ogdoade du Plérôme est en réalité une tétractys composée de quatre syzygies. Or, comme l'explique Irénée (*Haer.* I,16,1) à propos de Marc le Mage, la tétrade (1 + 2 + 3 + 4 = 10) est puissance de la décade et, en additionnant les nombres pairs de 2 à

---

[28] Cf. *Tite* 3,5: (Dieu nous a sauvés) «selon sa miséricorde (ἔλεος) par le bain de régénération (παλιγγενεσία)».

[29] Dans la *Paraphrase de Sem* (*NH* VII, 5,26.28; 6,25; 7,5.11 etc.) ὑμήν s'emploie en trois sens: sens physique (membrane dans le ventre de la Nature), sens cosmologique (sphère marquant la limite du monde supérieur), sens sotériologique (point de la progression spirituelle où les pneumatiques reposent provisoirement en attendant la consommation finale).

[30] Cf. Sagnard 1947, 334−357.

10 (2 + 4 + 6 + 8 + 10 = 30), celle-ci engendre la triacontade. Ces spéculations et d'autres du même genre laissent entrevoir, dans une certaine mesure,
comment les trente éons valentiniens auraient pu procéder d'une Décade
semblable à celle que Philon ou les *Hermetica* tirent de *Gen.* 5,1–30.

Mais saurait-on trouver des indices plus concrets attestant le lien entre le
mythe valentinien de la chute des éons et l'histoire des générations antédiluviennes? Nous voudrions attirer l'attention sur certains parallèles qui nous
paraissent significatifs dans la structure de ces deux récits.

La chute de l'Homme n'est pas totale après l'explusion du paradis en *Gen.*
3,24. Le texte biblique distingue nettement la lignée de Caïn, le meurtrier, de
la véritable postérité d'Adam, les Hommes nés de Seth. Ce n'est qu'en *Gen.*
6,1–4, lorsque les Fils de Dieu commencent à se mêler aux filles des hommes,
que la race des Hommes se pervertit. Certaines traditions apocryphes accen-
tuent le contraste entre la lignée de Seth et celle de Caïn, tout en insistant encore
plus nettement sur la progressivité de la chute.

Ainsi, dans la *Caverne des Trésors*, Adam et Eve, chassés du paradis, dont
la porte est fermée par Dieu jusqu'à la rédemption promise à la fin des
temps,[31] demeurent sur une sainte montagne toute proche, d'où l'on entend
encore la voix des anges. A la mort d'Adam, les fils de Caïn descendent dans
la plaine où avait eu lieu le meurtre d'Abel.[32] Mais les fils de Seth, restant sur
la montagne et persévérant dans la piété, se conduisent en Hommes «parfaits»
et sont appelés «Fils de Dieu». Toutefois, au temps de Yéred, le cinquième
depuis Adam, cent fils de Seth descendent de la montagne et se mêlent aux filles
de Caïn.[33] C'est là pour eux une chute définitive, car ils ne peuvent plus
remonter. Les Hommes succombent de plus en plus nombreux, si bien qu'après
la mort d'Enoch, fils de Yéred, son fils Mathusalem demeure seul sur la montagne avec les patriarches des deux générations suivantes, Lamech et Noé.[34]
Bientôt seul juste avec ses descendants, en tout huit personnes, celui-ci construit l'arche sur un ordre divin et doit abandonner la sainte montagne, où per-
sistaient encore les derniers restes de la gloire du paradis.[35] La porte de l'arche
est alors refermée.[36] Ainsi la chute de l'humanité, la rupture avec la splendeur
originelle n'est définitive et totale qu'au moment où commence le Déluge.

La progressivité de la chute est également soulignée dans le *Poimandrès* et
ordonnée selon la même chronologie.

Si, en *CH* I,14–15, l'Homme primordial, purement spirituel, en s'unissant
à Nature, vient habiter la forme sans raison et fait apparaître l'Homme double,

---

[31] Cf. Bezold 1888, 7.
[32] *Ibidem*, 8.
[33] *Ibidem*, 15.
[34] *Ibidem*, 17.
[35] *Ibidem*, 21.
[36] *Ibidem*, 22.

celui-ci demeure néanmoins, dans son être essentiel, Vie et Lumière, à l'image du Dieu Intellect. La situation se détériore au cours des sept générations suivantes: les Sept Hommes planétaires ont un corps matériel; ils cessent d'être Vie et Lumière pour devenir Ame et Intellect (*CH* I,17). Enfin la chute est consommée juste avant la citation de *Gen.* 9,1, quand Dieu sépare les sexes et décrète la mort de ceux qui ne sauront pas se reconnaître eux-mêmes comme immortels. Comme dans la *Caverne des trésors*, de la fermeture de la porte du paradis à la fermeture de la porte de l'arche, la chute est donc marquée par une décadence progressive située entre deux brusques ruptures: la dé-chéance du premier Homme et la séparation des sexes, qui correspondent, dans le texte biblique, à l'expulsion du jardin d'Eden et à l'anéantissement du Déluge.

La chute des éons valentiniens, selon Ptolémée, se déroule exactement sui-vant les mêmes étapes. Il faut se garder, en effet, d'une lecture superficielle de ce mythe qui imputerait la chute uniquement à Sophia, le trentième éon. D'après Irénée (*Haer.* I,2,2), la passion dont souffre celle-ci «avait pris nais-sance aux alentours de l'Intellect et de la Vérité», c'est-à-dire plus précisément après la deuxième syzygie. En effet, en *Haer.* I,2,1, nous apprenons que «seul l'Intellect se délectait à voir le Père et se réjouissait de contempler sa grandeur sans mesure. Il méditait d'en faire part également aux autres éons ... Mais Silence l'en retint, par la volonté du Père, car elle voulait amener tous les éons à la pensée et au désir (πόθος) de la recherche de leur Pro-Père susdit. C'est ainsi que les éons désiraient d'un désir plus ou moins paisible voir le Principe émetteur de leur semence ...».

Ce récit énonce une situation de conflit et de désordre latents. L'Intellect avait voulu révéler aux autres éons une certaine idée de la transcendance du Père. Il en fut empêché par Silence. Nous savons par Irénée (*Haer.* I,11,1–p. 169) que ce conflit, atténué ici par Ptolémée, était plus évident chez Valen-tin,[37] qui situait une première Limite «entre l'Abîme et le restant du Plé-rôme». En réunissant les données de Valentin et de Ptolémée, on peut se risquer à reconstruire le scénario suivant: au début l'Intellect jouit de l'intimité de Père; puis il commet quelque indiscrétion et il est séparé du Père par une première Limite. C'est à peu près ce qui arrive à Adam, lorsqu'il goûte à l'arbre de science et que la porte du paradis se referme sur lui.

Un calme relatif revient alors dans le Plérôme. Néanmoins la situation dé-crite par Ptolémée indique bien que le désir des éons a quelque chose d'irra-

---

[37] Bien que la découverte des écrits valentiniens de *NH* I incite à redoubler de prudence dans l'appréciation du témoignage d'Irénée sur le valentinisme et qu'on doive particulièrement se garder de confondre avec la doctrine du maître les enseignements de son disciple Ptolémée, rapportés d'après des sources qui ne sont pas forcément bien informées, nous croyons pouvoir admettre comme un témoignage authentique, portant sur un point très précis, la remarque de *Haer.* I,11,1 (Irénée, éd. 1979, p. 169) sur les deux Limites chez Valentin.

tionnel. En effet, ils veulent «voir» le Père, qui, précisément, est «insaisissable pour la vue» (οὐ καταληπτὸς ἰδεῖν). On ne saurait être surpris que, par une sorte de jeu de mots, ce désir (πόθος) se change progressivement en une passion dangereuse (πάθος), qui devient manifeste à partir du trentième éon. La suite du drame est connue: l'Ἐνθύμησις de Sophia est rejetée en dehors du Plérôme, autour duquel une seconde Limite est établie.

Ainsi, comme dans *Gen.* 1–8, dans la *Caverne des trésors* et dans les *Hermetica*, la chute s'opère en deux phases principales marquées par deux Limites et séparées par un intervalle de calme relatif. Simplement le Plérôme valentinien n'est plus une Décade, mais une Triacontade, en raison de spéculations arithmologiques, dont le principe est sans doute beaucoup plus ancien que Valentin ou Marc le Mage: il suffit d'observer l'attention que Philon y prête déjà.

Au terme de cette enquête, nous constatons que les *LXX*, Philon, les traditions apocryphes recueillies dans la *Caverne des trésors*, les *Hermetica*, *Eugnoste* (+ *SJC*) et le témoignage d'Irénée sur les valentiniens nous fournissent des points de repère suffisants pour nous permettre de comprendre comment on est passé d'une réflexion sur les générations antédiluviennes, et spécialement sur *Gen.* 5, au mythe gnostique de la procession et de la chute des éons.

A l'intérieur de cette chaîne, les écrits hermétiques, *CH* I, *Ogd.Enn.* ainsi que *CH* XIII, jouent un rôle essentiel, non pas en tant que sources, mais en tant que maillon significatif, à mi-chemin entre le récit encore très anthropomorphique de *Gen.* 1–10 est les abstractions savantes du valentinisme. En effet, s'il est à notre avis très probable qu'*Eugnoste* (+ *SJC*) dépend directement d'une source hermétique, le problème ne se pose pas dans les mêmes termes pour le valentinisme: on a pu estimer par exemple que l'épître valentinienne citée par Epiphane (*Panarion* 31,5,1–8) dépend directement d'un Eugnoste grec préalablement interpolé par les valentiniens.[38] D'autre part, la σοφία νοερὰ ἐν σιγῇ de *CH* XIII,2 ressemble beaucoup aux noms des premiers éons valentiniens. Toutefois les spéculations sur la Décade et sur la Limite apparaissent déjà chez Philon; l'Ogdoade est un symbole de régénération dès les *Epîtres de Pierre*, la *Lettre de Barnabé*[39] ou Clément d'Alexandrie; dans l'*Epître à Tite*, Paul, tout en combattant «les folles recherches, généalogies, querelles et

---

[38] Cf. Epiphane, éd. 1859, p. 314–320 (*Panarion* XXXI, 5–6) et le stemma proposé par M. Tardieu (1984, 61) après quelques remarques sur l'histoire du texte d'*Eugnoste*. Mais indépendamment de la question des interpolations valentiniennes dans *Eugnoste*, il se pourrait qu'*Eugnoste* et le valentinisme aient eu des bases mythologiques communes, qu'on retrouve également dans l'hermétisme. Les liens entre *Eugnoste* et l'hermétisme nous paraissent incontestables. Quant aux liens entre l'hermétisme et le valentinisme, on pourrait rappeler l'observation ancienne de F. Sagnard (1947, p. 590 s.): «Il faut ici faire mention d'une autre littérature qui présente des rapports marqués avec la gnose valentinienne: ce sont les écrits hermétiques».

[39] Sagnard 1947, 379.

disputes au sujet de la Loi» (*Tite* 3,9), proclame comme le fera plus tard *CH* XIII, la régénération (παλιγγενεσία) par la miséricorde (ἔλεος) de Dieu (cf. *Tite* 3,5, *CH* XIII,3).[40] Nous avons donc là, semble-t-il, un fonds d'exégèse juive qui a influencé aussi bien le *NT* qu'Hermès et Valentin.

Simplement, dans les documents valentiniens, le récit de la Genèse, réinterprété, épuré de ses anthropomorphismes les plus voyants, accordé avec les spéculations pythagoriciennes sur la science des nombres et farci d'abstractions ou d'allégories jugées dignes des meilleurs philosophes, serait parfaitement méconnaissable si nous ne disposions pas des étapes intermédiaires, transmises notamment par les *Hermetica*. Alors que dans le *Poimandrès*, sur lequel nous avons fondé l'essentiel de notre démonstration, l'arrière-plan mythologique du texte biblique se reconnaît encore assez aisément, la Décade hermétique de *CH* XIII, 9 se réduit à une série d'abstractions où il devient assez difficile de replacer les hypostases de *CH* XIII, 2 et des autres écrits hermétiques.[41] Entre *CH* I et *CH* XIII, *Ogd.Enn.* donne tous les repères nécessaires pour reconnaître, sous leur déguisement philosophique, les entités mythologiques du *Poimandrès* et de la *Genèse* et pour mettre en place la Décade qui sous-tend aussi bien le système d'Eugnoste que l'arithmologie valentinienne.

ABRÉVIATIONS

Ascl.	= Asclepius	: cf. NF, tome 2
BCNH	= Bibliothèque Copte de Nag Hammadi, Québec-Louvain	
CH	= Corpus Hermeticum	: cf. NF, tomes 1–2
DH	= Définitions hermétiques arméniennes	: cf. HHE, tome 2
Eug.	= Eugnoste, dans NH III.IV	: cf. Tardieu 1984
FH	= Fragmenta Hermetica	: cf. NF, tome 4
Haer.	= Contra Haereses	: cf. Irénée
HHE	= Hermès en Haute-Egypte, 2 vol.	: cf. Mahé 1978. 1982
NF	= Nock (A.D.)—Festugière (A.-J.), Hermès Trismégiste, 4 vol., Paris 1945–1954	
Ogd.Enn.	= L'Ogdoade et l'Ennéade, NH VI[6]	: cf. HHE, tome 1
ParSem	= La Paraphrase de Sem, NH VII[1]	
QG	= Quaestiones in Genesim	: cf. Philon
RHT	= La Révélation d'Hermès Trismégiste, 4 vol.	: cf. Festugière 1942–1953

---

[40] Cf. *supra* note 28.
[41] Cf. *supra* note 20.

SH   = Stobaei Hermetica   : cf. NF, tome 4
SJC   = Sophia Jesu Christi, NH III⁴ et
        Codex Gnostique de Berlin, BG³   : cf. Tardieu 1984

BIBLIOGRAPHIE

BEZOLD, C.
    1888   *Die Schatzhöhle*, Leipzig 1888 (réimpression: Philo Press, Amsterdam s.d.).
BRÉHIER, E.
    1956   cf. Plotin.
CLÉMENT D'ALEXANDRIE.
    éd. 1948   *Extraits de Théodote* (éd. F. Sagnard), Paris 1948. (*SC*, 23).
DODD, C.H.
    1975   *L'interprétation du quatrième évangile*, Paris 1975 (traduction française, par M.
                Montabrut, de *The Interpretation of the Fourth Gospel*, Cambridge 1953).
ÉPIPHANE
    éd. 1859   *Panarion* (éd. F. Oehler), *Corpus Haeresiologicum*, tome 2, Berlin 1859.
FESTUGIÈRE, A.-J.
    1942–1953   *La Révélation d'Hermès Trismégiste*, Paris 1942–1953 (4 volumes).
IRÉNÉE
    éd. 1979   *Contre les hérésies*, livre I (éd. A. Rousseau/L. Doutreleau), Paris 1979, 2
                volumes (*SC*, 263–264).
JAMBLIQUE
    éd. 1966   *Les mystères d'Egypte* (éd. E. Desplaces), Paris 1966
MAHÉ, J.-P.
    1978. 1982 *Hermès en Haute-Egypte*, tome 1, Québec 1978; tome 2, Québec 1982
MAHÉ, J.-P.
    1984   «Fragments hermétiques dans les papyri Vindobonenses graecae 29456 rᵒ et
                29828 rᵒ», dans E. Lucchesi et H.D. Saffrey, *Mémorial André-Jean Festugière.
                Antiquité païenne et chrétienne*, Genève 1984 (*Cahiers d'Orientalisme*, 10),
                51–64.
MAHÉ, J.-P.
    1986 a   Παλιγγενεσία et structure du monde supérieur dans les *Hermetica* et le traité
                d'*Eugnoste* de Nag Hammadi, dans *Deuxième Journée d'Etudes Coptes, Stras-
                bourg 25 mai 1984*, Louvain—Paris 1986 (*Cahiers de la Bibliothèque Copte*, 3),
                137–149.
MAHÉ, J.-P.
    1986 b   La création dans les *Hermetica*, dans *Recherches Augustiniennes* 21, Paris 1986,
                3–53.
MERCIER, CH.
    1979   cf. Philon, *QG*.
MUSSIES, G.
    1982   The Interpretatio Judaica of Thot-Hermes, dans M. Heerma van Voss e.a.
                (edd.), *Studies in Egyptian Religion Dedicated to Professor Jan Zandee*, Leiden
                1982.
PHILON

    Quaestiones in Genesim
                – éd. du texte arménien, avec traduction latine par J.B. Aucher, Venise 1822
                  [Nous avons consulté l'exemplaire personnel de Ch. Mercier, portant l'in-
                  dication manuscrite de variantes du texte arménien].
                – éd. des fragments grecs (éd. F. Petit), Paris 1978 (*Oeuvres de Philon
                  d'Alexandrie*, 33).
                – traduction française du texte arménien par Ch. Mercier, 2 volumes, Paris
                  1979. 1984 (*Oeuvres de Philon d'Alexandrie*, 34 A et 34 B). [nous ren-
                  voyons entre parenthèses aux pages de cette édition]

PLOTIN

         Ennéades II, éd. trad. E. Bréhier, Paris, 2ème éd., 1956.

PUECH, H.-CH.

1978   *En quête de la Gnose*, tome 1, Paris 1978.

QUISPEL, G.

sous-presse   Hermetism and the New Testament, especially Paul, manuscrit remis à *Aufstieg und Niedergang der Römischen Welt*, 205 p. dactylographiées [copie communiquée par l'auteur].

SAGNARD, F.

1947   *La Gnose valentinienne et le témoignage de saint Irénée*, Paris 1947.

TARDIEU, M.

1984   *Ecrits gnostiques. Codex de Berlin* (*SGM*, 1) Paris 1984.

TOBIN, T.H.

1983   *The Creation of Man, Philo and the History of the Interpretation*, Washington 1983.

'IF YOU DO NOT SABBATIZE THE SABBATH . . .'

THE SABBATH AS GOD OR WORLD IN GNOSTIC UNDERSTANDING (EV. THOM., LOG. 27)

BY

T. BAARDA (UTRECHT)

INTRODUCTION—THE TEXT OF LOGION 27

1. Logion 27 belongs to the few sayings of the Gospel according to Thomas which have been preserved both in a Coptic and in a Greek form:[1]

P.OXY.I^{v}:4–11		*NH II.2; 86:17–20*
ΛΕΓΕΙ/ Ι̅C̅	1	
ΕΑΝ ΜΗ ΝΗCΤΕΥCΗ/ΤΑΙ	2	ⲉⲧⲉⲧⲙ̄ⲣ̄ⲛⲏ/ⲥⲧⲉⲩⲉ
ΤΟΝ ΚΟCΜΟΝ	3	ⲉⲡⲕⲟⲥⲙⲟⲥ
ΟΥ ΜΗ / ΕΥΡΗΤΑΙ	4	ⲧⲉⲧⲛⲁϩⲉ ⲁⲛ ,
ΤΗΝ ΒΑCΙΛΕΙ/ΑΝ	5	ⲉⲧⲙⲛ̄ⲧⲉ/ⲣⲟ
ΤΟΥ Θ̅Υ̅	6	
ΚΑΙ	7	
ΕΑΝ ΜΗ / CΑΒΒΑΤΙCΗΤΕ	8	ⲉⲧⲉⲧⲛ̄ⲧⲙ̄ ⲉⲓⲣⲉ ⲙ̄ⲡⲉⲥⲁⲙⲃⲁⲧⲟⲛ
ΤΟ CΑΒ/ΒΑΤΟΝ	9	ⲛ̄ⲥⲁⲃ/ⲃⲁⲧⲟⲛ
ΟΥΚ ΟΨΕCΘΕ	10	ⲛ̄ⲧⲉⲧⲛⲁⲛⲁⲩ ⲁⲛ
Τ̅Ο̅ / Π̅Ρ̅Α̅	11	ⲉⲡⲉⲓⲱⲧ'

2. The two texts differ slightly. The Coptic text lacks the introduction 'Jesus said' in line 1; it has a scribal error in line 2, where the reading ⲉⲧⲉ- (2.sg. fem.Praes.I) should be emended with the *editio princeps*[2] into ⲉⲧⲉⲧⲛ- (2.pl. Praes.II); further, it omits the qualification 'of God' in line 6, which may have been typical for the Coptic text as can be seen in logion 3 where the Coptic translation also omits 'of God' where the Greek text must have contained the words in question.[3] Whether or not the Coptic translator read in his Greek copy the conjunction 'and' is impossible to say; in the Greek it may have the function of an introduction of a second saying.[4] The Coptic construction in

[1] B.P. Grenfell, A.S. Hunt, *The Oxyrrhynchus Papyri* I, London 1898, 3; Pahor Labib, *Coptic Gnostic Papyri in the Coptic Museum at Old Cairo* I, Cairo 1956, Plate 86.

[2] A. Guillaumont, H.-Ch. Puech, G. Quispel, W. Till, Yassah 'Abd al-Masīh, *The Gospel according to Thomas*, Leiden 1959, 18 app. (*l*. 17).

[3] For the Greek text (reconstruction) of logion 3, cf. J. Fitzmyer, *Essays on the Semitic Background of the New Testament*, Missoula 1974 (London 1971), 355–433, 374f.

[4] See e.g. C. Taylor, *The Oxyrrhynchus Logia and the Apocryphal Gospels*, Oxford 1899, 8;

lines 8−9 (including for the first time the reading CAMBATON in Coptic)[5] offers the possibility of various renderings, but we take it to be an attempt to do justice to the Greek text as preserved in the Oxyrhynchus Papyrus.

3. On the basis of the two texts we may suggest the following translation of the logion:

Jesus said:	G 1
'If you do not fast the world,	G/C 2−3
you will not find the kingdom of God'	G 4−6 (C 4−5)
and:	G 7
'If you do not sabbatize the Sabbath,	G/C 8−9
you will not see the Father'.	G/C 10−11

4. One cannot say that the meaning of this logion is clear at first sight. The parallelism between the two parts of the logion might suggest that the two sayings are to express the same idea. If the two apodoses refer to the same spiritual reality, it is tempting to suggest that the collector understood the two protases also as synonymous, even though the expressions used in them seem to point into a different direction. This makes the logion a rather enigmatic one. The purpose of this contribution is meant as an attempt at solving this enigma.

5. As a matter of fact, this is not the only obscure saying in the collection of sayings preserved in the Gospel of Thomas. Since the collector borrowed the material from oral tradition, from various written Gospels that circulated among christians in his days, and finally from some esoteric revelations known in gnostic circles, the present reader of the collection is often puzzled by the question why *Thomas* selected precisely these sayings and how he wished them to be understood. I refuse to accept that he merely wished to preserve all kind of material that he found, so as to save it from oblivion. He must have chosen these sayings, because they suited some purpose. In his introduction he speaks of the *secret* words of the living Jesus. Since many of the words which are included were not at all secret, but open for reading to everyone who wished to read them in the various Gospel texts that circulated in the second century (even pagan authors had access to them), he must have used the word 'secret' in the sense of *esoteric* with respect to their meaning. They should not be interpreted at surface level. Only the gnostic reader can understand the deeper meaning. The meaning is not clear at first sight, but asks for 'seeking' with the promise that 'whoever finds the interpretation of these sayings will not taste death.'[6]

6. It is my conviction that the Gospel according to Thomas both in its Greek and in its Coptic form is the product of a gnostic author. This does not imply

---

Fitzmyer, *o.c.*, 392; J.-É. Ménard, *L'Évangile selon Thomas*, Leiden 1975, 120.

[5] Fitzmyer, *l.c.*

[6] Ménard, *o.c.*, 77f.

that the material used by the collector could not be of a very early date or even genuine tradition of words of Jesus. Each of the sayings has to be investigated with the methods of literary analysis and historical criticism in order to establish its antiquity and authenticity.[7] Logion 27, as a whole or any of the sayings contained in it, could have been the product of very early tradition or even a genuine set of sayings of Jesus. It is, in this case, very improbable that the collector himself should have faked his readers by making up some saying that suited his own goals. But that he pursued his own goal when he adopted this logion from earlier traditions seems obvious, if one tries to study the possible background of the saying.

7. With background one may focus on two ways of interpretation. One approach is the *diachronic* investigation. What is the provenance of the logion or of the two sayings contained in the logion, before the logion became part of the present collection? Is it possible to conclude anything about its form and functioning in the earlier strata of tradition or perhaps of its meaning in the *viva vox* of the teaching of Jesus? In my view—which I hope to express elsewhere—the saying or the two elements of the saying belonged to a very archaic Jewish-Christian tradition which may have preserved items of the preaching of Jesus, in which both the practice of fasting and the observation of the sabbath were said to be conditions for the life of the believer.

8. The approach in this study is the *synchronic* one. What is the meaning and function of the logion within the context of the collection itself, or at least within the context of the doctrinal views which have created a collection like the Gospel of Thomas. We will concentrate on the function of the conditions 'if you do not fast the world' and 'if you do not sabbatize the sabbath.' What is the relation between the two clauses? What do they ask from the readers? In attempting to find an answer to these questions, I struck the problem of the meaning of *Sabbaton* in Gnostic texts, and since it became clear that the solution of the difficulties in logion 27 might perhaps lie in the definition of Sabbaton, I anticipated the treatment of the logion by an examination of this word in Gnostic texts that are related to the Gospel of Thomas.

I. The Sabbath as God — The Demiurge of the cosmos

I. The Demiurge as 'Sabbath' in Tertullian's Adversus Valentinianos

1. The first text which attracts the attention is a passage from Tertullian's treatise against the Valentinians (ch. 20, 1f.).[8] The author describes there the ac-

---

[7] Cf. my discussions of logia 22, 42 and 72 in *Early Transmission of Words of Jesus*, Amsterdam 1983, resp. 276ff., 179ff., 131ff.

[8] J.-CL. Frédouille, *Tertullien, Contre les Valentiniens*, Paris 1980, 124 (xx.1−2a, *ll.*1−10).

tivity of the Creator-God according to the Valentinian system, rather closely following one of his source texts, Irenaeus' *Adversus Haereses*,[9] as one can easily see from our synopsis:

(1) Igitur Demiurgus	1	... τὸν Δημιουργόν... (44:2)
extra pleromatis limites constitutus,	2	ἐκτὸς τοῦ πληρώματος (43:5f.)
in ignominiosa aeterni exilii uastitate	3	
nouam prouinciam condidit,	4	ποιητὴν ὄντα (43:6, 8, 10)
hunc mundum,	5	
repurgata confusione	6	
et distincta diuersitate	7	διακρίνοντα γὰρ τὰς δύο οὐσίας
duplicis substantiae illius detrusae	8	συγκεχυμένας (43:6f.)
animalium et materialium	9	πάντων ψυχικῶν τε καὶ ὑλι-
Ex incorporalibus corpora aedificat,	10	κῶν (43:6)
grauia leuia,	11	κούφων καὶ βαρέων (43:10)
sublimantia atque uergentia,	12	ἀνωφερῶν καὶ κατωφερῶν (43:10, 44:1)
caelestia atque terrena.	13	τά τε οὐράνια καὶ τὰ γήϊνα (43:8f.)
Tum ipsam caelorum septemplicem scaenam	14	ἑπτὰ... οὐρανοὺς κατεσκευα-κέναι
solio desuper suo finit.	15	ὧν ἐπάνω τὸν Δημιουργὸν εἶναι λέγουσιν (44:1−2)

'The Demiurge, therefore, / placed outside the borders of Pleroma, / in the igno-minious desolation of eternal exile, / founded a new territory, / this world, / after having purified the chaos / and having separated what was different / in that dual, driven down, substance / of psychic and hylic matter. / From incorporeal elements he built bodies, / heavy (and) light, / rising aloft and verging, / celestial and terres-trial. / Then he completed the very sevenfold stage of heavens / with his throne above it.'

2. Our interest lies in what Tertullian observes on the name of the Demiurg (20,2):[10]

(2) Vnde et sabbatum dictum est	16	καὶ διὰ τοῦτο ἑβδομάδα καλοῦ-
ab hebdomade sedis suae,	17	σιν αὐτόν (44:2f.)
ut Ogdoada mater Achamoth	18	τὴν δὲ μητέρα τὴν Ἀχαμωθ Ὀγ-
ab argumento ogdoadis primigenitalis.	19	δοάδα ἀποσώζουσαν τὸν ἀριθ-μὸν τῆς ἀρχεγόνου καὶ πρώτης τοῦ πληρώματος Ὀγδοάδος (44:3−5).

'That is why he is called *sabbatum* (σάββατον) because of the *hebdomad* of his residence, just as the Mother Achamoth (is called) Ogdoas, due to the first-created Ogdoas ....'

---

[9] Irenaeus, *Adversus Haereses* I, 5.1f. (ed. W.W. Harvey I, 43:5−44:2); for the sources of Tertullian cf. Frédouille, *o.c.*, 27f.

[10] Frédouille, *o.c.*, 124 (xx.2, *ll.*8−10); Harvey I, 44:2−4.

3. Whereas Tertullian abbreviates the description of *Achamoth,* he expands the notice on the name of the Demiurge. Irenaeus had mentioned the fact that the Valentinians called the Creator-God Ἑβδομάς, which agrees with the observation in Hippolyte's *Refutatio*: καλεῖται δὲ καὶ Τόπος ὑπ' αὐτῶν καὶ Ἑβδομάς καὶ Παλαιὸς τῶν ἡμέρων.[11] These names have a Jewish or biblical provenance, עתיק יומיא, שבת, מקום, two of them, at least, being designations of God. Therefore, the Gnostics used these names, including *Topos*[12] and *Hebdomas*,[13] as designations of the Demiurge. At the same time, however, they could give them a local meaning, e.g. when they refer to the residence of the Demiurge (in Irenaeus's words) ... τὸν Δημιουργὸν δὲ εἰς τὸν ἐπουράνιον Τόπον, τουτέστιν ἐν τῇ Ἑβδομάδι.[14] Both words have an ambiguous meaning, denoting both the created Cosmos of the seven heavens and its Creator. Such an ambivalence cannot surprise us in gnostic texts which as so often betray knowledge of the *Timaios* of Plato. The *Cosmos* is a living creature, a second *God*, but according to the Gnostics this God is no other than the bad Demiurge himself.[15]

4. One might think that Tertullian's expansion of the text of Irenaeus is due to his own free paraphrase of the Greek phrase. If so, he must have been aware that *Hebdomad*, rendered by him first with *Sabbatum*, was both the name of the Demiurge and the name of his creation and residence (cf. 23,1: 'subest enim Demiurgus in *hebdomade sua*'),[16] so that he used this term for his residence. However, it is quite possible that his deviation from the text in Irenaeus was based on other information, either from another heresiological source or from his knowledge of some gnostic document. He may have known a tradition in which the *hebdomad* was the cosmic planetary sphere and *Sabbath* the name of its creator and ruler, such as is expressed in the Apocryphon of John

---

[11] Hippolytus, *Refutatio omnium haeresium* VI, 32.7 (P. Wendland, *Hippolytus Werke* III, Leipzig 1916, 116:6f.); one should not necessarily follow the textual emendation τόπος ⟨μεσότητος⟩.

[12] For Τόπος being the Demiurge, cf. F. Sagnard, *Clément d'Alexandrie, Extraits de Théodote*, Paris 1948, 140ff. (Extraits 34,1.2; 37f.; 39; 59,2); Idem, *La Gnose valentinienne et le témoignage de Saint-Irénée*, Paris 1947, 543, 546. For 'the Old of Days' cf. *ibid.* 176.

[13] For *Hebdomas* = 'Sabbath' see below I,*I*,4 (n. 16).

[14] Irenaeus, *Adv.Haer.* I, 5.4 (Harvey I, 46:6–8); ἐπουράνιον is Harvey's conjecture, the Ms. reads ὑπερουράνιον. I would like to propose the emendation ὑπουράνιον as an alternative.

[15] See Plato, *Timaios* 34AB, 38C – E, 41A, 68E, 92C, R. Bury, *Plato* IX (Loeb 234), Cambridge – London 1981, 64f., 176, 252; cf. for Plato and Philo, D.T. Runia, *Philo of Alexandria and the Timaios of Plato*, Amsterdam 1983 (Diss.), 157ff.; J. Mansfeld, Bad World and Demiurge: a 'Gnostic' motif from Parmenides and Empedocles to Lucretius and Philo, in: R. van den Broek, M.J. Vermaseren, *Studies in Gnosticism and Hellenistic Religions presented to G. Quispel*, Leiden 1981, 261–314. Cf. also G.E.R. Lloyd, *Polarity and Analogy*, Cambridge 1971, ch. IV, esp. 232ff., 256ff.

[16] Frédouille, *o.c.,* I, 128 (23:1f.), 144 (31:2).

'This is the *hebdomad* of *Sabbaton*.'[17] This suggests to me the *first* conclusion: the name 'Sabbath' could have been the name of the Demiurge in the Valentinian system known to Tertullian.

5. The most recent commentary of this passage, that of J.-Cl. Frédouille, which carefully compares Tertullian's descriptions with the Valentinian sources, is not helpful at this point. This commentator is apparently puzzled by the name *sabbatum*: 'ce nom du Démiurge n'apparaît ni dans nos sources patristiques (Irénée, Hippolyte, Extraits de Théodote), ni, semble-t-il, dans les traités de Nag Hammadi ....'[18] The following observations might convince him that there is no reason to consider Tertullian's notice as completely isolated.

II. The Demiurge as 'Sabbath' in the Heavenly Dialogue

1. The first gnostic document that can ascertain the fact that the Demiurge was called 'Sabbath' is the beginning of a passage from the 'Heavenly Dialogue' quoted by Celsus in his *Alèthès Logos* and preserved by Origen in his work against Celsus, *Kata Kelsou* VIII:15f.[19] I will not enter into detail in this treatment of the text, which I have discussed at length elsewhere.[20] The gist of the beginning of the fragment preserved is that there is a higher divinity (represented here by the Son, the Son of Man, Some Other) than the Demiurge:[21]

1. εἰ ἰσχυρότερός ἐστι θεοῦ υἱός,
2. καὶ κύριος αὐτοῦ ἐστιν ὁ υἱὸς τοῦ ἀνθρώπου,
3. καί τις ἄλλος κυριεύσει τοῦ κρατοῦντος θεοῦ,
4. πῶς πολλοὶ περὶ τὸ φρέαρ,
5. καὶ οὐδεὶς εἰς τὸ φρέαρ;

'If the Son is stronger than God,[22] / and (if) his Lord is the Son of Man, / and (if) Some Other will reign over the mighty God, / how does it come that many are around the well, / and nobody is in the well?'

2. The phrase that interests us here is the second clause of the protasis of this

---

[17] See below I,*III*.2.

[18] Frédouille, *o.c.*, II, 301.

[19] P. Koetschau, *Origenes Werke* II, Leipzig 1899, 232–234.

[20] Cf. the forthcoming publication *The Heavenly Dialogue in Celsus' Alèthès Logos (Origen, Contra Celsum VIII:15–16)*, A Lecture held for the Royal Dutch Academy in 1986.

[21] This text differs from that of Koetschau, *o.c.*, II, 232:12–16, and also from the text of M. Borret, *Origène, Contre Celse* IV, Paris 1969, 206 (15:4–7), in that it reads τις ἄλλος instead of τίς ἄλλος (*l.*3) and interprets the line as the third subordinate clause of the protasis, and not as a parenthesis. For the reasons see *Heavenly Dialogue* § 8,1–6.

[22] See for this interpretation of the Greek phrase *Heavenly Dialogue* § 6,1–10.

hypothetical sentence. Origen, in his comments, repeats this clause with a slighty paraphrastic change, when he denies the allegation of Celsus that Christians would or could formulate such a phrase, 'And none of us—he says—is so crack-brained as to say, "the Son of Man is Lord of God." '[23] Origen rightly assumes that αὐτοῦ refers to 'God' in the first clause. But how could one say that the Son of Man is Lord of God? Such a pronouncement could only have been made by some heretic. This alleged heretical provenance is accepted and supported by the commentators of Origen's or Celsus's work. Already Mosheim (1745)[24] and Keim (1873)[25] referred to the fact that the figure of the Son of Man was a dominant concept in gnostic circles according to the heresiologists, and it has often been assumed that the Heavenly Dialogue was written or used among the Ophites. Whatever the precise origin may have been, there can be no doubt that the pronouncements behind the three hypothetical clauses rest on the dualism which distinguished between the supercelestial God, the Father of All, the God Man and his Son, the Son of Man, on the one side, and the Demiurge, the Father of the created Cosmos, Jaldabaoth, on the other side. This dualism enables the Gnostics to say that the Son is stronger than God (a statement based on the gnostic interpretation of Lk 11:21f.)[26]

3. It is my conviction that the second clause is also based on a saying of Jesus in the Gospel of Luke, namely 6:5, where it is said:[27]

Κύριός ἐστιν τοῦ σαββάτου ὁ υἱὸς τοῦ ἀνθρώπου,

which is reformulated in the fragment of the Heavenly Dialogue as:

Κύριος αὐτοῦ (sc.τοῦ θεοῦ) ἐστιν ὁ υἱὸς τοῦ ἀνθρώπου.

The difference between the two statements implies that 'the Sabbath' was interpreted as a name of 'God', that is, of the God of the Cosmos, the Demiurge. This means that the religious, ethical pronouncement of Jesus was reinterpreted in a cosmological, soteriological sense. So it became a verdict pronounced by the Revealer which made it clear to the gnostic believer that the supercelestial God—Man and Son of Man[28]—was superior to the celestial Demiurge and his creation, so that one should not have fear of the archons of this world.

---

[23] Koetschau, o.c., II, 233:10f.; Borret, o.c., IV, 206 (15:27f.).
[24] J.L. Mosheim, Origines, (...) Acht Bücher von der Wahrheit der christlichen Religion wider den weltweisen Celsus, Hamburg 1745, 825, n. 4.
[25] Th. Keim, Kelsos-Celsus, Wahres Wort, Zürich 1873 (repr. Darmstadt 1969), 123, n. 1; 230.
[26] Cf. Heavenly Dialogue, § 6,8–9.
[27] Cf. Mt 12,8; Mk 2,27 (= Lk 6,5 v.1.).
[28] For this expression cf. below § I,III,3 (n. 48).

This brings me to the *second* conclusion: the name 'Sabbath' is understood as a designation of the Demiurge in the Heavenly Dialogue, just as was the case in Tertullian's description of the Demiurge.

III. The Demiurge as 'Sabbath' in the Apocryphon of John

1. The third document to which I want to draw the attention is the 'Apocryphon of John,' preserved in no less than four recensions, three of them found in the Nag Hammadi Library.[29] It is quite obvious that this writing is a document akin to the source which Irenaeus has used for his survey of the Valentinian doctrine. In this Apocryphon the Creator of the Cosmos appears under the name Jaldabaoth, his creation consists of the seven heavens—the planetary spheres—in which seven archons sway their rule. These seven—each in his own sphere—form and dominate the whole created reality. They bear biblical or Jewish names, Atoth, Elohim, Astophaios, Jahu, Sabaoth, Adonai, and finally the seventh, who bears the names *Sabbede*,[30] *Sabbateōn*,[31] *Sabbataios*[32] and *Sabbadaios*.[33] It is obvious that these names are related to *Sabbaton*.[34]

2. These seven archons, who reign over the cosmic reality,[35] symbolize the various aspects of the Cosmos, and of its ultimate Creator Jaldabaoth. None of them has an absolute sovereignty, for in fact it is Jaldabaoth who reigns over them (ⲁϥⲣ̄ ⲭⲟⲉⲓⲥ ⲉⲣⲟⲟⲩ),[36] so that he can speak of himself as 'a God above them' (ⲛⲟⲩⲧⲉ ⲉⲍⲣⲁⲓ̈ ⲉⲝⲟⲟⲩ).[37] The physiognomy of Jaldabaoth is a rather complex one, since he is able to adopt the figure and face of each of these seven archons,[38] for he resides above them, and is so to speak each of them and all of them. The seven archons together form the *Hebdomad*, and the *Hebdomad* in its turn belongs to *Sabbaton*, or to put it into the words of the Apocryphon:[39]

II.I; 11:34f. ⲧⲁⲓ̈ ⲧⲉ ⲧⲍⲉⲃⲇⲟⲙⲁⲥ ⲛ̄ⲧⲉ ⲡ̄ⲥⲁⲃⲃⲁⲧⲟⲛ

III.1; 18:7f. ⲧⲁⲓ̈ ⲧⲉ ⲑⲉⲃⲇⲟⲙⲁⲥ ⲙ̄ⲡⲥⲁⲃⲃⲁⲧⲟⲛ

---

[29] Cf. M. Krause, P. Labib, *Die drei Versionen des Apokryphon des Johannes*, Wiesbaden 1972, esp. 37–46.

[30] Codex II:1; Krause-Labib, *o.c.*, 141 (11:33); Codex IV lacuna.

[31] Codex II:1; Krause-Labib, *o.c.*, 144 (12:25); Codex IV lacuna.

[32] B.G.8502:2 (W. Till, *Die gnostischen Schriften des Koptischen Papyrus Berolinensis 8502*, Berlin 1955), 42:6, 44:4.

[33] Codex III:1; Krause-Labib, *o.c.*, 73 (18:6).

[34] See below § I,*IV.2.*

[35] Cf. e.g. Codex III:1; Krause-Labib, *o.c.*, 72 (17:17ff.), 73 (18:8f.).

[36] Cf. e.g. Codex II:1; Krause-Labib, *o.c.*, 142 (12:6).

[37] Cf. e.g. Codex III:1; Krause-Labib *o.c.*, 74 (19:17).

[38] Cf. e.g. Codex II:1; Krause-Labib *o.c.*, 142 (11:35f.,12:1).

[39] Krause-Labib, *o.c.*, 141f.; 73; cf. 214 (Codex IV:1, 18:24f.: ⲑⲉⲃⲇⲟⲙ[...]; B.G.8502:2, 42:8f.

This statement is usually rendered with 'this is the sevenness of the week,'[40] that is, the planetary week which rules the Cosmos.[41] However, if we remember the statement of Tertullian, that the name of the Demiurge was *Sabbatum*, on account of the fact that he resides over the seven heavens, the *Hebdomad*,[42] we might posit another interpretation of these words: 'It is the *Hebdomad* of *Sabbaton*,' the seven heavens, planets, spheres, over which the Demiurge Jaldabaoth—now under the name *Sabbath*[43]—reigns.

3. The gnostic treatise reveals that this Demiurge, who is the God of the Jews and of the christian church, is an arrogant God, who as *Saklas*—the foolish God[44]—or *Sammael*—the blind God[45]—does not perceive the ultimate reality of the supercelestial God above him. That is why he can boast that he is God, a jealous God, besides whom there is no other God.[46] Jews and the christians of the church share his ignorance, stupidity and blindness, but the gnostic believers know that there is a reality beyond this Creator-God, beyond the planetary heavens of the created Cosmos. They are in fact 'the certain christians' of whom Celsus says that they 'have misunderstood sayings of Plato, so that they boast of a God who is above the heavens, while they (attempt to) transcend the heaven in which the Jews believe.'[47] The God of the Jews and ordinary christians is limited to the *hebdomas* of which *Sabbath* is the seal and symbol. In the cosmological teaching even the blind Demiurge becomes aware of the other, supercelestial God, when it is revealed to him

qϣOOП ᾹбI ПРⲱME ⲀⲨⲱ ПϣHPE ᾹПРⲱME

There exists "MAN" and the "SON OF MAN,"[48]

the divinity which is known with many names such as the Father of All, the *Anthrōpos*, the first Man, the Son of Man, the Father-Mother-Son triad, and which is the supreme deity which reigns both over the visible and invisible

---

[40] Cf. Krause-Labib, *o.c.*, 73b; F. Wisse, The Apocryphon of John, in: J. Robinson, *The Nag Hammadi Library*, Leiden 1977, 98–116, 105:14.

[41] Cf. Codex III:1; Krause-Labib, *o.c.*, 73 (18:8f.).

[42] Cf. Irenaeus, *Adv.Haer.* I,5.4 (see n. 14); Sagnard, *Gnose valentinienne*, 174. For the relation between the gnostic idea of the 'archons' who form and rule the cosmos and the view of Philo concerning the archons and Plato's view about the 'young gods,' cf. Runia, *o.c.*, 214, 207f.

[43] We may also compare the figure of *Pronoia Sambathas, i.e. the Hebdomad* as the feminine name of Jaldabaoth in 'On the Origin of the World'(NH II:5, 101:26f, H.-G. Bethge-O.S. Wintermute, On the Origin of the World, in: J. Robinson, *o.c.*, 160–179, 164.

[44] See *Heavenly Dialogue* § 7,6.1.

[45] See *Heavenly Dialogue* § 7,6.1.

[46] See *Heavenly Dialogue* § 7,6,1–2.

[47] Origen, *Contra Celsum* VI:19, Koetschau, *o.c.*, II, 89:18–20; Borret, *o.c.*, III, 224 (19:1–3).

[48] Codex II:1 (14:4f.), Codex III:1 (21:17f.), Codex IV:1 (22:17f.), Krause-Labib, *o.c.*, 148f., 75 (fragm.), 219; cf. H.-M. Schenke, *Der Gott "Mensch" in der Gnosis*, Berlin 1962, 6f. and *passim*.

realities.[49] This is the divine Being of whom the Heavenly Dialogue spoke, when it said that the Son is stronger than God, and that the Son of Man is Lord of God, that is, of the Demiurge.[50] It seems obvious that the Apocryphon of John enables us to draw the *third* conclusion: the name 'Sabbath' (*Sabbaton*) is used to denote the Creator-God of the Apocryphon of John, who usually is called Jaldabaoth. The name *Sabbaton* is in some way related to the names of the seventh archon, *Sabbede, Sabbataios* or *Sabbateōn*. The seven archons form the *Hebdomad* of *Sabbaton*.

IV. The Demiurge as 'Sabbath', final observations

1. The observation of Frédouille, that the testimony of Tertullian concerning the name *Sabbatum* for the Demiurge was quite isolated, is contradicted by the gnostic sources. The Heavenly Dialogue and the Apocryphon of John made it clear that *Sabbaton* was one of the names of the Demiurge. The three testimonies taken together make it quite clear that the first thesis—*Sabbath* is the name of the Creator-God in gnostic doctrine—was valid.

2. A further observation has to be made on the names of the seventh archon, *Sabbede, Sabbadaios, Sabbataios, Sabbateōn*, which are related to *Sabbaton*, but differ from it. I would suggest that *Sabbede* (from *Sabbete* = *Sabbetai*)[51] could have originated in the Hebrew word שבתי or שבתאי (which originates from שבת), that is, the planet 'Saturn' or 'Kronos', lit. the Sabbath's planet.[52] The identification of the Jewish 'Sabbath' with the day of Saturn[53] or the day of Kronos[54] is well-known from the writings of Roman and Greek authors.

3. Pagan authors also identified the God of the Jews with the deity Saturn.[55] This may have been the consequence of the identification of the seventh day

---

[49] See *Heavenly Dialogue* § 7.8.2.

[50] See *Heavenly Dialogue* § 7.9.1.

[51] This may have been the oldest form of the name, which has become graecizised as *Sabbataios, Sabbadaios, Sabbateōn = Sabbataiōn*.

[52] Cf. R. Goldenberg, The *Jewish Sabbath* in the *Roman World*, in: *ANRW* II (XIX:1), Berlin – New York 1979, 414–447, 446; R. van den Broek, The Creation of Adam's Psychic Body in the Apocryphon of John, in: R. van den Broek / M.J. Vermaseren, *Studies* (n. 15), 38–57, 41; idem, *De Taal van de Gnosis*, Baarn 1986, 64f., 67.

[53] See for the testimonies of Tibullus, Frontinus and a scholiast on Vergil's *Georgica*, M. Stern, *Greek and Latin Authors on Jews and Judaism*, I–III, Jerusalem 1974–1980, resp. I §§ 126 (319n), 229 (510), II, § 543 (664), cf. § 537c (654).

[54] See for the testimonies of Cassius Dio *ibid.*, II, §§ 406 (349, 352n.), 414 (359f.,361), 430 (373,377); cf. Th. Reinach, *Textes d'auteurs grecs et romains relatifs au Judaisme*, Paris 1895, 180ff.,194.

[55] Cf. the testimony of Tacitus, Stern, *o.c.*, II, § 281 (25, 38n.); Saturn is one of the seven stars that rule the mortals' fate, moving along the highest orbit and having the greatest potency; for the identification of Saturn with the Phoenician *El*, cf. Herennius Philo of Byblos, Stern, *o.c.*, II, § 326 (142f.).

with the day of Saturn, *Saturni dies*, ἡ τοῦ Κρονου ἡμέρα, which could have
suggested that 'the day of Sabbath' was the day devoted to the God 'Sabbath'.
Sabbath understood as the name of the Jewish God may have been the cause
for the identification with the Phrygian God *Sabazius* ('. . . Judaeos qui Saba-
zi Iovis cultu Romanos inficere mores conati erant . . .'),[56] and consequently
with *Dionysus*[57] and *Juppiter*.[58]

4. It is tempting to connect this idea of Sabbath as God with a phrase in
Juvenal's *Saturae* (xiv.96–106), which speaks of 'some people who have had
a father who reveres the Sabbath (*metuentem sabbata*)' and consequently
'worship nothing but the clouds and the God of heaven.'[59] In most commentaries to this text the verb *metuere* 'to fear' gave rise to the comparison with
expressions as 'fearers of God' or 'fearers of Heaven,'[60] without drawing the
conclusion that in this phrase 'sabbata' could have been a designation of the
Jewish God. In itself the verb could have been used in the sense of 'observing
the Sabbath,'[61] but since the fearing of the Sabbath is connected here with the
reverence of the heavenly God and because of the fact that 'the seventh day'
is mentioned only later in the text (105f.) as one of the aspects of the observance of the Mosaic law, one might seriously consider the possibility that 'sabbata' (cf. Aramaic שבתא) was meant as a designation of God.[62]

5. Whether the latter hypothesis is justified or not, it is obvious from the foregoing observations that the identification of the Jewish God with 'Sabbath' is
not only found in the gnostic sources. It was most likely to be found in the
greco-roman world even among the literated people, the more so among the
uneducated people whose knowledge of the Jewish religion was probably poor.

---

[56] See for the testimony of Valerius Maximus, Stern, *o.c.*, I, § 147b (358, 359n.); Reinach,
o.c., 258f. (§ 141). Stern and Reinach derive Sabazios from Sabaoth; however, the origin of this
identification of the Jewish God with Sabazios is most probably Sabbath (Shabbas), cf. M.P. Nil-
son, *Geschichte der Griechischen Religion* II, Munich 1961, 662; K. Latte, *Römische Religionsgeschichte*, Munich 1960, 275.

[57] Cf. the testimony of Plutarch, Stern, *o.c.*, I, § 258 (553f.,560n.).

[58] Cf. Varro's testimony, Stern, *o.c.*, I, §§ 72b (209f.n.), 72c (210f.), 75 (211f.); see also
Ep.Arist. 16 (H.G. Meecham, *The Letter of Aristeas*, Munich 1935, 7:16–18).

[59] For Juvenal, cf. Stern, *o.c.*, II § 301 (102–107); for *sabbata*, cf. A. Pelletier, Σαββατα,
Transcription grècque de l'Araméen, *Vetus Testamentum* 22 (1972), 436–447.

[60] Cf. Stern, *o.c.*, I, § 301 (103–106).

[61] Cf. e.g. Josephus, *Ant.* 12,6.2,τὴν τοῦ σαββάτου τιμήν; cf. also Elchasai in Hippolytus,
Ref. IX, 16.2 ἔτι δὲ τιμήσατε τὴν ἡμέραν τοῦ σαββάτου.

[62] For *sabbata* as a sing.noun, cf. Persius, *Sat.* 5 (*l.*184) 'recutitaque sabbata' (Stern, *o.c.*, I,
§ 190 (436f.)); Horatius, *Sat.* I, 9.69 'hodie tricesima sabbata' (Goldenberg, *o.c.*, 436f., 437
n. 86). If the name 'Sabbata' in Juvenal is a singular noun, it has to be taken as an indeclinable
noun denoting the name of the God of the Jews, not as a plural of *sabbatum*. For 'Sabbath' as
name of God in Jewish mysticism, cf. A.J. Heschel, *The Sabbath*, ⁵1979, 20 (ref. *Zohar* 88b,
128a).

II. The Sabbath as the World—The cosmos of the Demiurge

I. The Sabbath in the texts of the Nag Hammadi Library

1. Frédouille,[63] in his comments on the passage in Tertullian's treatise against the Valentinians, not only mentioned the fact that he could not trace a parallel in the Nag Hammadi texts (which was too hastily concluded, as we have demonstrated in § I.*III*), but he also referred to the fact that in the 'Gospel according to Philip' logion 8, the word ΣΑΒΒΑΤΟΝ had quite a different meaning, viz. the *pleroma*, which forms a contrast with the Demiurge and his world.[64] Now the problem is that *EvPhil* 8 is mutilated to such an extent that it is difficult to make firm conclusions with respect to the use of *Sabbaton*. In order to substantiate the positive sense of the word, Frédouille's spokesman Ménard[65] refers to the 'Gospel of Truth' (*EvVer*) as another proof text of this positive meaning of *Sabbaton*.[66] Therefore, we shall have to examine this text,[67] which belongs to the few texts of the Nag Hammadi Library which contain the Greek loan-word *sabbaton*. We have seen that it occurred in the 'Apocryphon of John'[68] (a text which was not registered in the Index, because it was rendered with 'week'),[69] in the 'Gospel according to Philip' (*NH* II.3; 52:34 in logion 8), in the 'Gospel of Truth' (*NH* I.3, 32:18.24) and in the 'Gospel of Thomas' (*NH* II.2; 86:19, in logion 27, the passage under discussion).[70] There is one other text in the Nag Hammadi collection, the 'Exposition of Knowledge' (*NH* XI.1; 11:18.31.33), which should not be overlooked, since it may give us the clue to the Gnostic understanding of the word *Sabbaton*.

II. The world as 'Sabbath' in the Exposition of Knowledge

1. The most explicit definition of *Sabbaton* occurs in the first treatise of the eleventh codex, the 'Exposition of Knowledge' (11:18f.):[71]

---

63 Frédouille, *o.c.*, 301.

64 J.-É. Ménard, *L'Évangile selon Philippe*, Paris 1967, 48 (Pl.52 (= 54), 34).

65 Ménard, *o.c.*, 127.

66 J.-É. Ménard, *L'Évangile de Verité*, Leiden 1972, 59 (*NH* I:3, 32:18.24).

67 See § II,*III* -cf. T. Baarda, The Sabbath in the Parable of the Shepherd (Evangelium Veritatis 32:18–24), *Nederlands Theologisch Tijdschrift* 41 (1987), 17–28.

68 Cf. § I,*III*, ad n. 38.

69 Robinson, *Nag Hammadi Library*, Index, 489a; F. Siegert, *The Nag Hammadi-Register*, Tübingen 1982, 299 refers to *NH* III, 1.18:17.

70 For *Sanbathas*, see n. 43; cf. also 'The Problem of the "Sambathions,"' *Corpus Papyrorum Judaicarum* III, Cambridge (Mass.) 1964, 43–87.

71 Translation of J.D. Turner, The Interpretation of Knowledge, in: Robinson, *o.c.*, 427–434, esp. 430:33. Cf. *The Facsimile Edition of the Nag Hammadi Codices*, Codices XI, XII and XIII, Leiden 1973, 17; Dr. J. Helderman who kindly informed me about the wording of the

...мⲛ̄ ⲡⲥ[ⲁⲃⲃⲁ]/ ⲧⲟⲛ ⲉⲧⲉ ⲡⲉ[ⲓ̈ ⲡⲉ ⲡⲕⲟ]ⲥⲙⲟⲥ...

'and the Sabbath, which [is the] world'

This is a most interesting identification, since it may help us to understand some of the other passages mentioned above. The author of the treatise had previously written (9:28−37),[72] that the true gnostic believer should not mention someone 'father' on this earth, because he or she, being the Light of the world, should not follow this world, but only the will of the true Father, the unique One, in heaven. 'For what use is it if you gain the world and forfeit your soul?'[73] As long as men were still in darkness, they worshipped many fathers, because the knowledge of the true Father lacked them. The readers of the treatise are reminded of the fact that 'the world is not theirs,'[74] for the Revealer had come down to take them to the great height (the *pleroma*) from which they had fallen and were taken to the *pit* (the material world).[75] It is then that the author identifies *world* and *sabbath*. The gnostic reader who has ears to hear is reminded of a saying of Jesus about the sheep fallen into the *pit* on *sabbath* day (Matthew 12,11 par.).[76] The author continues by saying, 'for the Father does not keep Sabbath but does work on the Son and through the Son He continues to provide himself with Aeons.'[77] The beginning of this phrase is admittedly an allusion to the pronouncement of Jesus in John 5,17, by which the healing of a man on sabbath is defended. The same combination of allusions to Mt 12,11 and Jn 5,17 occurs in *EvVer* (see below), where it is also used to emphasize the saving activity within the world of the Demiurge.[78] The true Father (and the Son through whom He works) does not, as the Demiurge—who created his own world and his own Aeons[79]—did, rest on the Sabbath, but is continuously active in rescuing the pneumatics and the psychics who receive knowledge, from this material world of the Creator-God. The Sabbath is not the time, in other words the World is not the place, where one can find the true Father idle, for He remains engaged in the saving activity through the Son.

The conclusion of this examination must be that the Sabbath in the 'Expo-

---

Codex approved of this rendering, but suggested as an alternative rendering 'and the Sabbath, *scil.* the world' (Letter Febr. 13, 1987).

[72] Turner, *o.c.*, 430:7−12.
[73] Cf. also Matth. 16:26a, Mark 8:36, Luke 9:25.
[74] Turner, *o.c.*, 430:18.
[75] Turner, *o.c.*, 430:25−27.
[76] See below *Ev.Ver.* (*NH* I:3, 32:18ff.).
[77] Turner, *o.c.*, 430:40, 431:1f.
[78] Cf. J. Helderman, *Die Anapausis im Evangelium Veritatis*, Leiden 1984, 239, n. 138 ('Es handelt sich hier um eine Erlösungsaktivität des Vaters').
[79] Cf. J.D. Turner, Trimorphic Protennoia (NH XIII:1), in: Robinson, *o.c.*, 461−470, 464:24ff., 35ff.

sition of Knowledge' is not a designation of the *Pleroma* or *Ogdoad*, but it is clearly an indication of the *Cosmos* of the Demiurge, or the *Hebdomad*, the planetary spheres of the Creator-God.

III. The world as 'Sabbath' in the Gospel of Truth

1. The second passage to be mentioned is the interesting paraphrase of the parable of the Shepherd in the Gospel of Truth, especially the part of it in which we are told that the Saviour works even on Sabbath day to rescue the sheep fallen into the pit (32:18−24),[80] which reads thus:[81]

> Even on the Sabbath, for the sheep / which he found fallen into the / pit he laboured ⟨for it⟩. He gave life / to the sheep by having brought it up / from the pit ...

As I have shown elsewhere, there can be no doubt that the author in his retelling of the parable made use of elements of Mt 12,11 (the sheep fallen into the pit on Sabbath) and Jn 5,17 ('My Father works until now, and I am working also' that is, on Sabbath).[82] The author of *EvVer* focuses here on the saving work of the Son, which was symbolized in the healing activity on Sabbath (cf. Jn 5:16). It is interesting to see that the author uses his version of the parable to instruct his gnostic readers about the lesson of the parable: 'in order that you might / know in the heart—you are the sons of the / truth-in-the-heart— what is the Sabbath, on which it is not proper / for salvation to be inactive, / ....'[83] This is the message of the parable: the process of salvation is a continuing one on the Sabbath. If they really know this, they will themselves perceive their task: 'in order that you might speak from / that day from above / in which there is no night, / and from the light / which does not sink, because it is perfect'/.[84] The believers will become missionaries in this world, because they cannot do anything else than follow the Son in his saving activity on Sabbath, because they are determined by another day, the day from above, the *Ogdoad*, which is not only a reality above them but is their own reality, 'Speak then from the heart that / you are the perfect day / and (that) in you dwells / the light that does not cease. / Speak of the truth with those who / search for it ....'[85] They share the saving work of the Son who became a way for those who had erred, a discovery for those who were searching (cf. 31:28ff.). From all this it is quite obvious that the sabbath is not the perfect day, because it is the time or place in which there is still ignorance and error, and consequent-

---

[80] H.W. Attridge / G.W. MacRae, The Gospel of Truth, in: H.W. Attridge, *Nag Hammadi Codex I*, Leiden 1985, 55−102 ad 32:18−24.

[81] Cf. T. Baarda, The Sabbath, 24 (§ 11).

[82] *Ibid.* 24 (§§ 12f.).

[83] *Ibid.* 26 (§ 15, *NH* I:3, 32:22f.,38f.).

[84] *Ibid.* 26 (§ 15, *NH* I:3, 32:26−30).

[85] *Ibid.* 26 (§ 15, *NH* I:3, 32:31−37).

ly it is the time and place in which the gnostics, although they have already reached the perfect day (they are the perfect day), still have to work to save others from the ignorance and darkness on the Sabbath.[86] This interpretation of the passage in question differs, as far as I can see, from all earlier interpretations,[87] but it seems to me that there cannot be a different interpretation of the 'sabbath' (e.g. *pleroma, eschatological day*) than I have presented here, if one would like to do justice to the text.

The conclusion, therefore, is that the *Sabbath* in the 'Gospel of Truth' is in agreement with the definition given in the 'Exposition of Knowledge' (where we also met with the combination of Mt 12,11 and Jn 5,17) the world of the Demiurge, from which man has to be rescued.

III. FAST THE WORLD—SABBATIZE THE SABBATH IN LOGION 27

I. Sabbath—God—Cosmos.

1. Our examination has made it quite probable that a gnostic believer understood 'Sabbath' as a designation of either the Cosmos as creation of the Demiurge or of the Demiurge, Jaldabaoth, himself. We have mentioned the fact that the created world could be understood—under the influence of the *Timaios*[88]—as a living creature (ζῷον) or as a second God (δεύτερος θεός) in hellenistic philosophy,[89] in the cosmology of Philo of Alexandria[90] and in Hermetic literature.[91] This interpretation of the Cosmos as God was originally meant in a positive way, so as to make the world an image (εἰκών) of God, by which—to use a Hermetic phrase[92]—through close and pious perception man could obtain the vision of the true God. When Celsus tries to attack the monotheism of the Jews—who adore the heaven (οὐρανός = שמים as a name of God) but refuse to accept the sun, moon, planets and stars as deities[93]— Origen mentions in his refutation the fact that the Greeks postulate 'the whole cosmos' (τὸν ὅλον κόσμον) to be a God, the *first* God according to the Stoics, the *second* God according to the Platonists, the *third* according to others.[94]

---

[86] For the missionary activity of the Gnostics, cf. Helderman, *o.c.*, 108.

[87] Cf. Baarda, The Sabbath, 27f. (§§ 16–17).

[88] Cf. n. 15.

[89] Cf. Runia, *o.c.*, 128ff.

[90] Cf. Runia, *o.c.*, 157f.

[91] G. van Moorsel, *The Mysteries of Hermes Trismegistus*, Utrecht 1955, 16f. Cf. for ζῷον as designation of the world *ibid.* n. 30; cf. P. Festugière, *La révélation d'Hermes Trismégiste*, II, Paris 1949, 65f.

[92] Van Moorsel, *o.c.*, 16 refers to XII:21, εἰ δὲ θέλεις αὐτὸν καὶ θεωρῆσαι, ἴδε τὴν τάξιν τοῦ κόσμου καὶ τὴν εὐκοσμίαν τῆς τάξεως.

[93] Origen, *Contra Celsum* V:6, Borret, *o.c.*, III,24,26 (6:1–7).

[94] Cf. Borret, *o.c.*, 29, n. 1–3 for the testimonies of Cicero, Seneca, Numenius, Proclus a.o.

Therefore, it cannot surprise that the gnostic believer understood the Cosmos as a God.

2. However, there is a difference. The identification of creation with its Creator is, in their systems, embedded in a sharp dualism. This is, for example, the case with Marcion, who apparently understood the biblical notion of 'world' as identical with 'the God of this world.'[95] He interpreted Paul's words ἐμοὶ κόσμος ἐσταύρωται κἀγὼ κόσμῳ (Gal. 6,14b)[96] in this sense, as can be seen from Tertullian's treatment of this passage: 'sed et *mihi, famulo creatoris, mundus crucifixus est,* non tamen "deus mundi," *et ego mundo,* non tamen "deo mundi." '[97] It is obvious that Marcion understood κόσμος as designation of the Demiurge, just as in the gnostic texts which we have examined 'Sabbath' refers to both the cosmos and Jaldabaoth.[98] The confluence of creation and Demiurge enabled the gnostic writers to use 'Sabbath' for both. But contrary to the major trend in Greek philosophy the gnostics do not idealize the world when they call it God, due to their dualistic and pessimistic view of both this creation and its Creator. Even in Hermetic literature, in which usually is spoken of the world in a positive way (xii.15: πλήρωμα τῆς ζωῆς),[99] one sometimes strikes a different tone (vi.4: πλήρωμα τῆς κακίας).[100] This latter evaluation of the world is prevalent in gnosticism, a bad world and a bad Demiurge.[101]

3. As a matter of fact, the depreciation of the world is not peculiarly gnostic. Although not in a dualistic form, but in an ethical sense it is present in the ascetical *trajectories* of early christianity.[102] One cannot deny that the roots of this reticence about and reserve of the 'world' are found in the earliest strata of christian preaching and teaching, not only in Paul's letters (cf. Gal. 6,14 just mentioned) and in Johannine literature (cf. e.g. 1 John 2,15),[103] but also in part of the early Jesus traditions.[104] The world, or rather this world, is an op-

---

[95] A. von Harnack, *Marcion,* Leipzig ²1924, 103, 307* (Gal. 6:14; 1 Cor. 4:9); 308* (2 Cor. 3:14), 309* (2 Cor. 11:14), 311* (Eph.2:2, 6:12); E.C. Blackman. *Marcion and his influence,* London 1948, 76f.

[96] Gal. 6:14b is often referred to as a parallel to Logion 27 of Thomas, cf. already Grenfell-Hunt, *o.c.,* 11.

[97] Tertullian, *Adv.Marc.* V, 2–4, esp. V, 4.15; E. Evans, *Tertullian, Adversus Marcionem,* Oxford 1972, 512–535, esp. 534:6–8.

[98] Similar to *hebdomas* as a designation of the Demiurge and of his Cosmos, the planetary sevenness created by him, see above § I,*I,*3f.

[99] Van Moorsel, *o.c.,* 16 (XII:15).

[100] Van Moorsel, *o.c.,* 16 (VI:4).

[101] Mansfeld, *o.c.,* 263 speaks of the *interpretatio Gnostica.*

[102] Cf. the final document of the conference of Milan 1982, presented in U. Bianchi (ed.), *La tradizione dell' Enkrateia, motivazioni ontologiche e protologiche,* Rome 1985, xxiii – xxxi and passim.

[103] Usually mentioned as a parallel to Logion 27 of Thomas, cf. Grenfell-Hunt, *o.c.,* 11; cf. M. de Jonge, *De Brieven van Johannes,* Nijkerk 1968, 91ff. for the 'Johannine' attitude towards the 'world'.

[104] The world in contrast with the human soul, Mark 8:36 parr.

position to the divine reality of the kingdom of God. This view of the world as a methaphor of everything that is contrary to the will of God[105] has got a wide spread in christian or even islamic traditions ascribed to Jesus, e.g. in the agraphon preserved by Al-Ghazzali:[106]

قال عيسى عليه السلام	Jesus, about whom be peace, said:
لا تتخذوا الدنيا ربا	Take not the world as Lord.
فتتخذكم عبيدا	lest it take you as slaves.

The world is apparently seen as a personalized power that can dominate man and dissociates man from the freedom which God gives.

4. This negative attitude towards the world, especially in gnostic dualism, is also present in the Gospel of Thomas.[107] A good example of its pejorative use is found in the parallel sayings 80 and 56, in which Jesus says:[108]

Whoever has known the κόσμος,	Whoever has known the κόσμος,
has found the σῶμα,	has found a πτῶμα,
and whoever has found the σῶμα,	and whoever has found a πτῶμα,
of him the κόσμος is not worthy.	of him the κόσμος is not worthy.

The world is an organism, a body, but for the collector of 'Thomas' it is not as in the *Timaios* a living organism, a ζῷον, but—if one has the spiritual eye of the gnostic believer to see the truth—a corpse, a dead body. Therefore, the gnostic knows that the world has to be forsaken: 'Whoever has found the κόσμος, and become rich, let him deny the κόσμος,' logion 110.[109] To become rich means to share the divine reality (cf. logia 29 and 85).[110] He who does not know himself is in poverty, in fact, is poverty (logion 3, cf. 29).[111] Therefore, the gnostic, that is the one who lives on the Living one (log.111b), is the one of whom Jesus says, 'whoever finds himself, of him the κόσμος is not worthy' (111c).[112]

5. One logion of special interest in this respect is saying 21,[113] which paraphrases a theme found in the Synoptics:

(21b) If the Lord of the house knows   Mt 24,43a//Lk 12,39a

---

[105] Cf. H. Sasse, κοσμέω κτλ., *TWNT* III, Stuttgart (repr.) 1950, esp. 889ff.; R. Bultmann, *Theologie des Neuen Testaments*, Tübingen ³1958, 254ff.,378ff.

[106] M. Asin e Palacios, *Logia et Agrapha Domini Jesu apud Moslemicos Scriptores* I, Paris 1917, 37f. (367f.).

[107] Cf. J. Zandee, Silvanus and Jewish Christianity, in Van den Broek-Vermaseren, *Studies*, 498–534, 532.

[108] Logion 80 (*NH* II:2, 95:12–14), logion 56 (*ibid.* 90:30–32); Guillaumont, a.o. (ed.), *o.c.*, 44f., 30f.

[109] Logion 110 (*NH* II:2, 99:4f.); Guillaumont, a.o., *o.c.*, 54f.

[110] Cf. also logion 81 (*o.c.*, 20, 44f., 46f.).

[111] Logion 3 (*NH* II:2, 80:19–81:5, esp. 81:2–5), Guillaumont a.o., *o.c.*, 2f.

[112] Logion 111 (NH II:2, 99:6–10, esp. 9f.), Guillaumont, a.o., *o.c.*, 54f.

[113] Logion 21 (*NH* II:2, 84:33–85:19, esp. 85:6–14), Guillaumont, *o.c.*, 14f., 16f.

that the thief is coming,	Mt 24,43c//Lk 12,39c
he will stay awake before he comes	Mt 24,43d
and will not let dig him through	Mt 24,43e//Lk 12,39d
into his house	Mt 24,43f//Lk 12,39e
of his kingdom,	
to carry away his goods.	Mt 12,29d//Mk 3,27d
You then must watch for the κόσμος,	
gird up your loins	Lk 12,35a (log.103)
with great strength,	
lest the brigands find a way	(log.103)
to come to you.	(log.103)

In this elaboration of the Synoptic texts *the thief* is symbol of the *Cosmos*, for which one has to watch. The world is first personified as a thief, and he who has ears to hear knows that Jesus is referring to Jaldabaoth (cf. Marcion's interpretation of Lk 12,39: in personam disponit *Creatoris*, according to Tertullian);[114] then, the world is personified as a plurality, 'the brigands,' apparently referring to the seven archons, the hebdomad of Sabbath, who are responsible for the "materializing" of man (cf. *Apocryphon of John*, III,26:21 parr.).[115] The world in Thomas is not only the material creation with its evil, but also the Demiurge and his archons. Ménard's comment on this logion, 'ici le voleur n'est ni le créateur, comme le pensait Marcion ..., ni Satan ..., mais le monde ... avec ses archontes'[116] makes an unnecessary contrast.

II. The parallelism in Logion 27

The apodosis clauses

1. As has been observed already, the Saying consists of two almost parallel conditional clauses, of which each protasis begins with ἐὰν μή[117], whereas the apodoses contain almost similar sanctions. From the very beginning scholars have concluded that the two sentences 'are clearly intended to balance each other.'[118] Whether or not the two sentences were originally disconnected is of no interest for the interpretation of the present logion, since they are now closely united and to be treated as such.
2. The two apodosis clauses sound rather familiar to us, because they have faint echoes in the canonical Gospels. 'To find the kingdom' corresponds with

---

114 Tertullian, *Adv.Marc.* IV:29; cf. Harnack, *o.c.*, 215*.
115 Cf. § I,*III*.2.
116 Ménard, *o.c.*, 112.
117 For logia with ἐὰν μή + aor.subj., cf. Matth. 5:20; 18:3, Justin, *Apol.* 61:4 (cf. John 3:3.5), in connection with the conditions for the entrance into the Kingdom (the negative conditions are the reverse of the beatitudes in Luke 6:20b, Matth. 5:8).
118 Grenfell-Hunt, *o.c.*, 11.

the exhortation 'to seek the kingdom' (Mt 6,33 parr).[119] 'To see the Father' reminds us of 'they will see God' (Mt 5,8)[120] or the Johannine expressions in John 14,8f. ('show to us the Father,' 'who has seen me, has seen the Father').[121] The use of the absolute form 'the Father' is not only found in John but also, and predominantly, in Gnostic texts.[122] The idea of 'finding the kingdom' is used in logion 49 of Thomas 'Blessed are the solitaries and elect, for you shall find the kingdom,' where finding means 'to return to the kingdom'[123] which implies that they originally came from the kingdom—a Gnostic theme.

3. One may ask whether the collector of 'Thomas' understood the clauses

you will not find → the kingdom

you will not see → the Father

as synonyms, or meant to convey a climactic parallelism: the finding of the kingdom as being the decisive step before the *visio Dei*. If he understood them as synonyms, he may have interpreted the protasis clauses as synonymous conditions as well; if he found in them a climax, this may be relevant for the interpretation of these clauses as being different conditions.

The protasis clauses

4. The two protasis clauses are more problematic. If we take for granted the correctness of the Greek text,[124] the logion contains this parallelism:

ἐὰν μὴ – νηστεύσητε – τὸν κόσμον
ἐὰν μὴ – σαββατίσητε – τὸ σάββατον

The parallelism may explain the unexpected accusative of the first clause (one would expect τοῦ κόσμου),[125] which has been labelled as 'harsh', 'un-Greek', 'strange', 'a wrong or exceptional construction,' 'which causes a great difficulty,' 'which has not yet been satisfactorily explained.'[126] One has to consider the possibility that τὸν κόσμον is understood by the collector as an accusative of relation 'with respect to,' and that also the accusative τὸ σάββατον

---

[119] Cf. Luke 12:31; for 'finding' cf. Matth. 13:44–46.

[120] Cf. John 1:18; 6:46; (1 John 3:2); 1 John 4:20; 3 John 11; cf. 2 John 2:15.

[121] Cf. John 6:46.

[122] Cf. e.g. *Ev.Ver.* 28:33; 29:1.

[123] Cf. Guillaumont, a.o., *o.c.*, 28 (89:28f.): ⲧⲉⲧⲛⲁϫⲉ ⲁⲧⲙⲛ̅ⲧⲣⲟ // ⲡⲁⲗⲓⲛ ⲉⲧⲉⲧⲛⲁⲃⲱⲕ ⲉⲙⲁⲩ.

[124] So-called emendations of the verb are ἐὰν μνηστεύσητε, ἐὰν μὴ μισήσητε, ἐὰν μὴ νικήσητε, of the object: τοῦ κόσμου, ἀπὸ τοῦ κόσμου, κατὰ κόσμον, τῷ κόσμῳ, τοῦ κοινοῦ, ἕως τῶν δυσμῶν, ἐλασμόν, τὴν νηστείαν.

[125] One of the usual emendations based on Clement, *Strom.* III, 15.99,4 μακάριοι οὗτοι εἰσὶν οἱ τοῦ κόσμου νηστεύοντες.

[126] These are the qualifications of resp. Fitzmyer, Quispel, Guillaumont, Grenfell-Hunt, Taylor, and Arndt-Gingrich-Danker.

must have that meaning—and not as so often has been assumed an accusative of the internal object.

5. In our view the two clauses have to be rendered in the following way:

'if you do not fast   with respect to the world
if you do not sabbatize   with respect to the Sabbath',

and understood—on the basis of our exegesis of the other Gnostic texts mentioned under I-II—as dealing with the 'world' and 'Sabbath' as designations of the same 'material' reality, the created Cosmos and its Creator, the Demiurge. This implies that the two religious terms 'to fast' (that is, abstain from food) and 'to sabbatize' (that is, to abstain from work) are used in a metaphorical way to denote the negative attitude of the Gnostic believer towards the creation as such and/or its Creator. My thesis is that the logion should be interpreted not as an ascetical or encratitic directive, certainly not as a Jewish-Christian device with respect to fasting and keeping the Sabbath, but in a cosmological sense as the denial of creation and/or its Creator. If one observes the structure of the logion, one finds the antithesis of

the Cosmos   *versus*   the kingdom [of God]
the created world   the other or real world
the Sabbath   *versus*   the Father
the creation or Jaldabaoth   the true God and his reality.

If one assumes the texts to offer synonym parallelism, the two sayings of the logion have the same meaning, but if one accepts a climactic parallelism one has to distinguish between the world and the Sabbath as its Creator *and* between the Kingdom of God and the Father.[127]

III. Fasting in Thomas

1. 'To fast the world'[128] is a rendering which preserves the harshness of the Greek text, usually softened by adding 'towards' or 'with respect to.' The Coptic translation ϵ-ⲡ-ⲕⲟⲥⲙⲟⲥ can have a variety of meanings such as 'to the world,' 'from the world' (not: 'in the world'),[129] but may have been the rather slavish rendering of the Greek accusative as well.[130] The expression is usually understood as a directive to follow some fasting practice, which implies that the logion is merely embedded in an ascetic 'trajectory' either in the

---

[127] This latter interpretation was proposed in the discussion by Prof. Dr. J.-P. Mahé.

[128] This literal rendering in Ch. Taylor, *The Oxyrrhynchus Logia and the Apocryphal Gospels*, Oxford 1899.

[129] Contra J. Jeremias and H.-Ch. Puech in E. Hennecke-W. Schneemelcher, *Neutestamentliche Apokryphen*, I, Tübingen 1959, 67 and 217, apparently based upon a mistranslation of *au monde*.

[130] One has interpreted it as *dativus relationis* (Schoedel-Grant, Fitzmyer, Lambdin, Leipoldt, Quecke), *separativus* (Wilson, Doresse, Guillaumont, Ménard, Quispel) or *obiectivus* (Quispel: nota accusativi).

church, or in some christian group outside of or at the edge of the church. In
my view, this may be true for the saying in some 'Vorlage' of the collection,
but the collector himself did not interpret it in this ascetical sense.

2. Fasting as an ascetical practice is not favoured by the collector. He presents
us with the following words of Jesus (Logion 104a):[131]

> They said to Him: 'Come, let us *fast*!'
> Jesus said: What then is the sin that I committed   (HE 3)
> or in what I have been defeated?'

Or in another passage (Logion 6a):[132]

> His disciples asked Him, they said to Him:
> (a) 'Do you want us *fast*,   (Mt 6,16)
> (b) and how should we pray,   (Mt 6,5)
> (c) give alms,   (Mt 6,2)
> (d) and what diet should we observe?'
> Jesus said: 'Do not lie,   (Tob 4,6)
> and do not (to others?) what you hate!'   (Tob 4,15)

The answer of Jesus is somewhat surprising. One would have expected an answer as now has been formulated in Logion 14:[133]

> Jesus said to them:
> (a') 'If you *fast*, you will beget sin for yourselves,
> (b') and if you pray, you will be condemned,
> (c') and if you will give alms, you will do harm to your spirits,
>   and if you go into any land and wander in regions,   (Lk 10,8a)
> (d') if they receive you, eat what they set before you ...'   (Lk 10,8b)

3. These passages demonstrate that within a Gnostic setting there is a rather
critical attitude towards religious duties or ceremonial prescriptions commonly found in Judaism and early christianity. Fasting, prayer, charity, diet laws
(for circumcision cf. Logion 53) are merely outward expressions of religion
which the Gnostic believer due to his interiorization of faith or knowledge,
does not value highly. As to fasting, there is no need for it since the Gnostic—
like Jesus his Revealer and model—does not commit sin, is not or no more
defeated. Therefore, if he would fast he would make himself known as a sin-
ner. Of course, there may be a situation in which fasting becomes necessary,
as is stated in Logion 104b:[134] 'but when the bridegroom comes out of the
bridechamber, let them then fast and pray ...,' that is, when the spiritual uni-

---

[131] *NH* II:2, 98:10–14.
[132] *NH* II:2, 81:14–19.
[133] *NH* II:2, 83:14–22.
[134] *NH* II:2, 98:14f.

ty of the Gnostic would be dissolved ('the one becomes two,' cf. Logia 11, (22), (48), 61b, 106) which is hardly assumable for the true Gnostic), one has to fast and pray again.[135] However, the true Gnostic is 'united', beyond the realm of sin, within the realm of the bridechamber.

4. If one takes into account this attitude towards the practice of fasting, one can easily see that Logion 27 in its present setting cannot be a device for ascetic or ceremonial fasting, but must necessarily be understood as a metaphor of a total and radical abstention from the material reality of this Cosmos. Even if the saying may have had an ascetic or encratitic meaning in the source of the collector, it is clear that he chose the saying for a different perspective. The ascetical meaning has been replaced by a cosmological understanding within the setting of this Gnostic florilegium: the total denial of present reality of the Cosmos and its Creator to enable the finding of the true reality of the kingdom and the Father.

IV. The Sabbatizing of the Sabbath

1. The expression 'to sabbatize the Sabbath' has prompted a score of interpretations, especially after the finding of the Coptic text. In my view, the Coptic text presents us merely with an endeavour to do justice to the Greek text which has to remain the starting-point for our interpretation. We have to admit that the Greek expression is not clear at first sight. The obvious rendering seems to be 'to celebrate the Sabbath.'[136] This has led many interpreters to find in it a Jewish-Christian saying in which Jesus prescribes the observance of the Sabbath, so that not a few scholars found in it an argument for assuming a Jewish-Christian flavour of the collection of Thomas.

2. There are, however, other renderings of the saying (especially due to the Coptic text) which slightly differ from the most obvious rendering: 'If you do not keep (celebrate, observe) the Sabbath as Sabbath' or 'If you do not make the Sabbath a Sabbath,'[137] in which one might hear a Jewish-Christian criticism of the wrong observation of the Sabbath, so that the sense may be 'If you do not truly keep the Sabbath'[138] or 'If you do not keep the true Sabbath'[139] or also 'If you do not make the Sabbath a real Sabbath.'[140]

3. Others, however, have found a spiritualizing of the idea of the sabbath-keeping, when they render the phrase with 'unless ye sanctify the whole week'

---

135 Cf. e.g. Ménard, *Thomas,* 204.
136 So e.g. Grenfell-Hunt, Hennecke, Santos Otero, Van de Sande Bakhuyzen, Preuschen[2], Godeschalk.
137 So e.g. Lambdin, Wilson, Gärtner, Quecke, Jeremias, Schippers, Erbetta, Ménard, Quispel.
138 So Schoedel's rendering (Grant-Freedman).
139 So Bruce.
140 Cf. e.g. Grenfell-Hunt, Doresse, Fitzmyer.

or 'and if you keep not the Sabbath for the whole week,'[141] which means that one's whole life should be a Sabbath.

4. All these solutions clearly demonstrate the difficulty in determining the precise meaning of the expression 'to sabbatize the Sabbath,'[142] One often (sometimes even when one assumes a Jewish-Christian sense) tends to spiritualizing the saying, referring to earlier or later Church Fathers who exhorted their readers to keep always (διὰ πάντος, πάντοτε) sabbath,[143] to keep the *true* sabbath[144] in a spiritual way.[145] The implication of such a spiritualization is then that one should abstain from sin, free oneself from the slavery of evil, from bad, unclean or shameless thoughts. This metaphorical or spiritual understanding of the saying has once been defined as an 'Aufforderung zur wesentlichen gnostischen Sabbatobservanz' which implies 'eine radikale Lossagung von der Welt, dem Materiellen überhaupt.'[146] This line of thought starts from a positive evaluation of the Sabbath.

5. I have tried to demonstrate that it is highly questionable that *sabbatizing the Sabbath* contains such a high esteem of the sabbath. Starting from the presumption that the present collection of sayings known as the Gospel of Thomas is a Gnostic florilegium, I have questioned the positive interpretation of the sabbath. Sabbath is understood either as the *world* as creation of the Demiurge or as the Demiurge himself, Jaldabaoth. In this interpretation of the saying *sabbath* and *world* are or are almost synonyms, and consequently the verbs *fasting (with respect to)* and *sabbatizing* are more or less synonyms.

6. The verb σαββατίζειν can be used as a synonym of the middle form of ἀναπαύειν,[147] as may be concluded from its use in the LXX:

Lev. 25,2   καὶ ἀναπαύσεται ἡ γῆ = ושבתה הארץ
Lev. 26,35(34)   σαββατιεῖ ἡ γῆ   = תשבת הארץ

We may also compare the parallelism in the Pseudo-Macarian formula's καὶ ἀληθινὸν σάββατον σαββατίζει // καὶ ἀληθινὴν ἀνάπαυσιν ἀναπαύεται.[148]

---

141 Cf. e.g. Taylor, Evelyn White, James, Leipoldt, Jeremias.

142 B. Gärtner, *The Theology of the Gospel of Thomas*, London 1961, 240.

143 Justin, *Dial.c.Tryph.*, 12:3 (E.J. Goodspeed, *Die ältesten Apologeten*, Göttingen 1914, 103); Ps-Macarius, *Hom.* 28:4 (E. Klostermann-H. Berthold, *Neue Homilien des Makarius / Simeon*, I, Aus Typus III, Berlin 1961, 167: 29f.); Tertullian, *Adv.Jud.*, iv:2 (ed. Kroymann, *o.c.*, II, 1347:9, 1348:1f.).

144 Justin, *loc.cit.* (Goodspeed, *o.c.*, 104); cf. Ps.-Macarius *Hom.* 35,1, in: H. Dörries / E. Klostermann / M. Kroeger, *Die 50 geistlichen Homilien des Makarios*, Berlin 1964, 263:1f. (= *l.*6f.).

145 Ps.-Ignatius, *Ad Magn.*, F.X. Funk / F. Diekamp, *Patres apostolici*, II, Tübingen ²1913, 124.

146 J. Helderman, *o.c.*, 108 (239 n. 136).

147 For σάββατον = ἀνάπαυσις, cf. e.g. Josephus, *Contra Apionem*, II, 27 (H.St.J. Thackeray, *Josephus I, The Life, Against Apion*, Cambridge (Mass.) – London (1926) Repr. 1976, 302); P. de Lagarde, *Onomastica Sacra*, I, Göttingen 1870, 204:39 (σάββατον· ἀνάπαυσις, ἁγιασμός, ἀργία).

148 *Hom.* 35,1 (263:1f.).

This may suggest for our logion the rendering 'If you do not come to rest (or: if you will not be at rest) with respect to the Sabbath, i.e. the world or its Demiurge, you will not see the Father.'

7. The 'rest' *(anapausis)* is the ultimate goal of the road for the Gnostic. Therefore it has an eschatological meaning. This is what is expressed in the Greek text of logion 2 'Let him who seeks not cease seeking until he finds, and when he has found, he will marvel, and when he has marvelled, he will reign, and when he reigns, he will find rest.'[149] At the same time this logion may suggest that the 'rest' is already part of the earthly existence of the Gnostic who has found and who is king. On his way to the final 'rest' the Gnostic is, because he knows that the Father is the 'Rest', himself already resting in the Father.[150] This resting in the Father implies the attitude of resting with respect to the realm of the Demiurge, this sinful world. The true believer does not consume this world, but he *fasts* with respect to this world; he does not exploit the sabbath (this world) or revere the Sabbath (the Demiurge), but he rests with respect to this world and its Creator, and therefore he will (later, but also in his present existence) enter the Kingdom and see the Father. 'While we are in this world, it is fitting for us to acquire the resurrection for ourselves, so that when we ship off the flesh, we may be found in the Anapausis and not walk in the Middle (that is, the realm of the spiritual death, the truly evil word). For many go astray on the road . . .,' is a similar message found in the Gospel of Philip.[151]

COROLLARIUM

The result of our inquiry into the 27th logion of the Gospel of Thomas is that his use of the 'Sabbath' as a parallel to the 'World' fits well in with the Gnostic understanding of the 'Sabbath' either as the Demiurge (I,*I–V*) or as the World as the created Cosmos of this Demiurge (II,*I–III*). Fasting and Sabbatizing denote the Gnostic attitude towards this world as the realm of matter which has become of no use for him: it is the *Kingdom of the Father* which has become his origin, existence and destiny. This kingdom of the Father is already spread out upon the earth—men do not see it, but the Gnostic sees it. That is why he fasts the world and sabbatizes the sabbath.

---

[149] Cf. for a discussion of this saying, Helderman, *o.c.*, 313.

[150] Cf. *Ev.Ver.*, 24:16–20; Attridge, *o.c.*, 92(93); cf. the discussion of Helderman, *o.c.*, 98–104.

[151] W.C. Till, *Das Evangelium nach Philippos*, Berlin 1963, 34(35); cf. Helderman, *o.c.*, 292 (I would suggest that the saying belongs also to his category *I*).

EUGNOSTUS AND ARISTIDES ON THE INEFFABLE GOD

BY

ROELOF VAN DEN BROEK (UTRECHT)

The gnostic treatise *Eugnostus the Blessed*, known in two versions from the Nag Hammadi Library (NH III,3 and V,1), deals exclusively with the divine realm, which is described as a happy, perfect world, not disturbed by any kind of evil.[1] In the introduction the author rejects the traditional proofs of God's existence and nature based on the ordering of the cosmos by countering these with the equally traditional arguments of the Sceptics. The true God is then described in the terms of a negative theology, though there are also some positive predicates, such as good, perfect, eternal, and blessed.[2] Under the unknown Father there are several lower androgynous beings, of which the first is called Immortal Man. Since we shall be looking at some aspects of *Eugnostus*' description of the supreme God, the development of the divine Pleroma does not concern us here.

In his *Codex de Berlin*, Michel Tardieu has made an important attempt to analyse the structure of *Eugnostus* and to discover its meaning. One of his views which did not convince me, however, is the one that holds *Eugnostus* to be a Christian work, influenced by the New Testament and in its present form also strongly by Valentinian gnosticism.[3] I am unable to see any distinct and

---

[1] The texts are available in *The Facsimile Edition of the Nag Hammadi Codices: Codex V*, Leiden 1975, and *Ibid.: Codex III*, Leiden 1976. The text of NH III has been edited by D. Trakatellis, Ο ΥΠΕΡΒΑΤΙΚΟΣ ΘΕΟΣ ΤΟΥ ΕΥΓΝΩΣΤΟΥ, Athens (private edition) 1977, 170–207. English translation of *Eugnostos* and its Christian adaption, the *Sophia Jesu Christi* (as found in NH III,4) by D.M. Parrott in: J.M. Robinson (ed.), *The Nag Hammadi Library in English*, Leiden 1977, 206–228. The other known version of the *Sophia*, in the Coptic Codex of Berlin (BG), was edited by W.C. Till, *Die gnostischen Schriften des koptischen Papyrus Berolinensis 8502*, 2nd rev. ed. by H.-M. Schenke, Berlin 1972, 194–295. A full bibliography on the *Sophia Jesu Christi* (and *Eugnostus* as well) in M. Tardieu and J.-D. Dubois, *Introduction à la littérature gnostique*, I: *Collections retrouvées avant 1945*, Paris 1986, 124–132. A French translation of both texts, with introduction and commentary, has been published by M. Tardieu, *Codex de Berlin*, SGM 1, Paris 1984, 47–67, 167–215, 347–402. The text of NH V is very fragmentary; in the following reference is only made to NH III.

[2] For the Introduction, see Tardieu, *Codex de Berlin*, 349–353, and R. van den Broek, Eugnostus: Via Scepsis naar Gnosis, *NTT* 37 (1983) 104–114. For an explanation of the occurrence of both negative and positive divine epithets in the same context, see J. Mansfeld, this vol., pp. 92 ff.

[3] Tardieu, *Codex de Berlin*, 65–66: "Rien dans *Eug* ne permet de supposer que l'auteur ait été un juif de la diaspora hellénistique. Toutes les formules et séries, qui dans *Eug* se rattachent au judaïsme, s'expliquent à travers la littérature néotestamentaire, paulinienne ou johannique." Ac-

indisputable Christian influence, whereas many of what seem to be Valentinian elements can be explained in another way, as I have tried to show elsewhere.[4] There is, however, in *Eugnostus* such a strong Jewish element that it seems far more likely that the unknown author, whom I shall henceforth call Eugnostus, was a Jew.

The first point to be discussed is the close relationship between Eugnostus' description of the unbegotten Father and that of God, the Father of Jesus Christ, by the apologist Aristides of Athens. Aristides' *Apology* is known to us through two short Greek fragments, a complete Syriac translation of a probably already revised Greek text, a short Armenian fragment—in four manuscripts—of the beginning, and a number of condensed sections of the original in the Greek romance of *Barlaam and Joasaph*, which is now generally ascribed to John of Damascus.[5] The first chapter of the apology, which

---

cording to Tardieu, the paragraphs 21–26 are due to a Valentinian revisor (60), while Valentinian glosses can also be detected elsewhere, e.g. in § 10 (364). I do not doubt, however, that the original text of *Eugnostus* was indeed interpolated at an early date, nor that some of its interpolations show a distinctly Valentinian stamp.

[4] R. van den Broek, Jewish and Platonic Speculations in Early Alexandrian Theology: Eugnostus, Philo, Valentinus, and Origen, in: B.A. Pearson and J.E. Goehring (edd.), *The Roots of Egyptian Christianity*, Philadelphia 1986, 190–203.

[5] Modern scholarship on Aristides' *Apology* began with two important discoveries, that of the Syriac translation by J.R. Harris, and that of the use made of the *Apology* in *Barlaam and Joasaph* by J.A. Robinson: *The Apology of Aristides on Behalf of the Christians from a Syriac Ms. preserved on Mount Sinai edited with an Introduction and Translation by J. Rendel Harris. With an Appendix Containing the Main Portion of the Original Greek Text by J.A. Robinson*, TS I,1, Cambridge 1891. This work contains the only existing edition of the Syriac text and the only English translations of the Syriac version and of the Armenian Edschmiazin Ms., by F.C. Conybeare. German studies of lasting importance are: R. Raabe, *Die Apologie des Aristides. Aus dem Syrischen übersetzt und mit Beiträgen zur Textvergleichung und Amerkungen herausgegeben*, TU 9,1, Leipzig 1893. A revision of Raabe's translation was published in E. Hennecke, *Die Apologie des Aristides. Recension und Rekonstruktion des Textes*, TU 4,3, Leipzig 1893, who for the Armenian version used a revision (by the Armenian Archdeacon Karapet) of the German translation of the Venetian text by F. von Himpel, Das Fragment der Apologie des Aristides (...). Aus dem Armenischen übersetzt und erläutert, *Theologische Quartalschrift* 62 (1880) 109–116. For his reconstruction of the Greek text Hennecke was assisted by U. von Willamowitz-Moellendorff. A thorough study and an independent reconstruction of the text was given by R. Seeberg, *Die Apologie des Aristides untersucht und wiederhergestellt*, Forschungen zur Geschichte des neutestamentlichen Kanons und der altkirchlichen Literatur V,2, Erlangen and Leipzig 1893, 159–414 (see also his *Der Apologet Aristides. Der Text seiner uns erhaltenen Schriften nebst einleitenden Untersuchungen über dieselben*, Erlangen and Leipzig 1894); for the Armenian texts Seeberg used the translations by von Himpel and Conybeare. The translations given in Seeberg's edition were adopted by J. Geffcken, *Zwei griechische Apologeten*, Leipzig and Berlin 1907, who wrote an extensive commentary on Aristides' *Apology* (28–96). Using Geffcken's text of the Greek portions, Goodspeed made another reconstruction of the text, with a Latin version of the parts not preserved in Greek, in his *Die ältesten Apologeten*, Göttingen 1914, 2–23 (less convincing than those by Seeberg and, in particular, Hennecke). The Greek fragments on papyrus are of chapters 5,3 and 6,1 (*Pap. Oxyr.* 1778) and of chapters 15,3–16,1 (*Pap. Lond.* 2486); they have no relevance for the problems dealt with in the present paper. An Italian translation of the Syriac text was made by C. Vona, *L'Apologia di Aristide. Introduzione, Versione dal Siriaco e Com-*

concerns us here, is for the greater part known only through the Syriac and Armenian translations, both of which seem to be rather free renderings of the Greek. According to Eusebius, *Hist. Eccl.* IV 3, the Armenian texts and the first part of the superscription of the Syriac translation, Aristides addressed his apology to the emperor Hadrian (117–137).[6] It has been argued, however, that this apology originally "was written by a proselyte to Hellenistic Judaism, probably in the time of Hadrian, not as an apology for Christians at all, but primarily as a counterattack upon polytheists and their religious notions and, secondarily, as a defense of the monotheistic worship and morals of the Jews. This definitely Jewish work of the second century was interpolated and 'edited' by a Christian writer, probably of the late fourth century, and was thus converted into what passed as an apology for Christianity."[7] It is true that the creed worked into chapter 2 has its closest parallels in later eastern creeds which are not earlier than about A.D. 360.[8] But it is quite conceivable

---

mento, Roma 1950 (with the Greek fragments, also those on papyrus, a new translation of the Venetian Armenian texts by A. Garabet, and a reprint of Conybeare's translation of the Edschmiazin Ms. (114–131)). For the authorship of the Greek *Barlaam and Joasaph*, see F. Dölger *Der griechische Barlaam-Roman, ein Werk des Hl. Johannes von Damaskos*, Ettal 1953. W.C. van Unnik, Die Gotteslehre bei Aristides und in gnostischen Schriften, *Theologische Zeitschrift* 17 (1961) 166–174, compared Aristides' doctrine of God with that of the *Apocryphon of John* and the *Sophia Jesu Christi*. In his opinion, there are agreements only in vocabulary, "wobei aber die Begriffe nicht in der gleichen Reihenfolge vorkommen" (172, but see below). Van Unnik rejected any direct influence of Greek philosophical ideas on the gnostic doctrine of God; according to him, the gnostics derived their negative theology from the non-gnostic Christian schools and then preached it "als die höchste *christliche* Offenbarung" (174). He did not yet know that *Eugnostus the Blessed*, the source of the *Sophia Jesu Christi*, does not show any specific Christian features but nevertheless has the same doctrine of God. In the following, the Syriac and Armenian texts are usually quoted in the translations by Harris and Conybeare, which, however, I have constantly compared with those given by Raabe, Hennecke, Seeberg and Vona. Where necessary, the Venetian edition of the Armenian Aristides is cited in Garabet's Latin translation.

[6] The Syriac text has a double title in two different colours of ink, of which the first says that the work was addressed to the emperor Hadrian and the second speaks of Ceasar Titus Hadrianus Antoninus. In the older studies the second address is mostly taken to be the most original, but O'Ceallaigh (see next note, 229–232) gave new arguments in favour of the authenticity of the first address. The question of the *Apology*'s original dedication has no bearing on our argument.

[7] G.C.O'Cealaigh, "Marcianus" Aristides, On the Worship of God, *HThR* 51 (1958) 227–254 (quotation on 227).

[8] The parallels noted by O'Ceallaigh, 239–241, are not all equally convincing. Decisive is the insertion of the disciples and the fulfilment of the 'economy' by the Lord between the Virgin Birth and the Crucifixion. This is found exclusively in three closely connected 'Homoean' creeds, of the fourth Synod of Sirmium (359), the Synod of Nice (359; not mentioned by O'Ceallaigh), and the Synod of Constantinople (360). For the texts, see A. Hahn, *Bibliothek der Symbole und Glaubensregeln der alten Kirche*, 3rd. ed. by G.L. Hahn, Breslau 1897 (reprint Hildesheim 1962), 204–206, 208–209; the creeds of Sirmium and Constantinople are also discussed and cited in J.N.D. Kelly, *Early Christian Creeds*, 3rd. ed., London 1972, 288–295. The wording of Sirmium is: γεννηθέντα ... καὶ ἀναστραφέντα μετὰ τῶν μαθητῶν, καὶ πᾶσαν τὴν οἰκονομίαν πληρώσαντα ... σταυρωθέντα. Syr. Aristides, 2,7: "born ..., and He had twelve disciples, in order that a certain *dispensation* of his *might be fulfilled* (Arm. Aristides offers an explanation of the οἰκονομία: "and He, by his illuminating truth, *dispending* it, taught all the world"). He was pierced (Arm.:

that a fourth-century reader felt himself compelled to adjust Aristides' poor christological statements to the orthodox standards of his own time. There are strong indications that the main body of this apology was written by a Jew indeed, but there is no evidence which precludes the view that this Jewish work, in a admittedly awkward manner, was already christianized in the second century. Then we need not dismiss as completely untrustworthy Eusebius' testimony, *Hist. Eccl.* IV 3: "Also Aristides, a faithful man, moved by the piety that characterizes us, like Quadratus, has left to posterity an apology of the faith addressed to Hadrian. This man's writing is also preserved by very many, even to the present time." The question of whether this apology was originally written by a Jew or by a Christian does not seriously affect our argument, however, since the doctrine expounded in chapter 1 could be adhered to by Jews and Christians alike.

As for the relationship between Eugnostus and Aristides, I should like to point out first that these authors must have derived their description of God from a common source, which most probably was also used by the author of the gnostic *Tripartite Tractate* (NH I,5). Aristides begins his discussion with an enumeration of six negative and two positive attributes of God, followed by a short discussion of two of them ('complete' and 'without beginning') and of two other items, dealing with God's namelessness and formlessness. The same terms in nearly the same order are the key-words in the *Tripartite Tractate*'s ample discussion of the nature of God, as can be seen from the juxtaposition of both texts in the appendix at the end of this study. Though it is conceivable that the author of the *Trip. Tract.* has made use of Aristides' *Apology*, it seems more probable that both he and Aristides are dependent on an earlier source.[9] This source may have contained a discussion of the divine epithets enumerated at the beginning of Aristides' description of God. The relationship between Aristides and Eugnostus, on the other hand, can be most easily demonstrated by putting part of their texts in parallel columns:

Aristides (Harris, 35)	Eugnostus, NH III,71,19–72,11
Now I say that God is not begotten, not made; a constant nature, without beginning and without end; *immortal*, complete, and incomprehensible.	For he is *immortal*, he is eternal,

---

"was *nailed on the cross*"; cf. Nice (359): σταυρῷ προσηλωθέντα) by the Jews." In the Syriac and the Armenian Aristides the disciples are not only mentioned before the fulfilment of the οἰκονομία and the crucifixion, but also after the Ascension, in connexion with their mission to the world. In *Barlaam and Joasaph* only the latter is referred to: οὗτος (sc. Χριστός) δώδεκα ἔσχε μαθητάς, οἱ μετὰ τὴν ἐν οὐρανοῖς ἄνοδον αὐτοῦ ἐξῆλθον ...; but the οἰκονομία is mentioned before the crucifixion: καὶ τελέσας τὴν θαυμαστὴν αὐτοῦ οἰκονομίαν διὰ σταυροῦ θάνατον ἐγεύσατο.

[9] I intend to come back to the negative theology of the *Tract. Trip.* in another study.

And in saying that He is complete, I
mean this; that there is no deficiency
in Him, and He stands in need of naught,
but everything stands in need of Him.

having no birth; for everyone who
has birth will perish: he is unbegotten,

And in saying that He is *without begin-*
ning, I mean this; that *everything*
which has a beginning, has also an
end; and that which has an end is
dissoluble.[10]

having no beginning; for *everyone who*
has a beginning has an end: he is
without beginning [litt.: nobody rules
over him = ἄναρχος ἐστίν].

He has no name; for *everything that*
has a name is associated with the
created.[11]

He has no name; for *everyone who*
has a name is the creation of another;
he is unnameable.

He has no likeness [Syr. *demuta'*,
'form', 'shape'], nor composition
of members; for he who possesses
this is *associated with things*
fashioned. He is not male, nor is
he female.[12]

He has no human form (μορφή); for
whoever has a human form (μορφή) is
the creation of another. He has a
shape (ἰδέα) of his own, not like the
shape (ἰδέα) which we have received
or which we have seen, but it is
another shape (ἰδέα), which greatly
surpasses all things and is better
than all these things. It looks in
all parts (or: on all sides) and sees
itself from itself. He is limitless,
he is incomprehensible. He is ever
imperishable, he has nobody who
resembles him.

Aristides has preserved the explanation of the term 'complete', while Eugnostus still has that of the term "unbegotten", with which he associates the
epithets 'immortal' and 'eternal'. Of course such an association is fairly ob-

---

[10] For the Armenian texts see below, 207.

[11] The Armenian text of the Edschmiazin Ms. reads (Conybeare 31): "In Himself He is nameless, for whatever is named is fashioned out of something else (note 2: or 'by another') and created." The Venetian texts have (Garabet 127): *Ipse sine nomine est, quoniam omnis res cui est no-*
men creata et facta est.

[12] Arms. Ms. of Edschmiazin (Conybeare 31): "Colour and form of Him there is not, for that
falls under measure and limit, unto whatsoever colour and form belong. Male and female in that
nature there is not, for that is subject to particular passions, in whatsoever that distinction exists."
Mss. of Venice (Garabet 127): *Colores et formas non habet, nam in quo haec inveniuntur, ipse*
est qui cadit sub mensuram et limitem. Masculinum et femininum non est in illa natura, nam in
quo hoc adest, ipse est qui sub partibus passionum est. If "neither male nor female" was part of
the common source of Aristides and Eugnostus—in the Armenian version the structure of the argument concerning this epithet is identical with that of the preceding ones—, Eugnostus must have
suppressed it. The Armenian Aristides says that what has colour and form "*falls under measure*
and limit." Eugnostus adds to his description of God's strange shape: "He is *limitless*" (see below, 212).

vious, but it may not be simply accidental that the same association is also found in the *Trip. Tract.*, NH I,52,8–9: "He is immortal since he is unbegotten." The fact that Aristides and Eugnostus both discuss God's being without beginning, without name and without form in the same order and with the same argumentation shows that they are dependent on a common source.

In Eugnostus the argumentation has a specific form which may reflect the one in the lost common source. It consists of three parts and is most clearly evident in the passage on the name of God: first it is said that God does not have a specific quality, then the reason why he does not have that quality is given, and this is, finally, followed by the appropriate negative predicate. He has no name (οὐκ ἔχει ὄνομα), for whoever has a name is the creation of another: he is unnameable (ἀκατονόμαστος ἐστίν). The same tripartite structure is still noticable in the explanation of 'unbegotten' and 'without beginning': He has no birth (οὐκ ἔχει γένεσιν),[13] for everyone, who has birth will perish: he is unbegotten (ἀγέννητος ἐστίν); and likewise: he has no beginning (οὐκ ἔχει ἀρχήν), for everyone who has a beginning has an end: he is without beginning (ἄναρχος ἐστίν—here the Coptic has a mistranslation: "nobody rules over him"). Only in the case of the form of God is the manner of reasoning and the conclusion not congruent with the preceding ones. I shall come back to this point later; first, there is more to be said about God's being without beginning and without name.

Both Aristides and Eugnostus argue that God has no beginning, since everyone who (or everything which) has a beginning also has an end. The Syriac Aristides has an addition which explains the implication of having an end: "and that which has an end is dissoluble." As a whole, the version in the Syriac text corresponds closely to a statement which was found in Eustathius of Antioch's *Contra Arianos*, II, frg. 58: Πᾶν τὸ ἀρχὴν ἔχον καὶ τέλος ἐπιδέχεται, πᾶν τὸ τέλος ἐπιδεχόμενον φθορᾶς ἐστιν δεκτικόν.[14] The addition of the Syriac text does not occur in the Armenian Mss. of Venice.[15] The Edschmiazin Ms., however, also has an addition at this point, albeit another one than is found in the Syriac translation; moreover, this manuscript has nothing corresponding to "for which has a beginning also has an end." It reads (Conybeare, 31): "In Himself He is without beginning, for he is beginning of everything whatever, and is perfect"—a well-known idea, found, for instance, in Tatian, *Or. ad Graec.* 4, 1: θεὸς ... μόνος ἄναρχος ὢν καὶ αὐτὸς ὑπάρχων τῶν ὅλων ἀρχή. These differences make it likely that Aristides'

---

[13] The Coptic reads *emñtef dzpo*, "having no birth," and *emñtf͞ arche*, "having no beginning," which connects these sentences with the preceding ones.

[14] See M. Spanneut, *Recherches sur les écrits d'Eustathe d'Antioche avec une édition nouvelle des fragments dogmatiques et exégétiques*, Lille 1948, 111 (= John of Damascus, *Sacra parallela* [PG 95, 1109B]).

[15] See Garabet, 127, and Hennecke, 4.

original Greek text did not have an addition explaining what it means to have an end, but that later generations saw here a gap to be filled.

The idea that God has no proper name is very common in the philosophical and religious literature of the first centuries of our era; it is expressed by pagan, Jewish and Christian writers alike.[16] Aristides and Eugnostus argue that everything which has a name belongs to the created, since having a name implies the prior existence of someone who gave that name. The same view is clearly expressed in the *Apocryphon of John*, 7: "He is unnameable because there is no one prior to him to name him."[17] This reasoning is also found in Justin Martyr, combined with the view that the names traditionally assigned to God do not express his essence but are based on his eternal activity, II *Apol.* 6,1–2: "No proper name has been bestowed upon God, the Father of All, since he is unbegotten, for whoever has a proper name received it from a person older than himself. The words 'Father', and 'God', and 'Creator', and 'Lord', and 'Master' are not real names, but rather terms of address derived from his beneficent deeds." The *Trip. Tract.* also takes the traditional names of God as terms of address which can be used to glorify him, even though not one of them really applies to him (NH I,54,2–11, see below, p. 218). Which names the author had in mind can be seen from NH I,100,24–30. There it is said that the Logos adorned the Archon whom he established over the All with all the names which characterize the Father: "For he too is called 'Father', and 'God', and 'Demiurge', and 'King', and 'Judge', and 'Place', and 'Dwelling', and 'Law'." Similar views are put forward by Theophil., *Ad Autol.* I 3–4, and Clem., *Strom.* V 82, who both mention the same names as Justin ('Father', 'God', 'Creator', and 'Lord'), together with other names which indicate God's powerful activity.[18] Just as Justin, Clement also mentions the other argument against the view that God has a proper name, *Strom.* V 83, 1: "Everything, then, which falls under a name is begotten," though he does not explicitly refer to the necessarily prior existence of a name-giver. The latter view apparently became part of the apologetic tradition; it is also found in Ps-Justin *Cohort. ad. Graec.* 21 (PG 6, 277AB): "No proper name can be applied to God, . . . no one existed before God who could have given him a name, ..." In the

---

[16] See the references in Hennecke, 53, Geffcken, 38–39, Vona, 73, and D.T. Runia, this volume, 69 ff.

[17] Ed. Till-Schenke (see note 1), 88–89.

[18] The names Κύριος, Πατήρ, Θεός, and Δημιουργός derive from the Greek philosophical (Platonist) tradition and are, for instance, also mentioned together in *Asclepius* 22 (and its source, the *Logos Teleios*, as found in Coptic translation in NH VI,66,35–38) and 26 (and the *Logos Teleios* in Greek and Coptic, NH VI,73,24–26); cf. J.-P. Mahé, *Hermès en Haute Egypte*, II, Bibliothèque Copte de Nag Hammadi, Section "Textes", 7, Québec 1982, 157, 185 (texts) and 216–217 (commentary), and (for *pater* and *dominus*) A. Wlosok, *Laktanz und die philosophische Gnosis*, Heidelberg 1960, 232–246. In the Armenian Aristides (Conybeare 30, Garabet 127), too, the Governor of the world is called "Lord and God and Creator" (see below, 210).

Apocryphon of John, 7, God's absolute priority has become the basic fact of his ineffability in general: he is illimitable, undifferentiated, immeasurable, invisible, ineffable, and unnameable, because there was no one before him by whom he could have been limited, differentiated, measured, seen, expressed, or named.

If Eugnostus and Aristides made use of the same source for their view that God is without beginning, without name and without form, the question may be raised whether there are also other similarities between their writings which point into the same direction. I think there are. Let us look more closely at the introductions to their respective works. Eugnostus starts his argument by referring to and then firmly rejecting the idea that God's existence and nature can be known from the διοίκησις of the cosmos. Though he does not explicitly say so, we may assume that he had to reject this view because, as a gnostic, he ascribed the origin of the world to a lower, most probably evil demiurge. Aristides likewise begins his work by mentioning the cosmological proof of God's existence, which he at first seems to embrace wholeheartedly. The διακόσμησις of the world and the observation that the world and all that is in it is moved by necessity (κατὰ ἀνάγκην, Arm. "by necessity and force") leads him to the conclusion that the Mover and Governor of all things must be God. The original Stoic colouring of the argument has been much better preserved by the Armenian than by the Syriac translation, which reads "by the impulse of another." Having said this much, Aristides immediately qualifies the cosmological argument by the statement that the nature of the Mover is incomprehensible. Here we have the same integration of the Aristotelian Mover into a negative theology as is found in Albinus / Alcinous, *Didasc.* 10, though Aristides does not speak of the *Unmoved* Mover. In this passage too the Armenian text seems to have preserved the original wording better than the Syriac. As was already pointed out by the editor of the Syriac translation, J. Rendel Harris, the original Greek text clearly alluded to a much-quoted sentence from Plato, *Tim.* 28c: "It is difficult to discover the Maker and Father of the universe and having found him it is impossible to declare him to all men."[19] The two translations run as follows:

Syriac (Harris 35)	Armenian (Conybeare 30)
And that I should investigate concerning this Mover of All, as how He exists—for this is evident to me, for He is incomprehensible in His nature—and that I should dispute concerning the steadfastness of His government, so as to comprehend it fully, it is not profitable for me; for	To enquire about Him who is guardian and controls all things seems to me to quite exceed the comprehension and to be most difficult, and to speak accurately concerning Him is beyond compass of thought and of speech, and bringeth

---

[19] See A.D. Nock, The Exegesis of *Timaeus*, 28C, *VC* 16 (1962) 77–86.

no one is able perfectly to comprehend it.   no advantage; for His nature is
                                               infinite and unsearchable, and im-
                                               perceptible, and inaccessible to
                                               all creatures.

In the Armenian translation the allusion to Plato's famous statement is still
clearly recognizable, whereas it has disappeared from the Syriac version.[20] In
the Armenian Aristides, as in all texts which make use of this passage from Plato, the emphasis is exclusively on God's hidden nature. In the Syriac text,
however, it is not only God's nature but also, and in particular, his government of the universe which is said to be incomprehensible. Both texts continue
with a conclusion which in the Armenian version follows more logically from
the foregoing than in the Syriac:

Syriac (Harris 35)	Armenian (Conybeare 30)
But I say concerning the Mover of the world, that He is God of all, who made all for the sake of man;	We can only know that He who governs by His providence all created things, He is Lord and God and Creator of all, who ordered all things visible in His beneficence, and graciously bestowed them on the race of man. Now it is meet that we serve and glorify Him alone as God, and love one another as ourselves.
and it is evident to me that this is expedient, that one should fear God and not grieve man.	

In the last sentence the version of the Syriac translation seems more Jewish
and original than that of the Armenian text, which looks like an adaptation to
the Christian double commandment of love.[21]

Of all this nothing is found in Eugnostus, probably because he did not
identify the ineffable supreme God with the Creator of this world. He asserts
that whoever is able to free himself from the conflicting opinions concerning
the ordering of the cosmos and, by means of another view, to come "to make
manifest the God of Truth and to be wholly in harmony concerning him, is an
immortal in the midst of mortal men" (NH III,71,8–13). Nevertheless, both
Aristides and Eugnostus start with a discussion of the possibility of real
knowledge of God from the creation and both conclude that such a possibility
does not exist. We saw that the Armenian Aristides says that God's nature is
unsearchable, imperceptible and inaccessible *to all creatures*; Eugnostus simi-

---

[20] Seeberg, 322, Geffcken, 35, and Vona, 134–135, take the Syriac translation as most closely
representing the original Greek text. Then the clear reference to *Tim.* 28c in the Armenian version
must be neglected, as done by Seeberg, 319–320, and Vona, 72 (who nevertheless in his note to
the passage remarks that many early Christian writers refer to *Tim.* 28c!) or explained away, as
by Geffcken, 35: "Nicht sowohl Platon: *Tim.* 28c . . ., liegt hier zugrunde, sondern vielmehr die
Abneigung der Stoa, namentlich der späteren Vertreter der Sekte, trotz ihrer materiellen Vorstel-
lungen von der Gottheit, das Transzendentale allzu sehr auszudeuten."

[21] Cf. *Testament of Benjamin* 3, 3: φοβεῖσθε Κύριον, καὶ ἀγαπᾶτε τὸν πλησίον.

larly declares, NH III,71,13–18: "The One who is, is ineffable. No sovereignty knew him, no authority, no subjection, nor did any creature from the foundation of the world, except himself."[22]

There are a number of reasons, then, to assume that Eugnostus and Aristides have both made use of a source which, in the traditional way, inferred from the orderly government of the universe that its Maker and Mover must be God, but at the same time asserted that, though we can see God's works, it is impossible to know his nature, and then went on to develop an explicitly negative theology based on the opposition between the unbegotten and the begotten. Their dependence on a common source explains the correspondences between Eugnostus and Aristides. The differences between them can be explained by Eugnostus' gnostic world-view, which forced him to reject the cosmological proof of God's existence with arguments developed in the Sceptical tradition.

I shall now return to Eugnostus' discussion of the form of God. As I have already observed, his argumentation at this point is not wholly congruent with that concerning God's being unbegotten, without beginning and without name. If he had continued to reason in the same manner he should have written: "He has no form, for whoever has a form is the creation of another: he is formless"—as in fact is said by Aristides. But Eugnostus says that God has no *human* form (μορφή) and that whoever has a *human* form (μορφή) is the creation of another. He does not say that God is *formless* but that "he has *a shape* (ἰδέα) *of his own*, not like the shape (ἰδέα) which we have received or which we have seen, but it is another shape (ἰδέα) which greatly surpasses all things and is better than all things." The exact meaning of "all things" is not clear; most probably Eugnostus simply meant to say that the form of God is better, more perfect, than all other forms. The most remarkable feature of this passage is that Eugnostus clearly assumes that God *does* have a form, which was most unusual in negative theology. Did he think of the pure form, the sphere? He continues with a remark which seems to point into that direction and which suggests that Eugnostus is influenced here, directly or indirectly, by the doxographic tradition concerning Xenophanes. He says of the form of God: "It sees in all parts (or: on all sides)." This expression *(esnau hi sa nim)* is so peculiar that the scribe of NH III, not only here (72,12) but also in the corresponding passage of the *Sophia Jesu Christi* (95,5), made a mistake and wrote *esnau ehise nim* ("it sees all labours"), but both times the error was noticed later, and corrected.[23] The Coptic word *sa*, 'part', 'side', translates the

---

[22] This view should be compared to those of Origen, *De princ.* IV 3,14 (Koetschau 346, 11 ff., Görgemanns-Karpp 776–778) and Silvanus, NH VII,116,27–117,3; see the remarks in R. van den Broek, *Origenes en de joden*, *Ter Herkenning* 13 (1985) 83–86.

[23] The scribe apparently took *hi sa* as one word, read it as *hise*, 'labour', 'suffering', and inserted the necessary preposition *e* after *nau*.

Greek word μέρος; *hi sa nim* means ἐν πᾶσι μέρεσιν. The version of the *Sophia Jesu Christi* contained in the Berlin Codex, 85,6–9, reads here *ñsa sa nim*, which means ἐπὶ πάντων τῶν μερῶν.[24] This reminds one strongly of the doxographic tradition concerning the doctrine of Xenophanes. For our purposes the quotation of two doxographic accounts will suffice.[25] Hippolytus, *Ref.* I 14,2 (*Vorsokr.* 21 A 33) says of Xenophanes' theology:

> He also affirms that God is eternal, one, identical in every respect, limited, spherical and perceptive in all his parts (πᾶσι τοῖς μορίοις αἰσθητικόν).

And Diogenes Laertius, IX 19 (*Vorsokr.* 21 A 1) writes:

> The substance of God is spherical, it has nothing which resembles man, but he sees as a whole and he hears as a whole, without respiring of course. He is wholly mind and thought (νοῦν καὶ φρόνησιν) and eternal.

That God is "perceptive in all his parts" (Hippolytus) or "sees in all parts" (Eugnostus) reflects one of Xenophanes' most famous fragments, *Vorsokr.* 21 B 24: "He sees as a whole, perceives as a whole, hears as a whole." If Eugnostus made use of the doxographic traditions concerning Xenophanes' theology, it also becomes understandable why he so strongly emphasized that God has no *human* form and, just as Diogenes Laertius, said that "he has nobody who resembles him." Xenophanes himself had said, *Vorsokr.* 21 B 23,2: "He is in no way like unto mortal men, either as to body or as to thought." There are no indications that Xenophanes had ever said that God has a spherical shape; the hellenistic doxographers must have inferred he had taught this when they fathered on him ideas which had been taught by his alleged pupil Parmenides.[26] Most probably, Eugnostus' peculiar ideas on the form of God derive from the doxographic vulgate concerning Xenophanes.

Eugnostus continues by saying that God is *unlimited*; the *Sophia Jesu Christi*, BG 85,9, has preserved the original Greek word, ἀπέραντος. Of course, the view that God is unlimited does not square with the idea that he is a sphere. The more consistent tradition is found in Hippolytus, quoted above (πεπερασμένον καὶ σφαιροειδῆ), and other authors.[27] However, ac-

---

[24] See W.E. Crum, *A Coptic Dictionary*, Oxford 1939, 314a.

[25] All relevant texts are to be found at *Vorsokr.* 21, and in M. Untersteiner, *Senofane. Testimonianze e frammenti*, Florence 1956. A thorough discusson of the conflicting doxographic accounts concerning Xenophanes is given by J. Mansfeld, Theophrastus and the Xenophanes Doxography, *Mnem.* Series 4, 40 (1987) 286–312.

[26] See Mansfeld, Theophrastus and the Xenophanes Doxography, 303. An overview of modern scholarship on Xenophanes' allegedly spherical God in Untersteiner, *Senofane*, LXIX–LXXIII, who himself explains this view from the physical notion of the περιέχον, LXXIII–LXXVI.

[27] Alexander of Aphrodisias, in Simpl., *In Phys.* 23,16 (*Vorsokr.* 21 A 31): πεπερασμένον αὐτὸ καὶ σφαιροειδές, and Theodoret, *Graec. aff. cur.* IV 5 (SC 57, 203, *Vorsokr.* 21 B 27): σφαιροειδὲς καὶ πεπερασμένον.

cording to Simplicius, *In Phys.* 23,16 (*Vorsokr.* 21 A 31), Nicolaus of Damascus, the Aristotelian court philosopher of Herod the Great, said that Xenophanes' first principle was "unlimited and unmoved (ἄπειρον καὶ ἀκίνητον)"; and in an Epicurean source used by Cicero, *Nat. deor.* I 28 (*Vorsokr.* 21 A 34), Xenophanes' God was said to be an infinite intellect ("*mente adiuncta omne . . . quod esset infinitum, deum voluit esse*"). There is no indication that these authors combined this view with the idea that God has a spherical shape. But in the Pseudo-Aristotelian treatise *De Melisso Xenophane Gorgia* (MXG), 3 (*Vorsokr.* 21 A 28) it is said of Xenophanes' God that "he is eternal, and one, and homogenous, and spherical (σφαιροειδῆ), neither unlimited nor limited (οὔτε ἄπειρον οὔτε πεπερασμένον), neither at rest nor moved." The origin of these polar attributes need not detain us here, since it has recently been explained by Jaap Mansfeld.[28] In this context it is sufficient to note that "neither unlimited nor limited" does not accord with 'spherical' either, and that, therefore, the contrast between Eugnostus' remark that God is unlimited and his suggestion (not: explicit statement!) that God is spherical is not wholly unprecedented. Eugnostus does not say that God is unmoved. This attribute, however, is found in the Armenian Aristides in a context which is strongly reminiscent of Xenophanes and for which there is no counterpart in the Syriac translation (Conybeare 31):

> He is unmoved and unmeasured and ineffable; for there is no place whence or with wich He could move; and He is not, by being measured, contained or environed on any side, for it is Himself that filleth all, and He transcends all things visible and invisible.

The beginning of this passage is reminiscent of another fragment of Xenophanes, *Vorsokr.* 21 B 26: "He always remains at the same place, without any movement (κινούμενος οὐδέν); it does not fit him to go now here, now there."

Both the Syriac and the Armenian Aristides continue by laying emphasis on God's absolute rationality:

Syriac (Harris 36)	Armenian (Conybeare 31)
Error and forgetfulness are not in His nature, for He is altogether wisdom and understanding, and in him consists all that consists.	Wrath and anger there is not in Him, for there is in Him no blindness, but He is wholly and entirely rational, and on that account He established creation with diverse wonders and entire beneficence.[29]

---

[28] Mansfeld, Theophrastus and the Xenophanes Doxography, 305–312.

[29] In *Barlaam and Joasaph*, Aristides 1,2–6 has been much compressed. The following corresponds to the passages quoted in the text: [ἀνώτερον πάντων τῶν παθῶν καὶ ἐλαττωμάτων] ὀργῆς τε καὶ λήθης καὶ ἀγνοίας καὶ τῶν λοιπῶν, δι' αὐτοῦ δὲ τὰ πάντα συνέστηκεν. Syr. has preserved λήθη, Arm. ὀργή; ἀγνοία might be an interpretation of the 'blindness' mentioned in the Armenian translation. R.M. Grant, *The Early Christian Doctrine of God*, Charlottesville 1966, 17,

The remark in the Armenian text that there is not blindness in God reflects Xenophanes' famous line on God as wholly seeing, etc. (fr. 24), which was interpreted in the doxographic tradition as an indication of his absolute rationality. Cicero, *Nat. deor.* I, 28 (God as an infinite Mind) and Diogenes Laertius IX, 19 (God as a wholly being νοῦς and φρόνησις) have already been cited. Reference must also be made to the Sceptic Timon, fr. 60,3 Diels (*Vorsokr.* 21 A 35): "more intellectual than (our) mind (νοερώτερον ἠε νόημα)," which our source for this fragment, Sextus Empiricus, *Pyrrh.* I 225, interpreted as λογικόν.

Eugnostus also concludes his discussion of God—which contains elements from other sources as well—by strongly emphasizing his complete rationality. According to him, God is not above Noûs, NH III,72,19–21: "He is unknowable, but he knows himself." Before anything came into existence "he embraced the totalities of the totalities and nothing embraced him" (73,6–8). Eugnostus continues with an elaborate description of the divine Mind, of which the Coptic has preserved the original Greek terms, 4 (73,8–16):

> For he is wholly νοῦς: ἔννοια and ἐνθύμησις, φρόνησις, λογισμός and δύναμις. They are all equal powers (ἰσοδυνάμεις), they are the sources of the totalities, and their whole kind is until their end in the foreknowledge of the Unbegotten.

Eugnostus has made use here of a psychological theory concerning the mental acts which lead to speech, or the production of a word, which was also used by Irenaeus, *Adv. Haer.* II 13,1–7, in his refutation of the Valentinian idea that the unknown Father's Ἔννοια produces his Νοῦς.[30] According to Irenaeus, the *noûs* is the mind in general, beginning and source of all mental activity (*principium et fons universi sensus*). The *ennoia* is the first of the *motiones* of the mind, followed by *enthymesis, sensatio* (= φρόνησις), *consilium* (= βουλή), *cogitatio* (= διαλογισμός, which can also be designated as λόγος ἐνδιάθετος), which finally proceeds as λόγος προφορικός (*cogi-*

---

n. 15, already called this passage of Aristides "a remote echo of Xenophanes."

[30] The relationship between this theory in Irenaeus and the doctrine of God in the *Sophia Jesu Christi / Eugnostus* and Manichaeism was first pointed out by A. Orbe, *Hacia la primera Teologia de la Procesión del Verbo, Estudios Valentinianos* I,1, Rome 1958, 366–386. Unaware of Orbe's study, I briefly discussed the same relationship in my article The Creation of Adam's Psychic Body in the Apocryphon of John, in: R. van den Broek and M.J. Vermaseren (eds.), *Studies in Gnosticism and Hellenistic Religions*, EPRO 91, Leiden 1981, 53–56; now also Tardieu, *Codex de Berlin*, 366–368 (without reference to Irenaeus). The Manichaean views are also discussed by P. Nagel, Anatomie des Menschen in gnostischer und manichäischer Sicht, in: P. Nagel (ed.), *Studien zum Menschenbild in Gnosis und Manichäismus*, Martin-Luther-Universität Halle-Wittenberg, Wissenschaftliche Beiträge 1979 / 39(K5), Halle (Saale) 1979, 82–85. The passage of Irenaeus has a close parallel in Maximus Confessor, *Opuscula theologica et polemica ad Marinum*, 8 (PG 91, 21A) and John of Damascus, *De fide orthodoxa* II, 22 (PG 94, 941D–944A), as was first seen by W. Lüdtke and pointed out by H. Jordan, *Armenische Irenaeusfragmente*, TU 36,3, Leipzig 1913, 51–55; see also A. Rousseau and L. Doutreleau, *Irénée de Lyon. Contre les Hérésies, Livre II*, I, SC 293, Paris 1982, 234–240 and 366–370.

tatio ... quae etiam in mente perseverans verbum rectissime appellabitur, ex quo emissibilis emittitur verbum).[31] It would interrupt my argument too much if I would enter into a detailed discussion of the difference between Eugnostus and Irenaeus. Eugnostus does not have an equivalent to *consilium*, and does not mention the λόγος in its successive stages.[32] He ends his list with δύναμις, which seems to have the sense of potentiality. But later on in his work, Eugnostus (NH III, 83,8–10), or in Tardieu's view an interpolator,[33] mentions 'will' and 'word', θελήσις and λόγος, as the last stages of the mental process instead of δύναμις. Eugnostus' five rational powers of God, including νοῦς and without δύναμις, became the five 'members' of the Manichaean Primeval Man.[34]

Irenaeus emphasizes that all these successive motions of the mind are in fact *unum et idem*, taking their origin from the one human νοῦς. But according to him, it would be completely wrong to assume that in God a similar succession of mental acts leads to the production of the divine Logos. God is identical in all his members, he is *similimembrius* (= ὁμοιομελής).[35] We are reminded here of the expression "all parts" of God, as used in the doxographic tradition concerning Xenophanes, and the whole passage of Irenaeus shows that he is making use of that tradition at this point of his refutation of the gnostics. God, he says in *Adv. Haer.* II 13,3, is:

---

[31] For the close relationship between διαλογισμός and λόγος ἐνδιάθετος, cf. Nemesius, *De natura hominis* 14 (PG 40,668A): ἔστι δὲ ἐνδιάθετος λόγος τὸ κίνημα τὸ ἐν τῷ διαλογιστικῷ γινομένον ἄνευ τινὸς ἐκφωνησέως (referred to by Orbe, 370, n. 31, and Rousseau-Doutreleau, SC 293, 368). Similar remarks in Maximus Confessor and John of Damascus (see note 30) are probably influenced by Nemesius.

[32] Maximus Confessor (PG 91, 21A) and John of Damascus (PG 94, 944A) do not mention an equivalent for *consilium* either; they enumerate the following κινήσεις of the mind: νόησις, ἔννοια, ἐνθύμησις, φρόνησις, διαλογισμός = λόγος ἐνδιάθετος (proceeding as λόγος προφορικός). I suggest that the original series might have been: νόησις, ἔννοια, ἐνθύμησις, φρόνησις, λογισμός, βουλή / διαλογισμός / λόγος ἐνδιάθετος, λόγος προφορικός, and that Irenaeus or his source erroneously left out λογισμός (if Maximus Confessor is not dependent on Irenaeus, which is by no means an ascertained fact, it must already have been omitted in Irenaeus' source). The internal dialogue of the mind, διαλογισμός, has a strong volitional aspect, which explains its association with βουλή (see G.W.H. Lampe, *A Patristic Greek Lexicon*, Oxford 1961, 302, and Rousseau-Doutreleau, SC 293, 369). In Eugnostus, the last stage of the mental process, after λογισμός, is summarized in the word δύναμις which is, later on in his work, replaced by 'will' and 'word' (see text); cf. also *Apocryphon of John*, 21: Νοῦς, Θέλημα, Λόγος.

[33] Tardieu, *Codex de Berlin*, 374.

[34] See the literature mentioned in note 30; for a synopsis of the terms for the members of the soul in the various Manichaean languages, see O. Klíma, *Manis Zeit und Leben*, Prag 1962, 212–213 (n. 13).

[35] On this term, see Rousseau-Doutreleau, SC 293, 241–244 (see also SC 263, 237–238, ad I,12,1), who with respect to II 13,3 (quoted in the text) do not deny "une dépendance plus ou moins indirecte et lointaine à l'égard de Xénophane," but primarily suggest a strong influence of Paul's image of the Church as a Body (1 Cor. 12,14–28). For the influence of the Xenophanes tradition in early Christian literature, see R.M. Grant, Place de Basilide dans la théologie chrétienne ancienne, *REAug* 25 (1979) 211–214 (also in several of his earlier writings, see the bibliography in Mansfeld, this volume, 107, n. 59); some other texts in which the Xenophanes tradition can be detected are given by Rousseau-Doutreleau, SC 293, 244.

simplex et non compositus et similimembrius et totus sibimetipsi similis et aequalis est, totus cum sit sensus et totus spiritus et totus sensuabilitas et totus ennoia et totus ratio et totus auditus et totus oculus et totus lumen et totus fons omnium bonorum, quemadmodum adest religiosis ac piis dicere de Deo.

In Eugnostos, at least at this point of his exposition, the divine rational powers are said to be ἰσοδυνάμεις, equal or equivalent powers; there is no gradation between them. He calls God wholly Νοῦς, and then mentions what Irenaeus calls the *motiones* of the mind. I suggest that, in Eugnostos, Νοῦς, is not yet one of the members of the divine Mind, as was later on taught in Manichaeism, but is still considered as the general, all-comprehensive principle, God himself, as a thinking Mind, and ἔννοια, ἐνθύμησις, φρόνησις, λογισμός, and δύναμις as his mental acts, thus expressing his complete rationality. Nevertheless, these acts do not coincide to the same extent as in Irenaeus view. Whereas Irenaeus says of God himself that he is the source of all good things (*totus fons omnium bonorum*, I 12,3; II 13,3), Eugnostos declares the ἰσοδυνάμεις of the divine Mind to be the sources of all things, contained in the Foreknowledge of God. He had already stated somewhat earlier that God encompasses all things. The same is said by Irenaeus in a similar context, *Adv. Haer.* II,28,4: *Cogitatio enim eius Logos, et Logos Mens, et omnia concludens Mens, ipse est Pater.*

The combination, found in Eugnostos and Irenaeus, of the doxographic tradition concerning the wholly rational God of Xenophanes with a psychological theory on the functioning of the human mind is not known from other sources. Aristides, who was shown to have made use of the same source as Eugnostos, emphasizes God's complete rationality but does not speak about the mental faculties (which, however, need not imply that they were not in his source). The application of the theory of the mental powers to the Mind of God may have been the work of someone who wished to elaborate the tradition concerning the completely rational God of Xenophanes. It was in this tradition that mention was made of equal parts or members (μέρη or μέλη) of God. God is *similimembrius* (= ὁμοιομελής), says Irenaeus, and so the equal powers, ἰσοδυνάμεις according to Eugnostos, of the Mind of God could be called his members. Here we have the original context of the Manichaean five 'members' of the heavenly Man.

The term 'members' is already used by Eugnostos with respect to the rational nature of the first hypostasis after the unbegotten Father, called Immortal Man, 12 (NHC III,78,5–15):

He has in himself a νοῦς of his own, an appropriate ἔννοια, ἐνθύμησις and φρόνησις, λογισμός and δύναμις. All existing parts (μέλος, plur.) are perfect and immortal. In respect to imperishableness, they are equal; in respect to power, there is a difference, like the difference between a father and a son, and a son and an ἔννοια, and the ἔννοια and the rest, as I said before.[36]

---

[36] The words "as I said before" do not belong to the following sentence, as is assumed by

The Son is conceived of as a second Noûs, whose 'members' or mental powers are said to be perfect and immortal, equally imperishable, but different with respect to power. Here we have a difference with the powers of the Father, which are said to be equal without any qualification. The heavenly Anthropos is the reflexion, the image of the unbegotten Father, and as such he represents a lower level of being, even though his powers are still perfect. In itself it would seem plausible to hold that the *human* mental powers were first ascribed to the heavenly *Man*, the Ἀθάνατος Ἄνθρωπος, and from him, only secondarily, transferred to the unbegotten Father.[37] But that position has become untenable now that we have seen that, at a certain stage of the doxographic tradition, the complete rationality of Xenophanes' God had been elaborated by applying to the divine Mind the rational powers of the human mind.

Like Eugnostus, Clement ascribed the rationality of the Father to the Son, and also in the terminology of the Xenophanes tradition. *Strom.* VII 5,5, he declares the Logos to be

> undivided, not cut off, not going from one place to another, always everywhere being and nowhere circumscribed, wholly mind, wholly paternal light, wholly eye, seeing all things, hearing all things, knowing all things, scrutinizing the powers with power.

Eugnostus and Clement show that both in gnostic and in Catholic speculation ideas and images developed in the doxographic tradition concerning Xenophanes' God were also applied to the second hypostasis of the deity.

APPENDIX: ARISTIDES AND THE TRIPARTITE TRACTATE

Aristides, *Apology* 1 (transl. from the Syriac by J. Rendel Harris, TS I,1 Cambridge 1891, 35).	*Tractatus Tripartitus*, NH I,51,1–54,32 (transl. from the Coptic by H.W. Attridge and E.H. Pagels, in: H.W. Attridge (ed.), *Nag Hammadi Codex I* (Texts), Leiden 1985, 193–199).
"Now I say that God is *not begotten, not made,*	[The Father alone is a father in the proper sense; no one is father to him:] "For he is *unbegotten* and there is no other who begot him, *nor another who created him.*" [All other fathers and creators have a father and creator themselves] (51,1–52,6).

Trakatellis, 187, Parrott, 215, and Tardieu, 181, since what follows had not yet been said before. Eugnostus refers to the members of Immortal Man he had just mentioned.

[37] Thus Tardieu, *Codex de Berlin*, 357, 366.

a *constant nature,*———————— "He is *without beginning and without end.*
without beginning and without Not only is he without end—He is *immortal*
end, immortal for this reason that he is unbegotten—but
                                 he is also *invariable in his eternal*
                                 existence, ..." [follows a passage on
                                 God's immutability, concluding with the
                                 words:] "who is the *unalterable, immutable,*
                                 one, with *immutability* clothing him" (52,
                                 6–33).
                                 "Not only is he the one called "*without a*
                                 beginning" and "*without an end,*" because
                                 he is *unbegotten* and *immortal*; but just
                                 as he has no beginning and no end as he
complete and *incomprehensible.* is, he is *unattainable* in his greatness,
                                 inscrutable in his wisdom, *incomprehensible*
                                 in his power, and *unfathomable* in his
                                 sweetness" (52,34–53,5).
And in saying that He is *com-* "In the proper sense he alone, the good,
plete, I mean this; that there the unbegotten Father and the *complete*
is no deficiency in Him, and *perfect* one, is the one *filled* with all his
He *stands in need of naught*, offspring and *with every virtue* and
but everything stand in need with everything of value. And he has more,
of Him. that is, lack of any malice, in order that
                                 it may be discovered that *whoever has any-*
                                 thing is indebted to him, because he gives
                                 it, ..." [an enumeration of several aspects
                                 of God's completeness follows] (53,5–54,1).

And in saying that He is without
beginning, I mean this; that
everything which has a beginning,
has also an end; and that which
has an end is dissoluble.
He has no name; for everything *Not one of the names* which are conceived,
that has a name is associated or spoken, seen or grasped, not one of them
with the created. *applies to him*, even though they are exceed-
                                 ingly glorious, magnifying and honoured.
                                 However, it is possible to utter these names
                                 for his glory and honour, in accordance with
                                 the capacity of each of those who give him
                                 glory (54,2–11).

He has no likeness [Syr. *demuta*', Yet as for him, in his own existence,
'form', 'shape'], nor composit- being and *form*, it is impossible for mind
ion of members; for he who pos- to conceive him (...). This is the nature of
sesses this is associated with the unbegotten one, which does not touch
things fashioned. He is not anything else; nor is it joined (to anything)
male, nor is he female." in the manner of something which is limited.
                                 Rather he possesses this constitution,
                                 without having a face or a form,—things which
                                 are understood through perception, whence
                                 also comes [the epithet] "the incomprehen-
                                 sible" (54,12–32).

THE KNOWLEDGE OF GOD IN ORIGEN

BY

JOHN M. DILLON (DUBLIN)

I propose to address the question of Origen's views on our knowledge of God from a rather special angle, but one which, I hope, will throw more light on the question than would a straight enumeration and evaluation of all relevant passages, and that is precisely the angle of *light*. I would like to consider in some detail the significance of the imagery of light used by Origen in connexion with our knowledge of God, both God the Father and God the Son, or the Logos, since I believe that by close attention to this we may able to discern accurately Origen's attitude to the possibility of our acquaintance[1] with God the Father.

The question of the knowledge of God, as we know, takes on increasing degrees of complexity in later antiquity, as the concept of the divinity itself becomes more complex. In particular, the gap which arises between the supreme God and the Demiurge or Logos creates an important distinction, addressed in various ways by different Platonists (Plutarch, Albinus, Numenius) and by Philo of Alexandria. Philo, for instance, makes a distinction (which he hardly invented himself) between knowing God's bare existence (*hyparxis*), which is possible for man, and knowing his essence (*ousia*), which is not, as well as between knowing him in himself and knowing him from his 'powers' (*dynameis*) or effects, including, inevitably, the Logos. We find an illuminating passage on these distinctions in *De Post. Cain.* 168–9, in an exegesis of *Deut.* 32:39, "See, see, that I am" (ἴδετε, ἴδετε, ὅτι ἐγώ εἰμι):[2]

> When we say that the Existent (*to on*) is visible, we are not using words in their literal sense, but it is an irregular use (*katachrēsis*) of the word by which it is referred to each of his powers. In the passage just quoted he does not say, "See me!"—for it is impossible that the God who truly exists should be cognised (*katanoethenai*) at all by the realm of generation (*genesis*)—but rather he says "See that I am," that is to say, see my existence (*hyparxis*). For it is quite enough for a man's reasoning faculty to advance as far as to learn that the cause of the universe is and

---

[1] I use this term to convey any variety of apprehension of the essence of God, as being a broader term than 'knowledge' or 'cognition', as including mystical contact, and yet narrower, as excluding any sort of indirect knowledge, such as knowledge of God's existence through his works or effects.

[2] For other useful statements of Philo's views on the knowledge of God, cf. *Leg. All.* I 36–38; *Leg. All.* III 100–102; *Congr.* 103–105; and especially *Praem.* 36–46.

exists (*hyparchei*); to be anxious to go further, and enquire about essence (*ousia*) or quality (*poiotēs*) in God, is monstrous simplemindedness. (Colson's trans., adapted).

He then goes on to call attention to *Exod.* 33:23, where God tells Moses "thou shalt behold my hinderparts, but my face thou shalt not see." This he sees as meaning that "all that follows in the wake of God is apprehensible (*katalēpta*) by the good man, while he himself alone is beyond apprehension (*akatalēptos*)." It is only the powers that accompany him that one may perceive, and these reveal not his essence (*ousia*), but only his existence (*hyparxis*).

I quote this at length because it constitutes a good introduction to the problem in Origen, as we shall see. His precise position on the modes and degrees of our knowledge of the divinity is well brought out, I think, by a study of the course of his argument in Book I of *Peri Archōn*, and in particular, as I suggested at the outset, by his use of the imagery of light there, so it is to that work that I will now turn.

On the vexed question of the nature of the *P. Archōn*, on which much has been written in recent years,[3] I must say that I am inclined to view the work as an attempt by Origen to state a reasoned Christian position on the topic of *archai*, or 'first principles,' arising out of his attendance at the lectures of Ammonius Saccas. I am led to this view, not just by a consideration of the subject matter, but by looking at the very way in which the work starts out. Origen begins abruptly, not with a positive statement of God's nature,[4] but with an an-

---

[3] Cf. B. Steidle, Neue Untersuchungen zu Origenes' Περὶ 'Αρχῶν, *ZNW* 40, 1942, 236–243; M. Harl, Recherches sur le Περὶ 'Αρχῶν d'Origène en vue d'une nouvelle edition: la division en chapitres, *Studia Patristica* 3 (= TU 78), 1961, 57–67; H. Crouzel, Intro. to *Origène: Traité des Principes*, Tome 1 (SC), pp. 15–22. The precise meaning of *archai* intended by Origen in this context has been the object of some uncertainty (cf. Crouzel's discussion, *op.cit.* 12–15, and Qu'a voulu faire Origène en composant le Traité des Principes? *Bulletin de Littérature Ecclésiastique* LXXVI (1975) 161–186, and 241–260). It seems probable to me that he sees himself as meaning what any Platonic philosopher would mean by this, viz. a discussion of the three acknowledged 'first principles,' God, Idea(s), Matter, together with topics arising out of those, and that is the subject-matter of the first section of the work (to II 3), *mutatis mutandis* (e.g. for 'Ideas', we have 'rational beings,' for Matter, the World). How well the title fits the other portions of the work is more problematic (a reference back to the discussion of free will in III 1 in the *Comm. in Rom.* (VII 15, PG XIV 1145A) as a separate *libellus* would seem to indicate that Origen thought of the work rather as a collection of essays).

Some light may be thrown on what particular connotation Origen attaches to the term *archai* by his remarks at *Comm. in Joh.* XIII 46, 302, where he presents the *archai* of any science or art as what the first discoverer, or 'sower', lays down, to be developed further and brought to completion (*telos*) by later generations ('reapers')—all this by way of exegesis of John 4:36. This 'dynamic' concept of the *archai* of a science imports another dimension, I think, into the traditionally static philosophical meanings of the term, as immutable basic principles or ultimate principles of reality. Certainly Origen is to some extent 'transposing' the traditional Platonic meaning of the term, as Crouzel suggests; the connotation "principles of the Christian faith" is superimposed on the basic meaning "first principles of reality." Cf. also *De Princ.* 4.1, 7, where *archē* is significantly glossed by *stoicheiōsis*.

[4] As one would expect in a statement of First Principles. On the immateriality of God, Cf.

swer to an accusation, plainly from a Platonic source, that Christians regard God as having a *corporeal* nature.[5] In combating this accusation, he has to face a series of passages of Scripture which seem to attribute to God material substance or characteristics.[6]

For instance, Moses says at *Deut.* 4:24: "Our God is a consuming fire,"[7] and Jesus says to the Samaritan woman at John 4:24: "God is spirit (*pneuma*), and those who worship him must worship in spirit and in truth." Now Origen's general line of defence is plainly that such passages must be taken figuratively, but that is not the first point that he makes. This first point I find rather interesting, and it is that which I wish to start from, since I think that it serves as a good instance of Origen's complex relationship to contemporary Hellenic[8] philosophy.

"These men," says Origen, "will have it that fire and spirit are body and nothing else. But I would ask them what they have to say about this passage of Scripture: 'God is light,' as John says in his epistle (1 *John* 1:5), 'and in him is no darkness.'

The point of adducing this passage about light is presumably that, in later Platonism, light is agreed to be incorporeal.[9] But this is, strangely enough, not a point which Origen cares to make explicitly. Instead, he goes on:

> He is that light, surely, which lightens the whole understanding of those who are capable of receiving truth, as it is written in the Thirty-fifth Psalm, 'In thy light shall we see light.' For what other light of God can we speak of in which a man sees light, except God's spiritual power (*dynamis*), which when it lightens a man causes him either to see clearly the truth of all things or to know God himself, who is called the truth? (trans. Butterworth).

Aetius, *Plac.* I 7, 31 (p. 304 Diels, *Dox.Gr.*), Apuleius, *De Plat.* I 5, 190–1; Numenius, Fr. 3 Des Places. (Albinus in *Did.* ch. 10 asserts, certainly, God's immateriality, but only at the *end* of his discussion).

[5] In the Preface, he begins, rather defensively, by identifying himself with Moses, who preferred, in the words of the author of *Hebrews* (11: 24–26), "the abused state (*oneidismos*) of Christ to the treasure-houses of the Egyptians," these latter being the much-vaunted doctrines of contemporary philosophy.

[6] These passages had certainly been adduced by anti-Christian polemicists (perhaps even by Ammonius, whom Porphyry, at least, maintained to have started as a Christian himself), though here Origen suggests only that they *might* do so (*scio quoniam conabuntur*). We know, in fact, that Celsus made these criticisms (*C. Cels.* VI 70–71), but had Origen read Celsus at this stage of his career? Ambrose sends him a copy of the book for refutation (*C. Cels. Pref.* 4), but this does not prove that he had no knowledge of it. We may note, by the way, that the point Origen seems here to adumbrate about the status of light does not recur in the *Contra Celsum* passage.

[7] He also describes him there as 'a jealous God,' but Origen leaves that aside in the present context.

[8] I use 'Hellenic' here instead of the commonly-used term 'pagan', which I find objectionable.

[9] Prof. J.C.M. Van Winden has challenged the validity of this point in conversation, and I agree with him that it is not, after all, a *necessary* explanation of Origen's line of argument. Origen's sole point could be, what it ultimately turns out to be, that all these modes of expression are to be taken figuratively, but it still seems to me that he is making a glancing reference to contemporary Peripatetic and Platonic doctrine.

Origen here has slipped unobtrusively from making one point to making another. The original purpose of introducing the example of light, to counter the references to fire and to *pneuma*, has been passed over in favour of an argument which applies to all three epithets equally, that they are not to be taken literally but metaphorically.

Why should Origen make such an apparently inconsequential move? I wish to propose two reasons, both of which illustrate his complex relationship to contemporary Platonism. The first is that, while he was well aware of contemporary Platonic doctrine on the incorporeality of light, he did not necessarily accept it himself; the second is that he also has very much in mind the Sun Simile of *Rep.* VI (507a–509c), which certainly since Alexander of Aphrodisias had been brought into conjunction with Aristotle's doctrines of the Active Intellect in *De An.* III 5 and of the Unmoved Mover in *Met.* XII, and had thus been incorporated in a coordinated Peripatetic and Platonist doctrine of God as Pure Activity (*energeia*) and as the *noetic* analogue of the Sun, bestowing both intelligibility and existence on all things, as well as knowledge on rational souls.

Let us explore each of these points in turn. First of all, the incorporeality of light. This is not a Platonic doctrine—neither in the *Republic* nor in the *Timaeus* is light presented as something incorporeal—but it is at least derivable from Aristotle, who, in *De An.* II 7, declares light to be 'the actuality of the transparent *qua* transparent.'[10] Aristotle simply wants to make the point that light is not a substance of any kind, but a condition of a substance (countering the doctrine of Empedocles), but for later Aristotelians and Platonists this incorporeality of light became something rather special, being connected with its preeminent role in the operation of the sense of sight, the most 'honourable' of the senses (cf. Plato, *Tim.* 45 *B–D*), and then being used as an analogy for the role of the Good (or in Alexander's theory, *Noûs*) in the activation of the human intellect in its cognising of True Being.

Thus it is that in Alexander's *De Anima* we find, first, at pp. 42, 19–43, 11 Bruns, a straightforward paraphrase of Ar. *De An.* III 7, but then, at 88, 26–89, 6, the use of the analogy of light to illustrate the principle that "whatever is eminently some kind of being imparts this kind of being to everything which is less eminently the same kind of being," to quote Philip Merlan's formulation.[11] The Active Intellect, being preeminently intelligible, imparts intelligibility to the 'material' intellect (that is, the immanent human intellect), which becomes intelligible by intelligising the proper objects of intellect, the forms in matter. Similarly, light, being preeminently visible, is the cause of the visibility of everything visible, as well as of the seeing ability of the eyes.

---

[10] 148b9–10: φῶς δέ ἐστιν ἡ τούτου ἐνέργεια, τοῦ διαφανοῦς ᾗ διαφανές.
[11] In *Monopsychism, Mysticism, Metaconsciousness*, The Hague 1969², 39.

This comparison of Alexander's plainly owes much to the Sun Simile of the *Republic*, and it in turn can be seen to have had considerable influence on Plotinus' view of the status of light in such passages as *Enn.* IV 5, 6–7, II 1, 7 and I, 6, 3.[12] The evidence of Origen would seem to indicate that this identification of light as *asōmaton*, against the indications of Plato's doctrine in the *Timaeus*, goes back to Middle Platonism, perhaps to Numenius, or at least to Ammonius Saccas.

For a Platonist, Aristotle's doctrine as presented in *De An.* II 7 is not satisfactory, since Aristotle declares light not to be a body, not for the purpose of exalting it, but simply to deprive it of any independent existence. Quite a different connotation can be put upon this bodilessness of light if one chooses to take this, as does Alexander, and later Plotinus, as indicating that light is pure Form without an admixture of matter. In Alexander this is actually only implied in the comparison of light with the Active Intellect, but in Plotinus it is quite explicit.[13] For Plotinus ordinary, physical light is, by reason of its freedom from admixture with body, the noblest element in the material universe.

Now as I say, Origen seems to recognise the existence of this doctrine of light, but he is not prepared to approve it. When it comes to employing the similes of the Sun and the Cave of the *Republic*, however, he has no such hesitation, although he employs them in a suitably disguised form. At *De Princ.* I. 1, 5, we find the following:[14]

Having then refuted, to the best of our ability, every interpretation which suggests that we should attribute to God any material characteristics, we assert that he is in truth incomprehensible and immeasurable.[15] For whatever may be the knowledge which we have been able to obtain about God, whether by perception or reflection, we must of necessity believe that he is far and away better than our thoughts about him. For if we see a man who can scarcely look at a glimmer or the light of the smallest lamp, and if we wish to teach such a one, whose eyesight is not strong enough to receive more light than we have said, about the brightness and splendour of the sun, shall we not have to tell him that the splendour of the sun is unspeakably and immeasurably better and more glorious than all this light he can see?

---

[12] See A.H. Armstrong, *The Architecture of the Intelligible Universe in the Philosophy of Plotinus*, Cambridge 1940, repr. Amsterdam 1967, 54–57; F.M. Schroeder, Light and the Active Intellect in Alexander and Plotinus, *Hermes* 112 (1984) 239–245.

[13] E.g. *Enn.* I 6, 7, 17–18: light is ἀσώματον καὶ λόγος καὶ εἶδος.

[14] I use Butterworth's translation, unless otherwise noted.

[15] *Incomprehensibilis* here probably translates ἀκατάληπτος; *inaestimabilis* may render ἀπερίμετρος, an epithet, which, though Greek, is only found in Apuleius' *De Plat.* ch. 5, but ἀδιεξήγητος or ἀπεριόριστος are also possibilities. It is interesting, though I do not know of what significance, that the conjunction of terms *incomprehensibilis* and *inaestimabilis*, referring to Aiōn, occurs in the Hermetic *Asclepius* (31, 23–4), but once again we do not know what Greek words are being translated, though A.J. Festugière proposes ἀπεριόριστος and ἀμέτρητος (La Révélation d'Hermès Trismégiste, IV: *Le Dieu inconnu et la gnose*, Paris 1954, 173).

Here, and in what follows, the influence of the Simile of the Cave is palpable enough, I think,[16] but there is another element here also, which is not present in Plato's image. Plato stresses the shock and discomfort of being brought from one's comfortable viewing of the shadows on the wall cast by the fire, first to the realisation that the fire is only a fire, and the figures only cardboard cutouts, and then to a view of the outside world dominated by the sun, but the end result is that one *can* view the sun, one *does* attain to a knowledge of the Good. For Origen, God is of such a nature as "the human mind, however pure or clear to the very utmost that mind may be, cannot gaze at or behold" (*ibid.*).

Now this is very much a part of the Christian doctrine of the 'invisibility' of God, but it finds an echo also in a passage of Numenius' dialogue *On the Good* (Fr. 2 Des Places), a work which Origen certainly knew (since he quotes from it in the *Contra Celsum*),[17] to the effect that we can gain the notion of anything bodily from comparison with things of a similar nature, but in the case of the Good, "no object present to us nor any sensible object similar to it gives us any means of grasping its nature." However, Numenius is actually leading up here to his lively description of the mystical vision of the Good, which he compares with a little fishing-boat which by close attention one can just pick out bobbing between the waves. Origen gives no such promise of a mystical vision in this life. The important thing is, though, that Numenius seems here to be giving an interpretation of the negative aspect of the Sun Simile—after all, Socrates *does* emphasise at the outset, in 506 C–E, that he cannot give an account of the Good itself, but only a series of images.

In the very next section (I 1,6), Origen seems to make further use of the Cave Simile, though sufficiently altered as to make identification less than obvious:

> But it will not appear out of place if to make the matter clearer still we use yet another illustration. Sometimes our eyes cannot look upon the light itself, that is, the actual sun, but when we see the brightness and rays of the sun as they pour into out windows for example, or into any small openings for light, we are able to infer from these how great is the source and the fountain of physical light.

This seems to owe something to *Rep.* VII 515e–516b, where the prisoner, newly freed from the Cave, cannot yet look upon the sun or bear the sunlight: "he would find it painful to be thus dragged out, and would chafe at it, and when he came out into the light, his eyes would be filled with its beams so that he would not be able to see even one of the things which we call real," and a

---

[16] Though long since formalised in Middle Platonic tradition, the Sun Simile is given by Albinus in *Did.* ch. 10 as prime example of the 'way of analogy,' while of the 'way of *anagogē*' (*via eminentiae*), which the Cave is certainly an instance of, he actually gives Diotima's speech in the *Symposium* as the example. Origen uses the comparison of the light of a lamp with the light of the sun elsewhere, at *Comm. in Joh.* II 120–121 and *C. Cels.* V II.

[17] I 15; IV 51.

gradual process of habituation is required. The difference, of course, is, once again, that in Plato one does come eventually to a vision of the Good, whereas in Origen one does not, at least in this life.[18] In fact, Origen has here subtly blended the imagery of the Cave with the later Stoic argument for the existence of God from the contemplation of his works (cf. Sextus Empiricus, *M* IX 75–87), which suits him rather better, especially as St. Paul himself had referred to it at *Rom.* 1:20: "Ever since the creation of the world his invisible nature, namely, his eternal power and deity, has been clearly perceived in the things that have been made." But for Origen the force of this argument, in relation to the Cave Simile, is that we can get no further than inference from God's manifestations and effects to His nature; we cannot know Him as He is.

Origen certainly approves of the central images of the *Republic*, as we can see from *Contra Celsum* VII 45–6, where he first quotes Celsus making use of the Sun and the Line, and then says, "We are careful not to raise objections to good teachings, even if the authors are outside the faith," but he is not committed to the full implications of the doctrine behind them, nor does he feel constrained from modifying them with other doctrines of his own. For instance, in the next chapter of Book I (2, 7) dealing with the Son or *Logos*, he identifies the process of habituation (συνηθέια) mentioned in *Rep.* VII 516a with the activity of the Logos (who is, after all, 'light from light'):[19]

> for it is through his brightness that the nature of the light itself is known and experienced. This brightness falls softly and gently on the tender and weak eyes of mortal man and little by little trains and accustoms (*adsuescens*) them to bear the light in its clearness; and when it has removed from them all that darkens and obstructs their vision, ... it renders them capable of enduring the glory of the light, becoming in this respect even a kind of mediator (μεσίτης, 1 *Tim.* 2:5) between men and the light.

Here, indeed, it seems as if, through Christ, we *are* enabled to see the Father, which would be fully in the spirit of the imagery of the Cave, but in fact Origen is allowing himself to be carried away slightly. This impression is severely qualified in what follows (sects. 8–10), particularly by the striking image of the immense statue, which is too big for us to view, and the miniature statue which is its faithful copy, but which we can see, and which gives us a true image (εἰκών, *similitudo*), but still only an image, of what we cannot see.[20]

---

[18] There seems almost an explicit contradiction of *Rep.* VII 516B, αὐτὸν καθ' αὐτὸν ἐν τῇ αὐτοῦ χώρᾳ δύναιτ' ἄν κατιδεῖν in I 1, 6: *mens nostra ipsum per se ipsum deum sicut est non potest intueri.*

[19] *Splendor ex luce* (presumably translating ἀπαύγασμα ἐκ φωτός) a phrase inspired by *Wisdom of Solomon* 7:26 and *Hebrews* 1:3. The same idea is expressed by Plotinus in slightly different terms in *Enn.* V 1, 6, 25 ff. (περίλαμψιν ἐξ αὐτοῦ ... οἷον ἡλίου τὸ περὶ αὐτὸν λαμπρὸν ὥσπερ περιθέον) Cf. also *Enn.* V 3, 12, 40 ff., and 15, 6.

[20] This is very much in the spirit of Origen's view of Christ as the 'image of the invisible God'

In all this we cannot, unfortunately, be sure that Rufinus is not indulging in a certain degree of censorship and 'laundering' of the text (as he certainly is seen to be doing in the few places where the original is available to us), but Origen seems to be struggling with the problem of how far God is knowable or unknowable, and to what extent Christ is the means to that knowledge, and Platonic imagery is both a help and a hindrance to him in this.

This is not quite the whole story, however. Origen gives ample indication, in ch. 1 of the *Peri Archōn*, that he is aware of the considerable development that had taken place over the previous centuries in the Platonic doctrine of the nature and the knowability of God.[21] He is influenced not only by his knowledge of the speculations of such Pythagoreanising Platonists as Moderatus and Numenius, and also possibly of the more 'main-line' Platonist Albinus, but also by his acquaintance with the works of Philo, who was himself influenced by contemporary Platonism. The consensus that appears to have been reached by 200 A.D. or so was that God was both absolute Unity (μονάς, εἷς, ἕν) but also an Intellect—an Intellect, however, which is to be distinguished from a second, active, demiurgic intellect or *logos* (Moderatus, Numenius and Albinus favour a second *noûs*, Philo, Plutarch and Atticus a *logos*), by being 'static' (Num. Fr. 15 Des Places) as opposed to 'in motion,' a fount and first principle of *noûs*, or, more vaguely 'something higher' (ἀνωτέρω) than *noûs* (Albinus, *Did.* ch. 10).

Such an entity can be known, if at all, only in some rather special way. Plato's famous dictum at *Timaeus* 28c about the difficulty of discovering the nature of God and the impossibility of communicating it to the general public gave much stimulus to negative theology of various kinds in later times (cf., e.g., *C. Cels.* VII 43), but it was not until the second part of the *Parmenides* was given a metaphysical interpretation, from the 1st century A.D. on, that the problem of how the First Principle could be cognised became an acute one for Platonists. At the end of the first hypothesis (142A), we reach the conclusion about the One that "it cannot have a name or be spoken of, nor can there be any knowledge or perception or opinion of it. It is not named or spoken of, not an object of opinion or knowledge, not perceived by any creature."

If it is to be cognised at all, then, it cannot be by any 'normal' cognitive process, such as *aisthēsis*, *doxa* or *epistēmē*. It will require a distinct supranoetic faculty, termed poetically by the Chaldaean Oracles (Fr. 1, 1 Des Places) 'the flower of the mind' (ἄνθος νοῦ), recognised by Plotinus as the *noûs* in a state of sober intoxication (*Enn.* III 5, 9; VI 7, 35), and also perhaps by Numenius in his eloquent description of the vision of the Good in Fr. 2 (mentioned above).

(*Col.* 1:15)—one of Origen's favourite texts (119 citations listed in *Biblia Patristica* 3). Cf. in particular *C. Cels.* VI 69, and below, *Princ.* II 4, 3.

[21] See Festugière's authoritative survey, *op.cit.* 1—140.

Origen, however, does not seem to have arrived at a formula for this special faculty. In his exhaustive study of Origen's terminology and doctrine of the modes and levels of knowledge (*Origène et la 'connaissance mystique'*),[22] despite the promising title (which he does, admittedly, enclose in inverted commas), Henri Crouzel cannot come up with any clear reference to a direct vision of God himself *in this life*. The term which best expresses the sort of direct intellectual contact envisaged by Origen for the beatific vision to be enjoyed by the saints after death is προσβολή,[23] but the significant thing here is that this same term is used by Plotinus, along with ἐπιβολή and ἐπαφή, for the sort of supranoetic contact which is attainable by the *noûs* while still in the body.[24] This is not to deny that Origen had mystical experience (Crouzel makes an eloquent case for his having had some, quoting in particular his first Homily on the *Song of Songs* (sect. 7)),[25] but the fact remains, I think, that for theological reasons he denied that the human soul or mind, while still in the body, could achieve the equivalent, in Platonic terms, of looking directly at the sun.

This has been, I fear, a rather superficial study, based only on one particular series of connected passages in one work (though a major one), of a very prolific and many-sided thinker, but, such as it is, it serves to bear out Crouzel's characterisation of Origen as a 'transformer' of Platonism, rather than a crypto-Platonist of any sort. One could, obviously, pursue this theme much further, in various directions. One directon that occurs to me is the paradoxical presentation of God as 'darkness' (*skotos*) in the *Commentary on John* (II 172), arising out of the exegesis of *John* 1:5, where precisely God is, after all, declared to be 'light shining in darkness.' By way of going one better, it would almost seem, than the traditional Platonic image of God as light and standing it on its head, but also in order to explain certain troublesome passages of the Old Testament, such as *Exodus* 19:9, 16, and 20:21, where God is described as enveloped in a thick cloud, and *Psalm* 18:11 "He made darkness his covering around him, his canopy thick clouds dark with water" (passages which, it seems, Gnostics such as Marcion had fastened on to support their argument that Jahweh was an evil Demiurge), Origen presents this 'darkness' and 'cloudi-

---

[22] Paris/Bruges 1963, 496–508.

[23] Interesting passages are *Fragm. in Joh.* XIII (GCS, IV p. 495), κατὰ προσβολὴν νοήσεως, *Exh. ad Mart.* XIII, where the 'friends of God' will enjoy direct knowledge ἐν εἴδει, προσβάλλοντες τῇ τῶν νοητῶν φύσει καὶ τῷ τῆς ἀληθείας κάλλει; *P. Euch.* XXV, 2, ὁ νοῦς προσβάλλει τοῖς νοητοῖς.

[24] E.g. *Enn.* III 8, 10, 33 (προσβολή); VI 7, 35, 21 (ἐπιβολή); V 3, 10, 42 (ἐπαφή).

[25] *Origène*, 162–4. Even here, though, Origen may after all only be talking about the frustrating experience of having at one moment a vision of the spiritual meaning of a certain text, only to lose it again on further reflection.

ness' as a symbol of God's unknowability to the human intellect; in himself, of course, he remains Light.[26]

But this is just by way of coda to my main theme. It seems suitable that a discussion of Origen's use of light imagery should end, paradoxically, with a discussion of God as darkness. My main purpose has been to suggest that Origen, by the judicious use and 'transformation' of Platonic light-imagery, manages to draw creatively on both of the conflicting tendencies observable in second-century Platonist (and Hermetic) doctrine on the knowability of God[27] on the one hand, the view of God as Demiurge, who makes himself known through his handiwork, the cosmos, and on the other, the God who is utterly transcendent, 'other' than everything material, who cannot be named or described or known by any faculty of the mind. Origen, as we have seen, presents us with both these types or levels of divinity, in God the Father and God the Son, or the Logos. The latter is knowable through his works and in himself, through that element in each of us which is an *eikōn* of him, even as he is an *eikōn* of the Father; the Father himself remains unknowable to us in this life, though we may hope for better acquaintance when we are free from the body, but the bare fact of his existence, his *hyparxis*, we can deduce both from his works and from our knowledge of the Son.

---

[26] Cf. Crouzel, *Origène*, 91–95. The concept of God as σκότος has an interesting analogy in the Pythagorean characterisation of the 'male-female' Monad, not only as Intellect and God, but also as Matter, Chaos, ἀλαμπία and σκοτωδία, as reported by Nicomachus of Gerasa (an author known to Origen) in his *Theologumena Arithmetica* (*ap.* Phot. *Bibl.* p. 143 Bekker).

[27] Cf. on this Festugière, *op.cit.*, 54 ff.

KNOWLEDGE OF GOD IN EUSEBIUS AND ATHANASIUS

BY

CHRISTOPHER STEAD (CAMBRIDGE)

The knowledge of God in Eusebius and Athanasius is a subject which in competent hands might form an impressive conclusion to our conference. To do it justice in a single paper is quite another matter; it opens up a wide range of enquiries, and touches on some of the most intractable problems of philosophical theology. For instance, are we to consider what can be *said* about God?—that is, what sort of human language can be so adapted as to describe the hidden and comprehensive reality which underlies our whole existence? Or should we be looking for some experience of contact with God which is necessarily so remote from our usual acts and thoughts that it cannot be described in normal terms and has to be indicated in the language of paradox? Or again, should we judge it a mistake to present these alternatives? I have suggested that knowledge of God may be conceived either in terms of rational statements or of mystical consciousness; but in pointing this contrast, I am using the categories of modern Western philosophy; we shall find, I think, that our chosen authors conceive their problem quite otherwise; their most important category being the intellect, *nous*, which implies both rational content and the directness of intuitive perception.

1. We need, therefore, to find a simple down-to-earth point of departure; and I propose to begin from a well-known passage in the *De Incarnatione*, c. 12. In this chapter Athanasius enumerates the various means of knowing God which had been devised by his divine providence; previous to the Fall, it would seem, and anticipating its possibility, God provided for man's negligence: προενοήσατο καὶ τῆς ἀμελείας τούτων, ἵν' ἐὰν ἀμελήσαιεν δι' ἑαυτῶν τὸν Θεὸν ἐπιγνῶναι, ἔχωσι ... τὸν δημιουργὸν μὴ ἀγνοεῖν. He mentions first what we may call ideal knowledge, which should have been sufficient for man if he had not sinned. Next comes the possibility of recognizing the Creator through attending to the works of his creation. Thirdly, God provided for the Law and the Prophets, whose teaching is more accessible, since in that case mankind can learn from other men. But since all these means were ineffective in the face of human wickedness, God finally adopted the expedient of renewing men through the presence of his own Image, the Logos, after whom they were first created; so the Word of God came down to earth in his own person: ὅθεν ὁ τοῦ Θεοῦ Λόγος δι' ἑαυτοῦ παρεγένετο, c. 13.7. There are thus four possible

ways of knowing God, if we may trust Dr. Meijering's analysis in *Athanasius contra Gentes*, p. 114; though Athanasius' treatment of the third way contains a rather complicated resumptive clause and refers to the 'saints', οἱ ἅγιοι, who may possibly be Christian teachers distinct from the Prophets, the μακάριοι διδάσκαλοι mentioned in c. 1. For the purpose of this paper I intend to consider only the first item on the list; I shall try to examine the ways in which Athanasius and Eusebius explain our ideal knowledge of God.

2. Any treatment of the *De Incarnatione* will naturally refer to its companion piece, the *Contra Gentes*; and we must take account of a certain difference in perspective between these two works, which compare rather differently with the thought of Eusebius. The divergence is especially marked in their early chapters, and it prompted a young Oxford scholar, as he then was, Dr. Andrew Louth, to draw a sharp contrast between them.[1] They differ, he maintains, in the account they give of the Fall of man, but also in the assumptions they make about our knowledge of God. 'The *Contra Gentes* gives an account of man's fall from a state of contemplation to a state subject to sensual pleasures. It is a timeless account. It is untypical of Athanasius—but typical of Alexandrian theology generally—in using allegorical exegesis. *De Incarnatione* is historical, realist, and turns, not on intellectual contemplation, but on the obedience and disobedience of man.'

I agree with Dr. Meijering that this contrast is overstated. In my own opinion, neither book presents a perfectly consistent picture. The case is rather, that in each of them Athanasius is drawing upon traditional themes, and selects rather different points for emphasis. But it is certainly not the case that the theology of one book contrasts *en bloc* with that of the other.

First, then, the *CG* certainly does not begin by considering the Fall of man in allegorical terms. One can see this clearly if one contrasts Athanasius with Philo. Philo repeatedly suggests that the first man symbolizes intellect, *nous*, and the first woman symbolizes sensation, *aisthēsis*.[2] But Athanasius does not tell us that the first man symbolizes anything at all; at most, we can say that he treats him as an example of a general truth. He states that God's purpose was that men should enjoy uninterrupted communion with him, and adds that this actually happened in the case of 'the first man ... who was called Adam in the Hebrew tongue;' the only hint of allegory here is a reference to the place which Moses figuratively called the Garden—τροπικῶς παράδεισον ὠνόμασεν, c. 2. Athanasius then states that men, οἱ ἄνθρωποι, neglected the contemplation of God and sought for satisfactions close at hand, in the pleasures of the body; and this again is illustrated by the case of the first man—τοῦ

---

[1] A. Louth, The Concept of the Soul in Athanasius' *Contra Gentes—De Incarnatione*, in: E.A. Livingstone, *Studia Patristica* 13 = *TU* 116, Berlin 1975, 228.
[2] Philo *Leg. All.* 1.92. 2.5–8, 16, 31, 38, 40, 70f. etc.

πρώτου πλασθέντος ἀνθρώπου—who at first attended to God and the contemplation of God, but then at the instigation of the serpent fell away. And this leads back to the general statement that in their pursuit of pleasure men began to devise various forms of idolatry and vice, where there is not the smallest doubt that Athanasius intends to describe actual practices of Egyptians, Greeks and Romans, including a reference to the Emperor Hadrian's favourite, Antinous.

Now of course the *DI* does present a rather different picture, and Dr. Louth is perfectly right in emphasizing the divine command of Genesis 2:16 and the stress on disobedience as opposed to the neglect of contemplation and pursuit of sensual pleasure. Indeed we could go further. Many readers of the *DI* find that it comes like a breath of fresh air; here at last, they think, is a straightforward biblical account, as opposed to the foggy generalities found in the *CG* and also in Eusebius. But I think we gain this impression because we have all been influenced by Augustine and his intense concentration on Romans, especially Romans 5:12, together of course with 1 Cor. 15:21–2. Athanasius does reproduce this Pauline perspective; but this is not the view of all the biblical writers. The Book of Wisdom, which Athanasius uses fairly freely, considers that human wickedness results from idolatry; the creation of man is mentioned only in general terms at 2:33 and 9:2; there is no mention of Adam by name; his creation appears only incidentally at 7:1, while his fall only comes to light at 10:1 in the claim that 'Wisdom delivered him out of his own transgression.' Even St. Paul in Romans *begins* with a general denunciation of human wickedness and discusses the role of the Law and the faith of Abraham before coming to Adam's transgression at 5:12–14; and this is specifically named as παρακοή first at 5:9. And of course there are other biblical traditions, including that which lays the blame on Eve.[3]

There is no call for surprise, then, if we find Eusebius writing largely in the tradition of the Wisdom writer, making general statements about human wickedness prompted by idolatry, and emphasizing the Origenistic theme of neglect and contempt rather than some single act of disobedience. The *Laus Constantini*, so far as I can discover, consistently follows this line. The *Praeparatio Evangelica* Book VII begins with a passage recalling the *CG* c. 3, in which mankind—or rather the Gentiles—are reproached for giving themselves over to bodily pleasures, and so learning to worship the sun and other heavenly bodies on which those pleasures depend; there follows a quotation of Wisdom 14:12, Ἀρχὴ γὰρ πορνείας ἐπίνοια εἰδώλων, which will recur in Athanasius, in *CG* 9 and 11. Eusebius occasionally refers to Adam by name, but hardly emphasizes his role as progenitor, or his failure and disobedience; this only appears rather incidentally at 7.18.8, τὸν δ' αὐθεκουσίῳ αἱρέσει

---

[3] 1 Tim. 2:14, Justin *Dial.* 10, Iren. 1.30.7, 3.22.4, 5.19.1 (*sec.* Massuet).

τῶν κρειττόνων ἀποπεσεῖν ... ἐντολῆς ὀλιγωρίᾳ, where the theme of neglect is still prominent. Adam, the earth-born γηγενής, seems undistinguished when contrasted with the perfectly righteous Enosh; the very name 'Adam' can symbolize τὸν κοινὸν καὶ πολὺν ἄνθρωπον (7.8.8.). In the *Demonstratio* there is no mention of Adam by name, and I think only one reference to his fall through the misuse of his free will.[4]

How does Athanasius appear by comparison? We can admit that there is some contrast between the two early works; the *CG* shows a rather closer agreement with Eusebius. But the contrast is far less acute than Louth makes out. Athanasius does not say, like Eusebius, that Adam represents the common man. Admittedly the *CG* describes the misdeeds of mankind in general, rather than a specific sin of Adam; but these general condemnations reappear quite frequently in the *DI*; the Fall is introduced by a general statement in 3.4; and although Athanasius quotes the divine prohibition of Gen. 2:16, he does not mention Adam by name until the genealogy in c. 35. The theme of idolatry, again, is still quite prominent.[5] Can one then see a contrast in that Eusebius and the *CG* dwell on the Origenistic idea of neglecting the contemplation of God rather than the specific sin of disobedience? Certainly the reference to disobedience as such are not very prominent in Eusebius; but the idea is found, e.g., in *PE* 2.6.12–15; again, the *CG* does not refer to the *parabasis* of men, and only once to their *parakoē*, c. 5. On the other hand the theme of neglect is well represented in the *DI*[5]. Men are still blamed, as in the *CG*, because they failed to devote themselves to the contemplation of God.

3. This contemplation is what I have called ideal knowledge; it was enjoyed by Adam in his unfallen state. Athanasius' view of Adam is closely bound up with his exegesis of Gen. 1:26. Like Philo, he explains that the εἰκὼν is God's Logos himself; in one passage, *c. Ar.* 2.49, he designates him τοῦ ἀληθινοῦ Θεοῦ εἰκὼν καὶ ὁμοίωσις. But man was created κατ' εἰκόνα καὶ καθ' ὁμοίωσιν, and the two phrases are treated as synonymous. This was a long-standing problem of exegesis; Irenaeus, Clement and Origen all offer two distinct interpretations, sometimes identifying the two phrases, sometimes distinguishing, so as to make ὁμοίωσις refer to a spiritual condition which we are to achieve by our own effort and virtue.[6] Origen puts this very clearly in *Comm. Joh.* 20.22.183,

---

[4] Eus. *PE* 2.6.12, 7.8.8–9, 11.6.10–15; *DE* 4.6.7; but cf. *PE* 7.18.5 cited below.

[5] Ath. *DI* condemns mankind generally, 11, 15, 36, 40 etc.; idolatry, 11f., 14, 20, 30f., 40, 46; neglect of contemplation, 4.4, 5.1, 11.4, 12.1, 14.7.

[6] Εἰκών and ὁμοίωσις equated: Iren. 3.23.2, 4.20.1, 5.1.3, 15.4; Clement *Protr.* 98.4, *Paed.* 3.66.2, *Str.* 2.19; Origen *Princ.* 1.2.6, 2.10.7, 11.3, 3.1.13, 4.4.10; *Hom. Gen.* 1.13, 13.4; *Hom. Lev.* 3.2; *Sel. Ps.* 4.3; *Hom. Lk.* 39; *Comm. Jo.* 2.23.144; Eusebius *HE* 1.2.4, *PE* 3.10.16, 7.12.10, 17.3f., *ET* 1.20.8.
Distinguished: Iren. 5.6.1, 16.1; Clement *Paed.* 1.3, *Str.* 2.22; Origen *Princ.* 3.6.1, *Hom. Ezek.* 13.2, *Comm. Jo.* 20.22.183, *Cels.* 4.30, *Orat.* 27.2; Eusebius *PE* 11.27 (?).

when he writes: κατ' εἰκόνα γεγόναμεν, ἐσόμεθα καὶ καθ' ὁμοίωσιν. But Eusebius I think shows a fairly marked preference for identifying the two phrases; typical is *PE* 7.18.5, τοῦτον μὲν οὖν κατ' εἰκόνα φασὶ θεοῦ καὶ καθ' ὁμοίωσιν πρὸς αὐτοῦ τοῦ θεοῦ ... ὑποστῆναι, and I have found only one passage (*PE* 11.27.4) which suggests that our ὁμοίωσις is something still to be achieved.

Very likely, therefore, it was Eusebius who taught Athanasius that Adam already possessed both image and likeness. Athanasius identifies these concepts, whether he is describing the creation of mankind in general, as in *CG* 2 and 34, ἡ ψυχὴ ... καθ' ὁμοίωσιν γέγονεν, and *DI* 11, ποιεῖ τούτους καθ' ὁμοίωσιν: or that of Adam in particular, who was τέλειος κτισθείς, *c. Ar.* 2.66, and whom God wished simply to persist in his original condition, *CG* 3, οὕτω καὶ μένειν ἠθέλησεν, with similar phrases at *CG* 34 and *DI* 4. There is no thought of ὁμοίωσις as a further perfection still to be acquired.

On this basis, Athanasius can describe man's ideal knowledge of God in highly optimistic terms in the second chapter of *CG*. We may note these points: (1) Man's creation ensures for him a knowledge of God. (2) This knowledge resides in the soul, (3) or more properly in the mind, *nous*. In either case, to exercize it, one must turn away from bodily sensations and attend to *noēta*. (4) Given this condition, the soul is self-sufficient; in its purity, it can reflect the Logos whom it resembles. These points, I believe, can all be found in Eusebius, though he states them more fully and less forcefully. Athanasius enormously improves on Eusebius; but his merit, in dealing with our present topic, lies in clarity and economy of statement rather than in originality of thought.

3.1. The first point is well stated in *CG* 2: ὁ παμβασιλεὺς Θεός, ὁ ὑπερέκεινα πάσης οὐσίας καὶ ἀνθρωπίνης ἐπινοίας ὑπάρχων ... τὸ ἀνθρώπινον γένος κατ' ἰδίαν εἰκόνα πεποίηκε· καὶ τῶν ὄντων αὐτὸν θεωρητὴν καὶ ἐπιστήμονα διὰ τῆς πρὸς αὐτὸν ὁμοιώσεως κατεσκεύασε, δοὺς αὐτῷ καὶ τῆς ἰδίας ἀϊδιότητος ἔννοιαν καὶ γνῶσιν. We note the apparent contradition; God is said to be beyond human apprehension, in the conventional version of Plato *Rep.* 509 b; yet he has given man knowledge of his own eternity. Similar statements can be found in Eusebius; but when carefully examined, Eusebius proves to be passing on two quite distinct traditions. First, he reproduces the old apologetic assertion that *all* men are really theists;[7] this appears very clearly in *ET* 1.20.6, τὸν δὲ ἐπὶ πάντων Θεὸν φυσικαῖς ἐννοίαις ἅπαντες ὁμολογοῦσιν ἄνθρωποι, which of course conflicts very sharply with the doctrine of an unknowable God. But secondly, there are relics of the tradition found in Philo of an ideal and sinless first man, incorporeal and asexual and naturally en-

---

[7] Minucius Felix *Oct.* 19, Eusebius *PE* 2.6.11, *ET* 1.20.6.

dowed with the knowledge of God. So Eusebius writes, *PE* 7.17.3: τῶν ἐν ἡμῖν τὸ μέν τι φασὶ θεῖον καὶ ἀθάνατον, ἄσαρκον τὴν φύσιν καὶ ἀσώματον, τοῦτον δὲ καὶ τὸν ἀληθῆ τυγχάνειν ἄνθρωπον, κατ' εἰκόνα θεοῦ καὶ ὁμοίωσιν γεγενημένον: and this ideal man is sharply distinguished from the earth-born Adam of Genesis 2 and 3. Athanasius here is simpler and more consistent; Adam for him is morally perfect, but he is a man like ourselves, equipped with a body and subject to bodily desires when he neglects his vocation of contemplating God. But Athanasius again is not wholly consistent; his combination of traditions presents us with an Adam who is supposed to be perfect, but whose virtue and spirituality is in fact corruptible.

3.2. Secondly, where do we possess the knowledge of God? 'In the soul,' seems the obvious answer. Athanasius is clearly affected by the idealized view of the soul propounded in Plato' *Phaedo*, which attributes true perceptions to the soul and makes the body the source of error.[8] This view is developed in *CG* 2–4, and appears again in 31–4. God is incorporeal, and knowledge of God depends upon our dissociating ourselves from corporeal things, *CG* 2.3. Athanasius even affirms that the body 'could not consider what is outside itself—οὐκ ἂν τὰ ἔξωθεν ἑαυτοῦ λογίζοιτο—for it is mortal and transitory,' c. 32. In c. 4 he says, more reasonably, that our bodily members can be occupied *either* with reality *or* with unreality; our eyes *can* be used to admire the creation, and our ears to listen to the laws of God. But this point is soon forgotten; Athanasius continues to point out the religious benefits of our sense of sight without reminding us that our eyes are parts of the body.[9]

3.3. When Athanasius idealizes the soul, he almost invariably refers to it as the seat of reason, *nous*. The notion that man perceives God through his *nous* is especially frequent in the early chapters of the *CG*, for instance when he declares Adam κατὰ τὴν ἀρχὴν ἀναισχύντῳ παρρησίᾳ τὸν νοῦν ἐσχηκέναι πρὸς τὸν Θεόν, 2.4. Eusebius takes the same view, which of course is exceedingly common and is well represented in Philo, for instance in *opif.* 69, where the *nous* takes the place of God's image in man: ἡ δὲ εἰκὼν λέλεκται κατὰ τὸν τῆς ψυχῆς ἡγεμόνα νοῦν. The connection of soul and mind is variously represented; in their idealized state they can be simply coupled together; so Eusebius *PE* 3.10.16, ψυχὴ λογικὴ ... καὶ νοῦς ἀπαθής: and Athanasius alludes to the Logos who sees both soul and mind, *DI* 14.4. Sometimes the mind seems to be conceived as part of the soul, or its directive part; so *CG* 34, men can ascend, ἀναβῆναι, τῷ νῷ τῆς ψυχῆς; thus the soul consorts with angels 'confident in the purity of its mind,' τῇ τοῦ νοῦ θαρροῦσα καθαρότητι, ibid. 33. Much the same view can be suggested without explicit reference to the *nous*; the phrase ψυχὴ λογική is common enough in Athanasius, as it is in Eu-

---

[8] *Op.cit.*, 64 c–67 d; cf. Eusebius *PE* 2.6.12f., 3.10.15.
[9] Athanasius *CG* 4.4, 35f., 40 fin., 45; *DI* 12.3, 32.1, 45.3.

sebius; and both authors use intellectualist terms like ἔννοια, κατανοεῖν and λογίζεσθαι to indicate our knowledge of God, together with associated metaphors like θεωρεῖν and θεωρία, and the Platonic image of the *nous* as ὄμμα τῆς ψυχῆς, to which I shall return.

The use of the actual word ὁρᾶν is naturally rather more restricted, but it does occur, encouraged perhaps by the quotation of Mt. 5:8, in *CG* 2: in its state of innocence, the mind is raised aloft, ἄνω μετάρσιος γίνεται, καὶ τὸν Λόγον ἰδών, ὁρᾷ ἐν αὐτῷ καὶ τὸν τοῦ Λόγου Πατέρα. Conversely, in c. 7 the guilty soul is described as καμμύσασα τὸν ὀφθαλμὸν δι᾽ οὗ τὸν Θεὸν ὁρᾶν δύναται, a biblical phrase often repeated in his later works.

Athanasius thus appears to treat the *nous*, not only as the eye of the soul, but as its only source of good impulses. I think he only once refers to other powers in the soul in complimentary terms.[10] Accordingly, as Charles Kannengiesser has observed, when Athanasius comes to speak of human corruption, it is always the soul that is involved; so *CG* 3.4, 4.4, and *DI* 11.4, ἐθόλωσαν ἑαυτῶν τὴν ψυχήν. The soul is infected when it rebels against the guidance of the *nous*, or when it neglects to keep its attention fixed on God; but there seems to be no suggestion that the *nous* itself can be corrupted. No suggestion, that is, within this particular topic of discussion; in practice, when criticizing his opponents, Athanasius is quite ready to say that their minds are unsound, οὐχ ὑγιαίνοντες, or crippled, πεπηρωμένοι, or perverse, διαστρέφεσθαι;[11] and there is a mention of the corrupt *nous* of 2 Tim. 3:8 in the Letter to Adelphius, c. 1.

But the optimistic view of *nous* is reflected in what Athanasius says about *noēta*; these are always presented as ideal realities and truths—which indeed is the normal use of the term. In the *CG* 4 there seems to be no distinction drawn between ἀποστῆναι τῆς τῶν νοητῶν θεωρίας and ἀποστῆναι τῆς πρὸς τὰ καλὰ θεωρίας, and both these phrases seem to be equivalent to the ἀποστρέφεσθαι τὴν πρὸς τὸν Θεὸν θεωρίαν of *DI* 15.1, or indeed ἀποστρέφεσθαι τὸν Θεόν, ibid. 11.4.

3.4. A specially striking phrase which appears at the end of *CG* 2 claims that the purity of the soul is capable of reflecting God through itself as in a mirror: ἱκανὴ δὲ ἡ τῆς ψυχῆς καθαρότης ἐστὶ καὶ τὸν Θεὸν δι᾽ ἑαυτῆς κατοπτρίζεσθαι. This brings together three suggestive ideas: (a) the self-sufficiency of the soul, (b) its purity, and (c), the metaphor of the mirror.

(a) The self-sufficiency theme recurs in c. 30, slightly modified by biblical texts which limit its application to Christians, who have faith and have the kingdom of God within them. In c. 2 the claim is far bolder; the context sug-

---

[10] Ἐπιθυμία condemned, *CG* 34 al.; with θυμός, *Vit. Ant.* 21 init; contrast *Ep. ad Marc.* 27, *PG* 27, 40A.

[11] Soul corrupted, *CG* 3.4, 4.4, *DI* 11.4. Mind corrupted, *Decr.* 21, *Dion.* 12.3, *c. Ar.* i.2.

gests that the soul's power of rising above perceptible things, which the body desires, and consorting with itself—ἑαυτῷ συνών—makes it capable of uniting with the divine and intelligible realities in heaven, just as Adam 'associated with the saints in the contemplation of intelligible reality,' ἐν τῇ τῶν νοητῶν θεωρίᾳ. Athanasius appears to draw no distinction between the soul's contemplation of the *noēta* and its contemplation of the Logos, in whom the Father himself can be seen.

(b) The theme of purity in the soul is of course a very common one, which indeed Athanasius has already mentioned earlier, in *CG* 2. There is a biblical basis in Wisdom 7:24, though strange to say the noun καθαρότης occurs only once in the New Testament, where it refers to the flesh, and not at all in Philo. Purity is closely associated with knowledge; so Eusebius *DE* 4.8.3, νῷ διαυγεῖ καὶ ψυχῇ κεκαθαρμένῃ, followed by Athanasius *Decr.* 24, καθαρᾷ τῇ ψυχῇ καὶ μόνῳ τῷ νῷ. More exactly, both authors associate purity with the so-called 'eye of the soul,' which needs to be cleansed in order to contemplate reality: the ὄμμα τῆς ψυχῆς of Plato *Rep.* 508, 533 d. Plato speaks here (and at 540 a) of redirecting or of training the eye; but the metaphor of cleansing is used at 527 d and is again suggested when he speaks of removing accretions from the soul, ibid. 611. The metaphor is used by Eusebius at *PE* 2.4.4. and again at 2.6.12, διανοίας ὄμμασι κεκαθαρμένοις ... συνενόησαν. Athanasius imitates this phrase with the slight rewording ὀφθαλμὸς τῆς διανοίας, *CG* 27, *DI* 30, and the metaphor of intellectual vision is quite elaborately developed in *CG* 34 and *DI* 57, where Dr. Meijering aptly compares Plotinus 1.6.9; the eye cannot see the sun unless it becomes sunlike.

(c) Athanasius associates the pure eye of the soul with the metaphor of a mirror, κάτοπτρον, *CG* 2, 8, and 34. This has a complex history, which includes Wisdom 7:26, where the word is ἔσοπτρον: Philo *migr.* 98, which shows that the comparison of the soul to a mirror, κάτοπτρον, was an accepted commonplace in his day; and St. Paul, especially the much discussed phrase in 2 Cor. 3:18, ἀνακεκαλυμμένῳ προσώπῳ τὴν δόξαν τοῦ κυρίου κατοπτριζόμενοι. Scholars have been unable to decide whether κατοπτριζόμενοι means 'beholding' or 'reflecting'; the verb is something of a rarity, though it occurs in Philo *L.A.* 3.101, where the sense 'beholding' is the more natural. Bettter evidence can be found in Christian authors, who are naturally drawn to the arresting phrases of St. Paul. Meijering refers to Theophilus and Clement; of whom Theophilus undoubtedly provides the closer parallel, since he connects the mirror with cleansing our eyes so that we can see the sun (*Aut.* 1.2; cf. *CG* 34, *DI* 57). In my opinion, however, the most important parallels are found in Gregory Thaumaturgus and in Eusebius. Gregory describes the soul learning to contemplate itself as in a mirror and thus beholding the divine mind: αὐτῆς τῆς ψυχῆς ἑαυτὴν ὥσπερ ἐν κατόπτρῳ ὁρᾶν μελετώσης, καὶ τὸν θεῖον νοῦν ... ἐν ἑαυτῇ κατοπτριζομένης (*pan.Or.* 11.142). Eusebius quotes a passage from the *First Alcibiades* of Plato (p. 133, at *PE* 11.27.5) where the full text adds some suggestive new touches to the comparison. The eye itself is a mirror, since one can see things reflected in the pupil of the eye (133 a); in fact, says Socrates, the eye can only see itself in some such way; nevertheless there are better mirrors available (133 c); likewise, although the soul itself is a mirror in which it can see itself, the purest and brightest mirror is the god who is present within it. We shall criticize this reasoning a little later; for the moment, we note that this passage suggests, more clearly than most, that there is an identity between the observer and the reflecting medium. I think we can conclude that there is no point in discussing the precise significance of κατοπτρίζεσθαι in 2 Cor., since the whole comparison turns on the claim that the soul can observe itself as in a mirror. It follows that the soul, as observer, sees itself, but the soul, as observed, reflects itself. Both senses are perfectly appropriate. *Cadit quaestio*.

3.5. As a footnote to what I have called the optimistic theory, we need to note a contrasting perspective which comes into view in the *DI*. Two points we have noted so far are the natural purity of the soul expounded in *CG* 2, and the suggestion that the crucial move in attaining a knowledge of God is the ascent from *aisthēta* to *noēta*. On the first point, the *DI* seems to present a sharp corrective, in cc. 3−4 and 11−12. Here the whole human race is seen as handicapped by its created and its corporeal nature, which make it incapable of continuing in existence, let alone attaining a conception and knowledge of God, without special assistance; so that their share in God's image results from an additional act of pity (ἐλέησας) independent of their creation (πλέον τι χαριζόμενος, c. 3). As in the *CG*, they have an ability which is sufficient, αὐτάρκης, to provide the knowledge of God; but in the *DI* this is not the natural purity of the soul, but a special gift of grace, ἡ κατ' εἰκόνα χάρις (c. 12), designed to offset its inherent weakness. As to the second point, it seems that in the *DI* Athanasius simply loses interest in the *noēta*; they are not mentioned; in fact there are only two further references to them, it appears, in all Athanasius' personal output.

It would be very easy to interpret this contrast as a divergence between the two works, assuming a more Platonic standpoint in the *CG*, perhaps inspired by Eusebius, as against a more biblical perspective in the *DI*. But this would be a serious mistake. For first, the theme of human incapacity is clearly stated in the *CG* itself, in c. 35: God is above all created being, whereas the human race was created from nothing, so that they were liable to be deprived (ἀτυχεῖν) of knowledge of him. And this theme of natural incapacity is already foreshadowed in Eusebius; see for instance *DE* 4.6.6, the Father appointed the Logos ὡς ἂν μὴ παντελῶς ἡ τῶν γενητῶν ἀποπέσοι φύσις, δι' οἰκείαν ἀτονίαν καὶ ἀδυναμίαν τῆς ἀγενήτου καὶ ἀχωρήτου πατρικῆς οὐσίας διεστῶσα. Similar teaching is found in the *Laus Constantini*, which of course I would not claim was prior to the *CG*; in contrast to the divine being, human nature was ἐξ οὐκ ὄντων προβεβλημένη πορρωτάτω τε διεστῶσα καὶ μακρὸν τῆς ἀγεννήτου φύσεως ἀπεσχοινισμένη (c. 11). This contrast is a mere commonplace, and is probably more typical of Eusebius than the theme of ideal human innocence, which, we have seen, is not represented by the earth-born Adam, and is later displayed only occasionally by virtuous heroes like Enosh.

As for the status of *noēta*, there are favourable estimates to be found in Eusebius, as at *PE* 3.10.11, where he argues that even the works of God's creation are σμικρὰ ἔτι καὶ βραχέα, ταῖς ἀσωμάτοις καὶ νοεραῖς οὐσίαις παραβαλλόμενα. But there are two striking passages at least where he puts the opposite case; at 11.21.6, expounding Plato *Rep.* 509 b, he claims that the νοηταί οὐσίαι derive their being from the transcendent Goodness, ὥστε μὴ ὁμοούσια αὐτὰ τίθεσθαι, ἀλλὰ μηδὲ ἀγέννητα νομίζειν. At 13.15.3 he complains of Plato's inconsistency, in first making the intelligibles ἀγενήτους, but then saying that they derive by emanation from the first cause: οὐδὲ γὰρ ἐκ τοῦ μὴ ὄντος αὐτὰς γεγονέναι διδόναι βούλεται.

Thus what we provisionally noted as new points in the *DI* are in fact anticipated in Eusebius. But I do not wish to argue that Athanasius introduced corrections as a result of reading Eusebius. It seems to me more likely that both writers are inconsistent because they reproduce conflicting items of traditional teaching without noticing the disharmonies that modern scholars detect.

4. We have tried to describe the teaching of Athanasius and Eusebius on our knowledge of God, with frequent quotation from both writers. But to complete the picture, we need to stand back a little and ask ourselves how much we have learnt, and what questions still need to be asked. Granted that we have a share in God's image, the Logos, how is this εἰκών, or more properly the state of being κατ᾽ εἰκόνα, manifested in our minds, and what effects does it produce?

4.1. This teaching is clearly built on the traditional maxim that like is known by like. I have not yet discovered an explicit statement of this general principle either in Origen or Eusebius or Athanasius; but it is clearly presupposed by a phrase we cited from *CG* 2, διὰ τῆς πρὸς αὐτὸν ὁμοιώσεως; and it underlies the striking illustration of *DI* 57, where Athanasius claims that in order to look at the sun one must cleanse the eye so that it becomes bright; in the background is Plato's theory of vision propounded in *Timaeus* 45, as well as the passage cited by Dr. Meijering, Plotinus 1.6.9, Posidonius in Sextus 7.93, and Irenaeus 4.36.6.

As a theory of vision, this is plainly mistaken. Good sight requires good clear eyes, rather than eyes which resemble their objects. It is no advantage to be dim-sighted if one is trying to decipher faded and illegible writing. But in the intellectual and moral field there is rather more to be said for the theory;

one cannot appreciate intelligence unless one is in some degree intelligent, or unselfishness if one is wholly self-regarding. And we can appreciate the mistakes and confusions of other people, not indeed by simply sharing them, but by intelligent reflection on our own.

Origen does indeed suggest that we can learn something about God simply by reflecting on the nature of the mind, *ex nostrae mentis contemplatione*; the mind has no need of space in which to move, or of physical magnitude, or of visible appearance (*Princ.* 1.1.6–7). This claim suggests a purely theoretical consideration, a psychology, for which good moral dispositions are not required; but it is generally taken for granted that the use of the intellect implies a detachment from bodily concerns and an attachment to pure and intelligible virtues; thus Origen continues: *quod propinquitas quaedam sit mentis ad deum, cuius ipsa mens intellectualis imago sit, et per hoc possit aliquid de deitatis natura sentire, maxime si expurgatior sit a natura corporali.* Rather similar indications are given in *Cels.* 7.33.

The modern critic may well be surprised to learn that the mind can apprehend theological truth by mere discursive reflection on itself and its activities; he might argue, moreover, that the Fathers held that God is perfectly simple; thus on the principle that like is known by like, they *must* have recommended some form of simplification or concentration of thought such as was advocated by Plotinus. There are indeed some passages which might allow this interpretation, such as *CG* 2; but on the whole I think the texts do not encourage it. The Fathers worked mainly with a fairly simple antithesis of body and mind. If sensual thoughts are discarded and the mind be occupied with itself and its own proper objects, they make no further demand. I have found no texts of our period which clearly suggest that some intellectual pursuits should be embraced and others avoided. And their doctrine that the Father must be approached through the Logos would seem to exclude any depreciation of expressed and formulated thought in favour of a Plotinian simplicity of formless contemplation.

Does the mind's likeness to God entitle us actually to describe God as mind? This was a much debated problem. On the whole, Origen accepts this view; God is *intellectualis natura simplex*, *Princ.* 1.1.6, as rendered by Rufinus.[12] Eusebius is more cautious, and reveals his hesitations at *PE* 3.10.3–4; one must not think of God as a kind of directive mind residing within the world. However at *ET* 2.17.4 he appeals to the commonplace that the human mind is mysterious, though its operations are familiar.[13] This enables him to say, surprisingly, that God's Logos is comprehensible to all men, τοῖς ἐκτός

---

[12] God as Mind, Origen *Princ.* 1.1.6 a., Eus. *PE* 3.10.14, but cf. ibid. 10.3.

[13] Mind mysterious, though its actions familiar: Philo *LA* 1.91, *Mut. Nom.* 10, *Somn.* 1.30, 56; Eus. *ET* 2.17.4.

πᾶσιν καθίσταται γνώριμος, while he refers to the Father as τόν ἀφανῆ καὶ ἀόρατον νοῦν. This tradition, however, does not make even the Father completely unknowable; as we have observed, he can be 'seen' by the transclucent mind and soul; as Athanasius puts it, καθαρᾷ τῇ ψυχῇ καὶ μόνῳ τῷ νῷ.[14]

4.2. If we now ask, what sort of activity will enable us to receive virtue and wisdom, the answer would seem to be, by meditating on their celestial prototypes conceived on the model of Platonic Forms, but also vaguely personalized and sometimes assimilated to the angels. In other words, it is usually a contemplative devotion that is required, with practical good works thrown in as a laudable but regretted interruption. There is seldom any suggestion that we might profitably imitate the Logos in his creative and providential functions; our authors never suggest that the artist or craftsman may gain a distinctive knowledge of the Logos through the exercize of his professional skill; the painter in particular remains a source of literary metaphors rather than a respected fellow-traveller on the heavenly road. Regarded in this light, is there not after all something to be said for what we all instinctively detest, namely the sycophantic comparisons which Eusebius draws between the Logos and the Emperor?

4.3. We have referred to the imagery of the mirror. Athanasius teaches that man, in his original state of innocence, can gain knowledge of the Logos by considering his own mind, an activity which we still refer to as reflection or introspection. It is of course misleading to think of self-awareness as a kind of sense-perception; as the ancients clearly recognized, each of our senses has its own distinctive sense-qualities; see for instance Origen Princ. 1.1.7; but self-awareness can involve them all. Sometimes, it may be, I take notice of my own visual experience; but alternatively, I may catch myself recalling a melody; the idea that I *see* what is going on within my mind is obviously absurd in the latter case, so it should be excluded also in the former.

On the other hand, it was a commonplace that sight is the best of the senses; and it is often used metaphorically for other kinds of knowledge. Visual metaphors turn up in the most unexpected places. One example is the statement found in the CG that we have a φαντασία θεοῦ. In this context φαντασία must of course indicate a true impression, a sense which the PGL does not record;[15] it occurs five of six times in the CG (c. 2 twice, 7, 9, 45) but elsewhere in Athanasius only at c. Ar. 2.78, conjoined with τύπος, as the image of himself which the divine Wisdom impresses on creation. But I have found two examples in Eusebius (PE 7.17.5, LC 4) and it is not uncommon in Philo; an es-

---

[14] God knowable by mind: Eus. DE 4.8.3 (?), PE 3.10.18; Ath. Decr. 24.
[15] Φαντασία reliable (tacet PGL!): Philo Opif. 166, LA 3.61, Heres 119, Mut. Nom. 3; Eus. PE 7.17.5, LC 4; Ath. CG 2.2 (twice), 7.3, 9.2, 45, c. Ar. ii.78. This usage is common in Greek philosophy; see LSJ.

pecially interesting parallel is *Mut. Nom.* 3, τὸ δεχόμενον τὴν θείαν φαντασίαν τὸ τῆς ψυχῆς ἐστιν ὄμμα, and *LA* 3.61 takes the self-exculpation of Eve in Gen. 3:13 to mean that the sense-qualities, symbolized by Eve, are trustworthy, whereas pleasure, the serpent, is a deceiver. Visual symbolism is very commonly used in discussing the knowledge of God, and if we wish to find in Athanasius an acceptable use of it, we must somehow discount the misleading implications of the idea that the mind sees itself. Some writers indeed maintain the opposite view, perhaps alluding to Socrates' parable of the eye seeing its own reflection; for of course, although the eye can see itself reflected in *an* eye, it cannot see itself reflected in itself, unless we imagine that it is reflected three times in succession. Hence, it was said, the eye can see everything else, but not itself; similarly the mind can know everything, but not itself (Philo, *LA* 1.91). This tradition is reproduced in those writers who hold both that God is mind, and that God is unknown.

Nevertheless we should not underestimate Athanasius. He is admittedly limited by the idiom of his own time; but we must not think that every inconsistency is a sign of incompetence; we must allow for deliberate paradox, or perhaps rather the willing acceptance of traditional paradox; an example, I think, is *CG* 2, where Athanasius in effect tells us that the soul can rise above itself by remaining within itself: ὅτε ὅλος ἐστὶν [ἄνω] ἑαυτῷ συνων ... τότε δὴ ... ἄνω μετάρσιος γίνεται.

Eusebius again tells us (*PE* 7.17.5) that man was created in the image and likeness of God μετά τινος διαφερούσης ὑπεροχῆς, as compared with the animals: διὸ καὶ θεοῦ ἐννοίας εἰς φαντασίαν ἰέναι σοφίας τε καὶ δικαιοσύνης καὶ πάσης ἀρετῆς ἀντιλήψεις ποιεῖσθαι, and then after recalling the story of our transgression (ἐντολῆς ὀλιγωρία, πλημμελεῖν, ἀποσφάλλειν) he adds: διὸ χρῆναι τὸ καθαρὸν αὖθις καὶ τὸ θεοείκελον ἀνακτήσασθαι τῆς ἐν ἡμῖν νοερᾶς οὐσίας.

The basic theory of our knowledge of God is, I believe, very simple. It is that in a state of innocence we have an idea of God, as Father or Ruler or Supreme Being, and we possess virtues such as wisdom and justice, implanted by God's Logos, which we also attribute to God, thus giving content to our basic ἔννοια. But the theory is complicated, partly by the confusing influence of the notion that the mind can *see* itself, and so *see* reflections of the divine Logos; and partly by the confusions attaching to the phrase νοερὰ οὐσία. For it seems that a thing can qualify to be νοερὰ οὐσία simply by being, as we should say, mental or psychological in character. On this interpretation, very little is gained if we say that our human virtues are νοεραὶ οὐσίαι; this *could* mean that they are mere illusions. But Eusebius and Athanasius will think that we only recognize these virtues by relating them to their divine archetype; hence to see them within ourselves is also to be carried beyond ourselves to the realm of *noēta*, the objective and eternal Forms of all things. But even this is not the end of the story, at least for Eusebius. For it is possible to see these *noēta* as created beings, comparable with the angels, but not *homoousios* with God. And Athanasius passes quite easily from the thought of τοῦ νοῦν ἐσχηκέναι πρὸς τὸν Θεόν to that of συνδιαιτᾶσθαι τοῖς ἁγίοις ἐν τῇ τῶν νοητῶν θεωρίᾳ, which seems to suggest that unfallen man can associate with the angels in the contemplation of a higher reality. Wisdom and Justice, then, are the created prototypes of human virtues, sometimes depicted as the trees of the first intelligible paradise; but they are also ἐπίνοιαι of the Logos himself, who is αὐτοσοφία and αὐτοδικαιοσύνη.

In conclusion, I return to the problem which I raised at the beginning. My tentative opinion is that the ideal knowledge of the Logos, as described by Eusebius and Athanasius, is *not* based on any recognizably mystical experience, such as we detect in Philo and much more clearly, say, in Gregory of Nyssa. The evidence, which might suggest this is, I think, inadequate. Athanasius does of course recommend detachment from the body and its concerns; he is an enthusiast for the solitary life, as practised by Anthony; and he endorses the traditional theme that God is inexpressible and incomprehensible. But he makes no reference to the divine darkness of Sinai, such as we find in Philo and is creatively developed by Gregory of Nyssa. His ideal monk is no quietist, but is actively involved in noisy and troublesome encounters with demons. And it is interesting to note that he reinterprets Plato's maxim about philosophers practising death.[16] Plato thinks that philosophers should disregard the body and attend to the intelligible world, just as if they were finally freed from the body's distractions. Athanasius of course reproduces this idea; but he understands Plato's maxim as an injunction to prepare for martyrdom, which he regards almost as a social activity, so much stress is laid on the great company of ones fellow-sufferers for Christ. The encouragment to concern oneself with *noēta* suggests to me, not a distinctively mystical consciousness, but something much more like the traditional catholic practice of meditating on the cardinal virtues. And lastly, we should not build too much on his admission that the divine nature is inexpressible, for inexpressible knowledge is more commonplace than we are apt to suppose. Origen tells us that we can distinguish between tastes, though we have no words to describe them. Indeed even a dog can know the way to Larissa, if that is where his master lives; though to be sure, he cannot know that it *is* the way to Larissa! It may, then, be a necessary condition for knowledge of God that it be inexpressible; but it is certainly not a sufficient condition. This estimate of Athanasius, and of Eusebius too, may perhaps be criticized as robbing them of a distinction with which we would like to invest them; but it has the advantage of bringing them closer to realms of thought which we ourselves can understand.

---

[16] *Phaedo* 64 A, 67 E, 81 A; Ath. *DI* 27.3, 28.1. Cf. Philo *Gig.* 14, *Det.* 34, Iren. fr. 11, Clement *Str.* 3.17.5, 4.58.2 (which anticipates Athanasius' literalist interpretation), 5.67.2.

LES DIEUX ET LE DIVIN DANS LES MYSTÈRES DE MITHRA

PAR

ROBERT TURCAN (LYON)

I

En remerciant mes collègues hollandais pour m'avoir invité à célébrer les 70
lustres de leur prestigieuse université, je voudrais d'abord rendre hommage à
la mémoire de notre regretté collègue et ami, le professeur Martin J. Vermaseren, qui a tant fait pour le progrès de nos études. Je voudrais aussi souligner
d'emblée l'opportunité des interrogations que nous propose le sujet du présent
colloque.

Car les historiens du polythéisme ont peut-être trop tendance à axer leurs en-
quêtes sur les rites, leurs modalités, leur signification ponctuelle, leurs variations ou leurs adaptations à telles situations connues, sans trop se préoccuper
le plus souvent de la notion que les Anciens pouvaient avoir des dieux et du
divin. Qu'est-ce qui différenciait fondamentalement, sur ce point, les représentations liées aux cultes romains traditionnels des croyances inhérentes aux
liturgies mystériques d'origine orientale?

On en a parlé, certes, en termes brillants et généraux. Les spécialistes ont ja-
dis et naguère esquissé, voire aventuré des hypothèses. A cet égard, certaines
pages de F. Cumont demeurent inoubliables et continuent de nous influencer.
Mais l'intérêt de notre colloque est de nous forcer à revoir les choses de plus
près, en mettant l'accent sur ce qui conditionne psychologiquement le culte et
la piété, sur ce qui en constitue la raison d'être. Il est évidemment plus facile
d'étudier le rituel que le spirituel. Tout ce qu'une religion positive a de voyant
et tangible en quelque sorte, surtout dans son expression populaire, est moins
discutable scientifiquement et mieux approprié que l'imaginaire mental aux in-
ductions qui ont les apparences de la rigueur historique.

Or il faut bien redire, même si c'est d'une plate évidence, que la documentation textuelle et figurée concernant le polythéisme gréco-romain est *cultuellement* foisonnante (quoiqu'inégalement explicite ou exploitée), mais *théo-
logiquement* décevante.

Sans doute, nous avons le témoignage des philosophes, des intellectuels ou
des rhéteurs. Mais leur discours abstrait, idéologique ou technique dissimule
ou transpose on ne sait quelle intuition du divin. Quant aux dédicaces, elles
gardent le secret des sentiments religieux que masque la routine des for-
mulaires, sauf exceptionnellement, lorsqu'une épithète, une épiclèse singulière

transcrivent tel aspect de la divinité qui tient au cœur du dévot. Même (et surtout) le *De natura deorum* de Cicéron ne nous dit rien finalement de l'idée
qu'on se faisait alors, qu'il se faisait lui-même de la «nature» des dieux: on a
même l'impression qu'il refusait de s'en faire une idée!

L'archéologie figurée et les expressions concrètes de la dévotion populaire
nous informent souvent beaucoup plus directement, sinon plus précisément,
du type de divin ou de divinité auquel correspondaient telle iconographie et tel
acte liturgique. Car même si la routine a du poids dans toute pratique religieuse (mais un poids qu'il convient d'analyser et d'interpréter différentielle-
ment, suivant les individus ou les contextes), on voue tel culte à une divinité
en fonction de l'idée qu'on se fait—même obscurément—de sa puissance, de
sa compétence, de sa bonté, de sa sollicitude, de son action dans les affaires
humaines. Le pharisaïsme le plus opaque, le ritualisme le plus mécanique impliquent toujours une certaine image (si pauvre qu'elle puisse être) du dieu
qu'on veut se concilier ou neutraliser. Le rite est un langage et l'iconographie
a le sien. Tout langage est conventionnel. Celui des théologiens n'est pas moins
extérieur que celui des monuments et des actes cultuels. Le traitement exégé-
tique de cette documentation apparemment muette et qu'il s'agit de faire parler a donc, me semble-t-il, sa légitimité.

II

Ce type d'enquête s'impose peut-être singulièrement à l'endroit des religions
d'origine orientale qui ont gagné différents secteurs du monde romain avant
et après notre ère, avec un succès inégal dans le temps et dans l'espace, suivant
les circonstances historiques et les milieux sociaux. Mais ce succès a coïncidé
presque toujours avec un nouvel état des esprits, avec une autre façon de poser
le problème de Dieu, des dieux et du divin, de la relation des dieux avec les
hommes et le monde, de leur place dans le monde, du sens de la vie et du destin.

Or de tous ces cultes d'origine orientale, celui de Mithra nous apparaît
comme le plus soucieux de répondre d'une façon à la fois claire et complexe,
imagée et systématique, mythique et quasiment philosophique aux questions
qui pouvaient préoccuper certaines couches de la population romaine ou
romanisée. La documentation mithriaque est par elle-même assez riche, mais
relativement homogène, assez homogène pour nous autoriser à induire du langage des stèles et des idoles les convictions fondamentales communes aux initiés. Elle est aussi plus explicite dans sa complexité même que l'iconographie
du culte métroaque, voire que celle des cultes égyptiens.

Il s'agit d'un culte polythéiste (Dieu sait si les polémistes chrétiens et si les
Mithraea consciencieusement saccagés au IVe siècle nous le rappellent avec in-

sistance).[1] Et pourtant ce polythéisme n'a rien à voir avec celui du paganisme classique, grec ou romain. Il suppose une tout autre conception de la pluralité du divin et du divin lui-même. Le mithriacisme se différencie aussi sur ce point des autres religions dites «orientales» comme des autres cultes à mystères. On a trop tendance depuis F. Cumont à uniformiser conceptuellement les cultes «orientaux» sous la rubrique d'une même typologie comme «religions de salut».[2] C'est encore plus vrai en général du polythéisme gréco-romain que les apologistes chrétiens nous ont trop habitués à considérer comme un tout solidaire et homogène.

III

Il n'y a pas un polythéisme, mais des polythéismes dans le paganisme gréco-romain des premiers siècles de notre ère. Tous les dieux ne sont pas sur le même plan dans la conscience et la pratique religieuses des idolâtres, et quel que soit leur niveau de pensée. Tous les cultes comportent ou impliquent une hiérarchie, même le culte romain traditionnel où cependant les *numina* détiennent chacun une compétence précise, leur part de puissance sur laquelle aucun autre ne saurait empiéter.

Très tôt s'affirme une tendance à reconnaître une sorte d'homologie fondamentale et nécessaire entre la monarchie céleste du «dieu grand» ou «très grand», comme l'appelle Celse, et la souveraineté terrestre de l'*imperator*. Aux IIe et IIIe siècles de notre ère convergent les aspirations jusqu'alors diffuses ou diversement ressenties à cette cohérence, dans une vision solidaire des mondes humain et divin qui finira par s'imposer dans les milieux intellectuels.

Mais, parallèlement à cette idéologie, la piété quotidienne contribue à transformer certains aspects du paganisme. A lire tels témoignages de la tradition littéraire ou épigraphique, on a le sentiment que les individus affectionnent souvent un dieu, une déesse, et que la religion personnelle tend vers une forme d'hénothéisme ou plutôt vers une pluralité d'hénothéismes aussi divers que les adorateurs. Il ne s'agit pas toujours d'hénothéismes à strictement parler, c'est-à-dire de systèmes théologiques consacrant la suprématie d'une divinité; car même si un Romain considère Jupiter comme souverain du ciel et du monde, il peut concentrer son attention cultuelle sur un dieu qu'il sait inférieur, mais qui importe directement, actuellement et singulièrement à sa vie. Dans le courant de son existence, un païen de l'époque impériale peut d'ailleurs changer de dévotion, suivant la conjoncture, et privilégier successivement des déités différentes. Mais il n'adore pas tous les dieux en même temps ni avec la même

---

[1] R. Turcan, Les motivations de l'intolérance chrétienne et la fin du mithriacisme au IVe siècle ap. J.-C., *Actes du VIIe Congrès de la F.I.E.C.*, II, Budapest 1983, 224.

[2] R. Turcan, Salut mithriaque et sotériologie néoplatonicienne, dans: *La Soteriologia dei culti orientali nell'Impero Romano* (EPRO, 92), Leyde 1982, 173 ss.

ferveur. Dans le temps comme dans l'espace, les dieux s'ordonnent et se subordonnent cultuellement suivant une hiérarchie mouvante, en fonction de préférences personnelles ou circonstancielles.

L'une des caractéristiques essentielles des religions «orientales» est justement qu'elles majorent toutes (avec des variantes plus ou moins significatives) l'importance, la puissance d'un dieu ou d'une déesse, d'un couple ou d'une triade. Mais dans les couples, comme dans les triades, une divinité a la prééminence: Isis, Cybèle, Jupiter Dolichénien ou Jupiter Héliopolitain. A cet égard, le dionysisme des Orphiques et plus tard des mystères bacchiques marquait déjà fortement la prépondérance d'un dieu dans le mythe fondateur.

Une distinction fondamentale s'impose à l'endroit de ces cultes par rapport aux positions philosophiques ou aux prédilections personnelles, quelles qu'en aient pu être les motivations: un mythe fonde et légitime la supériorité de Mithra, de Cybèle ou d'Isis, un mythe que la philosophie païenne tend souvent à rationaliser. Ce mythe fondateur est solidaire d'une cosmologie et d'une sotériologie qui donnent un sens à la vie comme à la mort du myste.

C'est bien là précisément ce qui exaspère certains chrétiens comme Firmicus Maternus, lorsque dans son *De errore profanarum religionum* il reproche aux cultes orientaux la déification systématique des quatre éléments.[3] Chez chacun des peuples incriminés, un élément prévaut sur tous les autres: l'eau chez les Egyptiens, la terre chez les Phrygiens, l'air chez les Syro-Phéniciens, le feu chez les Perses. Et une *ratio physica* justifie chaque fois cette primauté en même temps qu'elle étaye philosophiquement la liturgie des mystères. L'apologiste déplore dans cet hénothéisme le fait de substituer la créature au créateur, même si en réalité ils se confondent dans le cas de la Terre, mère des dieux. Mais il est assez remarquable qu'il dénonce globalement cette tendance des religions orientales à centrer la piété sur une déité fondamentale. En fait, il s'en prend moins à leur théologie et aux artifices de l'allégorie qu'à l'idolâtrie. Comme aux autres chrétiens du IVe siècle, c'est un problème de *praxis* cultuelle[4] que posent à Firmicus les variantes du paganisme. Car lorsqu'avec d'autres apologistes il parle d'un *summus deus*,[5] on a l'impression que le Dieu de Firmicus est certes un dieu souverain, mais auquel restent subordonnées certaines puissances divines, et donc que son christianisme est en un sens aussi une forme d'hénothéisme. On en dira autant du Dieu d'Arnobe.[6] Harnack disait qu'au IVe siècle le christianisme et le paganisme avaient deux mythologies, mais une seule théologie ....[7]

---

[3] R. Turcan (éd.-trad.), *Firmicus Maternus, L'erreur des religions païennes*, dans: la Coll. des Universités de France, Paris 1982, 34 ss.

[4] Turcan, Les motivations, 211 ss.

[5] Turcan, *Firmicus Maternus*, 179 s.

[6] *Adv.Nat.*, I, 26; VII, 35.

[7] Cité par E.R. Dodds, *Pagan and Christian in an Age of Anxiety*, Cambridge 1965, 118, n. 5.

IV

Cependant, cette façon qu'a le polémiste chrétien de solidariser les cultes levantins ne doit pas nous faire illusion,[8] non plus d'ailleurs que les généralisations analogiques et simplifiantes des historiens modernes. Il y a des différences notables entre les hénothéismes propres à ces religions «orientales». La prééminence de Cybèle est originelle et invariable, comme celle des dieux syriens (Jupiter Héliopolitain, Hadad et surtout Elagabal), ce qui n'est le cas ni d'Isis ni de Mithra. Isis s'est légitimée dans et par une histoire, par la quête, le remembrement et la revivification d'Osiris qui garantit celle de ses fidèles. Mais la déesse s'est légitimée seule et une fois pour toutes, comme souveraine du monde, *regina caeli*, comme la dénomme Apulée.[9]

Dans le mythe et l'iconographie mithriaques s'affirme au départ une succession de prééminences, un cycle du divin en devenir, qui rappelle celui des théogonies grecques et notamment de la théogonie orphique.[10] Les stèles à scènes multiples nous montrent presque toutes inévitablement la séquence des dieux qui assument chacun à tour de rôle une responsabilité dans l'histoire du monde.

C'est d'abord Saturne qui règne souverainement, puis Jupiter à qui il remet l'arme absolue, le foudre qui lui permettra de terrasser les géants anguipèdes, démons du désordre et du mal.[11] Après quoi, c'est Mithra qui émerge du roc, qui occupe le premier plan pour faire jaillir la source miraculeuse et fructifier la végétation. Il y a donc mutation de souveraineté dans le cosmos, en ce sens que Mithra prend le monde en charge, même si Jupiter reste le dieu suprême qui domine la geste du Tauroctone du haut de l'Olympe sur les stèles de Sarrebourg et d'Osterburken,[12] par exemple. A chaque étape de la grande aventure de l'Etre correspondent une ou plusieurs figures divines. C'est la séquence que paraît illustrer le grand relief d'Osterburken: Saturne, Kronos ou Chronos, c'est-à-dire le Temps originel; puis le Ciel et la Terre; les Parques ou le Destin; Jupiter foudroyant les démons anguipèdes, peut-être l'Océan (si l'on admet l'identification traditionnelle);[13] enfin Mithra qui sort du rocher.

Ce qui distingue essentiellement le cycle mithriaque des théogonies grecques, c'est d'abord qu'il est orienté, commandé par la vigilance divine envers les êtres vivants et qu'il débouche sur l'action directe d'un dieu dans le monde.

---

[8] Contrairement à ce qu'affirmait F. Cumont, *Les religions orientales dans le paganisme romain*, Paris ⁴1929, 189.

[9] *Met.*, XI, 2, 1. Cf. le commentaire de J.G. Griffiths (*EPRO*, 39), Leyde 1975, 114 s.

[10] O. Kern, *Orphicorum fragmenta*, Berlin ²1963, 130 ss., n°s 54−59.

[11] R. Merkelbach, *Mithras*, Meisenheim 1984, 107 s. (où le mythe est censé correspondre au grade du Lion: ?).

[12] *CIMRM*, I, n°966; II, n°1292; R. Merkelbach, *op.cit.*, 350 s., fig. 112.

[13] *CIMRM*, II, p. 119, n°1292, 4 f.: «Reclining Oceanus». Il s'agit d'une représentation différente de celle qu'on trouve sur la stèle d'Heddernheim (*CIMRM*, II, p. 77, n°1127 C), avec l'inscription: *Oceanum*.

C'est ensuite que ce processus concorde avec le cours inéluctable des astres, fréquemment représentés au-dessus de Mithra tauroctone. Cette histoire du salut s'accomplit conformément à un ordre bio-cosmique en quelque sorte providentiel. D'autres dissemblances évidentes distinguent plus spécialement Mithra des autres dieux grecs ou gréco-romains. Le dieu naît de la pierre miraculeusement, sans l'union d'un couple divin, comme dans les autres théogonies; sans l'intervention d'une femme ni de l'amour, quoi qu'en écrive saint Jérôme qui assimile indûment cette pétrogénèse à l'histoire d'Erichthonios.[14] Mithra surgit comme une émanation nouvelle du divin pour sauvegarder la vie dans le monde. Enfin, cette incarnation est celle d'un dieu qui assume désormais la responsabilité du monde, celle d'un *kosmokratôr*.[15] L'échelle symbolique et mystérique dont nous parle Celse[16] représente une semaine sidérale à l'envers, du samedi (c'est-à-dire de Saturne) au dimanche (jour du Soleil, donc de Mithra), et ce règne final du dieu de la lumière correspond à la prophétie des Mages dont Nigidius Figulus[17] et Lactance ont fait état.[18] La souveraineté de Mithra coïncide avec le salut final de la Création.

V

Ces mutations cycliques dans la prééminence de tel ou tel dieu sont corrélatives aux révolutions planétaires. Il ne s'agit pas d'un drame comme dans la gnose et les autres cultes orientaux, mais d'un processus solidaire du cosmos, comme en témoignent le cercle zodiacal et les autres représentations qui environnent la geste mithriaque.[19] Il ne s'agit pas non plus des vicissitudes de l'âme incarnée, comme dans l'exégèse allégorique appliquée par l'empereur Julien[20] au mythe d'Attis mutilé et souffrant, mort et en quelque sorte «ressuscité».[21] Le dieu des mystères persiques n'est pas soumis aux épreuves d'une passion, comme Dionysos, comme Osiris ou l'amant de Cybèle. C'est le cosmos tout entier, toutes les créatures vivantes qui sont en cause et solidaires de l'action des dieux, du dieu invincible, dans l'histoire mithriaque.

---

[14] *Adv.Jovinian.*, 2, 14. Cf. M.J. Vermaseren, *The Miraculous Birth of Mithras, Studia Archaeol. G. Van Hoorn oblata*, Leyde 1951, 94.

[15] R. Turcan, *Mithras Platonicus (EPRO, 47)*, Leyde 1975, 78 s., 144 *add.* p. 82 s.

[16] *Ibid.*, 58 s. (Orig., *C. Cels.*, VI, 22).

[17] *Ibid.*, 56. Cf. A. Swoboda, *P. Nigidii Figuli operum reliquiae*, Amsterdam ²1964, 83, fr. 67.

[18] J. Bidez / F. Cumont, *les mages hellénisés*, Paris 1938, I, 218 s.; II, 370 s. (Hystaspe, fr. 15) et n. 3.

[19] R. Turcan, Le sacrifice mithriaque, dans: *Le sacrifice dans l'Antiquité (Entretiens sur l'Antiquité classique*, Fondation Hardt, 27), Vandoeuvres-Genève 1981, 363 s.

[20] Cf. en dernier lieu G. Sfameni Gasparro, *Soteriology and Mystic Aspects in the Cult of Cybele and Attis (EPRO, 103)*, Leyde 1985, 61 s.

[21] Cf. R. Turcan, *Numismatique romaine du culte métroaque (EPRO, 97)*, Leyde 1983, 51; Firm.Mat., *De err.prof.rel.*, III,1 (*revixisse*).

Cette action consomme et couronne l'œuvre des dieux. Mithra intervient et agit dans le monde pour le sauver: *salutaris*.[22] C'est le sacrifice du taureau, détenteur (semble-t-il) du principe humide d'origine lunaire,[23] qui revitalise la faune et la flore. Le chien, le serpent, le lion qui s'abreuvent au sang de la victime, les épis de blé qui s'épanouissent de sa blessure ou de sa queue, les arbres et leurs frondaisons ramifiées autour de la tauroctonie signifient assez clairement cette fonction régénératrice du sacrifice. Et le vers peint dans le *Mithraeum* de S. Prisca, même si la lecture de

Et nos servasti (a)eternali sanguine fuso

n'est pas intégralement assurée,[24] ne laisse aucun doute sur le rôle du Tauroctone qui préserve par l'effusion du sang divin la vie menacée des créatures.

A la différence des autres dieux du paganisme gréco-romain, Mithra s'intéresse à la création, à toute la création. Il n'exauce pas tel ou tel fidèle, dans telle circonstance, pour répondre à un vœu, à une invocation occasionnelle. *Servasti* implique une intervention passée, dans l'histoire, une fois pour toutes et pour tous: *et nos* ....[25] Mithra ne surgit du rocher qu'en vue de cette action au service des êtres vivants. Elle n'est pas suscitée par une épreuve qui le rapprocherait des mortels, comme c'est le cas pour Isis ou Déméter. Déméter souffre de la disparition de sa fille, elle refuse la loi de Zeus, et c'est la sollicitude de ses hôtes éleusiniens qui lui inspirera le don du blé et des mystères, du «bon espoir» aux initiés qu'attend un sort privilégié dans l'au-delà. Mais ni sa «passion», ni son intervention dans la vie et pour la vie des hommes ne procèdent d'une volonté providentielle. Mithra vient au secours des créatures pour obéir à une loi divine, pour l'accomplir, mais sans rien souffrir des épreuves humaines.

Dans le culte d'Isis, comme dans le culte de Cybèle, c'est la déesse qui sauve et qui prévaut sur le dieu, la déesse mère et épouse. Attis reste un dieu parèdre et subordonné, sauvé par Cybèle qui l'emporte au ciel et l'exalte finalement dans l'immortalité bienheureuse.[26] Ce n'est pas un dieu actif dans le monde et pour le monde, du moins avant l'hymne gnostique des Naassènes[27] et la théosyncrasie du paganisme tardif, qui l'identifieront avec le soleil.[28] Il faudra les spéculations néoplatoniciennes de Julien pour en faire une sorte de démiurge descendant ici-bas pour tout féconder.[29] Le sacrifice qu'Attis fait de sa virilité

---

[22] *CIMRM*, I, n°s 213 (?), 333[1], 348.

[23] R. Turcan, *Mithras Platonicus*, 74.

[24] U. Bianchi, dans: *Mysteria Mithrae* (*EPRO*, 80), Leyde 1979, 53 et fig. 12–13; E. Paparatti, *ibid.*, 911 ss., pl. XXIII. Cf. Le sacrifice mithriaque (*supra*, n. 19), 362 s.; G. Sfameni Gasparro, Il sangue nei misteri di Mithra, dans: *Sangue e Antropologia Biblica nella Patristica* (*Roma, 23–28 nov. 1981*), II, Rome 1982, 864 s.

[25] Salut mithriaque, 176.

[26] *Supra*, n. 21.

[27] Hippol., *Philos.*, V, 9. Cf. H. Hepding, *Attis* (*RGVV*, 1), Giessen 1903, 35.

[28] G. Sfameni Gasparro, *Soteriology*, 99.

[29] *Ibid.*, 61.

exemplifie la consécration totale des galles à la Mère des dieux. Ce n'est pas un sacrifice garantissant la sauvegarde ou la réanimation du monde comme celui de Mithra, même si son sang fait fleurir les premières violettes à l'équinoxe de printemps.[30] La *ratio physica* des allégoristes païens[31] voudra déchiffrer dans l'éviration d'Attis la moisson des blés qui nourrissent l'humanité et qui semés germent, renaissent annuellement. Mais son propre sacrifice est une passion et non pas une action salvatrice comme celui de Mithra. Cette passion est liée au cycle périodique de la végétation; mais le dieu n'œuvre pas directement et personnellement pour préserver ou promouvoir la vie, non seulement celle des hommes, mais de toutes les espèces animales ou végétales que désaltère le sang du taureau.

Comme Attis, Osiris se sacrifie ou se laisse sacrifier, est sacrifié, au lieu d'accomplir le sacrifice comme Mithra qui dynamise ainsi et conforte le monde animé. Dans le mythe égyptien, c'est Isis qui ranime le «dieu bon». C'est elle aussi qui conséquemment domine et gère le monde, qui secourt les hommes et de qui dépend leur sort inéluctablement et sans restriction aucune. Comme Sérapis dans les papyrus magiques, elle est même au-dessus du Destin, et dit bien à Lucius chez Apulée qu'elle seule a le pouvoir de prolonger sa vie *ultra statuta fato tuo spatia*.[32] Sa grâce divine prévaut sur l'enchaînement des causes naturelles, comme si la bonté souveraine de la Mère avait le pouvoir de rompre le cycle de la Nécessité. Cette souveraineté gratuite et totale la différencie de Mithra dont la mission s'accomplit sous la garantie des dieux et des astres, en vertu d'un fatalisme céleste. On a certes nié, comme le fait R. Merkelbach,[33] que le mithriacisme ait intégré les dogmes de l'astrologie, sous prétexte que cette religion fondée sur le volontarisme et le libre arbitre procéderait d'une réinterprétation platonicienne des croyances iraniennes, sans impact aucun des théories stoïciennes. En fait—j'y reviendrai—le platonisme est secondaire dans l'exégèse du mithriacisme. En revanche, la valorisation du feu dans la théocosmologie du Portique s'accordait foncièrement avec le culte de l'élément igné qu'atteste l'archéologie des sanctuaires mithriaques.[34] Mais surtout l'épigraphie et l'iconographie nous y confirment l'importance que les mithriastes attachaient à l'état du ciel, et les études de R. Beck[35] corroborent ce que F. Cumont conjecturait du fatalisme sidéral adopté par les adorateurs du *Deus*

---

[30] *Ibid.*, 39: Arnob., *Adv.Nat*, V, 7 (257, 3, Marchesi). Cf. F. Cumont, *Lux perpetua*, Paris 1949, 45.

[31] Cf. notre *Firmicus Maternus* (n. 3), 193 s.

[32] Apul., *Met.*, XI, 6,7. Cf. J.G. Griffiths, *The Isis-Book* (n. 9), 166 s.

[33] *Mithras*, 200.

[34] M.J. Vermaseren / C.C. Van Essen, *The Excavations in the Mithraeum of the Church of S. Prisca in Rome*, Leyde 1965, 266 ss.; R. Turcan, *Feu et sang. A propos d'un relief mithriaque*, *CRAI*, 1986.

[35] Interpreting of the Ponza Zodiac, I–II, *Journ. of Mithr. Studies*, I, 1976, 1 ss.; II, 1978, 87

Invictus. Le témoignage de Celse sur l'échelle montrée aux initiés suffirait d'ailleurs à réfuter les négations de R. Merkelbach, car les planètes y sont rangées dans l'ordre d'une semaine à rebours, et nous savons bien que cette hebdomade est d'origine astrologique.[36]

Mais Mithra n'est pas au-dessus des astres, comme Isis, même s'il a le Cosmos en charge, même s'il tient d'une main le cercle zodiacal et de l'autre la sphère du monde sur le relief de Trèves.[37] Son action concorde avec les révolutions sidérales, comme nous le démontre l'orbe des constellations au-dessus de la tauroctonie, avec le Bélier à l'orient qui marque une coïncidence équinoxiale évidente non moins qu'essentielle aux yeux des mithriastes.[38] L'action du Tauroctone est conforme au destin du monde, à ses lois et à l'ordre universel, comme l'action du sage stoïcien s'accorde strictement à la Providence et au Logos. Sur ce point, le témoignage tardif—mais précieux—de Proclus[39] complète ceux des inscriptions et de l'imagerie mithriaques. Le commentateur néoplatonicien de la *République* écrit, en effet, que dans les «mystères persiques de Mithra» les invocations à Thémis lui associent constamment la Nécessité, *Anagkè*. Il fait état de trois invocations (πρῶται—μέσαι—τελευταῖαι), et l'on ne peut s'empêcher de songer à la trinité dont parle Denys l'Aréopagite,[40] *Mithras Triplasios*, ou à l'arbre sommé de trois *pileati* sur la stèle de Dieburg.[41] Ces trois invocations correspondent apparemment aux trois aspects solaires de Mithra qui culmine à midi entre Cautès et Cautopatès.

Curieusement, d'après les livres sur *La nature* qu'on attribuait à Zoroastre, on identifiait *Anagkè* avec l'air.[42] Cette donnée est une citation du platonicien Kronios auquel se réfère Porphyre dans *L'antre des Nymphes*[43] (où le culte de Mithra réinterprété par Numénius[44] retient singulièrement, comme on sait, l'attention du disciple de Plotin). Sur les stèles mithriaques, l'air est représenté par les quatre Vents autour du zodiaque et de la tauroctonie. On songe alors au rôle des Vents dans l'incarnation des âmes selon les poèmes orphiques dont fait état Aristote[45] et aux exégèses qu'en proposait Platon en se réclamant de

---

ss.; Sette Sfere, Sette Porte and the Spring Equinoxes of A.D. 172 and 173, dans: *Mysteria Mithrae*, 515 ss.

[36] A. Bouché-Leclercq, *L'astrologie grecque*, Paris 1899, 476 ss.

[37] *CIMRM*, I, n°985; R. Merkelbach, *Mithras*, 336, fig. 90. cf. *Mithras Platonicus* (n. 15), 78, n. 127.

[38] *Ibid.*, 54 ss.

[39] *In Plat.Remp.*, II, 345, 4 ss. Krol = Bidez-Cumont, *Les mages hellénisés*, II, 155 (fr.0 9 f.).

[40] *Ep.*, 7. Cf. *Mithras Platonicus*, 123.

[41] *CIMRM*, II, n°1247; R. Merkelbach, *Mithras*, 358, fig. 122 (3e compartiment à droite, à partir du haut).

[42] Procl., *In Plat.Remp.*, II, 109, 7 ss. Kroll = Bidez-Cumont, *op.cit.*, II, 159 (fr.0 13, ligne 14) et commentaire 160, n. 3.

[43] *Ibid.*, (ligne 24). Cf. Porph., *De antro Nymph.*, 2–3 et 21 (55, 17; 56, 7; 71, 1, Nauck²).

[44] *Mithras Platonicus* (n. 15), 62 ss.

[45] O. Kern, *Orphicorum fragmenta*, 95 s., n°27.

Zoroastre, si l'on en croit Clément d'Alexandrie.[46] Ces exégèses faisaient passer par le zodiaque aussi bien les âmes qui sombrent dans le monde de la genèse que celles qui en sortent. Si la tauroctonie est au premier degré l'image du sacrifice qui nourrit la création animale et végétale, c'est au second degré celle de la *bougonia* qui fait naître les abeilles, symboles des âmes selon Virgile[47] et Porphyre.[48] Mithra apparaît donc comme un dieu qui anime le monde en le peuplant d'âmes, en multipliant la vie incarnée dans les espèces.

On retrouve ici encore un dogme stoïcien, l'idée que le sang est le siège de l'âme.[49] Contrairement aux Orphiques pour qui l'incorporation des âmes est une chute douloureuse, une forme de déchéance, de mort ou d'expiation, cette animation du monde est pour les mithriastes positive et bénéfique. On a noté depuis longtemps que dans la tradition iranienne la création n'est pas, comme dans certains courants théosophiques occidentaux, affectée d'un coefficient négatif: elle constitue à l'inverse un moyen de lutter contre l'esprit du mal.[50] À l'époque où les sectes gnostiques et même certains penseurs néoplatoniciens comme Porphyre lui-même dépréciaient ou maudissaient le monde incarné,[51] les mithriastes glorifiaient en leur dieu celui qui les sauvait par le sang vivifiant du taureau, non pas pour les libérer du fatalisme sidéral, mais conformément à la loi divine dont les astres transcrivent l'expression dans le ciel. Cette cohérence bio-cosmique du divin—qui n'est pas étranger, ni a fortiori opposé au monde des corps et des mortels—contraste foncièrement avec le dualisme de ceux-là mêmes qui, tels Numénius et Porphyre, exploitaient à l'appui de leurs argumentations allégoriques certaines références au mithriacisme, pour l'annexer à leur platonisme syncrétique.[52]

VI

Cette théologie vitaliste qui excluait la division, le drame, la rupture intérieure, le mal de vivre, les nostalgies et autres souffrances existentielles, n'avait rien d'abstrait ni d'intemporel. Le pivot en était un dieu sacrifiant, grand-prêtre exemplaire, initiateur des immolations que les mystes réactualisaient avant leurs repas communautaires. La tauroctonie n'a évidemment rien à voir avec le sacrifice personnel d'un dieu rédempteur, dont l'effet salvifique et en quelque sorte transcendant échappe à l'entendement. La rédemption par la croix est par elle-même un mystère, le mystère suprême du christianisme. Rien de tel

---

[46] *Strom.*, V, 14, 103, 2 (II, p. 395 Stählin) = Bidez-Cumont, *op.cit.*, II, 158 (Fr.0 12).
[47] *Mithras Platonicus*, 72 s.
[48] *Ibid.*
[49] *SVF*, II, Leipzig – Berlin ²1923, 217 s., n°s 778, 781–783. Cf. notre *Feu et sang* (*supra*, n. 34.)
[50] *Mithras Platonicus*, .83.
[51] Cf. *Salut mithriaque et sotériologie néoplatonicienne* (n. 2), 180.
[52] *Mithras Platonicus*, 81 ss.

dans le mithriacisme. Le sacrifice de Mithra est directement, physiquement nutritif et roboratif, tout comme les aliments que partagent ses fidèles réunis dans les antres pour un banquet de communion entre eux et avec leur dieu, présent en image picturalement ou sculpturalement.[53]

Le Tauroctone ne rachète pas des créatures dégradées par le péché pour les libérer d'un maléfice moral ou d'une malédiction, mais pour leur épargner le dépérissement et ranimer le monde déficient. Il y a quelque chose de matérialiste dans cette conception du sacrifice divin, qui ne relève pas d'un symbolisme théosophique ni d'un mystère ineffable. Les initiés se fortifient mutuellement, avec les dieux, en mangeant ensemble les chairs sacrifiées, comme Mithra et le Soleil avaient consommé celle du taureau dont le sang avait réconforté la nature menacée de mort. Les mystes mangent en compagnie des dieux, car la force vitale assure et garantit la force d'agir au service de Mithra. La *vis* soutient la *virtus*.

Cette *virtus* caractérise le dieu des antres persiques plus précisément que les divinités des autres cultes orientaux: une *virtus* qui s'exerce au profit des êtres vivants, des créatures d'Oromasdès. C'est la raison d'être de Mithra en tant que dieu. Il ne sort du rocher que pour secourir. Aussi est-il invoqué comme dieu «bon»[54] et «salutaire»,[55] *numen propitium*[56] ou *praesens*[57]: «présent» aux soucis de ses fidèles, quoique «céleste» et «éternel». La providence divine s'incarne dans la personne et l'action de Mithra, toujours efficace parmi les hommes et vivante en ce monde. Le dieu n'a rien d'une puissance lointaine, inconcevable, rien du Père Inconnu de la gnose. Là où exceptionnellement (dans une inscription d'Ostie) on le trouve qualifié de deus *indeprehensivilis* (pour *indeprehensibilis*),[58] cette épithète n'a pas le sens d'incompréhensible ou d'insaisissable aux sens et à l'intelligence, mais signifie tout simplement qu'on ne peut le surprendre, le prendre en défaut, c'est-à-dire le vaincre. C'est une variante de l'épiclèse *Invictus*, et il n'y a pas lieu de rapprocher le dieu du *Timée* (28 c), comme le fait aventureusement R. Merkelbach.[59]

Une épithète assez fréquente et significative est celle de *sanctus, sanctissimus*.[60] En dehors de l'épigraphie mithriaque, on relève des exemples de ce qualificatif appliqué à des dieux.[61] En pareil cas, on ne le traduira pas sim-

---

[53] *Le sacrifice mithriaque* (n. 19), 356 s. Cf. notre *Note sur la liturgie mithriaque*, RHR, 194, 1978, 155.

[54] *CIMRM*, I, n°900 b; II, n°2276.

[55] *Supra*, n. 22.

[56] *CIMRM*, I, n°891.

[57] *Ibid.*, n°s 214, 305; II, n°2265. Cf. ἐπηκόῳ: I, n°433.

[58] *Ibid.*, I, n°311. Cf. P.G.W. Glare, *Oxford Latin Dictionary*, IV, Oxford 1973, 881, *s.v.*

[59] *Mithras*, 233.

[60] *CIMRM*, I, n°s 305, 333[1-2], 562, 575, 627, 658, 687; II, n°s 24 b, 117, 367, 1376, 1783, 1788, 2206, 2238, 2350. Cf. aussi S. Panciera, dans *Mysteria Mithrae*, 132.

[61] F. Cumont, *Les religions orientales* ... (n. 8), 146, 260, n. 65; S. Panciera, *loc.cit.*

plement par le français «respectable» ou «vénérable». *Sanctus* se dit de ce qui est «consacré» (surtout par le sang, d'après une glose de Servius)[62] et donc «garanti», qui a les garanties de la divinité. C'est d'ailleurs pourquoi ce participe passé du verbe *sancire* s'applique aussi à l'empereur.[63] On a donc le sentiment que dans un contexte cultuel *sanctus* concerne ce qui possède la divinité à un degré éminent, celui qui a mérité d'être dieu; qui ne l'est pas ontologiquement de toute éternité, en vertu d'un statut originel ou d'une essence, mais d'une existence, d'une action dans l'histoire et pour le monde. Mithra est *sanctus*, consacré dieu en somme parce qu'il s'est acquis des droits à la reconnaissance de toute la création, au respect et à l'adoration des hommes qui ont reconnu son pouvoir invincible, sa toute-puissance bénéfique et salutaire:

omnipotenti sancto caelesti numini praesenti

comme le proclame une dédicace d'Ostie.[64]

D'autres divinités «orientales» sont saintes, comme l'a noté F. Cumont[65] à la suite de L. Clermont-Ganneau.[66] Mais l'épithète n'a pas dans les religions sémitiques la même valeur que le latin *sanctus* dans un contexte mithriaque. Mithra est *sanctus* parce qu'il a fait ses preuves effectivement comme dieu vaillant et secourable, par sa *virtus*.

Ce dieu actif, qui s'intéresse aux hommes et qui par conséquent intéresse cultuellement les hommes, est né dans le monde. Il a eu dans le monde une existence historique, mais continue d'être présent à ses fidèles dans les repas communautaires consécutifs aux sacrifices qui rééditent la tauroctonie archétypique. Le renouvellement du sacrifice prolonge et renforce l'efficacité régénératrice et revitalisante de l'immolation initiale. Les mystes de Mithra sont ainsi censés participer au salut commun. Ils sont associés à l'action divine. On ne peut s'empêcher de songer à certains aspects du manichéisme dont se gausse saint Augustin,[67] notamment à ces «élus» qui, en mangeant tels fruits et légumes, en absorbent la substance lumineuse pour la libérer et la sauver. Ce salut par «les dents et le ventre» relève au moins en partie du même vitalisme fondamental, même si la notion de lumière à libérer est plus typiquement gnostique.[68]

Si, dans le vers précité de S. Prisca, la lecture de l'épithète (*a*)*eternali* appliquée au sang du taureau était confirmée, elle ouvrirait une perspective

---

[62] *Ad Aen.*, XII, 200 (II, p. 599, 17 ss. Thilo-Hagen).
[63] H. Fugier, *Recherches sur l'expression du sacré dans la langue latine*, Strasbourg, 1963, 278 ss.
[64] *CIMRM*, I, n°305.
[65] *Les religions orientales* (n. 8), 260, n. 65.
[66] *Etudes d'archéologie orientale*, II, Paris 1896, 104. Cf. Y. Hajjar, *La triade d'Héliopolis-Baalbek. Iconographie, théologie, culte et sanctuaires*, Montréal 1985, 227.
[67] *De moribus Manich.*, 15, 36–37.
[68] H. Jonas, *La religion gnostique*, trad.fr., Paris 1978, 65 s., 85 ss., 214 ss., 291 ss.

éclairante sur la nature essentiellement vitale du divin dans la théo-cosmologie mithriaque. En effet, ce sang qui régénère les espèces animales et végétales ne peut guère être qualifié d'éternel que parce qu'il véhicule cette substance divine qui anime le monde, comme le *pneuma* des stoïciens est ce souffle igné qui anime le sang.[69] Dans le sang du taureau, il y a tout à la fois la substance humide de la Lune et la force du feu solaire qui frappe Mithra sacrifiant sur plusieurs exemplaires peints ou sculptés de la tauroctonie:[70] d'où la présence constante des deux luminaires dans cette image du salut. Le divin, c'est la vie. C'est le sang qui sauve la vie grâce au «dieu bon».

VII

Mais quelle est la relation de ce dieu sauveur au dieu suprême?

Numénius et Porphyre[71] en font un «démiurge»: exégèse arbitraire que ne confirment ni l'épigraphie ni l'iconographie mithriaques.[72] les dédicaces qui célèbrent en lui un *genitor* ou un *genitor luminis*[73] ne concernent pas le créateur du monde, mais le géniteur de la lumière jaillissant avec lui du rocher, ou le responsable de la génération qui fait entrer les âmes dans le monde de la genèse par la tauroctonie. Ces épiclèses exaltent l'animateur de l'univers qui, par le sang, fait passer la lumière dans les espèces. Porphyre[74] dit bien que Mithra est γενέσεως δεσπότης, ce qui concorde à point avec la documentation proprement mithriaque, mais ne coïncide pas avec la fonction de démiurge. Le monde existe déjà quand Mithra sort du rocher pour le sauvegarder.

Alors que fait le dieu suprême? Comme souvent dans l'histoire des religions, on vérifie ici que le dieu créateur et souverain est un *deus otiosus*.[75] S'il se confond avec Jupiter, on constate sur les stèles de Sarrebourg et d'Osterburken[76] qu'il assiste d'en haut (de haut et sans intervenir) aux exploits de Mithra et à la tauroctonie. Un monument curieux, excellemment commenté naguère par Martin Vermaseren, un bronze du Vatican qui proviendrait de l'hypogée des *Herennii* à Bolséna,[77] nous montre Mithra immolant le

---

[69] *SVF*, II², 217, n°s 773, 775, 778 ss.

[70] *Salut mithriaque* ... (n. 2), 177, 186, n. 31. Cf. en particulier M.J. Vermaseren, *Mithriaca* (*EPRO*, 16), III. *The Mithraeum at Marino*, Leyde 1982, 66 et pl.IV.

[71] *Mithras Platonicus*, 77 ss.

[72] *Ibid. Contra*: C. Giuffré Scibona, *Mithras* demiourgos, dans: *Mysteria Mithrae*, p. 615 ss. (aucun argument épigraphique ni archéologique).

[73] *CIMRM*, II, n°s 1676, 2007–2008; R. Merkelbach, *Mithras*, 201.

[74] *De antro Nymph.*, 24 (73, 6, Mauck²).

[75] D. Sabbatucci, *Il mito, il rito e la storia*, Rome 1978, 15 ss., 22 ss.

[76] *CIMRM*, I, n°966; II, n°1292; R. Merkelbach, *Mithras*, 352, fig. 113. Autres exemples: *ibid.*, fig. 130, 134, 164 (avec des interprétations discutables).

[77] *CIMRM*, I, n°659. Cf. M.J. Vermaseren, Mithras-Sabazius-Cybele, *Mededel. van de Kon. Acad. v. Wetensch., Lett. en Sch. Kunsten van België, Lett.*, 46, 1984, 1, 27 ss.

taureau sur le buste d'un dieu barbu, que la pigne autorise à identifier avec
Zeus-Sabazios.[78] Ainsi, le Tauroctone apparaît comme une sorte d'hypostase
agissante et vivifiante du dieu Père. Celui-ci, θεὸς ὕψιστος, porte le dieu qui
abreuve et anime le monde, comme Zeus Héliopolitain porte sur son corps en-
gainé les bustes de planètes qui éclairent le ciel[79] ou comme le dieu cosmique
dont parle Plotin[80] et dont la poitrine est constellée d'astres étincelants. C'est
une façon de figurer la subordination d'une force divine immanente au grand
dieu transcendant, en même temps que la relation intime qui les unit, comme
si en agissant au sein de Zeus-Sabazios Mithra incarnait sa puissance géné-
ratrice.

On ne peut manquer ici de s'interroger sur les raisons qui peuvent expliquer
les titres de démiurge et père universel que Numénius donnait au Tauroctone.
Porphyre[81] nous réfère certes à Eubule, l'auteur bien mal connu d'un livre
sur les mystères de Mithra. Mais les expressions qu'il emploie sont typiquement frappées au coin du style de Numénius.

En principe, le philosophe d'Apamée distingue trois dieux: le Père, le
Créateur (ποιητής) et la Création (ποίημα) ou le monde.[82] Chez Platon (*Tim.*,
28 c 3), le Créateur et le Père ne sont qu'un seul et même dieu. Le second dieu
de Numénius est en mouvement (κινούμενος): c'est le démiurge du devenir
par opposition au démiurge de l'essense qu'est le Bien ou premier dieu.[83] Ce
deuxième dieu qui circule dans le ciel est assimilé au Soleil, chorège des astres.
Or Numénius sait évidemment que Mithra est *Sol Invictus*, et ce dieu qui
anime la création, qui fait s'incarner les âmes pour vivifier le monde lui apparaît conséquemment comme une sorte de démiurge.

Dans le texte mis au compte d'Eubule, mais revu et corrigé, repensé par
Numénius,[84] Mithra est désigné comme créateur et père de l'univers: τοῦ πάντων ποιητοῦ καὶ πατρὸς Μίθρου. C'est l'ordre même des mots chez Platon
dans le *Timée*, là où le démiurge nous est donné comme ineffable.[85] On prend
ici Numénius en flagrant délit d'application du *Timée* aux mystères de Mithra,
que la documentation inscrite ou figurée des *spelaea* ne caractérise jamais
comme un démiurge. Mais il reste vrai que Mithra est expressément nommé
«Oromasdès» sur le denier regravé de *Verulamium* (St-Albans)[86] et que plu-

---

[78] E.N. Lane, *Corpus cultus Iovis Sabazii* (*EPRO*, 100), II, Leyde 1985, 40, n°84.

[79] Y. Hajjar, *op.cit.*, (n. 66), 84 ss.

[80] *Enn.*, III, 2, 14. Cf. R. Turcan, *Une allusion de Plotin aux idoles cultuelles, Mélanges H.-
Ch. Puech*, Paris 1974, 307 ss.

[81] *De antro Nymph.*, 6 (60, 5, Nauck²).

[82] Fr. 21 (p. 60) de l'éd.-trad. E. des Places, dans: *la Coll. des Universités de France*, Paris
1973. Cf. A.-J. Festugière, *La révélation d'Hermès Trismégiste*, IV, Paris 1954, 275 s.; *CH*, XVI,
18.

[83] *Ibid.*, p. 127; Numen., fr. 16 (p. 57) E. des Places.

[84] Porph., *De antro Nymph.*, 6 (p. 60, 7 Nauck²); *Mithras Platonicus*, 77 ss.

[85] *Tim.* 28 c: τὸν μὲν οὖν ποιητὴν καὶ πατέρα τοῦδε τοῦ παντὸς εὑρεῖν ... κτλ.

[86] *CIMRM*, I, n°827 et fig. 221; R. Beck, *Mithraism since F. Cumont, ANRW*, II, 17, 4,
Berlin – New York 1984, 2049 et pl. XXII.

sieurs dédicaces l'identifient avec Zeus ou avec Jupiter *Optimus Maximus*.[87]
D'autres le qualifient de *Caelestis*[88] et surtout d'*Omnipotens* ....[89]

Autrement dit, le dieu qui agit dans le monde, sur le monde ou pour le monde, afin de le sauvegarder (*et nos servasti* ...) en le revigorant, finit par s'annexer la souveraineté, par absorber en quelque manière la divinité suprême ou se confondre avec elle. Le dieu sauveur prévaut sur le créateur ou s'identifie avec lui, comme dans certains cas le Christ finit par occulter Dieu le Père. Un dieu qui se dévoue à la création tend à assumer une fonction quasiment démiurgique, tout de même qu'en restaurant, régénérant l'humanité, Jésus apparaît comme un recréateur et, en tant que Logos, s'identifie même avec la puissance créatrice du Père.

En voyant que les mithriastes égalaient ou assimilaient leur «dieu bon», le Tauroctone géniteur de la lumière, à Jupiter Très Bon et Très Grand, les platoniciens de l'époque antonine ne pouvaient s'empêcher de songer au Bien de Platon, démiurge et créateur. Ils y étaient d'autant plus incités que, dans la *République*, Platon compare le Bien au Soleil[90] et que les mithriastes adoraient en Mithra *Sol Invictus*. Dans l'esprit de Numénius comme de tous les philosophes et théosophes de son temps, un dieu qui agit dans le monde ou en contact avec le monde ne peut correspondre qu'au démiurge, le dieu suprême régnant au-dessus de tout rapport direct avec la matière et la vie.[91] Mais tout en distinguant ses trois dieux hiérarchisés, Numénius reste fidèle à Platon, puisque son premier dieu ou premier intellect est démiurge de l'essence et pense le monde en tant que Bien, comme Oromasdès crée le monde et les êtres vivants en tant qu'esprit du Bien. Numénius devait savoir que dans les antres on tendait à doter Mithra des pouvoirs de Zeus-Oromasdès. Aussi appelle-t-il le Tauroctone «créateur et père de toutes choses»,[92] comme le démiurge du *Timée*. Cette désignation n'a pas la valeur d'un témoignage mithriaque, mais transcrit en termes platoniciens une croyance des mithriastes enclins à faire de leur dieu bienfaisant le maître omnipotent de l'univers.

En affirmant non sans raison que dans les mystères de l'époque romaine Mithra est «der oberste Gott», R. Merkelbach[93] ajoute hâtivement: «von Ahura Mazda ist keine Spur». C'est faux épigraphiquement et même iconographiquement, si Jupiter terrassant les géants anguipèdes joue le rôle d'Oro-

---

[87] *CIMRM*, I, n°s 463, 473, 475, 881; II, n°s 1467, 1881, 2007. Cf. aussi I, n°333¹ (*Domino Sancto Optimo Maximo Salutari*); II, n°1788: D(*eo*) S(*ancto*)/O(*ptimo*) M(*aximo*)/ SOLI IN-VIC/ TO ... etc.

[88] *CIMRM*, I, n°305.

[89] *Ibid.*, n°s 175, 305; II, n°s 1469, 1913, 1941.

[90] *Resp.*, VI, 506 e, 508 b. Cf. *Mithras Platonicus*, 79 s.

[91] A.-J. Festugière, *op.cit.*, 123 ss. Cf. *CH*, XVI, 18.

[92] *Supra*, n. 84.

[93] *Mithras*, 75.

masdès.[94] Mais il vaut mieux dire qu'Oromasdès est éclipsé par Mithra ou que Mithra s'annexe les prérogatives du dieu Père et monopolise finalement tous les pouvoirs divins.

Ce processus de promotion du dieu sauveur en dieu souverain n'est pas propre au mithriacisme. On le vérifie par exemple dans le cas d'Isis, qui devient Mère Universelle, qui «fait surgir les îles ou les continents»[95] et finit par détenir un pouvoir cosmique absolu, parce qu'elle incarne la vie et le salut, la bonté divine présente et efficiente, comme Mithra ou le Christ. En elle sont en quelque sorte subsumés tous les dieux et toutes les déesses: *deorum dearumque facies uniformis* (Apulée).[96] Dans les temples du culte égyptien, cependant, on adore également—quoiqu'avec moins de zèle et de ferveur, semble-t-il—des dieux comme Sérapis, Anubis, Osiris, Harpocrate. Mais dans les antres, à l'exception de certains dieux étrangers au culte persique, les dédicaces concernent Mithra. Celles qui portent les noms de Cautès et de Cautopatès honorent les hypostases du même *Sol Invictus* ou d'une même trinité.

VIII

Mithra est qualifié de *Summus*[97] (comme le Dieu d'Arnobe, de Lactance ou de Firmicus Maternus).[98] On l'appelle aussi *dominus*,[99] «le Seigneur» ....
En fait, l'hénothéisme mithriaque est très proche d'un monothéisme cultuel, sauf que de rares consécrations à Ahriman (*Deo Arimanio*)[100] nous posent le problème du dualisme. Je ne pense pas, comme R. Merkelbach,[101] qu'on puisse se tirer d'affaire en supposant que le latin *Arimanius* transcrirait le nom du compagnon védique de Mitra, *Aryaman*, par suite d'une confusion impossible à démontrer, car le grec *Areimanios* correspond bien à Ahriman. On sait que la littérature pehlevie attribue le meurtre du taureau primordial à Ahriman; et dans la mesure où le Tauroctone joue ce rôle, on est tenté de les identifier l'un à l'autre, comme J. Duchesne-Guillemin n'hésitait pas à le faire.[102] Mais aucune des dédicaces à *Arimanius* ne juxtapose son nom à celui de Mithra. Aucun témoignage ne les solidarise l'un avec l'autre, ni n'impute au premier la tauroctonie. On a voulu reconnaître Ahriman dans l'*Aiôn* léontocéphale

94 *Ibid.*, 107 ss. Cf. *Mithras Platonicus*, 131.
95 A.-J. Festugière, *Etudes de religion grecque et hellénistique*, Paris 1972, 152.
96 *Met.*, XI, 5, 1. Cf. J.G. Griffiths, *op.cit.* (n. 9), 143 ss.
97 *CIMRM*, I, n°s 206, 515–516, 553; II, n°395 A.
98 Cf. notre éd.-trad. de *Firmicus Maternus* (n. 3), 179 s.
99 *CIMRM*, I, n°s 333², 767; II, n°1483. Cf. *supra*, n. 74.
100 R. Turcan, *Les motivations*, (n. 1), 220.
101 *Mithras*, 104.
102 Aiôn et le Léontocéphale, Mithras et Ahriman, *La Nouvelle Clio* 10 (1960), 1 ss.; Id., *La religion de l'Iran ancien*, Coll. «Mana», Paris, 1962, 256 s.

qu'enlacent les spires d'un serpent.[103] En réalité, il personnifie le feu céleste et solaire, donc un aspect de Mithra géniteur de la lumière, qui surgit du roc une torche à la main et que le relief de Nesce[104] représente même naissant des flammes. Sur les stèles peintes, il est vêtu de rouge, couleur de feu.[105] Si la soif et le dessèchement menacent la Création, on ne voit pas que le feu relève dans le mithriacisme d'une puissance maléfique, puisque les Lions en sont responsables[106] et que l'*Aiôn* porte précisément une tête de lion. Un cippe du Palazzo Barberini[107] est dédié *Leoni sancto / deo praesenti*: épiclèses appropriées à une idole léontocéphale en même temps qu'à une déité bénéfique et secourable (*praesenti*).

Alors, les dédicaces gravées en l'honneur d'Ahriman peuvent être le fait de mithriastes qui voulaient soit neutraliser apotropaïquement la puissance des Ténèbres, soit s'acquitter d'un vœu pour avoir été épargnés par l'esprit du Mal dans telles circonstances qui nous échappent. Ce dualisme cultuel qui s'inscrit, certes, dans la tradition païenne et notamment dans le droit fil du souci très romain d'apaiser les puissances redoutables, n'est pas en contradiction flagrante avec l'adoration éminente d'un dieu Bon et lumineux, vainqueur de la mort et des forces obscures qu'il faut bien s'efforcer de détourner à l'occasion, en attendant la Fin des Temps. Je me demande même si un dualisme fondamental n'est pas nécessaire pour soutenir l'énergie d'un hénothéisme militant comme celui des mithriastes, voire l'éthique de tout monothéisme qui n'est pas seulement une croyance, mais une raison de vivre courageusement, dangereusement dans l'effort et la fidélité. Il faut avoir quelque chose à vaincre pour vibrer d'ardeur et de ferveur, surtout dans un culte qui associe les initiés à l'œuvre du salut commun.

IX

Au total, Mithra contraste avec les dieux du paganisme traditionnel comme avec ceux des cultes orientaux sur plusieurs points.

1°) C'est un dieu cosmique. Il n'est pas lié à une géographie sacrée comme Isis à l'Égypte, Cybèle à Pessinonte ou au Bérécynthe, les Ba'als syriens à Doliché ou à Héliopolis. On sait évidemment—et les chrétiens se plaisent à répéter—que Mithra est perse. Il porte le costume perse ou du moins asiatique.

---

[103] *Contra*: G. Windengren, *Les religions de l'Iran*, Paris 1968, 260 ss. Cf. H.M. Jackson, *The Meaning and Function of the Leontocephaline in Roman Mithraism*, Numen (32) 1985, 17 ss.

[104] *CIMRM*, I, n°650; R. Merkelbach, *Mithras*, 322, fig. 73.

[105] A Capoue et Marino, par exemple: M.J. Vermaseren, *Mithriaca* (*EPRO*, 16), I, Leyde 1971, pl. III; III, Leyde 1982, pl. III. Manteau rouge sur la fresque du *Mithraeum* Barberini: *ibid.*, pl. XI – XII, XV.

[106] H.M. Jackson, *loc.cit.* (n. 103).

[107] S. Panciera, dans *Mysteria Mithrae*, 127 ss.

Eubule attribuait à Zoroastre la consécration du premier *Mithraeum* «en Perside».[108] La hiérarchie initiatique comporte un grade du «Perse». Mais rien dans l'iconographie ne solidarise le culte de Mithra avec une région ou un peuple. Partout, de l'Euphrate à l'Ecosse, les antres reproduisent l'image de la grotte archétypique sans référence à une lointaine patrie iranienne. Le Tauroctone est indépendant même mythiquement de toute localisation terrestre. La tauroctonie a une signification et une portée universelles. Elle est seulement liée à l'équinoxe de printemps,[109] et plusieurs *Mithraea* sont pour cette raison orientés à l'est idéal, pour qu'en entrant dans la constellation du Bélier le Soleil y frappe de ses rayons l'image du dieu invincible.[110] Ce dieu cosmique assume la totalité du monde sans discrimination tragique ou ontologique.

2°) C'est un dieu incarné, mais non engendré, expression miraculeuse de la sollicitude divine qui couronne et parachève une séquence de règnes solidaires d'une histoire de l'univers.

3°) C'est un dieu sacrifiant et non sacrifié, un dieu agissant qui ne se contente pas de gérer le monde et de le dominer, mais qui l'anime ou le réanime par l'eau et le sang, un sang qui véhicule la force divine.

4°) Enfin, ce dieu «invincible», qui transcende les frontières humaines et matérielles, mais qui n'a rien de transcendantal, a une omnipotence qui tend à rejeter dans l'ombre tous les autres dieux ou à les marginaliser, à les subordonner à son action. De médiateur entre le Créateur et la Création, parce qu'il assure la médiation du salut, il devient le dieu majeur, celui qu'on invoque préférentiellement, sinon exclusivement. Le triomphalisme absolu de sa geste et de sa mission régénératrices le subliment jusqu'à donner à penser que, si le mithriacisme relève bien iconographiquement du polythéisme, il ressemble aussi pratiquement—sauf les rares consécrations *Deo Arimanio* dont la signification reste problématique—à un monothéisme cultuel.

Il va de soi que ces caractéristiques du divin et du dieu mithriaques ne sont pas sans corrélation avec les conditions historiques de leur succès, avec le recrutement des mithriastes et ce qu'on pourrait appeler la «base sociologique» de cette religion. Les commerçants, les fonctionnaires, les soldats, les esclaves et affranchis de l'empereur qui ont laissé les traces épigraphiques de leur dévotion étaient souvent des ambulants, des migrants, des déracinés.[111] A cet égard, les sénateurs du Bas-Empire qui collectionnent ostensiblement les

---

[108] Porph., *De antro Nymph.*, 6 (60, 5 ss., Nauck[2]). Naturellement, les polémistes chrétiens arguaient de cette hérédité persique pour déconsidérer le culte mithriaque: Firmicus Maternus (n. 3), 204.

[109] *Mithras Platonicus*, 54 ss., 77 s., 83, 85 s.

[110] *Ibid.*, 84; R. Turcan, *Mithra et le mithriacisme*, Paris 1981, 75; R. Merkelbach, *Mithras*, 134.

[111] *Mithra et le mithriacisme* (n. 110), 123 s. Interprétation astrologique de ce recrutement: M.P. Speidel, *Mithras-Orion* (*EPRO*, 81), Leyde 1980, 38 ss.

titres sacerdotaux et initiatiques[112] n'ont rien à voir avec le mithriacisme authentique de la grande époque, celui des IIe et IIIe siècles après J.-C. On conçoit que, dans cet Empire cosmopolite, une population active et mobile, mais fréquemment liée à la personne et au service du prince, en vertu de cette *fides* qu'illustrait et que signifiait même le nom de Mithra (ou «contrat»),[113] ait adoré un dieu supranational et qu'on ait vénéré dans le divin la force de la *virtus* au service de la vie.

Au fond, le mithriacisme sacralisait une certaine idée de la romanité impériale, et c'est probablement l'une des raisons primordiales de son expansion, qui ne pouvait survivre à la conversion de Constantin.

---

[112] Bien vu par R. Merkelbach, *Mithras*, 247.
[113] *Mithra et le mithriacisme* (n. 110), 5−6.

LA CONCEPTION DE DIEU DANS LE MANICHÉISME

PAR

M. Tardieu (Paris)

La question du Dieu manichéen a servi à étayer des thèses contradictoires. Non seulement chez les modernes, qui concluent du dualisme au dithéisme.[1] Mais d'abord chez les manichéens. L'évêque manichéen d'Afrique, Faustus, n'a-t-il pas soutenu que, pour les tenants de sa religion, il n'y avait qu'un Dieu, seul et unique?[2] La documentation qui subsiste est assez riche pour y trouver argument à l'appui de l'opinion de l'évêque manichéen. Mais cela ne ruine pas, pour autant, la thèse opposée, massivement affirmée et développée.[3]

Le débat sur l'espèce de théisme auquel répondrait le manichéisme est artificiel, et occulte la question de fond: quelle est la représentation de Dieu concernée? Quelles en sont les conséquences? Conception à la fois hiérarchique et unitaire, tout à fait à sa place dans la fourchette historique du Colloque. Conception stable également, pour transparaître encore dans un texte aussi tardif que l'*Élégie du royaume de lumière* transmise dans l'hymnaire manichéen chinois de Londres.[4] Conception non négligeable, enfin, pour saisir un point des relations du manichéisme avec le platonisme et le muᶜtazilisme.

Tel que les manichéens se le représentent, le Dieu suprême ne se conçoit qu'à travers des catégories spatiales. Non seulement il occupe un espace bien défini au sommet de l'univers mais il est lui-même, en son essense propre, coextensif à cet espace. Il n'est rien d'autre que la totalité des parties qui constituent son domaine. En somme, un Dieu-espace à environnement compartimenté et hiérarchisé, où les distances marquées entre les entités ont pour but de montrer le déploiement de la «grandeur»[5] du propriétaire de ce monde clos et inacces-

---

[1] Le débat est résumé par G. Stroumsa, König und Schwein. Zur Struktur des manichäischen Dualismus, dans: J. Taubes (ed.), *Gnosis und Politik*, Paderborn 1984, 141, n. 3; l'auteur lui-même défend le point de vue monothéiste (142–146 et 152).

[2] Répondant à la question: «Dieu est-il unique, ou y en a-t-il deux?», Faustus répond: *Plane unus* (Faustus *ap.* Augustin, *Contra Faustum*, XXI 1, CSEL 25/1, 568, 9 Zycha). Faustus reconnaît, toutefois, que dans sa propre tradition certains appellent Dieu la nature adverse mais, ajoute-t-il, *non hoc secundum nostram fidem* (p. 569, 11–13).

[3] Échappant à l'alternative dithéisme-monothéisme, G. Monnot observe avec pertinence que le dualisme manichéen est «un monisme clivé, qui postule l'unité verticale rigoureuse: ce qui n'a pas toutes les qualités d'un principe doit découler d'un autre principe» (*Penseurs musulmans et religious iraniennes. ᶜAbd al-Jabbār et ses devanciers*, Paris 1974, 184, n. 4).

[4] Londres, Br. Lib. Or. Stein 2659; traduction anglaise par Tsui Chi, Mo Ni Hsia Pu Tsan, *BSOAS* 11 (1943), 174–219. La traduction ici utilisée sera celle de L. Leyrat, destinée à paraître avec introduction et notes dans les *SGM* (Paris); voir *infra* n. 15.

[5] Suivant l'usage araméen, le mot «grandeur» (syr. *rabbūtā*, gr. μέγεθος, copt. *mntnac*) est

sible. Les sources manichéennes sont unanimes sur ce point. La question de Dieu n'y est traitée en-dehors de l'environnement concerné, et de son rituel.

Cinq éléments composent toujours le Dieu manichéen. Le psaume CCXXIII pour le Bêma les énumère dans l'ordre suivant: le Père, les douze éons, les éons des éons, l'air vivant, la terre de lumière.[6] Dieu est cet ensemble, aucune partie ne peut être dissociée du tout. Se référant à un témoignage manichéen direct, Augustin transmet cette description détaillée: le Père est un roi, porteur du sceptre (*rex sceptriger*) et couronné de fleurs. Il est entouré de *duodecim saecula* (= les douze éons), décrits comme «douze grands dieux (*magnos deos*)» placés trois par trois aux quatre angles du trône. Ces douze sont eux aussi couronnés de fleurs. Ils chantent et jettent des fleurs devant la face de leur Père. Autour des *saecula*, se tiennent des *innumerabiles regnicolae*, formés d'armées de dieux et de cohortes d'anges. Ces habitants vaquent à la gloire de leur Père dans une *aura salubris* (= l'air vivant), qui constitue l'atmosphère d'une terre de lumière avec champs d'aromates, arbres, collines, mers et fleuves où coule un doux nectar.[7]

Cette description de Dieu et de son domaine provient d'un hymne liturgique manichéen. Le témoignage d'Augustin est formel: *proprie igitur cantas deum*, dit-il en introduisant la description.[8] Selon toute vraisemblance, il s'agissait d'un hymne qu'Augustin entendait chanter lors des célébrations auxquelles il participait en tant qu'*auditor*. La solidité de l'information fournie par Augustin est confirmée par Mani lui-même. Selon la version latine de l'*Epistula fundamenti*, l'espace divin se décompose ainsi: au premier rang est le Père; ses *sensus* enferment les douze *membra* de sa lumière, ou *diuitiae adfluentes* composées de *thesauri*. Autour du Père et des douze, se déploient les *beata et gloriosa saecula*, incalculables en nombre et en étendue, fondés *supra lucidam et beatam terram*.[9]

Le caractère hymnique de la description de Dieu fournie par le *Contra Faustum* XV 5−6 est confirmé, également, par les termes de l'élégie au Seigneur des dieux (*xwadāy yazdān niwāg*), transmise par le fragment parthe M 730 R I. Les douze *saecula*, ou *membra*, sont décrits ici comme «douze couronnes de lumière» (*dwādēs dīdēm rōšn*); ils portent les noms de «fils» (*puhrān*) et de «premiers-nés» (*noxzādān*) du Père. Les éons des éons, ou *innumerabiles regnicolae*, entourant les douze, sont l'ensemble des dieux, divinités et joyaux qui forment «la suite du roi du paradis» (*wahišt šahrdār padwāz*).[10]

---

le terme courant chez les manichéens pour désigner le Dieu suprême.

[6] Bêmatikos CCXXIII dans *Psautier* manichéen copte (II), 9, 12−16 (ed. C.R.C. Allberry, Stuttgart 1938).

[7] Voir Augustin, *Contra Faustum*, XV 5−6; 425, 13−25 Zycha et 426, 10−12.

[8] Augustin, *ibid.*, XV 5, p. 425, 12−13.

[9] Fragment cité par Augustin, *Contra Epistulam fundamenti*, 13, CSEL 25/1; 209, 11−28 Zycha.

[10] M 730 R I, *ap.* E. WALDSCHMIDT et W. LENTZ, Manichäische Dogmatik aus chinesischen

Quelques termes techniques du fragment parthe se retrouvent dans l'exposé du Dieu manichéen chez Ibn al-Nadīm:

> En ce qui concerne le Dieu qui est dans cette terre-ci (= la terre de lumière): il y a douze grandeurs, auxquelles ils donnent le nom de premiers-nés (*abkār*). Leurs formes sont toutes comme sa forme (= la forme du Père). Ce sont des connaissants (*ᶜulamāʾ*), des intelligibles (*ᶜāqilūn*) ... Et il y a des grandeurs, auxquelles ils donnent les noms de piliers (*ᶜimād*), mondes (*ᶜālamūn*), forts (*ᶜaqwiyāʾ*) ... Et la brise (*nasīm*) est la vie du monde.[11]

Les *abkār* (= *noxzādān* en parthe) sont les douze *saecula*, ou *membra*. Les piliers sont les éons des éons, ou *innumerabiles regnicolae*, intermédiaires entre les douze et l'air vivant.[12] La brise (*nasīm*) est l'*aura salubris* composant l'atmosphère de la terre de lumière. Plus important que la correspondance des termes est l'apport de l'exposé d'Ibn al-Nadīm à l'histoire de la conception de Dieu. L'encyclopédiste arabe a, un effet, utilisé ici une source traduisant en concepts métaphysiques les symboles concrets de la représentation traditionnelle de Dieu: les «premiers-nés», c'est-à-dire les douze éons placés aux quatre angles du trône, sont les formes connaissantes et intelligibles de la forme du Père. Il est douteux, cependant, que le procédé d'interprétation employé (traduction conceptuelle d'images) et la terminologie (qui est néoplatonicienne) proviennent des manichéens eux-mêmes. Ce cas isolé pourrait s'expliquer par la nature de la source utilisée par Ibn al-Nadīm.[13]

Un fragment sogdien de cosmogonie, édité par Henning,[14] présente un portrait de Dieu, très proche également de celui fourni par le *Contra Faustum* XV 5−6. Le fragment commence avec là mention du troisième terme de l'habitat divin, les «bienheureuses régions» (*ʾfrytyt ʾwt̠ ʾkt*) où habitent les dieux lumineux, anges, éléments (*mardaspandat*), puissances. Les quatrième et cinquième termes, le «pur air» (*ʾwswgc bryʾ*) et la «lumineuse terre» (*xʾnʾ rwxšnʾ zʾy*) sont décrits sur le modèle de l'air et de la terre dans l'hymne latin: fleurs et aromates remplissent les champs, et les rivières font couler un doux nectar.[15]

---

und iranischen Texten, *SPAW*, Philos.-hist. Klasse, 1933, 553.

[11] Ibn al-Nadīm, *Kitāb al-fihrist*, ed. R. Tağaddud, Téhéran 1971, 396, 2−4.

[12] Le leçon *ᶜimād*, «piliers» du MSS 1934 d'Istanbul, adoptée par l'édition critique de Tağaddud, est confirmée par le psaume CCXXIV pour le Bêma (12, 25 Allberry); les puissances de la lumière chargées de la liturgie céleste y sont appelées, pareillement, «piliers forts», *n-stulos n-jōre = al-ᶜimād al-ᶜaqwiyāʾ*.

[13] C'est-à-dire al-Kindī, qui aura utilisé spontanément la terminologie néoplatonicienne pour transposer en concepts les images manichéennes.

[14] M 178 I R 1−V 32, édité par W.B. Henning, A Sogdian Fragment of the Manichaean Cosmogony, *BSOAS* 12 (1948), 307 = *Selected Papers*, t. 2, Téhéran-Liège 1977, p. 302.

[15] Henning a noté que cette description est passée dans les quatrains de l'*Élégie du royaume de lumière*, composée par le Mushe Wei Mao: «La terre de ce royaume est pure et véritable, dépourvue d'obstacles. Le sol précieux de diamants est sans frontières ... Les jardins et les parcs de ce royaume sont spacieux et purs. Des effluves parfumés et étranges flottent autour de jardins et vergers ... Ce parterre de diamants rayonne éternellement, jettant un scintillement omniprésent sur

Le Dieu de ce paradis céleste est le «grand Roi» (*mzyx 'xšywnyy*),[16] dieu Zarwān.

Le portrait du dieu-roi, trônant en présence de sa cour céleste,[17] est une composition littéraire transposant au monde divin l'ordonnancement de la cour de Perse. Le cérémonial des divertissements royaux, tel que le *Kitāb al-Tāğ* en attribue l'étiquette à Ardašīr, fournit la disposition ternaire suivante: «Les chevaliers et les princes du sang appartenaient à la première classe; par rapport au roi, elle se tenait à dix coudées du rideau. La deuxième classe, qui se tenait à dix coudées de la deuxième, était constituée par les courtisans, les familiers, et les narrateurs du roi, choisis parmi les nobles et les savants. La troisième classe, à dix coudées de la deuxième, comprenait les bouffons, les amuseurs, et les bateleurs».[18] À chacune de ces classes, correspondait une classe du musiciens et de chanteurs.[19]

Il est vain de chercher une correspondance de terme à terme entre cette étiquette et la disposition de la cour céleste de Dieu chez les manichéens. D'autre part, le rideau qui joue un rôle essentiel devant le trône du Sassanide,[20] n'existe pas dans la cour du Dieu manichéen. La distance et la sécurité de ce Dieu n'y sont pas, en effet, marquées par un rideau—la disposition circulaire de la cour céleste en exclut l'usage—, mais par une frontière qui sépare au Sud la terre de lumière du monde de la ténèbre.[21] Dans le monde clos de la cour divine, tout est homogène et continu.[22]

Mani n'a donc pas transposé, terme à terme, en Dieu l'étiquette de son contemporain siégeant au palais de Ctésiphon mais il s'est inspiré du motif. L'éti-

---

l'intérieur et l'extérieur; les territoires précieux s'étagent en royaumes sans nombre» (Hymnaire chinois de Londres, 567–578; traduction L. Leyrat; voir *supra* n. 4).

[16] M 178 I R 1; c'est par la mention du grand Roi, laquelle terminait l'exposé des *duodecim membra*, que commence le fragment sogdien.

[17] Une autre représentation concrète de Dieu en position assise est celle du «juge»; voir *Kephalaia* coptes, LXXXIX, 221, 33–22, 1 (ed. A. Böhlig, Stuttgart 1940).

[18] Ch. Pellat, *Le Livre de la couronne attribué à Ğāḥiẓ*, Paris 1954, 52; G. Schoeler (*ZDMG* 130 (1980) 217–225) attribue l'ouvrage à al-Ḥāriṯ al-Taġlibī (ob. avant 250 H. / 864).

[19] *Ibid.*, 53–54.

[20] *Ibid.*, 56–57; cf. A. Christensen, *L'Iran sous les Sassanides*, Copenhague-Paris 1936, 392–399; point de vue comparatif dans Th. Klauser, Der Vorhang vor dem Thron Gottes, *JbAC* 3 (1960), 141–142.

[21] Sur la frontière Sud de Dieu, voir Titus de Bostra, *Adv. Manichaeos*, I 11 (ed. P. de Lagarde, Berlin 1859, 6, 3–5 = version syriaque, 8, 9–11); Simplicius, *In Epicteti Enchiridion*, XXVII; 71, 16–17 Dübner (Paris, 1877); ʿAbd al-Ğabbār, *al-Muġnī*, t. 5, Le Caire 1965, 10, 13–16 (trad. G. Monnot, *Penseurs musulmans*, 153); al-Šahrastānī, *K. al-milal wa-l-niḥal*, t. 1, Le Cairo 1951, 621 (trad. G. Monnet dans D. Gimaret et G. Monnot, *Shahrastani. Livre des religions et des sectes, Traduction avec introduction et notes*, Louvain 1986, 656).

[22] Ainsi, le Père est dit *perpetuus* en sa racine, selon l'*Epistula fundamenti* (ap. AUG., *C. Ep. fund.* 13; 209, 13–14 Zycha). La continuité et l'homogénéité dans la cour divine sont marquées par la disposition des protagonistes en cercles concentriques autour du trône, alors que dans la salle d'audience du palais impérial, les familiers, séparés du souverain par le rideau, sont placés devant.

quette du grand Roi, dont chaque Iranien savait qu'elle était grandiose et précise, demeurait le symbole le plus parfait de l'étiquette divine. Les éons fleuris et chanteurs dans la cour céleste, disposés, trois par trois, aux quatre angles du trône, reposent sur la représentation que l'imaginaire iranien se faisait des réceptions et divertissements dans la salle à coupole où le Roi des rois recevait ses invités.[23]

Ce Dieu construit à l'iranienne est un Dieu de poète. Il est significatif, en effet, que toutes les sources manichéennes parlant de Dieu sont des hymnes, ou des sommaires tirés d'hymnes. Peinture naïve, fondée sur la vérité de l'analogie et du symbole, une telle représentation restait un produit facilement exportable. On en a la preuve avec le développement du thème dans les poèmes parthes, sogdiens et chinois. Vers l'Occident également, le portrait ne pouvait choquer. Le langage utilisé et le choix des symboles se retrouvent dans la conception de Dieu à l'œuvre dans l'hymne au Père des immortels, cité dans le deuxième livre de la *Philosophie tirée des oracles* de Porphyre.

L'oracle conçoit le Père sur le modèle d'un monarque: il est βασιλέστατος.[24] Le trône de ce δεσπότης est «le dos éthéré des mondes tournoyants».[25] Trois classes d'anges sont disposées circulairement autour de son trône: d'abord «les rejetons des saints souverains».[26] Une classe d'êtres servent, ensuite, de ministres et portent les messages à la puissance du grand Roi, c'est-à-dire à son intellect.[27] La troisième classe a pour fonction de louer Dieu par des chants.[28] Le scholion, qui suit l'oracle dans la *Théosophie* et qui provient très probablement de Porphyre,[29] distingue nettement les trois classes mais inverse l'ordre donné dans l'oracle: ceux qui se tiennent toujours devant le trône (= les chanteurs), ceux dont la fonction de ministres les met à distance moyenne entre chanteurs et porteurs, ceux qui sont à proximité immédiate du trône (= les porteurs).[30] Selon l'étiquette que le *Kitāb al-Tāǧ* place à l'époque d'Ardašīr, les plus proches du trône étaient les princes du sang, venaient ensuite les narrateurs, enfin les chanteurs.[31] D'autre part, l'oracle cité par Porphyre se ter-

---

[23] Le nombre douze et la disposition circulaire des entités de la cour divine peuvent apparaître d'autant plus une représentation du ciel des fixes, symbolisé par la coupole dans la salle du grand Roi, que la théorie manichéenne de l'interpénétration des éléments (στοιχεῖα) dans le monde divin reproduisait une disposition zodiacale; voir en ce sens le *Kephalaion* copte LXXI, 175, 26–176, 8.

[24] Porphyre, *De philosophia ex oraculis haurienda*, II, transmis par la *Theosophia*, § 27, v. 13 (ed. H. Erbse, *Fragmente griechischer Theosophien*, HAA 4, Hamburg 1941, 174, 4). H. Lewy, *Chaldaean Oracles and Theurgy*, 2ᵉ éd. par M. Tardieu, Paris 1978, 9–16, interprète à tort l'oracle comme chaldaïque et en référence exclusive à l'angélologie juive.

[25] *Theosophia*, § 27, 2; 173, 21 Erbse.

[26] *Ibid.*, § 27, 12; 174, 3.

[27] *Ibid.*, § 27, 15–16; 174, 6–7.

[28] *Ibid.*, § 27, 17–19; 174, 8–10.

[29] Voir P. Hadot, *Porphyre et Victorinus*, t. 1, Paris 1968, p. 394, n. 1.

[30] *Theosophia*, § 28; 174, 11–15 Erbse.

[31] Ch. Pellat, *Livre de la couronne*, 52.

mine par l'invocation du Père comme «forme à l'intérieur des formes» (ἐν εἴδεσιν εἶδος).[32] Autrement dit, il n'y a pas rupture entre les classes d'anges qui forment la cour céleste, et le grand Roi lui-même. Les uns et les autres participent de la même nature intelligible. La formule: «forme à l'intérieur des formes», a son équivalent chez Ibn al-Nadīm: «*Leurs* formes (*ṣuwar*) sont toutes comme *Sa* forme (*ṣūra*): ce sont des connaissants, des intelligibles».[33] C'est une terminologie néoplatonicienne, et non manichéenne.

Le monarque, qui sert de modèle à la conception de Dieu de l'oracle cité par Porphyre, ne peut être que le grand Roi, c'est-à-dire l'empereur iranien. Cette représentation n'est pas un cas isolé. Un contemporain de Mani, Plotin, l'utilise également pour faire le portrait de Dieu: «Il siège sur un beau trône ...; devant ce grand Roi, s'avancent dans son cortège: d'abord des personnages de second rang, puis devant eux se trouvent toujours des individus de rang supérieur et méritant plus de considération, puis ceux qui occupent autour du roi des charges plus royales, ensuite ceux qui ont rang de dignité après lui; à la suite de tous ceux-là, le grand Roi en personne apparaît tout à coup».[34] Ce passage, qui fait partie des traités de controverse de Plotin contre les gnostiques, a pour but de montrer que la multiplication en Dieu des généalogies n'est pas respectueuse du caractère, à la fois sobre et grandiose, de la cour divine.

Comme chez Mani, c'est bien l'image de l'étiquette en usage à la cour du grand Roi perse, qu'utilise ici Plotin, et non, comme l'ont prétendu R. Beutler et W. Theiler, à la suite d'A. Alföldi,[35] celle d'un cérémonial de la cour de Gallien. La métaphore du grand Roi des Perses comme représentation de Dieu et de sa cour se trouvait dans la propre tradition culturelle de Plotin. La description la plus précise de la majesté de Dieu siégeant au sommet de l'univers, sur le modèle de l'étiquette (πρόσχημα) en usage à la cour de Perse, est attestée par le *Perì kósmou*.[36] L'auteur y passe en revue la suite des salles du palais et l'ordonnancement de l'étiquette des fonctionnaires impériaux: les uns à proximité immédiate du grand Roi, les autres un peu plus éloignés: gardiens, écouteurs, intendants, commandants, maîtres de la chasse. La cour décrite concernerait, selon l'auteur du *Perì kósmou*, celle de Cambyse, de Xerxès et de Darius. Cela paraît fort improbable. Il aura plutôt, lui-même (ou sa source), pour rehausser le prestige de cette tradition, transféré à l'époque des Achéménides un rituel en vigueur sous la dynastie parthe.

---

[32] *Theosophia*, § 29; 174, 18 Erbse.
[33] Ibn al-Nadīm, *Fihrist*, 396, 3 Tağaddud. Le ʿāẓẓūn du texte de Tağaddud est une graphie défectueuse de ʿāqilūn (apparat, 396, n. 2).
[34] Plotin, *Enneades*, V 5, 3, 9–13.
[35] Dans R. Harder, *Plotins Schriften*, 3/b, Hambourg 1964, 404.
[36] Pseudo-Aristote, *De mundo*, 398 A 11–B 8 = Apulée, *De mundo*, 26.

À l'époque de Plotin et de Mani, le thème du grand Roi perse était devenue une métaphore familière aux lettrés d'Occident, pour parler de Dieu.[37] Suffisait-il, alors, que Mani l'utilisât, pour rendre son message attrayant, ou avoir une base commune avec les philosophes? Une théodicée poétique, construite sur un cérémonial perse et partagée avec la même ferveur religieuse par les platoniciens et les manichéens, aurait pu, à la rigueur, inciter ces derniers à fréquenter les écoles de philosophie. Les uns et les autres, en effet, sont en contact, en Haute-Égypte dans l'école d'Alexandre de Lycopolis à la fin du IIIe siècle,[38] en Syrie du Nord dans l'entourage de Simplicius au VIe siècle.[39] Le bout de chemin qu'ils pouvaient faire ensemble ne concernait qu'un symbole mais touchant à l'essentiel: un mode de représentation de Dieu à l'aide d'un motif iranien occidentalisé, auquel Plotin avait accordé un label d'autorité en l'utilisant contre ceux (gnostiques et chrétiens) qui introduisaient en Dieu des généalogies. La métaphore avait effectivement l'avantage, pour Plotin mais aussi pour Mani, d'exclure du monde divin filiations et progénitures interminables. Elle se contentait de montrer une procession ordonnée et limitée à un espace clos. Or ce fut précisément pour avoir voulu marquer cette clôture, que l'image devint une chausse-trappe, même si, comme nous allons le voir, les manichéens se refusèrent toujours à la considérer comme telle. Par conséquent, le bout de chemin entre philosophes et manichéens ne pouvait se produire, en raison même des conséquences que les manichéens tiraient de la représentation de Dieu comme roi de sa propre cour.

La métaphore des philosophes devenait, en effet, chez les manichéens, une disposition matérielle assurant la sécurité de Dieu, mais enfermant du même coup sa puissance dans les limites d'un domaine protégé. Illimitée dans sa terre vers le Nord, l'Est et l'Ouest, la puissance de Dieu s'arrêtait à la frontière méridionale de son royaume, c'est-à-dire là où commençait l'empire du mal.[40] Dieu n'était donc pas tout-puissant, puisque l'attribut d'infini ne pouvait lui être appliqué. Cette conséquence est très clairement tirée par l'évêque manichéen Faustus:

> quoniam quidem si non est malum, profecto infinitus est deus; habet autam finem, si malum est; constat autem esse malum. non igitur infinitus est deus; illinc enim esse mala accipiunt, ubi bonorum est finis.[41]

---

[37] Aelius Aristide, *Orationes*, XLIII 18; Maxime de Tyr, *Or.*, X 9; cf. F. Cumont, *Les religions orientales dans le paganisme romain*, 4e éd., Paris 1929, 299, n. 21 et H. Chadwick, *Origen. Contra Celsum*, Cambridge 1965, xviii – xix, qui cite Philon, *De decalogo*, 61; ajouter Arnobe, *Adv. nat.*, II 37.

[38] Sur ce document, voir en dernier lieu A. Villey, *Alexandre de Lycopolis. Contre la doctrine de Mani*, SGM 2, Paris 1985; Id. Controverses philosophiques à Assiout à la fin du IIIe siècle, *Cahiers de la bibliothèque copte* 3, Louvain 1986, 23–28.

[39] Sur ce point, voir M. Tardieu, Ṣābiens coraniques et «Ṣābiens» de Ḥarrān, *JA* 274 (1986), 24–25, n. 105.

[40] Voir *supra* n. 21.

[41] Faustus, cité par Augustin, *Contra Faustum*, XXV 1, *CSEL* 25/1; 726, 25–727, 2 Zycha.

Cette question de la finitude de Dieu fut un cheval de bataille des controverses anti-manichéennes. «Comment n'est-ce pas tout à fait impie», déclare Titus de Bostra,[42] «de circonscrire Dieu selon la substance, et de ne pas reconnaître et confesser qu'il est infini?» Simplicius range cette question parmi les «grands blasphèmes» jamais énoncés contre Dieu.[43] La vulnérabilité de Dieu à sa frontière Sud fait de lui un «craintif» (δειλόν), un «non-parfait» (ἀτελῆ).[44] Le débat sur la finitude sera au centre des controverses menées par les muᶜtazilites contre les manichéens.

Ainsi, la définition muᶜtazilite de Dieu, rapportée par al-Ašᶜarī, vise directement la conception des manichéens: «On ne peut qualifier Dieu de fini, il n'a point de limites, il ne se dirige dans aucune direction».[45] Deux sections du *Kitāb al-intiṣār* sont consacrées à cette question.[46] Al-Ḫayyāṭ cite en particulier un passage de la *Faḍīḥat al-muᶜtazila* d'al-Rawandī, dans lequel ce dernier faisait état d'une controverse entre le muᶜtazilite al-Naẓẓām et des manichéens affirmant que «la lumière et les ténèbres sont finies en étendue et en mesure dans certaines de leurs directions».[47] Proposition incontestablement manichéenne. Ce à quoi al-Naẓẓām aurait répondu qu'une limitation de Dieu dans une seule direction entraînait limitation dans toutes les directions, le Dieu suprême des manichéens était donc fini. C'est la conclusion à laquelle aboutissait, cinq siècles auparavant, l'évêque manichéen Faustus et qu'un contemporain mazdéen d'al-Naẓẓām, polémiquant lui aussi contre les manichéens, formulait en ces termes:

> Ce qui est enclos de tous les côtés est nécessairement fini; donc, Dieu, en tant qu'il serait conscient d'être totalement enclos, devrait être tenu pour fini, ou, s'il est infini, pour ignorant.[48]

---

[42] Titus de Bostra, *Adv. Man.*, I7; 4, 22−24 de Lagarde = version syriaque, 6, 9−11.

[43] Simplicius, *In Ep. Enchir.*, XXVII; 70, 35−36 Dübner: οἷα δὲ καὶ ὅσα βλάσφημα εἰς τὸν θεόν.

[44] *Ibid.*, 70, 37−39 et 71, 4−5.

[45] al-Ašᶜarī, *Maqālāt al-islāmiyyin*, 155 Ritter; trad. *ap.* A.N. Nader, *Le système philosophique des muᶜtazila*, Beyrouth 1956, 51.

[46] al-Ḫayyāṭ, *K. al-intiṣār*, XIX: «Discussion entre al-Naẓẓām et les manichéens (*manāniyya*) au sujet du fini»; XX: «Ibrāhīm réfute la thèse des athées relative au fini»; ed. A.N. Nader, Beyrouth 1957, 31−34 ch. ar. (texte), 30−33 (trad.).

[47] *Ibid.* XIX, 32, 16 ch. ar. (texte), 31 (trad.).

[48] *Škand-gumānīk vičār*, XVI, 72−74, (ed. J. de Menasce, Fribourg 1945, 256−257). De Menasce observe que l'auteur de cette apologétique mazdéenne, Martan Farrux i Ohrmazdātān, revendique comme maître, à plusieurs reprises, un docteur mazdéen qui aurait fréquenté la cour d'al-Ma'mun (*loc. cit.*, 11), où, comme on sait, les muᶜtazilites, alors à leur apogée, avaient pignon sur rue. Dans un article posthume, («Muᶜtazila et théologie mazdéenne» [1974] = *Études iraniennes*, Studia Iranica, Cahier 3, Louvain 1985, 205−211), de Menasce n'exclut pas, d'un point de vue général, une influence des muᶜtazilites sur les encyclopédistes mazdéens du IXᵉ siècle. La controverse anti-manichéenne serait, à mon avis, un lieu précis de l'influence des premiers sur les seconds. Car la méthode dialectique utilisée par le ch. XVI du *ŠGV*, entièrement consacré à la réfutation de la thèse manichéenne de la finitude de Dieu, et les arguments employés, sont celle

La métaphore charmante d'enfermer Dieu en sa terre, tel le grand Roi en son palais, laquelle constitua la réponse manichéenne à la question du mal, se terminait ainsi sur une catastrophe métaphysique.

---

et ceux des controverses muᶜtazilites anti-manichéennes, dont on a un écho dans la section XIX du *K. al-intiṣār*.

INDEX

I. Biblical and Jewish Texts
(including Apocrypha and Pseudepigrapha)

II. Greek and Latin Texts and Monuments

III. Coptic, Syriac and Other Oriental Texts